The National Museum of the American Indian

Critical Conversations

The National Museum of the American Indian

Critical Conversations

Edited by
Amy Lonetree and Amanda J. Cobb

UNIVERSITY OF NEBRASKA PRESS | LINCOLN & LONDON

Library of Congress
Cataloging-in-Publication Data
The National Museum of the American Indian:
critical conversations / edited by Amy Lonetree
and Amanda J. Cobb.
p. cm.
Includes bibliographical references and index.
ISBN 978-0-8032-1111-7 (pbk.: alk. paper)
1. National Museum of the American Indian (U.S.)
2. Indians of North America—Museums.
I. Lonetree, Amy. II. Cobb, Amanda J., 1970–
E56.N36 2008
973.04'97074—dc22
2008021684

Set in Quadraat and Quadraat Sans.
Designed by R. W. Boeche.

We dedicate this collection, with love and respect,
to the citizens of the
Ho-Chunk Nation of Wisconsin
and the
Chickasaw Nation of Oklahoma.

Contents

Illustrations

Following page 228

Acknowledgments

Amy Lonetree thanks Jon Daehnke and her family for their constant love and support. Amanda Cobb thanks her husband, Stephen Greetham, and her family for their love and unwavering encouragement. We both thank Jon and Stephen for sharing their editorial talents—this volume is a better product because of it.

Earlier versions of some of the essays in this volume appeared in *American Indian Quarterly* 29, nos. 3-4 (Summer–Fall 2005); *American Indian Quarterly* 30, nos. 3-4 (Summer–Fall 2006); *American Quarterly* 57, no. 2 (June 2005); *Museum Anthropology* 25, no. 2 (2002); *The Public Historian* 28, no. 2 (2006); and *American Anthropologist* 107, no. 4 (December 2005). We thank these journals for permission to reprint and, in particular, Devon Mihesuah for the opportunity to guest-edit our special issues of *American Indian Quarterly*, the genesis of this collection, a rewarding collaboration and a more rewarding friendship.

We thank the wonderful staff of the University of Nebraska Press for the expert advice and shepherding of this project. We extend our heartfelt thanks to the contributors for their patience, level of commitment, excellent essays, and unique insights; we have learned from each and every one of you.

Introduction

Amy Lonetree and Amanda J. Cobb

Beginnings

Critical Conversations grew out of two special issues of *American Indian Quarterly* that we guest-edited. Although both issues took the National Museum of the American Indian (NMAI) as their subject matter, the issues were markedly different in voice, perspective, and sense of audience. Through lengthy discussions we realized that each journal issue represented the ongoing conversations of distinct communities of scholars. These communities, working from specific interdisciplinary traditions and bodies of literature, find different sets of issues at stake in the study of the NMAI. We recognized that the NMAI is at the center of many such conversations—spirited, robust conversations rooted in specific traditions and perspectives.

Through a close analysis of our special issues, we identified four such sets of conversations that we used to shape and organize the collection, placing them in conversation with each other. The essays here exemplify the multiplicity of responses people have had to the National Museum of the American Indian (e.g., celebratory, critical, or political) and the diversity of theoretical and practical lenses they have used to engage with it (e.g., historical, museological, interpretive, or curatorial). This collection's strength comes not in a unity of voice but from the complexity of voices, each offering a unique perspective on a collective effort to take meaning from the NMAI.

The first conversation, "History and Development," includes essays written by scholars who explore the NMAI's history and evolution. The conversations in this section establish a foundation from which to begin an exploration of the museum's importance, particularly with respect to understanding the significant shifts in the relationship between Native Americans and museums as embodied by the NMAI.

The second conversation, "Indigenous Methodology and Community Collaboration," includes essays by NMAI curators on the exhibition development process. More than simple process descriptions, these essays offer a critical analysis of the work carried out by curators who ambitiously sought to collaborate with Indigenous communities from throughout the hemisphere.

The third conversation, "Interpretation and Response," features essays from a diverse group of scholars analyzing the NMAI's opening exhibitions. The NMAI's pathbreaking "Indigenous museology" has been both widely praised and criticized, and these essays reflect several divergent views.

The fourth and final conversation focuses on "Questions of Nation and Identity," which explore the museum as an important transnational site and consider the NMAI's complex identity as a museum of Native nations *and* as an institution of the U.S. government.

Each of these thematic sections can be read as a stand-alone conversation that addresses a set of questions and issues. Taken together, however, the four sections provide a richer, deeper, multifaceted, and more complicated study of this important site of Native American and American national history and memory. The result is not merely a compilation of essays from each special issue; instead, *Critical Conversations* invites readers to think about the NMAI from a variety of uniquely focused perspectives. Furthermore, this volume, a combination of revised essays from the special *AIQ* issues plus some new essays, invites readers to join each of these conversations, to make connections between and among them, and to identify other sets of conversations as well—there are certainly more than the four we present here. As a whole, *Critical Conversations* provides snapshots, taken from different angles, of a particular moment in the academy, in museums, and in Indian Country—a moment fraught with competing ideologies and beliefs about the ultimate significance of the NMAI.

In assembling this collection we sought to find balance and include multiple voices at every turn. One especially important criterion was the need to include both Native and non-Native perspectives in the mix. Given the many strong emotions and viewpoints the museum evokes, we believed it was critical that the various audiences it seeks to engage be brought to the table. As the existence of the museum itself is politically charged, any discussion of it is inherently so. We did not shy away from including divergent views and reactions to this site, as we ourselves feel very differently about the museum's complex identity and effectiveness. Our willingness to work together on this volume represents our desire to bridge these divergent conversations and fully explore the museum's significance.

We recognize that our choice of what to include and what to exclude privileges certain perspectives and voices. The contributors featured are not the only ones who have weighed in on this important site of Indigenous history and memory; other worthy essays by scholars, museum professionals, journalists, and Indigenous community members could have been selected. We regret that we could not include all of them here. Finally, the choices we made were governed both by what we thought was relevant, timely, and important and by the logistics and negotiations of completing a project of this size. We are confidant, however, that the essays selected are of great value in documenting the history of the NMAI and the initial response to its inaugural exhibitions.

Critical Conversations represents the first scholarly study of the NMAI produced outside the museum. This collection seeks to advance the scholarly discourse on the NMAI from a variety of academic perspectives and disciplines, including cultural studies and criticism, art history, history, museum studies, anthropology, ethnic studies, and Native American studies. As founding NMAI director W. Richard West has noted, the next step for the NMAI is to engage academics *across* disciplines "in the intellectual and museological questions that come out of the National Museum of the American Indian." This volume takes that step.

Critical Conversations is also one of the first volumes to examine Native Americans and museums with a primary focus on a single major national museum, and it expands on previous work that focused primarily on exhibitions or on tribal museums. Thus it builds on and engages with similar museum studies projects and contributes to the growing literature on the relationship between Native Americans and museums. The collection also complicates the content of the discourse by combining the voices of scholars and practitioners, which is rarely found in similar projects. Read in its entirety, we believe that *Critical Conversations* is useful to professors seeking to synthesize issues of theory and practice in their classrooms. Further, it places history, cultural criticism, and museology in conversation together, thereby highlighting both subject matter and research methods. We have no doubt, however, that general readers interested in American Indian history, American history, and national and cultural memory will also find much of this collection to be both relevant and useful.

The Conversations
History and Development

The NMAI's history is a complex story to tell, and the contributors in Conversation 1, "History and Development," explore the history of the institution from its early years, as the Museum of the American Indian, to its current formation. This history is critical to the NMAI's story and our understanding of its current formation. As scholar Ruth Phillips has observed, museums "have genealogies—family trees the tracing of which allows us to place contemporary projects in critically important perspective."[1] This section seeks to do just that: to explore the NMAI's deep history and genealogy, beginning with George Gustav Heye's all-consuming collecting practices, through the development of the largest collection of Native American material culture in the world, to the founding of the Museum of the American Indian in 1922. Contributors also examine the complex struggles among policy makers, tribal leaders, museum professionals, and politicians during the 1970s, when those disparate groups negotiated the fate of the Heye collection and the NMAI's establishment. Authors also explore the institution's ambitious attempts to fully collaborate with Indigenous groups from throughout the Western hemisphere in all phases of its development. As a group, the essays in Conversation 1 cover a significant amount of historical ground and provide the context necessary to engage with the institution's philosophy, scope, and impact.

Our conversation begins with the large-scale collecting practices of George Gustav Heye (1874–1957) in the late nineteenth century and the founding of the Museum of the American Indian to house this collection. The time period in which Heye set out to collect "all things Indian" is viewed as the nadir of Indian existence on this continent. Native people were believed to be "vanishing," and anthropologists and collectors thought of themselves in a race against time to collect the remnants of dying cultures. Heye represents the most ambitious and exploitive of these collectors. Museum anthropologist Ira Jacknis seeks to place Heye's collecting practices and the museum that he later established in disciplinary and geographic context. In "A New Thing? The National Museum of the American Indian in Historical and Institutional Perspective," Jacknis provides extensive historical information on the NMAI and the specifics of Heye's collecting practices. Heye's collection would eventually total eight hundred thousand pieces from Native peoples from throughout the hemisphere, and Jacknis puts the importance of that mass of cultural items in context by placing the museum in relation to other museums of similar size and scope. He follows the evolution of the museum under Heye until his death in 1957, to the period of crisis after his death, and to the collection's eventual transfer to the Smithsonian, where it became the National Museum of the American Indian. This essay focuses particularly on the period in which Native relations with museums were defined by exploitation, misrepresentations, and power imbalances. During this period, Indigenous people were "sources" to be collected—objects, bodies, languages, and ethnographic information—for consumption by museums that sought to reframe Indigenous history, culture, and lifeways into their own Western knowledge systems.

The relationship between Native Americans and museums experienced a major shift in the 1970s, when a groundswell of Native American activism in museums sought to challenge these objectifying and exploitive practices. One contributor, anthropologist Patricia Pierce Erikson, has termed this period of activism the "Native American Museum movement." Erickson argues that this movement encompasses a range of Indigenous activism, including (a) protesting stereotypical displays of Native American history and culture at mainstream institutions; (b) protesting the collecting, displaying, and holding of American Indian human remains; (c) seeking to change museums from the inside by having Native people enter into the curatorial profession; (d) challenging the authority of Western museums to represent Native American communities without including the Native perspective; and (e) pressuring for the repatriation of Native American cultural objects, human remains, funerary objects, and cultural patrimony.[2] The activism of this period eventually led to the establishment of tribal museums, the passage of the Native American Graves Protection and Repatriation Act (1990), Indigenous involvement in mainstream institutions, and the creation of the Smithsonian's National Museum of the American Indian.[3]

Erikson's essay in this collection, "Decolonizing the 'Nation's Attic': The National Museum of the American Indian and the Politics of Knowledge-Making in a National Space," explores the national influence of the Native American Museum movement, the internal debates that ensued at the Smithsonian Institution during the 1970s and 1980s regarding repatriation, and the NMAI's establishment. As Erikson claims, the creation of the NMAI "involved negotiation and debate between Congress and at least three key museum players: the Smithsonian's National Museum of Natural History, the Office of the Secretary at the Smithsonian Institution, and the Museum of the American Indian." The often contentious debates that ensued at the Smithsonian regarding the establishment of the NMAI left "Native American material culture and human remains . . . suspended in a complex web of political maneuvers." She goes on to argue that the establishment of the NMAI "marks one of the critical moments in rising Native American influence in a national arena," which has led to the "process of reenvisioning and remaking" museums. She is careful, however, to acknowledge that even though the extension of this influence offers important possibilities and authority, the NMAI is still part of the Smithsonian Institution and "overlap[s] with . . . a highly charged symbolic national space," which "make[s] it a potential site for co-optation, silencing of alternative knowledge structures, and homogenization of diversity among tribes."

Art historian Judith Ostrowitz explores the NMAI's ambitious attempts to collaborate with Indigenous people from throughout the Western hemisphere. Collaboration is becoming more the norm than the exception in the museum world, marking a new relationship between Indigenous people and museums. The NMAI represents the most ambitious collaborative project to date. A great deal of attention—including considerable confusion and criticism—has been placed on the NMAI's ambitious collaborative process that sought to bring Native people into all phases of the institution's development. In her essay, "Concourse and Periphery: Planning the National Museum of the American Indian," Ostrowitz provides detailed descriptions and analysis of the NMAI's initial concept, with emphasis on "the architectural program as well as ideas generated very early on for appropriate exhibition and operations strategies." She also provides reflections and analysis of the completed project. In her thorough investigation, Ostrowitz provides an important summary of the early collaborative process with Indigenous groups that culminated in their most important planning document, *The Way of the People*. This document has informed all aspects of the museum, including its architecture, exhibitions, public programming, and outreach to Indigenous communities.

Indigenous Methodology and Community Collaboration

The second set of conversations in the volume focuses on what is the most praised, the most criticized, and easily the most significant aspect of the NMAI: the Indigenous methodology and community collaboration processes. Each of the scholars in this conversation worked on a different aspect of the NMAI during its development, and each provides critical reflections of his or her work.

The scope and magnitude of the public's response to the NMAI—from various media, from universities, from Native communities, from museum visitors—has been almost overwhelming. The NMAI also has produced much of its own literature that explains, celebrates, and describes its goals, history and development, and exhibitions. The NMAI's curators and practitioners, on the other hand, have had little opportunity to respond to or publicly engage in the many spirited conversations of the more general public. The essays in this section seek to make transparent the processes that so many have found complicated, confusing, and obscure by bringing those involved in the development of those processes into a discussion of the NMAI with the larger community.

Much of the literature about Native museums is either very theoretical or very descriptive. To our minds, the authors in this section offer essays that combine theory and practical description in the best of ways: through thoughtful critical engagement and sincere, honest reflection. They consider their goals, choices, frustrations, and end results bravely, with grace and integrity.

Paul Chaat Smith (Comanche), the lead curator of the permanent exhibit Our Peoples, reflects on what he considers to be the exhibit's "goals, successes, and failures." Smith writes from the perspective of a Native person on the NMAI curatorial team charged with developing the major theme for Our Peoples: that "contact was the biggest thing ever, the most profound and momentous event in recorded human history." He describes the curatorial process of each major installation in detail, analyzing the initial vision, moments of choice, and the decisions made throughout. His essay, which he first wrote as a lecture for the NMAI's monthly curator series in 2005, adds a very human element to the NMAI as an institution, underscoring the fact that all museums, no matter how grand their scale, are ultimately produced by the individuals and groups of people on the ground facing innumerable challenges, working not merely to apply theory but to create an embodiment of it.

Cynthia Chavez Lamar (San Felipe) further humanizes the NMAI's curatorial methods in her essay, "Collaborative Exhibit Development at the Smithsonian's National Museum of the American Indian" by recounting and reflecting on her work as a Native curator collaborating with community curators on the Our Lives exhibition. Chavez Lamar's role was to work with community curators from eight remarkably different Native communities to develop a separate installation for each community. Significantly, Chavez Lamar details every step of the elaborate protocol established for the co-curation process, reflecting on challenges she faced personally. Ultimately, she realized "what it meant to represent Native peoples at the NMAI's historic opening" and confronted the fact that her role placed her squarely "between the NMAI and the Native communities."

Beverly Singer (Santa Clara) found herself in a similar position as the associate producer of the NMAI's preparatory film, Who We Are, a multimedia production in the museum's Lelawi Theater. Seen by millions of people each year, this film holds a monumental place in the history of ethnographic and Native filmmaking. In her essay, "The Making of Who We Are, Now Showing at the National Museum of the American Indian Lelawi Theater," Singer shares a story of collaboration among

Native team members, museum project members, and media producers. Elsewhere, she has emphasized that the film exists in the context
of "a highly competitive media landscape that constantly seeks to represent Indigenous peoples without their input." Her discussion, however, moves beyond the usual lamentation over stereotypes implicit in the
popular culture industry and explores a complex of protocol and willingness to let the Indigenous perspective speak for itself. She critically analyzes the production process, content decisions, and the role of
being a Native American filmmaker working on behalf of Indigenous
peoples and communities in the Smithsonian's highly politicized institutional environment.

Interpretations and Response

The authors in this section seek to contextualize Native and non-Native
responses and interpretations to the opening of the NMAI's Washington
site. The museum has generated a great deal of attention, particularly
since its inaugural celebration. The museum and its contents have been
widely praised and vigorously criticized by the media, the larger American
Indian community, museum professionals, the general public, and scholars. These varied responses to the NMAI, the self-proclaimed "museum
different," is recognition that however one may view this particular manifestation of the changing relationship between Native Americans and
museums, it is a site that has provoked— and continues to provoke—considerable attention and critique.

The contributors in this section are no exception. Their essays offer a
divergent set of responses to the museum from art historians, anthropologists and archaeologists, historians, and cultural critics. There is
no uniform view of the museum, nor is there a typical response: what
some view as effective and inspiring exhibits, others find problematic and
vastly disappointing. The range of responses and perspectives reminds
us of the NMAI's importance and power in shaping the public's understanding of Native American history, culture, philosophy, and identi-

ties. Conversations on its effectiveness and impact must continue as the museum charts its course for the future.

We begin the conversation in this section with two essays that devote considerable attention to engaging with the many criticisms that the museum has received, especially those made by journalists immediately following its 2004 opening. Many of those initial reviews expressed dissatisfaction with what the individual reporter perceived to be a confusing museum-going experience and a lack of historical information and context for the exhibitions. Most tellingly, these criticisms particularly attack the NMAI's privileging of Indigenous voice and perspective, which some critics believed reflected a lack of scholarly rigor.

The literary scholar Elizabeth Archuleta (Yaqui/Chicana) challenges these critics directly, emphasizing in her essay that the museum does indeed rely on scholarship, as reflected in the emphasis on Indigenous storytelling in its exhibitions. In "Gym Shoes, Maps, and Passports, Oh My! Creating Community or Creating Chaos at the National Museum of the American Indian?," Archuleta argues that the "exhibits resemble Indigenous storytelling traditions and literary techniques" and that this methodology requires that "visitors . . . set aside notions they previously held about museums and Indians, 'listen' to the stories being told in the exhibits, and trust that meaning will be made if they become involved as participants in the storytelling process." Knowledge is not "spoon-fed" to visitors at the NMAI, Archuleta argues, and it is therefore the responsibility of visitors "to take what they see and engage in their own research to learn more." She attempts to reconcile her perspective on the museum with the earliest reviews by journalists who read the museum's exhibits very differently and, in her opinion, were overly dismissive of certain notions of Indigenous sovereignty and curation methods.

In their essay "'Indian Country' on the National Mall: The Mainstream Press versus the National Museum of the American Indian," Janet Berlo and Aldona Jonaitis also attempt to reconcile their experiences of the museum with the earliest reviews of it. The authors address the following central question: "Why have reviewers attacked the museum so severely—and ... judged the museum so harshly?" Similar to Archuleta's piece, Berlo and Jonaitis challenge the view that this museum is devoid of scholarly analysis and examine the NMAI in relationship to changing museological theory and practices occurring throughout the world. Overall they describe the museum as an "intellectually serious and visually pleasurable experience," an institution that clearly reflects the changing museological standards firmly rooted in "postcolonial paradigms," which, they argue, mainstream journalists have failed to recognize.

Making meaning out of the NMAI and the widely divergent viewpoints is central to Gwyneira Isaac's discussion in "What Are Our Expectations Telling Us? Encounters with the National Museum of the American Indian." Isaac explores her four different encounters with the institution and attempts "to move beyond issues of representation and to address how museum meanings are made on the ground in ongoing encounters between displays and the ideational worlds their audiences bring with them into the museum space." She also addresses the postmodernist tenor of the new exhibitions at the NMAI through a close reading of the curated section of the Our Peoples gallery. She argues that "the exhibit exists not to give specific Native Americans a voice. It exists to argue that history itself is subjective and that the Native American experience of colonization cannot be understood until the nature of the varied histories themselves is understood." She believes that the museum is more interested in questioning ideas about singular versions of history than in providing evidence of specific historical events and processes.

Other scholars engage critically with specific exhibitions, examining both what made it to the exhibition floor as well as the many absences and silences that they believe surround some aspects of the Native American past and present. In "No Sense of the Struggle: Creating a Context for Survivance at the National Museum of the American Indian," Sonya Atalay (Ojibwe) explores the extent to which the NMAI's exhibits fail to offer hard-hitting representations of Native history that effectively portray the processes and lasting effects of colonization in Native communities. In her essay, Atalay recognizes the significance of emphasizing Indigenous agency and survivance-predominant themes throughout the NMAI's inaugural exhibitions. She argues, however, that the silences around the struggles that make that survival so amazing are absent and do a grave disservice to the subject peoples. As she states, "One cannot appreciate and experience the power of Native survivance if the stories and memories . . . are not placed in the context of struggle." The context necessary to understand fully Native survivance is absent at the NMAI, and Atalay argues that by not explicitly telling the hard truths of colonization, the museum fails in its educational mission.

Historian Myla Vicenti Carpio (Jicarilla Apache/Laguna Pueblo/Isleta Pueblo) in "(Un)disturbing Exhibitions: Indigenous Historical Memory at the National Museum of the American Indian" also criticizes the NMAI for not discussing colonization and its lasting legacies. She argues that by "minimizing the discussion of colonization, especially in a historical context," the museum "centers colonialism as the 'absent presence' in the NMAI." She further claims that the exhibits "lack a historical context that informs or explains the continuing impacts of colonization and ignores the continuing presence of colonization in our lives." She argues that these silences only serve to "[make] more conspicuously present the apologist mission of the NMAI," which fails to challenge the deeply embedded stereotypes that the general public bring with them to the museum. Most important, she contends that the museum fails to assist Native communities in their own decolonization efforts by not including a specific discussion of "how imperialism and colonialism have impacted us in the past and present," which she believes is critical in "decoloniz{ing} our own perspectives and values."

We close this section with an essay by Amy Lonetree (Ho-Chunk), "'Acknowledging the Truth of History': Missed Opportunities at the National Museum of the American Indian," which explores the NMAI's significance to the changing relationship between Native people and museums. Lonetree examines the importance of the museum's community-collaborative approach and offers her views on the inaugural exhibitions. Like Atalay and Vicenti Carpio, Lonetree is critical of the silences around the more painful stories of colonization and its legacy in our communities, as well as the inability to convey these ideas clearly to the public. She questions whether an abstract historical presentation is the appropriate strategy for conveying the important and painful story of colonialism and its continual effects in the Americas to a nation that has willfully sought to silence our versions of the past or to reframe Indigenous history to suit its own colonizing agendas.

Questions of Nation and Identity

The fourth and final set of conversations offered in this collection, "Questions of Nation and Identity," places the NMAI in a national context. The NMAI is simultaneously (a) a U.S. *national* museum, (b) a museum of and for the Indigenous *nations* of North and South America, and (c) a museum that will host millions of *international* visitors. The NMAI is, fundamentally, a transnational site—a site in which cultural and political boundaries seem, paradoxically, firmly fixed and fluid, highlighted yet obscured.

The authors in this section consider the fundamental identities and agendas of the NMAI, recognizing that, as its formal name, the Smithsonian's National Museum of the American Indian, clearly indicates, the NMAI is ultimately the property of the Smithsonian, an institution of the U.S. nation-state. As an institution of the nation-state, the Smithsonian serves a powerful nationalistic function. By offering officially sanctioned narratives of history and culture, Smithsonian museums shape the cultural memory of U.S. citizens as well as the perceptions of the United States held by international audiences. These narratives, without question, act in and promote the best interests of the nation-state.

And yet, as the authors in this section also recognize, perhaps the formal name does not carry such a clear connotation. In the case of the

NMAI, the term "national," for example, can signify the United States as a nation-state, the nation-states that make up North and South America, or the Indigenous nations of North and South America. Therefore, any reinterpretation of the term "national" also requires a reinterpretation of the multiple identities and agendas at play and in power.

For example, in her essay "The National Museum of the American Indian as Cultural Sovereignty," Amanda Cobb (Chickasaw) contends that Native Americans have ingeniously turned what has historically been an instrument of colonization and dispossession—a national museum—into an instrument of self-definition and cultural continuance. By providing a descriptive walk-through of the NMAI exhibitions and public spaces, as well as an examination of the original mission and curation process, she demonstrates that virtually every aspect of the museum was filtered through Native core cultural values. This filtering process, drawn heavily from the practices of tribal museums and cultural centers, undermines the extent to which the NMAI—a Smithsonian museum—is able to act in the "best interests" of the nation-state, disrupting and complicating long-standing national master narratives and, importantly, changing the master narratives. In effect, any overarching "national" agenda of the nation-state present in the NMAI has been fundamentally altered by the "national" agendas of the Native nations of the Americas, making the NMAI a powerful exercise in cultural sovereignty for Native nations.

On the other hand, in "Performing Reconciliation at the National Museum of the American Indian: Postcolonial Rapprochement and the Politics of Historical Closure," the cultural studies scholar Pauline Wakeham considers the way the nation-state uses the merging of "national" narratives with the narratives of Native American nations as a form of "reconciliation" that promotes the interests of the nation-state. In a close analysis of the NMAI's opening ceremonies and Native Nations Procession, Wakeham is concerned with the way "triumphant pageants impose a kind of historical closure on colonial violence, thereby attempting to silence recognition— and calls for redress—of the continued power asymmetries and systemic racism that affect Indigenous peoples and their struggles for social justice today." Wakeham's piece interrogates the manner in which the NMAI "stages performances of reconciliation" through the inaugural celebrations, and the problems inherent in framing the NMAI as a site of "museological reconciliation" that could potentially be conflated with "broader forms of political reconciliation."

Similarly, in her essay "'South of the Border' at the National Museum of the American Indian," anthropologist Robin Maria DeLugan (Cherokee) examines the representations of Latin American communities in the inaugural exhibitions, importantly questioning whether the NMAI signifies the continuing endurance of Native sovereignty or "the destruction of Native sovereignty and the co-optation of Native cultures in a gesture of nation-state largesse." DeLugan argues that through its stated commitment to representing Native voices, the NMAI challenges the traditional loyalty that a "national" museum has to the state. Furthermore, the NMAI as a hemispheric museum extends its commitment to support Native peoples throughout the Americas. DeLugan contends that "by situating the realities of Native peoples from 'south of the border' in local, transnational, and global matrices, the NMAI highlights factors and conditions that unite Native North, Central, and South America." The NMAI also provides an opportunity for these communities to present aspects of their experiences that they are not able to present in national museums within their respective home nations. However, she argues that if the NMAI is to truly reflect the realities of these tribal nations, it must also examine "the role of U.S. policies and practices" that had, and continue to have, a profound impact on the Indigenous people of Latin America.

Art historian Ruth Phillips also considers the transnational nature of the NMAI, turning her attention "north of the border" and placing the NMAI in conversation with the First Peoples Hall in the Canadian Museum of Civilization. In her essay "Inside Out and Outside In: Re-presenting Native North America at the Canadian Museum of Civilization and the National Museum of the American Indian," Phillips situates the two museums within the larger history of Natives and museums, contending that their similarities "testify to the epochal changes in the power relations between Indigenous peoples and settler institutions," significantly noting that such "changes participate in a global movement toward a postcolonial museology." However, Phillips emphasizes that each museum's exhibitions "point to historically contingent differences in the relationships between Indigenous peoples and the institutions and governments of Canada and the United States," thus firmly grounding her analysis in the specific. This enables her to consider the structures of power and curatorial processes that informed the development of each. By doing so, Phillips significantly reminds us that all "national" agendas are filtered through the individual curators whose own agendas play a critical role.

The cultural studies scholar Mario A. Caro turns his attention from the larger "national" agendas of the NMAI and instead focuses on the museum visitor's identity as a national subject. In "The National Museum of the American Indian and the Siting of Identity," Caro contextualizes what visitors bring with them, pointing out the ways in which a visitor's national identity is frequently multiple or in transition and calling into question the utility of the concept of master national narratives. In particular, he considers the significance of site—that is, a sense of belonging to a place—to a visitor's engagement with museums, arguing that the site-specificity of a museum has nationalist implications, particularly when considering the site of, for example, an on-reservation tribal museum. Although the tribal museum may reaffirm a sense of belonging or "homeland" for community members, Caro asserts that the site of the NMAI demands that visitors consider the role of the nation's capital in framing the presentation of Native cultures.

All of the scholars in these thoughtful and compelling essays offer reflections on a site of great historic and symbolic importance to Indigenous people. In the opening video in the Our Peoples gallery, the narrator encourages us to "view what's offered with respect. But also skepticism.

... Encounter it. Reflect on it. Argue with it." The authors of these essays take seriously that directive, and in the process they advance the discourse on this important site of Indigenous history, memory, and identity and will help to shape the future of the NMAI as it continues to evolve.

Editors' Note

The directorship of the NMAI has recently changed. Kevin Gover (Pawnee/ Comanche) assumed the role of director at the beginning of 2008 upon the retirement of W. Richard West (Southern Cheyenne) in 2007. Because the change occurred while this book was in production, some of the essays refer to West as the director. As a result, the collection provides a thorough analysis of the history of the NMAI from its inception as the Museum of the American Indian to its opening in 2004 to West's retirement in 2007.

Notes

1. Ruth Phillips, "Reply to James Clifford's 'Looking Several Ways: Anthropology and Native Heritage in Alaska,'" *Current Anthropology* 45, no. 1 (2004): 25.
2. Patricia Pierce Erikson with Helma Ward and Kirk Wachendorf, *Voices of a Thousand People* (Lincoln: University of Nebraska Press, 2002), 33.
3. The changing relationship between Indigenous people and museums and the important new developments mentioned have also been influenced by new directions in museum theory and practice. A few important works include: Michael Ames, *Cannibal Tours and Glass Boxes: The Anthropology of Museums* (Vancouver: University of British Columbia Press 1992); Ivan Karp and Steven Lavine, eds., *Exhibiting Cultures: The Poetics and Politics of Museum Displays* (Washington DC: Smithsonian Institution Press, 1991); Laura Peers and Alison Brown, eds., *Museums and Source Communities: A Routledge Reader* (New York: Routledge, 2003); Gail Anderson, ed., *Reinventing the Museum: Historical and Contemporary Perspectives on the Paradigm Shift* (Walnut Creek CA: AltaMira Press, 2004); Moira G. Simpson, *Making Representations: Museums in the Post-Colonial Era*, revised ed. (London: Routledge, 2001); James Clifford, "Museums as Contact Zones," in *Routes: Travel and Translation in the Late Twentieth Century* (Cambridge MA: Harvard University Press, 1997), 189–219; and Eilean Hooper-Greenhill, *Museums and the Shaping of Knowledge* (London: Routledge, 1992).

The National Museum of the American Indian
Critical Conversations

Conversation 1
History and Development

1. A New Thing?

The National Museum of the American Indian in Historical and Institutional Perspective

Ira Jacknis

In 1916 George Gustav Heye, a wealthy engineer and financier, founded the Museum of the American Indian in New York City. According to one curator, Heye (1874–1957) "managed over some sixty years to acquire the largest assemblage of Indian objects ever collected by a single person, ... now including more than 800,000 objects."[1] Heye served as director of the museum, which opened to the public in 1922, until 1956. In 1989, after several decades of financial problems and declining attendance, the Heye collections were transferred to the Smithsonian Institution, where they became the National Museum of the American Indian (NMAI).[2] The original buildings in upper Manhattan and the Bronx have now been replaced with three structures: the George G. Heye Center, which opened in lower Manhattan in 1994; the Cultural Resources Center in Suitland, Maryland (completed in 1998 and fully opened in 2003); and the main exhibit building on the Mall in Washington DC, opened in September 2004.

As my title suggests, my basic question is this: To what extent is and was the (National) Museum of the American Indian different or unique or new? To answer this question, we must compare the institution to other collections of Native American objects. Museums, however, come in many varieties of size, subject, and mission, and they change and evolve over time. They also have multiple functions. Among the primary aspects considered here are collection, exhibition, and education and outreach. In this essay, I place the Museum of the American Indian in varying disciplinal (anthropology, art, history) and geographic (city, region, nation) contexts.

Naturally, this vast undertaking requires many more pages than I have here, so my approach is to sketch out the big picture, composed of broad strokes instead of fine detail.[3] Although I consider the basics of George Heye's life and subsequent history of the Museum of the American Indian, this essay is meant to relate Heye and the MAI to a larger historical context.[4] Furthermore, this context is defined in terms of the institutions of the dominant society, not primarily those of Native cultures. Taking George Heye as our reference point, we can divide the history of the Museum of the American Indian into three periods: the time under Heye, the period after Heye's death, and the present, as the National Museum of the American Indian at the Smithsonian.

Native American Collections before George G. Heye

When Heye began his museum, Native American objects had already been the subject of four centuries of collecting.[5] During the first, extended period, from European exploration through the Civil War, collecting was both governmental and personal, and the principal agents were explorers, scientists, and merchants. Given the colonial situation, the very earliest collections are in Europe. One of the earliest American endeavors was the Lewis and Clark expedition of 1804–6, the first of many national reconnaissance surveys. The objects obtained on the trip went to President Jefferson and to Charles Willson Peale, whose Philadelphia museum served as an unofficial national repository. Like many museums before the Civil War, Peale's was a commercial operation, devoted to entertainment. Another institutional model was the many collections of local amateur societies, devoted to history or natural science. For example, the Peabody Museum, founded in Salem, Massachusetts, in 1799 as a maritime society, has significant Native American collections, especially from the Northwest Coast.[6]

Although the national collections at the Smithsonian were founded in 1846, it took at least until the Centennial of 1876 for the Smithsonian to accumulate significant American Indian artifacts.[7] At the Smithsonian, Native American cultures became the concern of the research Bureau of American Ethnology in 1879, assisted by the related U.S. National Museum, opened in 1881. Soon the primary venue for Native American collections would become the great municipal natural history museums, most notably New York's American Museum of Natural History, founded in 1869, and Chicago's Field Museum, founded in 1893.

It was also at about this time that anthropology became a specialized scholarly profession, in Europe as well as in America. Among the earliest homes for the discipline were the university museums of anthropology. Founded in 1866, the Harvard Peabody Museum of Anthropology is the oldest American museum devoted exclusively to anthropology. It was followed in 1889 by the University of Pennsylvania Museum and in 1901 by the University of California Museum of Anthropology (now known as the Phoebe Hearst Museum).

During the late nineteenth century, many state museums were founded in the West. Often located at the state university, they included anthropology. In addition to the University of California, Berkeley, the largest and oldest are the Washington State Museum (now the Burke Museum of Natural History and Culture) in Seattle, founded in 1885, and the Arizona State Museum in Tucson, founded in 1893.[8] All these museums tended to feature the Native artifacts of their respective regions. For instance, Arizona is solely an anthropology museum, dealing almost exclusively with the Southwest.[9]

These, then, would have been the relevant models for Heye as he set out. In some ways, his own collections would be like them; in other ways, they were different. From his developing practice, we can conclude that his closest model must have been the large collection in his home town of New York, the American Museum of Natural History, but as his interest developed he would have learned about the important collections at

Harvard, the University of Pennsylvania, and the Smithsonian. There were not many other places to see American Indian art on the East Coast, nor much more in Europe, where he traveled frequently, except in Berlin, which was then actively building its collection.

Each type of museum carried a different disciplinary message. History museums included Native and Anglo objects in a single narrative, even if it was a tale of conquest and disappearance. Natural history museums, on the other hand, were predicated on colonialist notions of survey, uniting the natural and cultural for the Native peoples encountered in contested lands. Art museums in the nineteenth century were generally reserved for Western culture and its direct ancestors. With some exceptions, such as the Boston Museum of Fine Arts, Asian arts were not yet granted full status; these were collected by only a few specialized museums, most in Europe.

While anthropology museums had the advantage of treating all of human culture on a comparative and autonomous level, their principal constraint was their general omission of Western cultures. In almost all of these museums, however, collections and exhibits were systematically arranged according to some disciplinary principle of classification. The dominant anthropological scheme—notably at the U.S. National Museum—was a putative evolutionary typology, from simple to advanced. In some museums—notably the Harvard Peabody—specimens were arranged according to geographic survey, with a distribution of types in space.

All these museums were also embedded in changing relations between dominant national powers throughout the Americas and their Aboriginal peoples. By the 1890s, when Heye began collecting, the American frontier was declared officially closed. With the cessation of the great Indian wars and the confinement of Native peoples to reservations, the dominant society adopted a range of ambivalent attitudes. On the one hand, the federal government implemented assimilationist policies that were designed to obliterate Native societies, including land allotment, boarding schools, and the banning of certain religious practices on reservations.[10] At the same time, however, many began to valorize Indian cultures. This period of romantic nostalgia witnessed perhaps the greatest period of private collecting. Stimulated by the Arts and Crafts movement, which valued handmade objects of natural materials, many people between 1880 and 1915 sought out Indian baskets, blankets, and pots. None, however, collected on the scale of George Heye.

George G. Heye and the
Museum of the American Indian (1897–1957)

Like many museums, the Museum of the American Indian has a prehistory, prior to its founding and subsequent opening. From a single Navajo hide shirt picked up casually in Arizona in 1897, Heye had, by 1914, become a full-time collector.[11] Two years later, he formally incorporated his private collection as a public museum, but it took until 1922 before the exhibits opened to the public. Without doubt, the 1920s were the museum's heyday, seeing the most extensive collecting, the opening of the public exhibits, and the erection of a storage building (called the Research Branch, or Annex) in the Bronx in 1926. In discussing the museum under George Heye, it may be useful to first consider features of the objects he collected before turning to his staff and his relation to contemporary anthropology.

In regard to their regional scope, Heye decided to focus his holdings only on the American continents, not the entire world, as most anthropology museums did. Yet, as Kidwell notes, when Heye started, American museums were actually losing interest in North American Indians.[12] The situation varied, however, from region to region, and for anthropological subdisciplines. At the two largest natural history museums, in New York and Chicago, collecting on the Northwest Coast did taper off by about 1905, but for the Plains it continued for another decade. For the Southwest, which is probably the most heavily collected region of Native America, it has never really stopped since the Smithsonian started in 1879. Compared to these other regions, the East tended to be ignored, but this was one area that Heye emphasized.[13]

Unlike the many smaller personal collectors of American Indian artifacts, Heye extended his American scope from the United States to the
rest of North, Central, and South America. About two-thirds of the collections are from the United States, a small percentage from Canada, and
the remaining from Latin America.[14] The Spanish-American War of 1898
generated an interest in Latin America among American anthropology
museums, and with his many expeditions to Mexico, the Caribbean, and
South America, Heye was, in fact, a pioneer of this trend.

Anthropological collections come from two very different sources:
ethnographic objects obtained directly or indirectly from Native owners, and archaeological specimens, which are generally removed from
the ground. It is an interesting and somewhat surprising fact that Heye's
main collecting interest was archaeology.[15] Most American museums of
the time focused on ethnology, if only because these objects tended to
be more colorful and varied and thus popular with visitors. There were
also more theoretical reasons. For instance, Alfred Kroeber at Berkeley
shunned archaeology because he believed that Native Californians had
not changed much during what he thought was their relatively short time
in the region. Heye, on the other hand, was particularly interested in the
Indian past. One consequence of this focus is that, like other museums
with important archaeological collections, such as Peabody and Penn, the
total size of his collection was vastly inflated compared to those composed
only of ethnography. There are several reasons for this: these objects are
often refuse or are otherwise abandoned; they can be obtained en masse
through excavation; and, perhaps most important, generally they do not
need to be individually purchased from a Native owner, who may still be
using the object.[16] Finally, collecting trends for archaeology were also
somewhat distinct from those for ethnography. For many regions, this
collecting peaked in the 1930s (in the 1950s for California), often following in the wake of development projects such as roads, dams, and buildings. Again, Heye's activity fits these trends.

Heye's artifactual sources, as in most anthropological museums, were diverse. Some objects he collected directly from Native people or, on occasion, on an archaeological expedition. He purchased many artifacts, especially ethnographic objects, from dealers, both local ones encountered on his trips—such as Grace Nicholson in California and William A. Newcombe in British Columbia—and merchants in distant cities such as London and Paris. The bulk of Heye's collections, especially the archaeology, came from his sponsored expeditions. Following the practice of the time, he also made exchanges with other museums (e.g., the Smithsonian, Pennsylvania, Field Museum, the private museum of Rudolf Haffenreffer).[17] As his museum became better known, particularly after 1930, he accepted donations from like-minded patrons and collectors.

To a greater degree than others, Heye's was a collection of collections. As a wealthy individual with a passion for rapidly building a huge collection, Heye was well known for his purchase of large, existing collections, as opposed to the more usual method of acquiring objects one by one.[18] He began the practice in 1903, when he bought an assemblage of southwestern archaeological pottery. It was this purchase that signaled his intention to expand his activity from a personal to a more scientific assemblage. Among the benefits of this practice was his acquisition of very old ethnographic collections, full of items that were no longer obtainable in Native communities. Even when negotiating for single items, Heye tended to buy in bulk, and his vacuum cleaner approach has been criticized for netting large quantities of undocumented, damaged, and unattractive objects. As curator Mary Jane Lenz notes, however, this practice may actually have increased the collection's research value. For, as Franz Boas maintained, anthropology shares with natural science an interest in the typical and in the full range of variation, as opposed to art's focus on individuality. Boas would also have agreed with Heye's desire that the "material must be old, no tourist material."[19]

One sign of Heye's disciplinary identifications was his creation in 1904 of a formal, written catalogue, and he continued to personally catalogue every object until his death.[20] The nature and degree of this documentation varied, however. Heye was notorious for his supposed lack of interest in such documentation, but the reality seems more contradictory. On the one hand, the archaeologist Samuel Lothrop reported that Heye often recorded guesses as fact, and one consequence of his frequent purchases of existing collections was that documentation was often lost.[21] On the other hand, Heye stressed to his collectors the necessity for field tags. In his correspondence with the art dealer Julius Carlebach, Heye repeatedly insisted on documentation. As he wrote in 1953, "The point of view for purchasing an ethnological piece is entirely different from the artistic point of view than it is from the scientific one," and he threatened to return some pieces unless he could get their provenience documentation.[22] In support of the research value of his collections, Heye also amassed relevant photographs, archives, and books (largely held by the separate but related Huntington Free Library in the Bronx).[23]

Turning now to George Heye's human and disciplinary context, we note that he maintained an ambivalent relation to the museum anthropology of his time. In 1907, after building a sizable collection, he joined in a cooperative arrangement with the University of Pennsylvania Museum. In exchange for public gallery space, "duplicate" specimens, and museum processing of his objects, Heye funded collecting expeditions and several staff positions.[24] The director assumed that in time these collections would be donated to Penn. In 1916, however, Heye withdrew his collections from Philadelphia to found his own museum in New York. When Boas, who had left the American Museum of Natural History in 1905 for a full-time professorship at Columbia, heard that Heye was about to establish his museum, he encouraged him to merge his collections with the large American Indian holdings at the Natural History Museum or to found a university museum at Columbia. Heye declined, citing his desire for an independent operation.[25] We must conclude that Heye supported Penn when he benefited from the relationship but rejected collaboration with Columbia when he had become large and experienced enough to go it alone.[26]

An analysis of Heye's roster of field collectors and professional staff is one of the clearest indications of his relationship to contemporary anthropology. Among his more prominent collectors, all on the permanent staff, were Marshall H. Saville, George H. Pepper, Mark R. Harrington, Frederick W. Hodge, and Samuel K. Lothrop. Heye hired Pepper and Harrington as curatorial assistants while his collections were at Penn.[27] Not surprisingly, however, most of the staff were hired after 1916, when Heye had access to funding from his fellow trustees.

Marshall Saville (1867–1935) and George Pepper (1873–1924) have been credited with being Heye's anthropological mentors,[28] and while this may be strictly true, both were about the same age as their patron (born 1874), who was in his twenties when he started to collect. Significantly, both had worked at the American Museum with Frederic W. Putnam (who was serving simultaneously as director of the Harvard Peabody Museum),[29] and both were archaeologists, Saville solely and Pepper primarily.

Marshall Saville studied anthropology at Harvard, working at the Peabody with Putnam in Mesoamerica. In 1894 he followed his mentor to the American Museum, again focusing on Central America, and in 1903 he joined the faculty of Columbia University.[30] After working with Heye in 1907 on an expedition to Ecuador, Saville joined the MAI staff in 1918, serving at both the MAI and Columbia until his retirement in 1932. George Pepper also worked with Putnam at both the American Museum and Harvard. After a 1904 expedition for Heye and another with Saville in 1907, Pepper was hired as curatorial assistant at the University of Pennsylvania in 1909. From 1910 until his death in 1924, Pepper worked for Heye. He was known for his collecting in the Southwest, archaeological as well as ethnographic.

Mark R. Harrington (1882–1971), who collected more than anyone on Heye's staff,[31] was yet another Putnam protégé. At the American Museum until 1903, he came to know both Saville and Pepper, as well as Boas, who guided his 1908 master's thesis. Hired as one of Heye's curatorial assistants at Penn, Harrington worked for his boss from 1911 until leaving for the Southwest Museum in 1928.

In addition to Saville, Heye hired two leading archaeologists: Frederick W. Hodge and Samuel K. Lothrop. Clearly the most prestigious appointment Heye ever made, Hodge came to the MAI in 1918 from the Smithsonian's Bureau of American Ethnology. At the museum, he served as assistant director and editor of the publication series until 1932.[32] The independently wealthy Lothrop was a specialist in Latin America, especially Mesoamerica. After earning his doctorate in anthropology from Harvard in 1921, he served on Heye's staff between 1924 and 1930 and was later associated with Harvard.

Several other notable anthropologists worked with Heye, although often for only short periods. Alanson B. Skinner was a specialist in the ethnology of the Indians of the East, especially the Great Lakes. After service at the American Museum (1907–15), he worked for Heye between 1915 and 1920, and again in 1924–25.[33] Jesse L. Nusbaum, known for his work in the Southwest, was employed by the MAI from May 1919 to June 1921. Ethnobotanist Melvin R. Gilmore, with a 1914 doctorate in botany, served on the staff from 1923 to 1928.

In characterizing these men, one notes that few of them were among the leading anthropologists of their day.[34] Although some had university training, few held doctorates (among the permanent staff, only Lothrop and Gilmore did).[35] In fact, many of Heye's field agents had no college at all and little formal training, for example, preparator William C. Orchard, staff assistant Charles O. Turbyfill, and staff photographer Edwin F. Coffin, all of whom made field collections.[36] Heye actually seems to have favored such self-trained men, just as he was self-trained in anthropology. In fact, when declining to join his museum with Boas and Columbia, Heye spoke of his support for the education of the general public over university training.[37] Admittedly, this was a time of transition in anthropology, as the discipline gradually professionalized. None of the early practitioners could have received a degree in the subject, and Heye's support enabled many talented men to obtain important field experience. The contributions of two men, Skinner and Pepper, were muted due to their early deaths at forty and fifty-one, respectively.

In addition to his permanent staff, headquartered in New York, Heye funded many local collectors on a more or less regular basis. Although these men made their living through other professions, they were often quite serious in their ethnographic collecting. Two of the most significant were William Wildschut, a Dutch-born businessman living in Billings, Montana, who collected among the Crow (1918–29), and Edward H. Davis, a rancher and hotelier from southern California, who made diverse collections from the Greater Southwest (1916–33).

Also among Heye's contract collectors were several Boasian anthropologists: Frank G. Speck, Samuel A. Barrett, and Thomas T. Waterman.[38] Notably, each collected for relatively short periods and relatively early in their careers (with the exception of Speck, who sent Heye objects for almost twenty years, from 1910 to 1929).

Broadening our view from the museum to the university, we note that Heye had no effective ties to the academy. It is true, as Kidwell claims, that he subsidized academic programs at Penn and Columbia, but this support was short-lived.[39] Instead, his primary support of academic anthropology came through his funding of a publications program under the editorship of Frederick Hodge.

This freedom from academia was double-edged. As Lothrop notes, this was a time when most anthropologists "were tied up by teaching."[40] For someone wanting to rapidly amass collections, full-time fieldwork was certainly desirable. On the other hand, the lack of students was an issue in the museum's gradual isolation. Not being at a university or effectively supporting university programs after the founding of his museum, Heye's institution succumbed to the fundamental problem suffered by all museums: they could not use the ready supply of new students for recruitment and to spread their influence. Without successive generations of new students, they could not easily reproduce themselves.

Heye, however, did have a distinctive, though informal, relationship to the anthropology of the time. It should be obvious that many of his staff had ties with Frederic W. Putnam (either at the American Museum or Harvard's Peabody) or with the Smithsonian. They were not part of Boas's circle at Columbia, who would soon come to dominate American anthropology. It is surely noteworthy that there were no real Boasians on the permanent staff, with the possible exceptions of Pepper and Skinner. Although Boas knew both from the American Museum, they were protégés of Putnam. And although Lothrop entered the program after Putnam's retirement, he was also a Harvard product. As the historian George Stocking maintains, there was a broad coalition between Boston (Harvard) and Washington (Smithsonian).[41] One of its traits was a concentration on archaeology, Heye's collecting focus. Boas in New York was known for his teaching in ethnology and language. Of Heye's staff collectors, only Harrington, Pepper, and Skinner did significant ethnographic collecting, and even for the former two, it was secondary to their archaeological work.

Not surprisingly, the most direct personal context for George Heye was his fellow trustees, old friends who, like him, were members of New York's elite.[42] All donated objects as well as funds. Among them were James B. Ford, a vice president of the U.S. Rubber Company; Harmon B. Hendricks, the owner of a metalworks; and Minor C. Keith, the founder of the United Fruit Company, which had substantial land holdings in Honduras. The most important, however, was Archer M. Huntington, the adopted son of railroad tycoon Collis P. Huntington. It was Huntington who encouraged Heye to incorporate the museum by offering him land on Audubon Terrace in upper Manhattan, where Huntington planned a cultural center consisting of the Hispanic Society, American Numismatic Society, American Geographical Society, American Academy of Arts and Letters, as well as the Museum of the American Indian.

The decades of depression and war (1930–45) were almost literally the dark ages of American museum anthropology. Most of the great collections were fairly static and neglected during this period. The American Museum, for example, focused on impressive dioramas and displays of dinosaurs, yet even it suffered during this period. In fact, for Heye the Depression started a year earlier, in 1928, with the almost simultaneous deaths of two of his most important trustees, Ford and Hendricks (followed by three more within the year). Although both left generous bequests, these could not replace the substantial outright funds they had previously donated. With the loss of this income, Heye was forced to choose between collecting and his scientific staff.[43] He decided to lay off almost the entire curatorial staff and to end scientific work. As several commentators have noted, this was a clear expression of Heye's priorities.

Some collecting continued, however, in the succeeding years. By the early 1930s, Heye was sending out modest expeditions, primarily for archaeology.[44] Even more important, he took the opportunity of hard times for other museums and collectors to purchase significant existing collections. These were cheaper to acquire because they did not need staff to gather them. On the other hand, at times he was forced to do his own deaccessioning. In the early 1940s, Heye sold parts of his collections, especially Eskimo and Northwest Coast pieces, to local dealers.

While other museums gradually recovered after World War II, especially for disciplines other than anthropology, Heye's museum did not. The Museum of the American Indian never regained the dynamism and activity it had achieved during the 1920s. Moreover, when George Heye began his collections, museums were the prime institutional home to anthropology, but by 1930 they had been largely supplanted by university programs. The rise and fall of Heye's fortunes coincided with the curtailment of his museum, further contributing to its growing marginalization.

After Heye: Crises at the Museum of the American Indian, 1957–1989

Although the fate of Heye's museum after his death was to some extent special and unique, in many respects it participated in dominant trends

in the collecting and display of Native American artifacts. Most fundamental, perhaps, was the gradual cessation of large-scale collecting,
especially among the largest, eastern museums. The collecting that did
continue was mostly of newly made objects by smaller institutions in
the West.

In the absence of new additions, these accumulated collections began
to attract the attention of researchers. There seems to be little evidence
that Heye's collections were so used during his lifetime, despite mentions in museum publications of such research.[45] Heye's interest seemed
to be in accumulation for study in an indefinite future. In this, however,
his museum was like most of the great anthropology collections made
in the early twentieth century. This was a period of acquisition, not one
of researcher study of museum collections. That came only in the 1960s,
with a retrospective view of Native American history and a growing appreciation for the uses of these accumulated collections (see below).[46]

Like the MAI, the largest anthropological collections in the East, most
notably those at the "big three" natural history museums (New York's
American Museum of Natural History, Chicago's Field Museum, and
Washington's Smithsonian), left their Native American exhibits virtu-
ally unchanged (with the exception of the Field's Arctic and Northwest
Coast Hall, opened in 1982).

Instead, the center of gravity regarding Native American collections
shifted west, especially to smaller museums, such as the Heard Museum
in Phoenix, and to the art museums of cities such as Denver and Seattle,
which are associated with strong regional Native cultures and, more
important, strong markets. For example, the Heard has thrived because
of the influx of collectors and wealth to the Sun Belt. As in many western
museums close to substantial Indian territories, here Indians are seen as
part of the local, regional identity. Over the twentieth century, there has
been a decline in the somewhat colonialist domination of metropolitan
museums, except perhaps in some of the great eastern art museums.

With the death of George Heye, the crisis at the MAI was partly financial but primarily institutional. The museum was never able to overcome the financial problems that had first set in around 1928. One of the inherent structural problems of a single-patron museum is the difficulty of continuation when that support wanes (see the next section). Although Heye had adequate funding from his fellow trustees during the 1920s, he was not able to replace them, and his own finances dimmed over time.

Administrative succession is a problem for all institutions, but it is even more critical for a personally founded and funded museum. The Museum of the American Indian has had relatively few directors in its almost ninety-year history: George G. Heye (1916–56), Edwin K. Burnett (1956–60), Frederick J. Dockstader (1960–75), Roland W. Force (1977–90), W. Richard West Jr. (1990–2007), and Kevin Gover (2007–present). Not counting Gover and with the exception of the interim appointment of Burnett, each represented a significant departure from the practices of his predecessor.

Burnett clearly represented a temporary solution. With no academic credentials, he had been the museum librarian and Heye's assistant. Dockstader, on the other hand, came with a doctorate from Case Western Reserve University (1951). He started out as a breath of fresh air, refurbishing the exhibits and publishing several books on the collection,[47] but Dockstader's later tenure was marred by a host of museological problems: claims of unethical deaccessioning of objects, a lack of inventory control, and unchanging displays and a consequent lack of visitors to a site in an unattractive neighborhood. Force, a Pacific ethnologist but an experienced museum director, was hired to resolve these accumulated problems.[48]

Like all museums, Heye's institution has to be considered in relation to others of its locality. Considering the issue of urban ecology, we may ask, To what extent did the MAI act as a local institution, catering to local audiences, and to what extent did it serve a national role? The great cultural complex on Audubon Terrace envisioned by MAI trustee Archer Huntington never matched their founders' dreams. Despite its great size,

Heye's museum had little relation to the other great Native American collection at the American Museum of Natural History or to the important but smaller one at the Brooklyn Museum. In fact, it never received the attention or visitorship that these did. One would imagine that many of its visitors were from out of town.

One solution to the MAI's problems was to merge with another institution. Several possibilities were explored, but the most serious offer was from the American Museum of Natural History. Ironically, Franz Boas had suggested the very thing when Heye founded his museum back in 1916, but Heye rejected the offer, having been in partnership once before, with Penn. Yet by the 1970s, this seemed like a compelling approach to the trustees. The American Museum was pushing for it, proposing the merger of their two American Indian collections. But this was ultimately rejected by the Heye administration; as before, they thought that the merger would not be on their terms or in their best interests.

Heye's Museum: Private and Public Ownership

During his lifetime, Heye's collection went though several changes in ownership and direction. Although it may have begun as a purely personal passion, upon the museum's incorporation in 1916 it was required to serve public functions as part of its charter. In this, the Museum of the American Indian differed from other private museums, which may not be open to the public, and if they are, rarely have a large professional staff, a complete catalogue, and a publication series. Clearly, Heye was modeling his institution on those such as the American Museum or the University of Pennsylvania. Heye's fellow trustees seem to have supported him completely, allowing him to serve as director for the remainder of his life. Although his funds could not fully support all the institution's activities, the Museum of the American Indian functioned as Heye's personal fiefdom until his death.

Heye's museum was certainly the largest "private" collection of American Indian artifacts, but it was not alone. Other significant collections of the early twentieth century included those founded by Rudolf Haffenreffer (Mount Hope, Rhode Island), Dwight and Maie B. Heard (Phoenix, Arizona), Mary C. Wheelwright (Santa Fe, New Mexico), Millicent Rogers (Taos, New Mexico), Mary and Francis Crane (Florida Keys, now in Denver), and Sheldon Jackson (Sitka, Alaska).[49] Heye's friend Rudolf Haffenreffer was clearly his most similar exemplar. Even more common were prominent art museums dominated by a founding collector. Among the best known are the institutions founded by Isabella Stewart Gardner in Boston, Henry Clay Frick in New York, and Albert C. Barnes in Merion, Pennsylvania; and there are many more.

As diverse as they are, these museums share important features. First, as noted by the historian Kathleen McCarthy, relatively marginalized fields such as anthropology, folk art, and modern art often attract patrons who are themselves marginal, such as women, the young, and those living in distant regions. (Of course, all this is relative; almost all subjects of collecting go through cycles of interest.)[50] In such arenas there was less competition from the wealthiest and most prestigious collector-patrons. Though Heye and his trustees were not as marginal as some, certainly their money went further for the purchase of American Indian artifacts than it would have for Old Master paintings.

Personal direction also encourages idiosyncrasy and freedom from disciplinary boundaries. With his control, Heye did not have to be exactly anthropological, although he followed this discipline more than any other. His single-minded control of the institution, from direction to cataloguing, also meant that he did not fully make use of trained professionals. Such freedom carries with it a negative side: a lack of support from that discipline. When Heye encountered financial and then staffing problems in the Depression, he was largely on his own.

Another problem that affects many such museums that have grown out of a founder's vision is that they often find themselves in now undesirable locations.[51] The Museum of the American Indian was never able to overcome its location in Manhattan's far uptown. Rudolf Haffenreffer's museum in Mount Hope, on the Rhode Island coast, is far from the Brown University campus, which it joined in 1955. The Southwest Museum in the Highland Park section of Los Angeles is perhaps the closest parallel to the MAI. The oldest museum in the city, the Southwest Museum was founded by Charles F. Lummis in 1907, although most of its finances came from others. It, too, had accumulated many fine collections over its distinguished history, but by the end of the twentieth century it was not attracting the funding and visitors it needed. Trustees at both the Southwest Museum and the MAI were confronted by a dilemma: on the one hand, they needed the assistance of a larger museum (or a very rich patron); on the other, neither desired to lose its autonomy and distinguished history. Finally, in 2003, the Southwest Museum became a unit of the Autry National Center (formerly the Autry Museum of Western Heritage).

Fundamentally, many of these private museums have a problem of succession, in the broadest sense. Unlike the U.S. Constitution, it seems that it is not so easy for personally founded museums to formulate both a vision and a means of support in order to extend their institutions beyond the lives of their original owners. In some cases—such as the museums founded by Phoebe Hearst and Gene Autry, to name two diverse examples—the museum successfully redefines its mission and the institution grows beyond the visions of its founders. When it does not, as was the case for the MAI, it often declines. Although there are some notable exceptions—such as the Heard on a larger scale and the Wheelwright on a smaller scale—most of these private museums have survived by merging with a larger and stronger institution. This, in the end, was the fate of Heye's museum.

A National Museum, 1989–Present

In 1989, the Museum of the American Indian became the National Museum of the American Indian, a part of the Smithsonian. Its new director, W. Richard West Jr. (Southern Cheyenne), has served from 1990 to 2007.[52]

The story of the Museum of the American Indian is very much an account of institutional changes. All museums have a life history, with ups and downs, but the Heye's history was particularly severe and dramatic: a rapid and great high and then a protracted low, followed by a radical transformation. Its ownership and control moved from totally private to almost completely public, the extremes of corporate embodiment.

This change in ownership coincided with temporal shifts in Native American cultures, their relation to the dominant society, and the collection and study of their artifacts. These larger trends would have affected the MAI whatever its status, as they have all Native American collections. As suggested by the anthropologist Edward Bruner, all ethnography embodies narrative strategies. For those concerned with Native American culture—Native as well as non-Native—there has been a shift over the twentieth century from a story of vanishing cultures to accounts of survival and resistance.[53] Beginning in the late 1960s and coming to fruition through the 1970s was the Red Power movement, broadly defined. Like other minority groups, Indians now demanded control of their representation. Very little of this was represented at the MAI during the Dockstader years. In 1977, after his departure, things started to change as the first two of thirteen Indian trustees was appointed: George H. J. Abrams (Iroquois) and Vine Deloria Jr. (Dakota).[54]

In considering the place of the Heye collection at the Smithsonian, one must examine the Smithsonian's other acquisitions of entire museums, for this was not the first time that the institution had grown by merger. There had been the much earlier donation of the Asian art collection of Charles L. Freer (donated in 1906 and opened in 1923) and the later one by Arthur M. Sackler (donated in 1982 and opened in 1987). Even closer parallels were the 1967 takeover of the Cooper-Hewitt collection of design and decorative arts in New York (founded in 1897), and particularly the 1979 acquisition of Washington's Museum of African Art (founded in 1964 and opened on the Mall in 1987).

Though relatively rare, such complete mergers are not unusual in the museum world. In many cases, the unions are perceived as filling in gaps in collecting. For instance, in 1976 the Museum of Primitive Art, founded by Nelson Rockefeller in 1957, joined with the Metropolitan Museum of Art, which had not previously collected the tribal arts of Africa, Oceania, and the Americas. Encyclopedic museums like the Met seem to be constantly adding entire departments of photography, modern art, or "primitive" art, objects that had not been defined as art at the museum's founding in the mid-nineteenth century.

The acquisition of entirely new collections and museums at the Smithsonian must be considered in light of the institution's constant redefinition of its mission. Its vast collections and the museums that house them have been especially fluid over their more than 150-year history.[55] Even at its birth following the bequest of British scientist James Smithson, its fundamental mission was uncertain and contested. In time, the Smithsonian was defined as the national museum. As the collections grew in size and scope, they were constantly subdivided and rearranged. Whole new subjects were declared desirable; for instance, until Freer donated his Asian art, the Smithsonian had not formally collected fine art, and it was only in 1964 that a museum of American history was opened. Coupled with these dramatic changes, however, is a great deal of institutional inertia, due partly to a lack of funding but more to the accumulated bureaucracy and the restrictions of congressional support.

One of the interesting consequences of this tangled institutional history is that in many cases the Smithsonian has accumulated multiple museums that collect and display the same kind of objects. Again, the primary parallel is with the African and Asian collections. In these cases, new museums—formed from new collections—opened in 1987: the National Museum of African Art and the Arthur M. Sackler Gallery for Asian art. African and Asian artifacts had long been separately collected and displayed as ethnology at the National Museum of Natural History. The Smithsonian attitude toward this overlap has been to let a hundred flowers bloom, that is, to encourage—or at least tolerate—multiple presentations.

The terms of the merger called for the naming of an independent board of trustees. Although this may be somewhat unusual at the Smithsonian, it is not unheard of, as the National Gallery is similarly independent. So there was plenty of precedent for keeping the Heye collection separate from the existing and important Native American collection in the Anthropology Department of the National Museum of Natural History. By maintaining its separate identity, the Heye collection could develop freely, as Heye and the last board of the MAI trustees had insisted on.

There are, however, two major problems with the Smithsonian anthropological approach to Native American cultures. First, like so many of its sister institutions (particularly the largest, in New York and Chicago), it is part of a natural history museum. As noted earlier, such presentations stem largely from colonialist notions that only some humans are part of nature. During the 1970s there were abortive plans for a national museum of man, but this idea never got beyond a sign outside the building that read "National Museum of Natural History" and "National Museum of Man." Separate national museums for anthropology and human cultures are actually the norm in most parts of the world. There are such museums in the capital cities of Canada, Mexico, France, Germany, and Japan, among many others. Even in Britain (where such collections are part of the encyclopedic British Museum) there was a separate Museum of Mankind from 1970 to 1997.

An even more unfortunate problem was that the American Indian displays at the Natural History Museum remained static for decades, until finally closing in May 2004. In 1999, the museum was able to open African Voices, a new hall of African cultures, but it has not been able to do the same for Native America. The recently closed hall had "ancient" roots, much of it having been prepared by William H. Holmes in 1903. It was revised by John C. Ewers in the mid-1950s, and there were many more minor changes since, but years of planning have not resulted in a new hall.[56] The thoroughly outdated and unappealing gallery was quite a contrast with the new national American Indian museum. The reasons for this inaction are unclear, and are probably multiple, but it seems evident that the ongoing fund-raising efforts during the past decade to build the new museum on the Mall competed with and swamped Smithsonian attempts to create a specifically anthropological presentation. More than this, it leaves some very important collections unseen and dangerously unknown by the general public.[57]

This recent spate of ethnically marked museums raises the issue of who and what determines which groups should be honored at the national museum by their own free-standing institution. Although it had been claimed that the NMAI would be the last Smithsonian museum to be built on the Mall, room has been found for a National Museum of African American History and Culture.[58] Is there any limit to these ethnically delimited museums? Certainly there is a spatial limit on the Mall, home to most of these institutions. In fact, many museums devoted to American ethnic groups, often with "National" in their title, are not part of the Smithsonian and have homes outside of Washington. For instance, the Japanese American National Museum (founded in 1985) is in Los Angeles. The problems of the Museum of the American Indian in New York were fortuitously taken advantage of in Washington, advanced by strong congressional support.

There is a tendency for national anthropology museums, especially in non-Western countries, to have the largest and most comprehensive such collection in the nation. The Smithsonian collection is clearly comparable to the national anthropology museums in the capitals of most large Western countries: Canada (Canadian Museum of Civilization), Mexico (Museo Nacional de Antropología), France (Musée de l'Homme), Germany (Museum für Völkerkunde), and the United Kingdom (the Ethnology Department of the British Museum).

For museums, the term "national" is ambiguous. On the one hand, it usually means simply that the collection is owned by the nation-state.

However, it may also mean that the museum is restricted to objects from within the country's borders. Anthropology, as a cross-cultural study of humanity, fits uneasily into this scheme. Interestingly enough, the other national anthropology museums in North America, in Ottawa-Hull and Mexico City, focus on the Native peoples of their country, whereas the European ones, all associated with major colonial powers, collect from all over the world.[59] The Smithsonian looks both ways, with an international focus in the Department of Anthropology in the Natural History Museum and the Museum of the American Indian resembling the two American institutions in its Americanist focus.

Unlike those, however, the NMAI is unique in including collections from throughout the Western hemisphere, from Canada to Chile. When one considers Heye's own interests, as well as the composition of his board, it is clear that this expansive viewpoint stemmed from a somewhat imperialist attitude lacking in Ottawa and Mexico City. When the Museum of the American Indian became the National Museum of the American Indian it accepted Heye's scope of collecting and was challenged to respond to it with exhibits and programs.

Comparative Collections:
Regional Representation and Size

Many collections of American Indian material are in regional museums, focusing on the Native peoples of their local area. This seems to be particularly true in the Southwest, which has the Southwest Museum in Los Angeles, the Museum of Man in San Diego, the Heard in Phoenix, and the Museum of Indian Arts and Culture, School of American Research, and Wheelwright Museum in Santa Fe. A regional focus also characterizes most of the state museums in the West. For example, the Hearst Museum at the University of California, Berkeley has the preeminent collection of California Indian material, just as the Burke Museum at the University of Washington focuses on the Northwest Coast and the University of Arizona emphasizes the Southwest.

There are several good reasons for such specialization. As is well known, there are substantial differences among Native American cultures, particularly in art and artifact styles. Taking as an example the dominant form of containers, we have wooden boxes on the Northwest Coast, plant fiber baskets in California, clay pots in the Southwest, and hide bags on the Plains. This diversity makes it hard to generalize. More practically, if an individual or small institution has limited funds, it is easier to build and manage a comprehensive regional collection than one for the entire continent.

This is true even for the largest institutions. Only a handful of museums have substantial representation of the entire continent, let alone all of North, Central, and South America. In fact, the Heye does not have the totally encyclopedic coverage that one may think. According to one former curator, "There are collections from all major culture areas of the Americas," but while "virtually all tribes of the United States" are represented, only "most" tribes from Canada and only "a smaller number" from Mexico and Central and South America are a part of the collection.[60]

The National Museum of the American Indian may be the largest museum devoted completely to that subject, but it is especially difficult to determine this. First, one would need to compare the sizes of just the Native American components of the largest collections, but such figures are not readily available. More important, it is almost impossible to determine the size of especially large collections. This is due in part to the sheer difficulty of the procedure, but a fundamental reason is the varying and almost arbitrary definitions of what a single object is.[61] For this reason, museums often give two totals: the number of catalogue entries, usually more definite, and the number of individual objects in the collection, more often an estimate.[62]

Among collections comparable to the NMAI (with about 890,000 objects), at the top in the United States are the three largest natural history museums: those in New York, Washington, and Chicago. Of the university anthropology museums, only the largest, the Harvard Peabody

Museum, has strengths in every region.[63] Those with a somewhat smaller size and scope include the university museums at Penn and Berkeley and the natural history museum in Milwaukee. Among art museums, the clear leader is the Denver Art Museum (around 16,000 objects), which, though relatively smaller, excels aesthetically and in documentation. In addition to the Museum of the American Indian, these eight institutions are the largest with comprehensive American Indian collections.

Disciplinary Distinctions: Art and Anthropology

As James Clifford reminds us, anthropology and art are but two discourses of Western disciplinary culture, whatever real differences they may have.[64] And both are apt to vary profoundly from the original conceptions of the makers and users of Native American objects. In Heye's day, few art museums collected Native American artifacts, unlike the museums of history, natural history, and anthropology. Due to specific historical situations, such artifacts were included in some smaller museums, such as those of Brooklyn and Cincinnati, but the art museums of the largest cities, such as New York, Boston, and Chicago, collected American Indian art not at all or only by accident. The first art museum to specialize in Native American objects was, not coincidentally, located in the heart of Indian country: the Denver Art Museum, beginning in 1925.[65]

George Heye expressed no doubts about his allegiance to anthropology. As he annunciated in his mission statement: "This Museum occupies a unique position among institutions, in that its sole aim is to gather and to preserve for students everything useful in illustrating and elucidating the anthropology of the aborigines of the Western Hemisphere, and to disseminate by means of its publications the knowledge thereby gained."[66] To accomplish this aim, Heye hired many trained anthropologists and established a department of physical anthropology.[67]

Yet all around him the museum treatment of Indian objects was changing. The primitivist revolution begun by Picasso with African art was spreading to America. One of the pioneers was René d'Harnoncourt, director of the U.S. Indian Arts and Crafts Board and later director of New York's Museum of Modern Art. In 1941, d'Harnoncourt and Frederic Douglas, curator of Denver's collection, put together an influential exhibit at the Museum of Modern Art: Indian Arts of the United States. At the same time, Heye was unwittingly encouraging this movement. As Heye was deaccessioning Eskimo and Northwest Coast objects to Julius Carlebach and other dealers, they were eagerly snapped up by a group of émigré French Surrealist artists living in New York during the Second World War. They, and the Abstract Expressionists who came after them, made great claims for the high aesthetic status of these objects.[68]

The current widespread presence of Native American objects in art museums is a relatively recent development, which began in the mid-1960s.[69] This positive reevaluation has certainly affected how Heye's collections are viewed by the general public. The NMAI's exhibits are now reviewed by the art critics of the *New York Times*, and, more important, the very same kinds of things on display in its galleries now fetch high prices among private collectors. The millions of dollars that it took to construct the new NMAI building on the Mall would never have been possible if these objects were still defined as anthropological specimens.

At the time of the museum's opening on the Mall, prominent staff denied the relevance of an anthropological perspective in its exhibits (despite the presence of several anthropologists among its curators).[70] Richard West often recounted the disappointed reaction of a visiting art museum director, acknowledging that the museum is not directed toward collectors or those interested merely in objects. Ironically, in its focus on culture over objects, the NMAI allies itself with Franz Boas and anthropology, against aesthetics, the art market, and art museums.[71] In fact, Boas's more holistic, people-centered view of anthropology museums distanced him from the acquisitive, object-obsessed Heye.

As we have seen, the Museum of the American Indian's freedom from a natural history perspective has long allied the museum with the several free-standing anthropology museums. On the other hand, its limited focus on Native America has given it a kind of cultural unity more often found in history museums; the MAI is not nearly as cross-cultural as most anthropological museums. In this, it resembles the scholarly field of Native American studies, which incorporates multiple academic disciplines. Most important, it recognizes the validity of alternative Native American realities. In the realm of museums, the Museum of the American Indian is thus more like a tribal museum.

Ironically, although NMAI practice since 1990 may have been motivated by an attempt to restore Heye's collections to a more original, Native context, this very reappropriation is fundamental to what one might call the "museum process." Objects are susceptible to constant reinterpretation as they move beyond their original makers and users.[72] Heye had done this to other private collections that he purchased, as he had to all the Native American objects that he—and others—collected. Paradoxically, although objects in a museum may be enduring, as are the institutions themselves, they are often radically revalued over time. Often museums do not explicitly acknowledge these reevaluations. In the case of the NMAI, there is no doubt.

The Tribal Perspective

As the National Museum of the American Indian has been defined by the enabling legislation and the practice of Richard West's administration, the Heye collection has became a fundamentally different kind of institution in regard to Native peoples. Given the emphasis of the other essays in this volume, I will not dwell on the current practices of the museum, but a few comparative comments are useful.

From all accounts, George Heye had little interest in contemporary Indians; it was the Native American past that motivated him. As one associate recalled, "He didn't give a hang about Indians and he never seemed to have heard about their problems in present-day society."[73] In his own practice he seems to have embodied some of the larger society's ambivalence toward American Indians, simultaneously destroying and preserving Aboriginal cultures. On a number of occasions he was involved in shady ethics. In 1914, he and his team were arrested—but acquitted—for grave robbing in New Jersey. On the other hand, he did hire at least one Native American, Amos Oneroad (Dakota), who became a close collaborator with Alanson Skinner.[74] Unfortunately, the best example of Heye's progressive behavior was not what it appeared to be. In 1938 he agreed to repatriate a medicine bundle to the Water Buster Clan of the Hidatsa.[75] It seems, however, that he could not bear to part with it, as he gave back generic bundle contents. In 1977 the museum returned what remained of the original. One might note that if Heye may have been a little more disrespectful than most, such practices were relatively common at the time. Convinced that American Indians would soon be extinct, culturally if not physically, even Franz Boas uncovered burials.

During the past two decades anthropology museums and other institutions holding objects from ethnic "source communities" have become more responsive to demands by such communities for control over their representation.[76] The shift in control of the Heye collections is thus part of a much wider museological trend,[77] and it is certainly in the expression of a Native voice that the National Museum most differs from its ancestor. Following the spirit of the Native American Graves Protection and Repatriation Act of 1990, which does not apply to the Smithsonian, the museum has a policy of expedited repatriation of skeletal and sacred collections. These archaeological collections, of such interest to Heye, now contain items that many Native people think should not be in museums, and relatively few are exhibited. For those sacred objects that it preserves, the museum tries to care for them according to Native protocols.[78] The NMAI offers a wide range of services to Native communities, and in this it is carrying forth and expanding several outreach programs that the Smithsonian has sponsored since 1973.[79] Onsite programs are aimed at elementary and secondary schools, student interns, artists, and museum professionals. External programs include community workshops and media productions in radio, books, sound recordings, and the Internet.

Museum staff at the NMAI liken this to their "fourth museum," apart from the actual buildings in New York, Maryland, and Washington.[80]

In some ways, one may view the NMAI as a kind of national tribal museum. As a type of museum, tribal museums are a particularly recent development.[81] There was a Cherokee tribal museum as early as 1828, but most existing tribal museums have been founded since the 1960s. Today there are more than two hundred tribal institutions in the United States and Canada. Many, in fact, avoid the term "museum" in favor of "cultural center," implying a broader scope that goes beyond the collection and display of artifacts. With the notable exception of the Mashantucket Pequot Museum and Research Center in Connecticut (opened in 1998), most suffer the problems of many smaller museums, such as a lack of collections, trained staff, funding, and facilities. With its relatively abundant resources, the National Museum can be of enormous assistance to its sister institutions.

As an institutional genre, the tribal museum is a Native American variant of the more general museum type of a community museum.[82] While most are addressed to fairly small-scale populations of interacting people, such as the Chinatown museums in New York and San Francisco, some are larger ethnic museums working in a national perspective, such as the Japanese American National Museum (Los Angeles) and the National Afro-American Museum and Cultural Center (near Dayton, Ohio).

At first glance, the NMAI seems more like one of these ethnic museums, being national and located in Washington. Yet it must also be something few other tribal museums are: multitribal. It cannot simply present one Native viewpoint, given the tremendous diversity within Native American cultures. One way out of this dilemma is a certain focus on the local Native peoples who originally inhabited the museum's homes in Washington and New York. For instance, the café in the Mall building is called Mitsitam, which means "Let's eat" in Piscataway and Delaware.[83] The other approach is multiple perspectives. For instance, the café contains five stations, each featuring a different geographic and culinary tradition. And this mode of multiple case studies underlies the bulk of the current exhibits.

While the NMAI clearly operates according to many Native programs and procedures, to what extent can this be mandated for a national museum, funded, at least in part, by the federal government? The fundamental direction, as one might expect, was laid out in the establishing legislation, which calls for more than half of the trustees to be Native American.[84] Thus Indians have a deciding say in the conception and running of the museum. They could conceivably choose a non-Native director and staff, but their basic priorities are clear. Another factor in opening up the museum to outside influences is the fact that, as is true of the rest of the Smithsonian, the federal government does not fund the museum's total budget. In fact, the NMAI was required by Congress to seek outside funding for its Mall building.[85]

A fundamental question for any museum is the identity of its audience. Are the museum's programs directed primarily to those inside or outside the culture being represented? Like many tribal museums, the NMAI embodies an institutional tension, serving as a venue for Native insiders to present their cultures to the many non-Native outsiders who visit the Mall museums. Even if it is largely staffed by Natives and many of its programs are for Natives, as a national institution it has to speak to the entire nation and world.

A Self-Conscious Model for Museum Practice

There are some things that the old Heye Foundation shares with the new National Museum of the American Indian. Some are relatively trivial, such as the ethnobotanical garden at the Bronx research branch, which anticipated the current plantings on the Mall.[86] Others are more structural and substantial. The Museum of the American Indian has always been big and wholly concerned with Native Americans. Because of the size of the collection, both versions have separate buildings for exhibits and collections storage. Since the time of Heye, the museum's trustees have insisted on a relative autonomy, which survives even as a branch of the Smithsonian. In this, it has been able to remain somewhat free of disciplinary categories such as art, anthropology, and history.

On the other hand, as many have noted, the museum would probably be unrecognizable to George G. Heye. First, and perhaps most important, it is focused on culture, not objects. And in place of the founder's interest in a distant past, represented by non-Natives, the current museum emphasizes the present as seen by American Indians themselves. Finally, it did this by moving from private ownership by one man to control by all Native Americans on behalf of the entire nation.[87]

Thus, the conclusion to my initial question is that, although the National Museum of the American Indian may not be a completely new thing, it is essentially unique. It resembles a wide variety of museums, containing aspects of these others, but there is really nothing exactly like it, even in other countries. Because of this, I suppose the conclusion must be that no matter what else happens in its long history, it will never be dull.

Notes

For assistance in the preparation of this essay I would like to thank Malu Beltrán, Rachel E. Griffin, Curtis M. Hinsley Jr., Steven Karr, Amy Lonetree, Mary Jane Lenz, and Ann McMullen.

1. Mary Jane Lenz, "George Gustav Heye: The Museum of the American Indian," in *Spirit of a Native Place: Building the National Museum of the American Indian*, ed. Duane Blue Spruce (Washington DC: National Museum of the American Indian, National Geographic Society, 2004), 87.
2. In this essay, I use the abbreviation MAI (Museum of the American Indian, also known as the Heye Foundation) to differentiate it from NMAI (National Museum of the American Indian), part of the Smithsonian.
3. Given the wide scope of this essay, a word is in order on my sources. In addition to specific historical sources, cited below, this essay derives from my thirty-plus years of work in anthropology museums and research on American Indian art and culture. I have worked at the Yale Peabody Museum, Field Museum, Smithsonian, Brooklyn Museum, and Hearst Museum, and have conducted extensive archival and collection research in other museums. This essay also draws on the research on Northwest Coast

collections embodied in my recent book, *The Storage Box of Tradition: Kwakiutl Art, Anthropologists, and Museums, 1881–1981* (Washington DC: Smithsonian Institution Press, 2002).

4. There are relatively few published sources on the Museum of the American Indian. Among the useful overviews are "Aims and Objects of the Museum of the American Indian, Heye Foundation," in *Indian Notes and Monographs* 36 (New York: Museum of the American Indian, Heye Foundation, 1929); "The History of the Museum," in *Indian Notes and Monographs, Miscellaneous Series* 55 (New York: Museum of the American Indian, Heye Foundation, 1956); U. Vincent Wilcox, "The Museum of the American Indian, Heye Foundation," *American Indian Art Magazine*, 3, no. 2 (Spring 1978): 40–49, 78, 79, 81; Tim Johnson, ed., *Spirit Capture: Photographs from the National Museum of the American Indian* (Washington DC: Smithsonian Institution Press, 1998); Duane Blue Spruce, ed., *Spirit of a Native Place: Building the National Museum of the American Indian* (Washington DC: National Museum of the American Indian, National Geographic Society, 2004); the special issue of *American Indian Art Magazine* 29, no. 4 (Autumn 2004); and Edmund Carpenter, *Two Essays: Chief and Greed* (North Andover MA: Persimmon Press, 2005).

5. There is no comprehensive review on Native American collecting, but see Shepard Krech III and Barbara Hail, eds., *Collecting Native America, 1870–1960* (Washington DC: Smithsonian Institution Press, 1999), and Beverly Gordon with Melanie Herzog, *American Indian Art: The Collecting Experience* (Madison WI: Elvehjem Museum of Art, 1988). For specific regions, see Douglas Cole, *Captured Heritage: The Scramble for Northwest Coast Artifacts* (Seattle: University of Washington Press, 1985); Nancy Parezo, "The Formation of Ethnographic Collections: The Smithsonian Institution in the American Southwest," in *Advances in Archaeological Method and Theory*, ed. Michael B. Schiffer (New York: Academic Press, 1987), 10:1–47; Don D. Fowler, *A Laboratory for Anthropology: Science and Romanticism in the Southwest, 1846–1930* (Albuquerque: University of New Mexico Press, 2000); Marvin Cohodas, *Basket Weavers for the California Curio Trade: Elizabeth and Louise Hickox* (Tucson: University of Arizona Press, 1997).

6. Castle McLaughlin, *Arts of Diplomacy: Lewis and Clark's Indian Collection* (Cambridge MA: Peabody Museum of Archaeology and Ethnology of Harvard University, 2003), 70; Mary Malloy, *Souvenirs of the Fur Trade: Northwest Coast Indian Art and Artifacts Collected by American Mariners, 1788–1844* (Cambridge MA: Peabody Museum of Archaeology and Ethnology of Harvard University, 2003).

7. Curtis M. Hinsley Jr., *Savages and Scientists: The Smithsonian Institution and the*

Development of American Anthropology, 1846–1910 (Washington DC: Smithsonian Institution Press, 1981).

8. In both Seattle and Tucson, however, it was years before the first anthropologist was hired: 1930 for Washington and 1915 for Arizona (although its director and curator, Byron Cummings, had been trained as a classical archaeologist).

9. Founded somewhat later, in 1932, was the University of New Mexico's Maxwell Museum in Albuquerque, also focusing on the Southwest.

10. Amy Lonetree, "Reckoning with the Past: Indigenous Peoples and Museums," invited lecture, Women Warriors: Native Historians Advancing the Indigenous Cause and Perspective Conference, Southwest Minnesota State University, Marshall, Minnesota, April 2005.

11. For further details on George G. Heye and his collecting, see J. Alden Mason, "George G. Heye, 1874–1957," *Leaflets of the Museum of the American Indian* 6 (New York: Heye Foundation, 1958); Kevin Wallace, "A Reporter at Large: Slim-Shin's Monument," *New Yorker* 36 (November 19, 1960): 104–46; Clara Sue Kidwell, "Every Last Dishcloth: The Prodigious Collecting of George Gustav Heye," in Krech and Hail, *Collecting Native America*, 232–58; Lenz, "Heye," 86–115; Edmund Carpenter, "9/3428: Three Chapters from an Unfinished Two-Volume Study of George Heye's Museum of the American Indian," *European Review of Native American Studies* 15, no. 1 (2001): 1–12; and Ann McMullen, "Re-Inventing George Heye: Nationalizing the Museum of the American Indian and Its Collections," paper prepared for the Newberry Library's "Contesting Knowledge: Museums and Indigenous Perspectives" symposium, September 2007. The early essays of Mason and Wallace were the principal sources for both Kidwell and Lenz, who are often cited here because of their easier availability.

12. Kidwell, "Dishcloth," 236.

13. Ann McMullen, "Wonders of the East: Woodlands Art and Artifacts at the National Museum of the American Indian," *American Indian Art Magazine* 29, no. 4 (Autumn 2004): 56–63.

14. W. Richard West Jr., "The National Museum of the American Indian: Adventures in the Post-Colonial World," plenary session of AAA annual meeting December 2, 2005, Washington DC.

15. Mason, "Heye," 13. Cf. Kidwell, "Dishcloth," 241; Lenz, "Heye," 93.

16. Of course, objects taken from burials may still be of interest to—not to say, owned by—their descendant communities, but during Heye's time the colonial imbalance of power allowed widespread collecting from such sites.

17. Lenz, "Heye," 105–6, 95, 106. Franz Boas, "The Occurrence of Similar Inventions in Areas Widely Apart," *Science* 9 (1887): 485–86, reprinted in *The Shaping of American Anthropology, 1883–1911: A Franz Boas Reader*, ed. George W. Stocking Jr. (Chicago: University of Chicago Press, 1974), 63.

18. For a useful summary of the principal collections that Heye purchased, see Carpenter, *Two Essays*, 44–51.

19. Lenz, "Heye," 95, 105. For Boas, see Jacknis, *Storage Box*, 40–43. Despite his aversion to "tourist art," Heye did acquire innovative items made for sale; see Mary Jane Lenz, "No Tourist Material: George Heye and His Golden Rule," *American Indian Art Magazine* 29, no. 4 (Autumn 2004): 86–55, 105; Bruce Bernstein, "The National Museum of the American Indian Collections," *American Indian Art Magazine* 29, no. 4 (Autumn 2004): 54.

20. Lenz, "Heye," 91.

21. Lothrop, "Heye," 67; cf. Kidwell, "Dishcloth," 252; Lenz, "Heye," 104–5, 95. Carpenter, in particular, in *Two Essays* stresses Heye's evident contempt for documentation and scientific rigor.

22. Kidwell, "Dishcloth," 252; Lenz, "Heye," 105–6.

23. In 2004, this collection was transferred to the division of Rare and Manuscript Collections of the Cornell University Library in Ithaca, New York. The Smithsonian had claimed it as part of the Heye museum but was unsuccessful in court.

24. Eleanor M. King and Bryce P. Little, "George Byron Gordon and the Early Development of the University Museum," in *Raven's Journey: The World of Alaska's Native People*, ed. Susan A. Kaplan and Kirstin J. Barsness (Philadelphia: University Museum, University of Pennsylvania, 1986), 16–53. Cf. Kidwell, "Dishcloth," 240.

25. Mason, "Heye," 16. Cf. Kidwell, "Dishcloth," 236–37, 242–43.

26. When it suited him, Heye did collaborate with other institutions in collecting. For example, in 1924 he sent Mark R. Harrington to Lovelock Cave, Nevada, to work with UC Berkeley's Llewellyn L. Loud, and he also jointly funded the excavations of the Smithsonian's Jesse W. Fewkes on St. Vincent and Trinidad.

27. The other two Penn assistants were William C. Orchard and Frank G. Speck. King and Little, "Gordon," 39–40.

28. Mason, "Heye," 13; see Kidwell, "Dishcloth," 236.

29. The most successful anthropological entrepreneur of his time, Frederic W. Putnam (1839–1915) served as director of Harvard's Peabody Museum from 1875 to 1909, while also directing anthropology programs at the Chicago World's Fair (1891–93), the American Museum of Natural History (1894–1903), and the UC Anthropology Museum (1901–9).

30. At the American Museum, Saville served as assistant curator (1894–1905), curator (1905–8), and honorary curator (1908–10).

31. Mason, "Heye," 20. Cf. Lenz, "Heye," 90. From 1911 to 1915, Harrington also served as a curator at Harvard.

32. Kidwell, "Dishcloth," 247.

33. Alanson Skinner is mentioned as having attended Columbia and Harvard, but there is no reference to his degrees and no record of a doctorate. Between 1920 and 1924 he worked for the Milwaukee Public Museum.

34. Kidwell, "Dishcloth," 247; Lenz, "Heye," 103. Other, less renowned collectors included Donald A. Cadzow, Theodore de Booy, Thomas Huckerby, and Foster Saville.

35. Another who held a doctorate (in biology) was the physical anthropologist Bruno Oetteking, who served Heye officially from 1921 to ca. 1928. Oetteking held a simultaneous faculty appointment with Columbia.

36. An artist from England, Orchard worked briefly for the American Museum before coming to Heye. He was skilled in object restoration and model making. See Frederick J. Dockstader, "Preface," in *Beads and Beadwork of the American Indian*, by William C. Orchard, Contributions from the Museum of the American Indian, Heye Foundation, 11, 2nd ed. (1929; New York: Museum of the American Indian, 1975), 13. Turbyfill, who originally ran a livery stable and hardware store in North Carolina, worked as Heye's general assistant and resident manager of the Research Branch in the Bronx; Wallace, "Slim-Shin." A former race car driver, Coffin first worked for Heye as a chauffeur before showing a talent for photography; see Natasha Bonilla Martinez, "An Indian Americas: NMAI Photographic Archive Documents Indian Peoples of the Western Hemisphere," in Johnson, *Spirit Capture*, 39.

37. Kidwell, "Dishcloth," 243.

38. Frank G. Speck (Ph.D., Pennsylvania, 1908), who studied with Boas, collected among Eastern tribes; see Natasha Bonilla Martinez, "Camera Shots: Photographers, Expeditions, and Collections," in Johnson, *Spirit Capture*, 92–97. Samuel A. Barrett (PhD, Berkeley, 1908) collected among the Cayapa in Ecuador in 1908–9. Thomas T. Waterman (a Berkeley student who got his Ph.D. at Columbia in 1914) collected among the Puget Sound Salish between 1919 and 1921 while teaching at the University of Washington (1918–20).

39. Kidwell, "Dishcloth," 243, 251.

40. Samuel K. Lothrop, "George Gustav Heye: 1874–1956 [sic]," *American Antiquity* 23, no. 1 (1957): 66.

41. George W. Stocking Jr., "Ideas and Institutions in American Anthropolo-

gy: Toward a History of the Interwar Period," in *Selected Papers from the American Anthropologist, 1921–1945*, ed. George W. Stocking Jr. (Washington DC: American Anthropological Association, 1976), 9.

42. Kidwell, "Dishcloth," 244.

43. Mason, "Heye," 19–20; cf. Martinez, "An Indian Americas," 45. Trustee Minor Keith died the next year, in 1929.

44. Mason, "Heye," 23. Cf. Kidwell, "Dishcloth," 249; Lenz, "Heye," 109.

45. "The History of the Museum," 4–5. In fact, one 1929 review went so far as to claim, "The main object of the Museum is not to appeal to the general public, welcome as it will be to view the exhibits; rather it is the aim to afford to serious students every facility for utilizing the collections in their researches" ("Aims and Objects," 18). In the end, the MAI probably served Heye more than either the scholarly or general public. See Carpenter, *Two Essays*, 25–26.

46. William C. Sturtevant, "Museums as Anthropological Data Banks," in *Anthropology beyond the University*, ed. Alden Redfield, Southern Anthropological Society Proceedings, 7 (Athens: University of Georgia Press, 1973), 40–55.

47. Frederick J. Dockstader, *Indian Art of the Americas* (New York: Museum of the American Indian–Heye Foundation, 1973); *Masterworks from the Museum of the American Indian–Heye Foundation* (New York: Metropolitan Museum of Art, 1973).

48. These interim years between the death of Heye and the Smithsonian takeover are extensively covered by Roland W. Force in his book *The Heye and the Mighty: Politics and the Museum of the American Indian* (Honolulu HI: Mechas Press, 1999). For another, more critical view, see Carpenter, *Two Essays*.

49. While most of these collections developed in place into formal museums, the Crane collection was acquired in 1968 by the Denver Museum of Natural History (now the Denver Museum of Nature and Science). For information on the Crane collection and many of these institutions, see Krech and Hail, *Collecting Native America*.

50. Kathleen D. McCarthy, *Women's Culture: American Philanthropy and Art, 1830–1930* (Chicago: University of Chicago Press, 1991), 140–41.

51. In the art world, the Barnes Foundation, located in a Philadelphia suburb, is another well-known example of a museum constrained by its founder's vision. John Anderson, *Art Held Hostage: The Battle over the Barnes Collection* (New York: Norton, 2003).

52. The story of the planning process for the new museum is recounted in George Horse Capture, "The Way of the People," in Blue Spruce, *Spirit*, 31–45.

53. Edward M. Bruner, "Ethnography as Narrative," in *The Anthropology of Experience*, ed. Victor W. Turner and Edward M. Bruner (Urbana: University of Illinois Press, 1986), 139–55.

54. Force, *Heye and the Mighty*, 466–67.

55. James Conaway, *The Smithsonian: 150 Years of Adventure, Discovery, and Wonder* (New York: Knopf, 1995); Steven Lubar and Kathleen M. Kendrick, *Legacies: Collecting America's History at the Smithsonian* (Washington DC: Smithsonian Institution Press, 2001).

56. The South American hall was also closed during the summer of 2004, so there are now no Native American displays in the museum. (In fact, with the closure of the Asian-Pacific exhibits, the only anthropology is found in the galleries for Africa and Ancient Civilizations.) For the hall's history, see John C. Ewers, "Problems and Procedures in Modernizing Ethnological Exhibits," *American Anthropologist* 57, no. 1 (1955): 1–12; John C. Ewers, "A Century of American Indian Exhibits in the Smithsonian Institution," *Annual Report of the Smithsonian Institution for 1958* (1959): 513–25; William W. Fitzhugh, "Ambassadors in Sealskins: Exhibiting Eskimos at the Smithsonian," in *Exhibiting Dilemmas: Issues of Representation at the Smithsonian*, ed. Amy Henderson and Adrienne L. Kaeppler (Washington DC: Smithsonian Institution Press, 1997), 206–45. For a comparative case, see Ira Jacknis, "'A Magic Place': The Northwest Coast Indian Hall at the American Museum of Natural History," in *Coming Ashore: Northwest Coast Ethnology, Past and Present*, ed. Marie Mauzé, Michael E. Harkin, and Sergei Kan (Lincoln: University of Nebraska Press, 2004), 221–50.

57. Evidently, the Natural History Museum still has plans for a Native American hall but continues to have funding problems. Joel Achenbach, "Within These Walls, Science Yields to Stories," *Washington Post*, September 19, 2004.

58. Although the museum has no collections, it already has a home on the Smithsonian web site: http://nmaahc.si.edu/.

59. While the Canadian Museum of Civilization features its Native peoples, it also includes material from other historic and ethnic groups in Canada. There are, however, no displays from outside the country.

60. Nancy B. Rosoff, "Smithsonian Institution, National Museum of the American Indian, Research Branch," in *Anthropological Resources: A Guide to Archival, Library, and Museum Collections*, ed. Lee S. Dutton (New York: Garland, 1999), 270. See also Wilcox, "Museum of the American Indian," 78, 79, 81.

61. At the Hearst Museum, for instance, some sets of Yurok arrows are each given separate catalogue numbers; others, seemingly identical, are given

one number with suffixes (a, b, c, etc.) for each object in the set. While theoretically this implies that the first are all individual items and the latter are part of a functional set, different cataloguing standards and procedures may have been applied over the years. The problem is only magnified when trying to compare one institution to another.

62. Here, for instance, are estimated sizes of the anthropology collections for some of the leading museums: National Museum of Natural History, Smithsonian, 472,394 catalogue entries, 2 million objects; Peabody Museum, Harvard University, 450,000 entries, 5 million objects; American Museum of Natural History, 530,000 entries; University of Pennsylvania Museum, 250,000+ entries, 1 million objects; Field Museum, 600,000 entries, 1.5 million objects; Phoebe Hearst Museum, UC Berkeley, 630,000 entries, 3.8 million objects; in addition to NMAI, 890,000 objects. Taken from respective publications and web sites. See also Cornelius Osgood, *Anthropology in Museums of Canada and the United States*, Publication in Museology 7 (Milwaukee: Milwaukee Public Museum, 1979), 71.

63. The museum claims to have more than 100,000 Native American objects, but this figure probably represents catalogue entries, not objects. Barbara Isaac, ed., *The Hall of the North American Indian: Change and Continuity* (Cambridge MA: Peabody Museum Press of Harvard University, 1990), 2.

64. James Clifford, *The Predicament of Culture: Twentieth-Century Ethnography, Literature, and Art* (Cambridge MA: Harvard University Press, 1988), 215.

65. Richard Conn, *Native American Art in the Denver Art Museum* (Denver CO: Denver Art Museum, 1979). For a summary of the interest in American Indian objects by American art museums, see Jacknis, *Storage Box*, 117–34, 188–92.

66. "Aims and Objects" 3.

67. Kidwell, "Dishcloth," 247.

68. Among this group was French anthropologist Claude Lévi-Strauss. Ira Jacknis, "A Magic Place," 238. See also Carpenter, *Two Essays*, 114–21.

69. The recent literature on Native American art worlds is huge. See Margaret Dubin, *Native America Collected: The Culture of an Art World* (Albuquerque: University of New Mexico Press, 2001), especially 83–99, focusing on the inaugural exhibits of the NMAI; Janet Catherine Berlo and Ruth B. Phillips, "Our (Museum) World Turned Upside-Down: Re-presenting Native American Arts," *Art Bulletin* 77, no. 1 (1995): 6–10.

70. According to Jim Pepper Henry, assistant director for community services, "We're not an anthropology museum. . . . We're a museum of living cultures. . . . This is a venue for native peoples to tell their own story.

You're not going to get the anthropological perspective." Gerald McMaster, deputy assistant director, said, "Anthropology as a science is not practiced here." Quoted in Achenbach, "Within These Walls," R01.

71. West, "The National Museum." For Boas's position on the museum priority of culture over objects, see Ira Jacknis, "The Ethnographic Object and the Object of Ethnology in the Early Career of Franz Boas," in Volksgeist as Method and Ethic: Essays on Boasian Ethnography and the German Anthropological Tradition, ed. George W. Stocking Jr. (Madison: University of Wisconsin Press, 1996), 185–214.

72. I explore these issues at greater length in my Storage Box of Tradition and "A Magic Place."

73. Junius Bird, quoted in Wallace, "Slim-Shin," 118; see also Kidwell, "Dishcloth," 251; Carpenter, Two Essays, 26.

74. Mason, "Heye," 15; Kidwell, "Dishcloth," 241, 247.

75. Mason, "Heye," 24. Cf. Kidwell, "Dishcloth," 250; Lenz, "Heye," 112–13; Carpenter, Two Essays, 98–108.

76. Laura Peers and Alison K. Brown, eds., Museums and Source Communities: A Routledge Reader (London: Routledge, 2003); Joy Hendry, Reclaiming Culture: Indigenous People and Self-Representation (New York: Palgrave Macmillan, 2005).

77. Museums in Canada—such as the Canadian Museum of Civilization (Hull), the University of British Columbia Museum of Anthropology (Vancouver), and the Royal British Columbia Museum (Victoria)—are clearly a model for the practice of the NMAI, whether acknowledged or not. See Michael Ames, "How to Decorate a House: The Renegotiation of Cultural Representations at the University of British Columbia Museum of Anthropology," Museum Anthropology 22, no. 3 (1999): 41–51; Ruth B. Phillips and Mark Salber Phillips, "Double Take: Contesting Time, Place, and Nation in the First Peoples Hall of the Canadian Museum of Civilization," American Anthropologist 104, no. 4 (2006): 694–704.

78. Nancy B. Rosoff, "Integrating Native Views in Museum Procedures: Hope and Practice at the National Museum of the American Indian," Museum Anthropology 22, no. 1 (1998): 33–42, reprinted in Peers and Brown, Museums and Source Communities, 72–79. James Pepper Henry, "Challenges in Maintaining Culturally Sensitive Collections at the National Museum of the American Indian," in Stewards of the Sacred, ed. Lawrence E. Sullivan and Alison Edwards (Washington DC: American Association of Museums, 2004), 105–12.

79. Patricia Pierce Erikson, with Helma Ward and Kirk Wachendorf, Voices of

a Thousand People: The Makah Tribal Center (Lincoln: University of Nebraska Press, 2002), 147–66.

80. Horse Capture, "Way of the People," 43.

81. For good reviews of American Indian tribal museums, see Moira G. Simpson, "Native American Museums and Cultural Centres," in *Making Representations: Museums in the Post-Colonial Era* (London: Routledge, 1996), 135–69; Christina F. Kreps, *Liberating Culture: Cross-Cultural Perspectives on Museums, Curation, and Heritage Preservation* (London: Routledge, 2003), 79–113; and Karen Coody Cooper and Nicolasa I. Sandoval, eds., *Living Homes for Cultural Expression: North American Native Perspectives on Creating Community Museums* (Washington DC: National Museum of the American Indian, Smithsonian Institution, 2006).

82. Ivan Karp, Christine Mullen Kreamer, and Steven D. Lavine, eds., *Museums and Communities: The Politics of Public Culture* (Washington DC: Smithsonian Institution Press, 1992).

83. This resolutely local acknowledgment of tribal sovereignty is becoming the norm with American Indian–related museums. For instance, the Canadian Museum of Civilization greets its visitors in the words of the Kitigan Zibi (formerly known as the River Desert Band of Algonquians). See Phillips and Phillips, "Double Take," 694.

84. W. Richard West Jr., "As Long as We Keep Dancing," in Blue Spruce, *Spirit*, 54.

85. Reportedly, the NMAI raised "$100 million of its $219 million from private sources (a third of that from Indian tribes made wealthy from gambling casinos)." Edward Rothstein, "Museum with an American Indian Voice," *New York Times*, September 21, 2004.

86. The Bronx garden was supervised by Heye's wife, Thea, and staff ethnobotanist Melvin Gilmore; Mason, "Heye," 19; cf. Lenz, "Heye," 101. The current landscaping was directed by Donna House (Navajo/Oneida); cf. Donna House, "The Land Has a Memory," in Blue Spruce, *Spirit*, 74–79.

87. Kidwell, "Dishcloth," 252–53; Lenz, "Heye," 115. For the contemporary perspective, see West, "The National Museum."

2. Decolonizing the "Nation's Attic"

The National Museum of the American Indian and the Politics of Knowledge-Making in a National Space

Patricia Pierce Erikson

From the "Margin" to the "Center"

Looking forward as well as backward, I have no doubt that the launching of the National Museum of the American Indian represents a fundamental turning point for the Smithsonian. It begins to correct a vast wrong, and all the myths and stereotypes with which we surrounded it in order to hide it— or at least not to have to confront it ourselves. It envisions a partnership of a new and unprecedented kind—with those whose history and culture, once torn away from them, will now be represented only with their full complicity. It creates a model of a dialogue with wider relevance than any in which we have participated, ending the separation between specialists as embodiments of authority and a passive audience, and leading in the direction of a museum without walls.

—Smithsonian Secretary Robert McC. Adams[1]

I believe that if the Museum of the American Indian, Heye Foundation is brought to Washington and located on the Mall in a brand new building it would bring it into competition with our own existing Department of Anthropology at the Smithsonian. . . . [Based on prior experience with Congress collapsing the Bureau of American Ethnology,] I would predict that in the future the Congress which would have to appropriate money for the support of both these organizations would insist upon their merging. . . . And I am confident that it would mean the end of our dream of a Smithsonian Museum of Anthropology, or of Man.

—Smithsonian Ethnologist Emeritus John C. Ewers, 1987[2]

The Smithsonian Institution has been called "the most highly regarded cultural icon in the nation."[3] Inhabiting the National Mall, it acts as the proud yet sometimes reluctant symbolic manifestation of the nation. In her testimony supporting the establishment of the National Museum of the American Indian before the Senate Select Committee on Indian Affairs in 1987, Ann Rockefeller Roberts testified to the nature of the Smithsonian as a symbol of and for the nation:

> *Washington is the symbolic center of our nation. It is the seat of our national government and furthermore it houses in its extraordinary museums the materials that reflect the general American experience. It is the place we go in order to understand who we are. We send our young in bus loads each year to teach them what it means to be American. . . . It is a giant living archive, a repository for our legacy—our past and present—our hopes for the future. It seeks to be complete—we need it to be complete— to describe the American experience in its entirety. That experience includes the legacy of the American Indians, the original inhabitants of this land.*[4]

All public museums can become arenas of contestation, but the Smithsonian is particularly susceptible. At a 1995 conference devoted to discussing how museums present controversial subjects in a democratic society, Richard Kurin quoted President Clinton as saying that "individuals could write or say whatever they want, but when the Smithsonian speaks it, the implication is that it is being done officially, of, and for, the nation as a whole."[5] Clinton noted that the Smithsonian either projects itself as or is perceived as a purveyor of "official knowledge." While the Smithsonian's stature is frequently rendered in these terms, its relationship with "the nation" and "the state" should not be oversimplified. Indeed, the history of the development of the National Museum of the American Indian reveals the complexity of this relationship.

Elsewhere I have explored how Native American community museums and cultural centers embody, represent, and reinforce tribal knowledge, sensibilities, and morality in ways that are not necessarily consonant with conventional museum practices.[6] I do not mean to say that tribal museums operate entirely outside of or apart from mainstream museology or academia. Indeed, at the same time that tribal institutions seek to challenge and reform dominant practices, they must also enter into dialogue with and draw from dominant practices in order to gain access to funding sources and to ensure recognition as a museum, with its inherent authority. I have also seen tribal museums reproduce dominant versions of history in their community.

For generations, Native knowledge structures have been marginalized relative to official versions of knowledge. This does not necessarily mean that these subjugated knowledges remain marginalized, however. On the contrary, Native American community museums have proven themselves to be innovative centers that attempt to infuse alternative ways of knowing into a public sphere. My assertion is that historically marginalized knowledge structures can spread from the putative margin to the symbolic center and institutionalize themselves there. I say "putative" because these ideas, beliefs, and knowledge structures are not separate or overlapping. We need to embrace a more complex model, one in which conflicting ways of understanding our world are interwoven. We can see how the threads emanating from Native communities are making their way into the fabric of the national public sphere by noting how Native Americans have achieved a greater voice in centralized social institutions, such as the national museum.

By virtue of their prestige and their professional influence, national institutions such as the Smithsonian are desirable places for challenging and forging notions of citizenship and humanity. The Smithsonian is a research and educational, private, nonprofit institution. However, it is not entirely separate from the state. It maintains significant fiduciary and governance links to the U.S. Congress. Although the staff members who work at the Smithsonian may enjoy the power afforded them by the reputation and authority of their institution, they must also negotiate their inherent vulnerability to congressional interference.

The *Enola Gay* controversy at the Air and Space Museum showed the degree to which Congress can meddle with the interpretive content of

Smithsonian exhibits. Thus, while the Smithsonian can serve as a means to influence the public through its exhibitions and programming, it is also a site vulnerable to influence from the political sphere. This complexity makes it an attractive place for those who wish to use it as an arena of debate or a platform for challenging dominant ideologies that have, in practice, contributed to the colonization of Native peoples.

My research interest has been how Native American philosophies have been moving into and juxtaposing themselves against centralized, official narratives about history and identity. Have these narratives negotiated power relations successfully enough to effect concrete changes in the national museum? Have relations between Native American peoples and museums been transformed? If so, on what levels, or to what degree, have these changes occurred? These were some of the questions directing my three months of research at the Smithsonian in 1995.[7]

The relationship between Native American peoples and museums spans centuries and has varied so extensively that it nearly defies general description. However, because American museums are a part of our social fabric, museum narratives and practices are informed by overall social perceptions of Native peoples. The stereotypes inherent in historic museum representations of "Indianness" have repeatedly overwritten the existence and persistence of actual Native American communities. Stereotypes replace complex and dynamic identities with often static and anachronistic pan- or pastiche-Indian ones. Frequently, the "imagined Indian" has inhered in persistent narrations of Native American extinction.[8] Over time many of these modes of representation have become embedded in a variety of institutional practices, particularly those of museums.[9]

Although tribes in the United States maintained communities that were spiritual and intellectual centers of tribal life, discontent raged over the living legacies of colonialism, the ongoing inequalities of American life. Many Native peoples complained that Indian stereotypes, well entrenched in American popular culture, only supported these inequalities. Across the country, tribes felt an increasing need for greater influence over popular representation of Native people. In the twentieth century, museums joined the ranks of contested sites of representation, along with textbooks, movies, and various "playing Indian" traditions.[10] The proliferation of tribal museums has coincided with a period when anthropology, including museum anthropology, has critically analyzed how power relationships have shaped the methodology, ethics, and research design of the disciplines.[11] Native American "source communities" increasingly sought to clearly define and disseminate members' lifestyles, values, and concerns for themselves and the public; the result has been widespread development of community-based museums or collaborative representational projects.[12]

As a graduate student in both anthropology and Native American studies during the 1990s, I became fascinated and impressed with the degree to which Native American self-determination movements had spread into museological terrain. I saw this occurring not only across North America, but in Latin America as well.[13] This Native American museum movement reflected a much wider, even global trend of "democratizing" or decolonizing museums.[14] Inspired by Michael Ames, James Clifford, and Ruth Phillips, I decided to explore how tribal communities developed their own community museums (and why) and how Native Americans were increasingly influencing non-Native or mainstream museum.[15]

Much has been written about the historic role of mainstream museums in Western societies: their concentration of priceless works of art, their collections of meaningful artifacts, and their assertion of themselves as authoritative producers of knowledge about the (colonized) world.[16] In the United States, and the Western Hemisphere more broadly, Native American people were vital to these collecting and ethnological practices.[17] Historically, mainstream museums have been considered the center of knowledge making; in this vision Native American communities are represented as the periphery or frontier of discovery, the content but not the authors.[18] This pattern of museum representation of North American indigenous peoples is analogous to representation practices associated with colonization and nation building elsewhere.[19]

Mary Louise Pratt has argued that those who have been marginalized and discriminated against rarely remain passive bystanders. Instead, they select elements of the dominant culture and create self-made portraits to engage with, accommodate, and negotiate with the dominant culture. She calls these self-made portraits "autoethnography"; the space of colonial encounter and negotiation she calls the "contact zone." She writes that although the people responsible for knowledge making (museum curators, for example) tend to understand themselves as representing and determining the periphery, they blind themselves to the way the so-called periphery constructs the center.[20]

This reflection on the National Museum of the American Indian NMAI provides the opportunity to discuss the appearance of the Native American movement at the Smithsonian Institution in the 1970s and 1980s, and how this relates to the development of the first phase of the NMAI at the Smithsonian, the Customs House or the George Gustave Heye Center. In Pratt's terms, I am trying to make visible the way the so-called periphery constructs museum representation at the symbolic center of the nation.

The National Mall, stretching from the U.S. Capitol in the east to the Washington Monument in the west, has been popularized as a kind of sacred space symbolizing the national public sphere. It is a space deliberately mapped, ringed by several museums of the Smithsonian Institution. Through implementing their plans for a national museum on this Mall, a number of Native American individuals and groups claimed a new space for national dialogue. In doing so, Native American peoples found receptive, non-Native museum professionals and politicians who valued various aspects of the Native American museum movement. None of this, however, occurred without contestation, or what John Ewers in 1987 called "competition" with other visions of the Smithsonian's future.

We can recognize that at least one source of museums' historic authority has been their reputation for discovering and creating knowledge and presenting it as objective truth.[21] Despite their assertions of "objective truth," museum representations are symbolic manifestations of the belief structures of those who fund, create, or authorize the exhibitions. Or is it that simple? Museums are also bureaucracies and cultural institutions that are embedded in a social order. Museums are themselves "social artifacts."[22] Therefore, they tend not to be monolithic; rather, they embody competing interests of different stakeholders. The public, of course, is not homogeneous either, despite some models that would have it that way. As public institutions, museums are open to contestation regarding how they will contribute to maintaining or overturning existing social orders. In this sense, museums become arenas for debate. They also are "crucibles" in which notions of citizenship, personal identity, community, and nationhood are negotiated and possibly forged.[23] Karp has persuaded many readers that, as issues of pluralism and diversity in the United States are squelched by conservatives in the political sphere, social debates and initiatives will be channeled into cultural spheres, such as the museum.[24] He argues that although museums are not officially political institutions, they become politicized.

The creation of a Smithsonian National Museum of the American Indian in 1989 involved negotiation and debate between Congress and at least three key museum players: the Smithsonian's National Museum of Natural History and the Office of the Secretary at the Smithsonian Institution, and the Museum of the American Indian, Heye Foundation in New York City. Each stakeholder desired bureaucratic restructuring and institutional improvement (for both the Heye Museum of the American Indian in New York City and the Smithsonian Institution), but each had a different vision of how that would proceed. In the process of this negotiation and debate, Native American material culture and human remains were suspended in a complex web of political maneuvers.

In the end, the negotiations to create the NMAI determined the future deposition of not only the enormous Heye American Indian collection, but also the National Museum of Natural History's Native American human remains and funerary materials. Furthermore, the creation of the NMAI influenced the future deposition of Native American human remains, funerary materials, and cultural patrimony in museums across the nation. Thus, the creation of the NMAI marks one of the critical moments in rising Native American influence in a national arena.

In essence, one chapter of the NMAI story entails a dilemma of the Anthropology Department in the Smithsonian's National Museum of Natural History. This dilemma reflects one experienced by the anthropological discipline in general: a perceived need to free itself from its nineteenth-century position within a natural history paradigm and adopt new theoretical models for analyzing and representing human cultures.

The Anthropology Department:
Framed in a Natural History Museum

Archival records at the Smithsonian and my interviews with staff members there indicate that a long-range goal of the Smithsonian's Department of Anthropology had been to form a Museum of Mankind. If accomplished, this would enable a measure of independence from the National Museum of Natural History (NMNH) in which it was housed and administered. While under the NMNH, the Department of Anthropology has had relatively little control over resources, policy, and allocation of exhibit space and funds. Anthropology at the Smithsonian has been one department within a multidepartmental natural history museum; not unlike the dynamics elsewhere, the priorities and interests of anthropology have been weighed against more biologically oriented research interests.

While the Anthropology Department has collaborated with other Smithsonian bureaus with related interests in culture and humankind (e.g., art, folk life, history), their institutional placement in natural history has challenged departmental growth and evolution. Consequently, the Department of Anthropology has attempted to establish a relatively autonomous bureaucratic presence multiple times in its history: in the late 1960s, the late 1970s, and again in 1982. This phenomenon of being stuck in a natural history paradigm has had far-reaching implications for anthropology's relations with Native Americans. I do not mean to imply that four-field anthropology has not benefited from biological and geological sciences. As a scholar with degrees in both geology and archaeology, I would be the last to make that claim. Instead, I am arguing that when a four-field discipline is housed within a museum with a natural history-driven mission, its multidisciplinary approach—particularly collaborative research in Native American cultures—can be challenged.

In the early 1980s, Native American individuals and tribes began to approach the Smithsonian, expecting receptivity to their interest in "renovating" the representation of Native American peoples in the National Museum of Natural History. Native American confidence in potential Smithsonian collaborations was high due to the following: (a) the Smithsonian had developed Native American cultural resource training programs in the early 1970s; (b) the American Indian Religious Freedom Act had encouraged scrutiny into any institutionalized practices that oppress indigenous religions; and (c) national networks of Native American museum organizations were developing from community-initiated projects and facilitating collaboration with local and regional museums.

Despite greater optimism, increased networking, and the widespread establishment of Native American community museums and cultural centers, the Smithsonian's ability to establish substantively collaborative relations was slow to develop. In March 1981, the chairman of the North American Indian Museum Association, Richard Hill (Tuscarora), approached the Office of Exhibits at the NMNH, stating an interest in "establish[ing] cooperative relations with your museum to assist in the planning of the projected renovation of your North American Indian Exhibits. We are most interested in sharing our knowledge, resources and contacts to assure a more accurate and sensitive public presentation of our cultures."[25] Hill's expectation was that the North American Indian Museum Association would be an appropriate association for assisting the Anthropology Department in establishing a Smithsonian Institution national advisory committee on American Indian cultures.

When Eugene Behlen, chief of the Office of Exhibits, enthusiastically passed on this offer to the department, the physical anthropologist Douglas Ubelaker replied:

> Our North Americanists have advised me that whereas advice and review by the North American Indian Museum Association may be important in developing future exhibits on North American subjects, the relationship should not be formalized. I recommend thanking them for their offer and indicating that we will contact them in the future as the need arises. A formal advisory committee is not called for at this point and may in fact prove difficult.[26]

Renovating the exhibit halls at that time hinged on either marshalling enough funds or breaking away to a separate anthropological museum. Neither was occurring at that moment. Nevertheless, an opportunity for collaboration was passed over, and a preliminary joint committee was not formed. This lost opportunity, and many others like it, formed a pattern that undoubtedly contributed to eventual Native American lobbying that circumvented the Department of Anthropology when the opportunity to found a separate Native American museum at the Smithsonian presented itself.

Four years later, in June 1985, the Anthropology Department chair was still able to state that, with the exception of some pioneering outreach programs that had been backed by piecemeal funding, "the Smithsonian has never collaborated with native groups or individuals interested in creating their own exhibitions at the Smithsonian Institution or elsewhere. Such an enterprise, however, would be a useful addition to the Natural History exhibits."[27] By and large, a backlog of collections management work and the high expectations for personal research placed outreach and collaboration lower on the priority list of Smithsonian curators. This was not an unusual pattern for museums generally.

However, during the 1980s, the National Museum of Natural History was increasingly criticized for the content of its aging exhibit halls. The

National Congress of American Indians complained in 1986 about an exhibit on the second floor of the NMNH that they described as

> highly offensive, in part due to the display of several hundred Indian skeletal remains, a practice ceased by most museums several decades ago. . . . We would prefer to see the Indian exhibit hall empty, with an accompanying explanation of why the exhibit has been removed than for the current exhibit to continue. An empty hall with a candid explanation would serve a better educational purpose for Smithsonian visitors than does the current exhibit. Ideally, a new Indian exhibit, done in consultation with Indian people to ensure accuracy and sensitivity, will be put in place.[28]

Eventually, the director of the NMNH conceded that the exhibits were "woefully inadequate displays." This critique prompted John C. Ewers, ethnologist emeritus and the creator of the American Indian hall exhibits, to petition the NMNH director in 1989:

> May I introduce myself as the individual who planned the exhibits in the two American Indian halls on the first floor of the Museum of Natural History more than 35 years ago. . . . I know that repeatly [sic] since those halls opened to the public I have expressed the opinion that each generation of curators should have the right and the duty to redo the exhibits as they see fit in the light of the increase of knowledge and the changes of emphasis in his or her discipline since the hall was last developed. . . . The exhibits in these two halls have been seen by perhaps two hundred million people since they were installed. . . . Yes, it is time for a change. In fact, it is way past time.[29]

Thus, there was growing consensus that the Anthropology Department needed to expand and renovate its exhibit space, especially in the contemporary context of a race-conscious society. It was clear to at least some staff members of the Department of Anthropology that the representation of Native American and other "ethnic" groups in a Natural History paradigm—given the implicit depiction of primitivism—was no longer appropriate. However, the financial means to accomplish this renovation were not made available.

Eventually anthropology staff members created a detailed design for a renovated version of the Museum of Natural History's American

Indian halls. Curator William Merrill submitted a proposal to the Special Exhibition Fund for the 1989 fiscal year to request support for planning entirely new American Indian exhibit halls, which would open in 1992. The proposal asserted that "The ethnology halls are replete with inaccuracies and tend to portray American Indians as 'frozen in time,' usually at the points in their histories at which they became stereotyped in the non-Indian mind."[30] To remedy this ethnographic stereotyping, the renovated exhibit planned to highlight the transformation of Native cultures through time, as opposed to portraying them in their respective "culture areas." The proposal advocated that a renovated exhibit should address the "politics of cultural representation" by examining the political and economic circumstances in which images of Native peoples had been constructed (especially representations by anthropologists). The suggestions in this proposal reflected the widespread and critical self-reflection within the anthropology discipline throughout academia during the 1980s.

The proposed renovation planning process involved visits to recently completed exhibits on Native Americans to identify new representational innovations. Community museums and cultural centers, such as the Makah Cultural and Research Center in Neah Bay, Washington, were among those identified as having influenced the exhibit renovation plan. Planning continued under the direction of NMNH anthropologist Joallyn Archambault (Dakota) and culminated in an exhibit design document entitled "Native Peoples of North America: Cultures in a Changing World." Some of its highlights included Native perspectives on their own cultures (such as Native American origin stories and cosmology); emphasis on contemporary Native American life through "'cultural icons,' ranging from a pickup truck to a section of oil pipeline"; and encouragement of the understanding that Native American cultural change is a part of global cultural change. It is important to recognize that although this proposed exhibit renovation never occurred, it was planned and designed in collaboration with Lakota, Tlingit, Inupiat, Yupik, Zuni, Tzeltal, Tzotzil, and Delaware peoples.[31]

What do we achieve by acknowledging the NMNH exhibit plans that were never implemented? It enables us to see that as the Columbus Quincentennial approached, the subjectivity of the National Museum of Natural History was far from monolithic. Had this exhibit plan been implemented, the NMNH's Native exhibits would have included Native perspectives along with anthropological analyses. Although it is difficult to say how far the pendulum would have swung toward allowing Native knowledge structures to influence exhibit design structure, part of the department was clearly open to this influence by the late 1980s. Indeed, other developments in the anthropological field made these collaborations desirable.

Other Native American community-anthropology collaborations at the Smithsonian were more successful when they avoided completely dismantling the American Indian halls. These include projects such as the Kiowa tribal catalogue project "Getting the Collections Back to the People" and a traveling exhibit organized by the Smithsonian Institution Traveling Exhibition Service. The Kiowa tribal catalogue project began in 1986; it was directed by curator William Merrill and implemented by Candace Greene, specialist for North American ethnology, and the Kiowa anthropologist Marian Hansson. The project's intent was to make accessible information about the Kiowa collections to the tribe as they prepared their own tribal museum and cultural projects. As Candace Greene explained to me, the collaborative nature of the effort transformed the project from one perceived as an "infringement" upon intellectual property rights to one perceived as "honoring" the tribe and building positive relations. The traveling exhibit Saynday Was Coming Along . . . Silverhorn's Drawings of the Kiowa Trickster was developed with the assistance of the extended family of the artist Silverhorn, who drew the images in the 1890s. The exhibit included family oral history as well as oral tradition recorded in the 1890s.

Despite these collaborative plans and projects, the American Indian exhibit halls remained largely shaped by nineteenth- and early twentieth-century anthropological paradigms. Furthermore, as negotiations to acquire the Heye collections heated up, it became clear that the Department of Anthropology was not comfortable legislating repatriation in a way that left anthropology at the margin of the decision-making process.

Thus the early stages of the negotiations to establish the National Museum of the American Indian entailed a contradictory response at the Smithsonian. Some recognized a potential NMAI as a solution to anthropology's dilemmas of trying to renovate its American Indian halls; others saw the NMAI as challenging several underpinnings of anthropology's intellectual tradition. Regarding the latter, Smithsonian anthropologists believed that the plan to found a national Native American museum might dislodge three disciplinary underpinnings: (1) a comparative science of humankind, (2) a commitment to academic freedom, and (3) museum anthropology's commitment to protect the public trust. The perceived challenge to academic freedom was labeled "anti-intellectualism." The repatriation of human remains and funerary objects represented a challenge to anthropological authority in framing what constituted knowledge, inquiry, and data.

Repatriation: Disrupting the Definition of Native American Remains as "Artifact"

The year 1986 was a critical juncture in the history of museums, particularly in how the state positioned Native American material culture and human remains. In that year, the Senate Select Committee on Indian Affairs began to explore the status of museum collections of Native American human remains and the issue of repatriation. Soon thereafter, Smithsonian Secretary Adams testified to the Senate that the Smithsonian Institution curated thousands of American Indian skeletal remains, which constituted 42.5 percent, or 14,523 objects, of the institution's physical anthropology collection. In addition, he testified that another 11.9 percent, or 4,061 objects, were Eskimo, Aleut, and Koniag. By comparison, 20 percent were identified as White, 5.1 percent as Black, and 20.6 percent as all others.[32] Newspapers around the country reported that tribal communities were appalled at the enormity of the Smithsonian's skeletal collections and that they were pushing for legisled repatriation.[33]

Prior to 1987, a number of repatriation bills had been submitted in both the House and Senate. These bills addressed a variety of issues, some of which were already under debate in state senates, but none had been passed at the federal level. Senator Daniel Inouye, who had just recently assumed the chair of the Senate Select Committee on Indian Affairs, seized on the human rights aspect of the Native American repatriation issue. With an advocate so strategically placed, the repatriation movement picked up momentum.

Senator Inouye's realization that thousands of Native American remains were housed as research materials at the Smithsonian led him to consider a proposal to rebury all of the remains and erect a memorial to them in the nation's capital. A search for existing memorials or monuments to Native Americans found that, other than busts commemorating specific individuals, there were no such commemorations in Washington.[34] Consequently, Inouye approached the National Capitol Planning Commission (under the National Park Service) to investigate the possibility of a Native American memorial on the National Mall. The commission pointed out that the one undesignated site remaining on the Mall was reserved for the Smithsonian Institution. Given that museums were the predominant forum for Smithsonian research and educational programming, the commission suggested that a Native American memorial be combined with a museum format.[35] At this point, the Committee on Indian Affairs' initiative to address Native American human remains in the nation's attic began to involve the National Mall, a space given symbolic significance in the nation. The initiative also converged with a very different agenda that had been developing in New York City, one that also revolved around Native American material culture.

Since the late 1970s, the George Gustav Heye Foundation–Museum of the American Indian in New York City had been having severe financial difficulties and was seeking possible resolutions. Heye (1874–1957) was a wealthy New York banker who had personally collected Native material culture throughout the Western hemisphere and had underwritten extensive archaeological expeditions. As a result of his passion to collect Native American material culture, he founded the Museum of the American Indian in 1916. The Heye collection amassed nearly one million ethnographic and archaeological pieces, as well as 86,000 prints and negatives. The overwhelming majority was from North America (70 percent) with the rest from Central and South America. As early as 1976, Nelson Rockefeller had commented to the Smithsonian regents that he had been impressed with Native Americans' concerns for their "growing sense of Indian identity and pride"; he suggested that because the Heye was in financial trouble, the Smithsonian Institution could acquire the Museum of the American Indian and establish a national Indian museum on the Mall. At that time, Smithsonian Secretary Ripley investigated merging the Heye with the Smithsonian, but recommended against it.[36]

The troubles of the Museum of the American Indian intensified through the 1980s. The Heye Foundation aggressively sought means to save a priceless collection of Native American materials. Ross Perot offered tens of millions of dollars to purchase the collection and move it to Texas, but this offer raised the ire of the New York public and politicians. Numerous solutions to save the collection were formulated and rejected.[37] At the same time, Senator Inouye was working on repatriation and the Native American memorial idea. The Heye-Smithsonian linkage came when Barber Conable, then chair of the Heye Foundation, invited Inouye and Smithsonian Secretary Robert McCormick Adams to New York City. On April 20, 1987, they toured the Heye's exhibitions and met with the Heye board. This meeting formally launched two years of very sensitive negotiations involving Congress, the Heye Foundation, and the Smithsonian Institution. When the negotiations ended, the relation of Native American material culture and human remains to the conventions of scientific research, and to definitions of national property and identity, were dramatically altered.

At the encouragement of the Smithsonian regents, Secretary Adams continued to investigate and to discuss, with the Heye Foundation and Congress, founding a Native American museum at the Smithsonian. Adams defended the Smithsonian's repatriation policy, which returned only those human remains that were identifiable as "named individuals." The Smithsonian entered the negotiations with the position that no legislative mandate of repatriation was warranted. However, the Senate Select Committee on Committee Rules and Administration, which has congressional jurisdiction over the Smithsonian, collaborated with the Senate Select Committee on Indian Affairs, thus forming a critical body of influence within Congress. With this intra-Congress collaboration in place, Native American lobbying could be all the more effective.

Discussions of a new museum on the National Mall that would include a memorial to Native Americans drew a quick response from the National Museum of Natural History. The NMNH did not condone the reinterment of Native human remains, nor the erection of a memorial, both of which had been proposed in the bill drafted to found the National Museum of the American Indian at the Smithsonian using the Heye collection. Ives Goddard communicated to his fellow curators the following sentiment:

> The mission of the Smithsonian is the increase and diffusion of knowledge. The construction and maintenance of a memorial crypt is not possibly consistent with this mission. Furthermore, the permanent physical removal of items in the National collections and their interment ("inter" is the word used) where they cannot be studied is irresolvably antithetical to the mission of the Smithsonian. It would be a violation of our charter and of our sacred trust for any Smithsonian resources to be devoted to such a purpose. The only way the Smithsonian can discharge its obligations in the present circumstances is to insure that a vigorous resistance is mounted against any proposal to alienate any part of the National collections under outside pressure, and to mount a vigorous campaign to educate Congress and the American public about the value of any parts of the National collections that are threatened.[38]

Disturbed by the prospect that a repatriation movement was gaining ground, Goddard drafted a form letter the next day to go out to tribal chairmen across the country. I don't know if the form letter was ever mailed, but its content provides insight into the arguments against repatriation. It gave recipients two choices to check off, leaving a third line blank. The first choice was that the Smithsonian would keep "Indian skeletons . . . where they will be stored and treated respectfully and used for scientific research on Indian health, history, and culture." The second choice was that the Indian skeletons would be removed from the museum and made unavailable for study, with the caveat that "as a result Indian people would receive less accurate and less complete scientific study than other groups of Americans."

Initially, Smithsonian Secretary Adams presented the "official Smithsonian position" as coinciding with anthropology's position on the repatriation issue. Adams would become a greater proponent of repatriation before leaving office.

At the November 1987 hearings Secretary Adams presented the following description of the Smithsonian's position. I quote Adams at length to establish the tenets of the argument:

> The [NMAI] bill clearly treats as a given the removal from the National collections of the Indian skeletons that can be identified to tribe and hence it addresses only the removal of the skeletal materials that cannot be identified to tribe. It is certainly discouraging to see what was discussed a few weeks ago as a worst case outcome taken by the other side as the baseline for further demands. . . . The case for the prior right of descendants would appear to be very strong, even if the directness of their descent is only tentatively established. But there is also plausibility to the claims of science. Only the analysis of these specimens, with marvelous new laboratory techniques that are being introduced more and more rapidly, holds out the promise of tracing the exact derivation of recent groups from their more remote ancestors. The difficulties multiply, in other words, as we shade off from certainty into uncertainty. At what point do the claims of possible descent weaken until the claims of advancement of scientific knowledge outweigh them? As Secretary of the Smithsonian, I am not empowered to surrender national collections

to individuals who claim, but cannot demonstrate, their legal standing as descendants [followed by twelve pages of description of the scientific value of human skeletal remains].

. . . Careful study of ["prehistoric" Native Americans'] skeletons offers insight into and understanding of them and those times, as well as of ourselves and the times in which we live, that are not available from other sources. To suggest, as sweepingly as Title II does, that these remains should cease in that offering is inconsistent with the Smithsonian's historic mandate "for the increase and diffusion of knowing" and with the precepts of modern scientific inquiry. . . . Having expressed these serious reservations, I should re-emphasize that the Smithsonian does not in any sense deprecate or deny the sensitivity that many Indian people feel with regard to its policies on skeletal collections. We shall continue to meet with those who are dissatisfied with the position taken here, not only to resolve individual claims but, through the accumulating lessons that these provide, to scrutinize and perhaps reconsider its more general features.[39]

Some of the pivotal points of the official Smithsonian position, then, were (a) that the power of determining ancestral identity would remain in the hands of science through "marvelous new laboratory techniques"; (b) that repatriation should be judged not solely on human rights terrain, but that the advancement of scientific knowledge presents another "higher good"; and (c) that a legislative mandate for repatriation should be avoided, and that the solution should be to proceed with case-by-case claims.

Secretary Adams's 1987 position largely coincided with that of the physical anthropologists in the National Museum of Natural History. They proposed an alternative to the National Museum of the American Indian: the establishment of their long-desired museum of mankind, which would include a "Gallery of the Americas" to showcase not only the newly acquired Heye collection, but also the extensive Native American collections that the NMNH already possessed.[40] Of course, the proposed museum of mankind was intended to scientifically compare and interpret cultures from other parts of the world, enabling the revelation of social processes universal to mankind. However, neither anthropology's proposed alternative to the NMAI nor the Smithsonian's concerns about repatriation found sympathetic ears on Capitol Hill.

Meanwhile, the controversy over repatriation signaled to museums across the country that some kind of mandate was forthcoming to regulate repatriation at the Smithsonian Institution and that it would set a precedent nationwide. Consequently, museum professionals approached the Senate Select Committee on Indian Affairs and asked for a one-year delay on any further repatriation legislation until a national dialogue could transpire. The committee responded favorably. Consequently, representatives of Native communities, museums, and Congress gathered in a series of meetings, sponsored by the Heard Museum in Arizona, to air the issues surrounding repatriation and the ethics of collecting Native American material culture. These dialogues led to some new understandings of the issues and at least a tentative understanding of differences in what is considered sacred.

This dialogue was summarized in the 1990 *Report of the Panel for a National Dialogue on Museum/Native American Relations*.[41] Although Native Americans had been raising these issues for decades, their voices finally influenced Congress in a substantive way. The findings of this report led to the Native American Graves Protection and Repatriation Act (NAGPRA, which passed in 1990. Some of the most important findings were the assertion that repatriation was a *human rights* issue, that judicially enforceable repatriation was thus appropriate, and that Native Americans ought to have greater access to information about what is in collections, how collections are curated and studied, and what their appropriate, final disposition ought to be.[42]

Key figures such as Walter Echo-Hawk (Pawnee) of the Native American Rights Fund and Suzan Shown Harjo (Cheyenne/Creek) of the Morningstar Foundation encouraged Secretary Adams to become a repatriation advocate. The eventual support of the Smithsonian's secretary was critical because the Department of Anthropology maintained a hard-line position against a mandate that would force the return of human remains and funerary objects whose cultural affiliation could be determined. The Smithsonian split within itself on the issues of repatriation and the significance of founding the NMAI. Meanwhile, Native groups organized public education drives and encouraged general electoral support for repatriation in congressional districts nationwide. Media attention appeared to undermine much of the resistance to the NMAI and to the subsequent NAGPRA legislation in Congress.

The NMAI Act (PL 101–185), which passed on November 28, 1989, and created the National Museum of the American Indian at the Smithsonian, mandated that the *entire* Smithsonian Institution, not just the new museum, had to inventory all human remains and funerary objects and to consider repatriating them upon the request of affiliated individuals or tribes. This sent the first shock wave through the Smithsonian and through the entire museological discipline. Furthermore, the new museum was established as a separate bureau of the Smithsonian, with its own board of trustees that reported directly to the Smithsonian regents. The NMAI Act also mandated, despite Secretary Adams's objections, that at least seven of the twenty-three initial NMAI trustees had to be Native American, with this number increasing to twelve after initial trustee terms expired. This led some to label the NMAI a "politically correct" venture.[43] Onondaga Chief Oren Lyons testified to Congress that Native American representation on the governing body of the NMAI was the only means by which institutional support for the museum's structure could emanate from Native worldviews:

> When we get to talking about museums, we use the term artifacts, and artifacts denotes a society or a time passed. It has been my observation and been our position that many of the objects that are in collections throughout museums and historical societies and private collections in this country and outside of this country are not artifacts but are indeed objects that would be used today in contemporary societies of Native American people. . . . We should have some input into what these definitions are going to be.[44]

This testimony clearly critiques the anthropological prerogative of defining the significance of Native American material culture and of framing it as a scientific artifact.

With the passage of both the NMAI Act and NAGPRA, a number of anthropologists and administrators in the National Museum of Natural History continued to maintain defensive positions, particularly when the National Museum of the American Indian Policy Statement on Native American Human Remains and Cultural Materials emerged. The statement that the collections "must be treated as the sole property of the affected Native American culturally-affiliated group" generated concerns about an erosion of academic freedom and a weakening of the perception of science as an altruistic endeavor. The Smithsonian's physical anthropology curator, Donald Ortner, wrote to Secretary Adams:

> The issues raised by the Americanists substantially transcend their individual or collective concerns. This is much more than a matter of curatorial or scholarly self interest. Western science and scholarship have flourished in part because of the free access to sources of information that were carefully preserved by various institutions. Any departure from this tradition needs to be evaluated with great care.[45]

A few days later, Frank Talbot, director of the National Museum of Natural History, also wrote to Secretary Adams:

> We hold the material in trust for the enlightenment of "all men" using [Joseph] Henry's phrase, and not for any group alone. The principle of "reasonable belief" also scares me. If this is a valid concept in affecting the disposition of material, would it, in this science museum, also be a valid reason for responding to a demand for "equal time" by creationists?[46]

Given the 2007 opening of the Creation Museum in Kentucky, Talbot's argument entails a prophetic element. How was a comparative science of mankind going to reconcile competing knowledge structures based in different belief systems?

Finally, the Smithsonian's Senate of Scientists Council joined the Department of Anthropology and the NMNH in lobbying Secretary Adams about the potential threat that NMAI policies posed:

> In many cases this [policy] will mean restriction of access unless permission is granted by the Native American group. This will undoubtedly lead to censor-

ship in cases in which research is found unacceptable by the Native American group owning the collection, if research is allowed at all. The Smithsonian should not be a party to the overt cultural or political restriction and restructuring of knowledge. It is in no one's best interest to stifle differing points of view.[47]

As the implications of the NMAI's establishment to issues of ownership, curation, material culture ownership, and influence in restructuring knowledge became more clear, the statements generally increased in their vehemence.

Despite being a new bureau of the Smithsonian Institution, the NMAI was still required to maintain an exhibitionary presence in New York, a stipulation solved by establishing the Heye Center for the American Indian exhibitions at the Alexander Hamilton Customs House in Lower Manhattan. This is effectively a New York branch of the Smithsonian's National Museum of the American Indian. This New York component of the NMAI, the first physically realized, opened in October 1994. Primarily, though, the plan was that the Heye collections would be showcased sometime after the year 2000 in the second component, a Smithsonian museum in the last space available on the National Mall. Collections storage, library, and archives would be housed in a third NMAI component, the Cultural Resources Center in Suitland, Maryland. The Cultural Resources Center would embody the final component of the NMAI: the Fourth Museum concept. The Fourth Museum concept was an effort to institutionalize collaboration with and openness to communities; the intention was to share responsibility of research development and collections use and interpretation with Native American communities through a variety of architectural, programmatic, and technological strategies.

As part of the political process of establishing the NMAI, the general public and Congress became aware, and critically so, of the extent of the skeletal collections in the Museum of Natural History and the research conducted on them. Through political lobbying and media appeals, Native Americans persuaded the public to accept limits on scientific justification for research on Native American skeletons. In terms of its relevance to the politics of knowledge-making, once the new NMAI bureau of the Smithsonian was established, it opened the door for alternative knowledge structures to enter and gain an institutional foothold in the national museum—an opportunity that had been difficult to realize elsewhere in the bureaucratic structure.

Anthropologists at the NMNH seemed to be characterizing the new museum as a political maneuver to undermine a comparative science of mankind and the analytical authority of anthropologists—in other words, censoring the free practice of positivism. This "antiscience/pro-Indian" characterization—often directed at the repatriation movement—ignores the fact that repatriation is far more than a political struggle over the authority to own, study, and interpret Native American materials and bodies. The Native American museum movement, as it manifested itself during the founding of the NMAI, called attention to human rights issues inherent in museum collecting histories and also advocated awareness that the construction of knowledge occurs in particular social contexts with particular power inequalities.

The Native American museum movement largely framed repatriation as a human rights issue couched in the context of a colonial history. This alternative framework extracts Native American skeletal materials from a positivist framework (body-as-artifact) and reinscribes the human remains as still having a status as "persons." Many have been disappointed that repatriation of human remains and material culture has been forced into legislative arenas for resolution. Given the materials involved, many would have preferred quiet and effective collaboration. Yet without legislative mandates, museums were responding cautiously and slowly, making their decisions based primarily on the paradigmatic framework that contextualized the collections in the first place. Both NAGPRA and the NMAI Act have been legislative responses to the Native American museum movement and its efforts to address institutionalized forms of ongoing colonial relationships vis-à-vis Native peoples.

As Richard Hill (Tuscarora) of the National Museum of the American Indian put it to me, "Indians have been like Don Quixote taking on museums with an empty gun. The law has been the hammer of change." In response to charges that repatriation and reburial interfered with the "intellectual gains of science," Hill added, "To those who say 'How can we understand Indians without understanding burials?' I say, 'How can you understand anything if you can't understand why it's a bad idea?'"[48] Litigation has been one strategy in a repertoire of resistance strategies, one that has been effective but has caused tremendous resentment in the museology and anthropology disciplines.

My intent has been to point out that the national museum is composed of competing subjectivities and that competing visions for the future played a significant role in the Native American museum movement's impact on the national museum's approaches to curating, interpreting, and presenting Native Americanness to the American public. In other words, particularly since the 1970s, there have been clefts or contradictions in the bureaucratic structure that provided significant opportunity for Native American ways of knowing to influence the institution. At the Smithsonian, these are discontinuities of mission, practice, and leadership:

> between the National Museum of Natural History and the National Museum of American History;
>
> between the National Museum of Natural History and the Department of Anthropology;
>
> between the Office of the Secretary and the Department of Anthropology; and
>
> between different anthropology subdisciplines or individuals within the Department of Anthropology itself.

These are the institutional locations of the competing subjectivities *within the national museum* that, collectively, have created the crucible for the creation of Native American training programs and the founding of the National Museum of the American Indian.

Reframing the Window onto Native Lives

The [NMAI] exhibitions challenge the traditional stance of the museum as the singular voice of authority on excellence and cultural meaning.

—Smithsonian secretary Michael Heyman at opening of George Gustav Heye Center, 1994

I believe that these distinct ways of understanding are stated most articulately and are discerned by museum visitors most clearly when the Native voice is permitted, from an interpretive standpoint, to speak for itself.

—NMAI director W. Richard West Jr. at opening of George Gustav Heye Center, 1994

Recent trends have been toward the creation of separate "mini-museums"—independent, ethnically-isolated museums, such as the National Museum of the American Indian, the African Art Museum. . . . Our experience with the "balkanization" of the Smithsonian is that this current direction will result in practical destruction of our capability to present a unifying view of human societies to the public, and will increasingly harm interdisciplinary and international research requirements.

—Department of Anthropology report to the Smithsonian Institution Council, 1994

One of the fundamental challenges posed by the Native community-based narratives embedded within the NMAI is a reflection on the nature of knowledge itself and what counts as valid knowledge or as a valid knowledge-maker and curator. Secretary Heyman stated above that the NMAI presented a challenge to the model of museums with a "singular voice of authority." On one level, this singular voice of authority refers to Western metanarratives that seek to intellectualize and encompass human experience in a universal, explanatory framework. The Native American strategy of seeking some sort of autonomous representational space—whether in a community museum or a specifically Native national museum—has been one strategy for challenging this universal, interpretive framework forged in a colonial context.

One goal of the broad Native American museum movement has been to reframe representations of Native cultures and thereby to restructure both popular perceptions and scientific paradigms. The founding of the NMAI was, in part, an effort to *recontextualize* Native material culture in the social milieu (including emotional and spiritual) in which it acquired meaning in the first place, and to do this in a symbolically significant, national arena. I recognized this recontextualization when I viewed the three inaugural exhibitions when the Heye Center component of the NMAI opened in October 1994.

The first exhibition, Creation's Journey: Masterworks of Native American Identity and Belief, argued for recontextualizing Native art in subjective meaning and a cultural milieu—what the exhibit calls "art in context." Creation's Journey attempted to overturn two dominant, Western interpretive frameworks, one aesthetic and the other scientific.

One exhibit panel articulated these two perspectives of Native art. Vivian Gray, a Micmac artist and the manager of the Indian Art Center in Ottawa, Ontario, wrote, "The consensus of many Indian artists from various tribal groups and languages is that art is not just the created object. Art is a way of life—a holistic experience." Mary Lou Radulovich (Ojibwe) wrote, "Art is part of life, like hunting, fishing, growing food, marrying and having children. This is an art in the broadest sense . . . an object of daily usefulness, to be admired, respected, appreciated, and used, the expression thereby nurturing the needs of body and soul, thereby giving meaning to everything." Here, art is not just the created object. Art is a way of life or a part of life. It is an object of daily usefulness whose expression nurtures the needs of the soul, thereby giving meaning to everything. These are powerful statements linking material culture and the mundane uses of it with notions of social relationality, aesthetics, spirituality, and meaning. Throughout the exhibit, material objects are paired with personal testimonies that contextualize the object in lived and remembered experience and feeling. For example, the following personal reminiscence of an Arapaho woman in 1930 accompanies an elaborately beaded cradle, circa 1910: "My mother used to tell me that when I was still a baby in the cradle, she would strap my cradle to her saddle and drive a herd of ponies across the prairies, sometimes all day long."[49] The cradleboard was accompanied by the text to a lullaby.

The inclusion of oral history (personal experience) as an interpretive approach to an aesthetically pleasing and functional object was very vivid in the exhibition. In the case of the cradleboard, interpretation went beyond communicating its function as a baby carrier, as a technology aiding female mobility, and perhaps as a status marker. It went beyond communicating its age and composition. In a simple yet effective way, the cradleboard provoked imagery of the mother remembering how she carried her child on the pony, remembering her determination to herd those ponies and to secure the child as she did, and later telling the adult child about it. It provoked an image of the cradleboard in use in a way that a simple statement of that fact could not have. Furthermore, it subtly conveyed the animate sense of the object and its *relational role* to the child, to her mother, to their lifeway, to their environment, and to the tribe in general. The object's pertinence to identity and cross-generational memories is suggested. Expressive culture, how Native Americans feel about objects and express themselves through objects, is therefore not a limited or subordinate area of inquiry, it is the crucible of individual and group experience in which the meaning of material culture is established, reinforced, and overturned.

The NMAI's Creation's Journey exhibit attempted to overturn the practice of univocal narrative voice. One of the representational techniques for encouraging reflection on the value of multivocality was the juxtaposition of Native views of art with non-Native, anthropological views of Native art. Between the first and second gallery of the exhibit visitors had to walk through an opening that was flanked by two panels. The first panel was inscribed with Native American perspectives on art; I quoted two of them above. The other side of the opening was flanked by a panel inscribed by a non-Native anthropological view of Native art:

> *The meaning of Indian art is quite different for the old or "traditional" objects and the new or "contemporary" works. The old art is the product of exotic societies, now extinct or so changed as to be difficult to understand on the basis of their modern representations. The new art is made by artists who belong to an ethnic minority but share most cultural forms . . . with the non-Indian members of the larger society.*[50]

Clearly, the curators chose an anthropological view that made a strong temporal separation between "traditional" Native art as a product of "exotic societies" and "contemporary" Native art as a product of an assimilated subculture largely discontinuous from a traditional, essential worldview. The curatorial juxtaposition of contrasting framings of Native art was continued on the labels that accompanied exhibited objects. The Creation's Journey exhibit intended to invite reflection on the multivalence of objects, that is, that art historians, anthropologists, historians, Natives, and non-Natives read cultural materials differently depending on the "cultural eyes and understandings" that are brought to the objects.[51] This was a critique of positivist metanarratives in general, as well as conventional museum practices in particular.

In Consultation, Collaboration, and Cooperation with Natives

As I said, the inclusion of Native Americans in the planning, curation, interpretation, and representation process disrupts conventional notions of what a scholar is and who gets to constitute the consciousness of the visitor. Bringing Native voices and narratives based on alternative epistemologies into a national museum has required building bureaucratic and procedural mechanisms to do so. Collaboration among Native American community members, scholars, artists, anthropologists, and museologists has been one of the mechanisms for bringing formerly subjugated ways of knowing into the planning of the philosophy, the physical structure, and the practices of the National Museum of the American Indian.

In the exhibit All Roads Are Good: Native Voices on Life and Culture, Native American guest curators, exhibit designers, and interpreters shaped what objects were chosen, how they were presented, and which narratives that accompanied them. In the exhibit catalogue, Assistant Director for Cultural Resources Clara Sue Kidwell (Chippewa) argued for the benefits of incorporating Native perspectives into the exhibit design and implementation process. I quote at length from her essay in the catalogue, in which she draws on personal experience as an analogy to the NMAI interpretation process:

> There is a rule about jingle dresses that my mother mentioned to me once. Jingle dresses are worn by women for dancing in the traditional Chippewa (Anishinabeg) way. They are festooned with rows of small, shiny metal cones that used to be, and occasionally still are, made from the lids of snuff tins. The skill of the dancer can be judged by the rhythm of the sound the dress produces. The rule my mother mentioned is that you don't mix jingles made from Copenhagen cans with those made from Skoal cans, because the tones of the two don't harmonize. The rule underscores the most important dimension of a jingle dress—it is made to be heard as well as seen, and to be heard, it must move. The rhythmic clink, the metallic flash in the sun, are part of the dress as surely as the materials of which it is made. . . . My great-aunt donated her jingle dress, along with other items, to a county historical museum in Minnesota, where it probably languishes in a box on a shelf. Even displayed, it would be a static thing, silent and motionless. Chippewa women, viewing that object on display, can enliven it in their minds through their memories of powwows and of family traditions that delineated how dresses were made, and by whom, and for what purpose. The non-Indian, or even non-Chippewa, viewer may see the colorful material, the shiny cones, and the painstaking hand-stitching, but could easily miss the real significance that the dress has.[52]

Kidwell illustrate the point that in validating Native cultural specialists as scholars and interpreters, museum exhibits can foreground the memories and ongoing significance of an object. In doing this, an exhibit can illuminate the meaning that is produced in the midst of the social relationships that encompassed the creation and use of the object. Thus, the insights the exhibit strives for were the nature of the sacred, human relationships with the environment and responsibility to one's community.[53]

To Protect, Support, and Enhance the
Development, Maintenance, and Perpetuation
of Native Culture and Community

The Fourth Museum concept is one of the means the NMAI used to move the national museum toward becoming a cultural center, and therefore becoming a resource for those communities who wish to develop, maintain, and perpetuate their culture and community. Another strategy for supporting these community endeavors is to present alternatives to official narratives and representations whose subtext communicates a paradigm of cultural evolution or inevitable cultural extinction. One of the projects, then, is to disrupt institutional structures or representational practices that imply (and therefore reinforce) notions that Native American cultures have been extinguished due to colonizing and acculturating processes.

The NMAI Customs House exhibit This Path We Travel: Celebrations of Contemporary Native American Creativity asserts that Native American experience with the project to civilize the American Indian-is as important a part of Native American culture and systems of meanings as identity and meaning prior to contact with Europeans and Euro-Americans. Two galleries of the exhibit represented Native American social spaces that have been shaped by the colonial encounter: a 1930s-era boarding school classroom and the living room of U.S. Department of Housing and Urban Development (HUD) house on a reservation. Exhibit planners conceived of the two galleries as "profane intrusions" into a formerly sacred, Native world.

The inscriptions on the boarding school classroom blackboard and on the desks invited visitors to reflect on the imposition of Euro-American schooling and the survival of Native identity despite this imposition. In the HUD living room, the setting familiarized the visitor with contemporary "Native American material culture", such as a television, a couch, a star quilt, a traveling trunk, Indian blankets, Native newspapers, and, ironically, a number of food products marked by stereotypic Indian labeling. Acknowledging the effects of assimilation projects on historical and contemporary Native American experiences was part of the effort to acknowledge both continuity and change in Native cultures.

Inclusion of contemporary Native narratives demonstrated to museum visitors the role of intergenerational relations and cultural memory in perpetuating cultural forms. For example, All Roads Are Good installations paired contemporary and historic objects to foreground cultural survival and historical continuations of cultural processes, despite change.

The Pomo basketweaving installation, for example, featured both cultural continuity and change. A video monitor presented basket weaver Susan Billy's interpretation of the historic and contemporary baskets on display, as well as her insights into the creative process. I was drawn to her storytelling on the video monitor, how she had long admired the Pomo baskets of her tribal heritage and how she had awaited the opportunity to learn to weave herself. I noticed that other visitors to the gallery were also drawn to her narrative and sought out their friends to come and listen, arguably atypical museum visitor behavior. Susan Billy's testimony emphasized that cultural processes are creatively regenerative:

> When I showed up the next morning [at my great-aunt Elsie Allen's house], she handed me an awl and knife and said, "These are the only tools you will need as a basket-weaver. They belonged to your grandmother and I realized last night that I was just taking care of them for you." It was a very emotional experience, quite overwhelming. I had these tools and I could just feel that I was where I was supposed to be. And I began to sit with her and learn from her for the next sixteen years. . . . I get very upset when I hear people say that weaving is a dying art and that nobody is doing it, because I'm here, I'm doing it. And I know that there are others also weaving. I feel that there is always somebody who is going to carry on that wisdom and that knowledge. Which reminds me that a lot of our songs have been lost. But they're only lost for now, they are not really gone. Elsie Allen used to tell me that the lost songs would come through at some time in the future, they will come through to young people in their dreams. The songs aren't gone—they may be in the rocks now, or somewhere down by the river, or someplace. She felt very strongly that they are just waiting for the right person to bring them out again.[54]

Susan Billy's narrative disrupted stereotypes that either situate Native American peoples in a timeless past or afford them a contemporary presence only by portraying them as hollow, broken communities.

The initial reception to the first, New York phase of the NMAI was mixed among non-Native museum professionals and art critics, as well as among various Native American individuals. After the NMAI opened its Heye Center installations in New York City, some critics pointed out the museum's departure from convention. One wrote, "[The exhibits have] no traditional sense of order. Objects are not arranged chronologically or geographically."[55] Another complained that the museum gift shop displayed the objects more respectfully than the exhibits did, including appending chronological dates.[56] Yet another stated, "In distancing itself from academic museum practices by which American Indian cultures have been disastrously ill-served, the National Museum of the American Indian has . . . tipped too far in the opposite direction. It is imperative that the museum rethink its strategies before establishing its Washington home. Meanwhile, visitors to the Custom House are advised to keep their eyes on the objects . . . and try to tune out nearly all of the rest."[57]

I encountered some of these critiques firsthand at a dinner meeting of the Material Culture Forum at the Smithsonian. I was seated with two staff members of the National Museum of American History. One complained, "I didn't feel that their exhibits were up to par at all. They were overinterpreted and underdocumented. They cited the name of the person composing the interpretation on every label. It got repetitive. The same names over and over again. . . . On each label it had both interpretation by an archaeologist or anthropologist and then by a Native American. It was too much." Another complained, "There wasn't the standard documentation, like when it was collected, who donated it, collected it, what the object was made of. Nothing like that was included. I wanted to know those things!" This dinner symposium was entitled "Objects and Things: Reconsidering the Route from the Present to the Past." My dinner companions were not fond of the way the NMAI was attempting to reconsider that route from the present to the past.

Not all NMAI critics are non-Native museologists, by any means. In the course of this project, a number of Native individuals expressed to me some of their concerns about the museum: (a) that the NMAI would never be able to measure up to the ideal standards it had set; (b) that the NMAI had already missed some important opportunities to effect revolutionary change; and (c) that the NMAI would absorb a massive amount of funding that could be better spent at the community level. One Native artist expressed her skepticism using an imaginary interview with the late anthropologist Alfred Kroeber, who had been a director of the University of California Museum of Anthropology. Hulleah J. Tsinhnahjinnie explains to Kroeber that she was involved in the NMAI's This Path We Travel exhibit and continued her conversation with him as follows:

> **Hulleah:** One must remember it [the NMAI] is still an institution of the United States Government. The lesson I learned from the project is to beware of satisfied Native bureaucrats, especially those who are the self-appointed authorities of Native thought.
>
> **Kroeber:** Mmm . . . But you did work with them.
>
> **Hulleah:** To understand bureaucratic reasoning one must work within the madness. Some might say that I have sold out by working on such an [sic] project. Working with the "awesome" institution has strengthened my belief and allegiance to the community/alternative art centers. Perhaps the agenda in selecting me as one of the participating artists for this project was based on the thought that "maybe Hulleah would become comfortable and enjoy the benefits of being a NMAI Indian" and "perhaps Hulleah would buy into the program of the universal anonymous indigenous myth." What was not taken into consideration was the confirmation of already existing doubts of patronizing "good intentions", Native or non-Native. The experience reinforced my "Don't fuck with me" attitude.[58]

In her skepticism of the NMAI and her allegiance to community centers, Hulleah Tsinhnahjinnie points to the distance between one's own community and the National Mall. As part of the Smithsonian Institution, the NMAI does significantly overlap with the formal, political sphere and with a highly charged symbolic national space. Although these qualities lend an unprecedented authority to Native voices in national arenas of representing identity, these very same qualities also make it a potential site for co-optation, silencing of alternative knowledge structures, and homogenization of diversity among tribes.

Conclusions

The initial process of establishing the NMAI as a distinct bureau of the Smithsonian Institution involved more than a struggle over the content of museum narratives. Establishing the NMAI entailed a debate over the concept of "the museum" itself: its purpose, its subjectivities, and its validation of what counts as knowledge. This compellingly demonstrates the power of counternarratives to effect substantive change. At stake were whether or not univocal subjectivity and the Western metanarrative (encompassing and authoritatively explaining otherness while simultaneously maintaining a rational distance from it) would guide the NMAI.

Native American self-determination efforts have contributed to the process of re-envisioning and remaking one of the fundamental educational forums in our society. Admittedly, there are multiple critiques and initiatives that are driving change in museology. Some of these have come from within the museums themselves; others have come from academia. Given the inherent possibilities of the Native American museum movement—for reshaping how the public thinks about Native American history, identity, and humanity and for reconfiguring Native Americans as participants in a self-defining process rather than as subjects of study—the importance of these accomplishments should not be underestimated. My attention to the NMAI should not be confused with the position that the Smithsonian is the ultimate point of decolonization. That would drastically oversimplify the multifaceted nature of the Native American museum movement. Much of the movement is directed at forming institutions at the community level, which will directly benefit the communities' interest in maintaining desired aspects of their

identity and of their coherence as a community. Nevertheless, attempts
to influence mainstream museums at the regional and national level are
a critical part of strategies to survive as a distinct people. Along with
textbooks, films, and other media, museums are targeted as important
sites of representation that influence public perception of and actions
toward Native peoples.

Notes

1. Robert McC. Adams to a major benefactor, quoted by W. Richard West Jr.
   at press conference for the opening of the Heye Center of the American
   Indian, October 25, 1994, Box 5, Smithsonian Institution Archives (SIA)
   ACC 04-170, National Museum of the American Indian Records.
2. Memorandum from Ethnologist Emeritus John C. Ewers to Secretary Adams
   through Anthropology Department Chair Adrienne Kaeppler, May 20, 1987,
   William Merrill personal archives.
3. Richard Kurin, director, Center for Folklife Programs and Cultural Studies, Smithsonian, "Closing Remarks," "Presenting History: Museums in
   a Democratic Society" conference, sponsored by the Smithsonian Institution and the University of Michigan, April 19, 1995, Ann Arbor, Michigan, p. 30 of Summary, Museum Reference Center Archives of the Center
   for Museum Studies, Smithsonian Institution.
4. Anne Rockefeller Roberts, *Joint Hearing before the Select Committee on Indian
   Affairs and the Committee on Rules and Administration in the United States Senate,
   National American Indian Museum Act (Part 2)*, November 18, 1987 (Washington
   DC: U.S. Government Printing Office, 1987), 197–98.
5. Kurin, "Closing Remarks," 31.
6. Patricia Pierce Erikson with Helma Ward and Kirk Wachendorf, *Voices of a
   Thousand People: The Makah Cultural and Research Center* (Lincoln: University
   of Nebraska Press, 2002).
7. The component of my doctoral research that analyzed the Smithsonian as
   one of my field sites was conducted in 1995 with the support of the Smithsonian Predoctoral Fellowship Program. I would like to thank Dr. William Merrill (National Museum of Natural History–Anthropology) and
   Nancy Fuller (Office of Museum Programs) for serving as advisors for my
   research. Many other curators and staff members shared their personal
   experiences and opened their personal files for me. I am grateful to all of
   them for their efforts to help me get to the bottom of this story. Although
   several members of the Smithsonian staff read and critiqued earlier ver-

sions of this manuscript, they did not necessarily agree with the analysis here. I trust others will add to or correct what I have contributed.

8. Richard W. Hill Sr., "The Indian in the Cabinet of Curiosity," in *The Changing Presentation of the American Indian: Museums and Native Cultures* (Washington DC: National Museum of the American Indian, Smithsonian Institution, 2000).

9. See Curtis Hinsley, *The Smithsonian and the American Indian: Making a Moral Anthropology in Victorian America* (1981; Washington DC: Smithsonian Institution Press, 1994); Shepard Krech II and Barbara A. Hail, eds., *Collecting Native America, 1870–1960* (Washington DC: Smithsonian Institution Press, 1999); Michael M. Ames, *Cannibal Tours and Glass Boxes: The Anthropology of Museums* (Vancouver: University of British Columbia Press, 1992); James Clifford, "Four Northwest Coast Museums," in *Exhibiting Cultures: The Poetics and Politics of Museum Display*, ed. Ivan Karp and Steven D. Lavine (Washington DC: Smithsonian Institution Press, 1991); Evan M. Maurer, "Presenting the American Indian: From Europe to America," in *The Changing Presentation of the American Indian: Museums and Native Cultures* (Washington DC: National Museum of the American Indian, Smithsonian Institution, 2000).

10. Philip Deloria, *Playing Indian* (New Haven CT: Yale University Press, 1998).

11. George E. Marcus and Michael M. J. Fischer, *Anthropology as Cultural Critique: An Experimental Moment in the Human Sciences* (Chicago: University of Chicago Press, 1986); Renato Rosaldo, *Culture and Truth: The Remaking of Social Analysis* (1989; Boston: Beacon Press, 1993).

12. Specific critiques of anthropology and academia include Lucy Biddle, "Keeping Tradition Alive," *Museum News*, May/June 1977, 35–42; Vine Deloria, "Custer Died for Your Sins," *Playboy*, August 1969; Deborah Doxtator, "The Idea of the Indian and the Development of the Iroquoian Museums," *Museum Quarterly*, summer 1985, 20–26; James A. Hanson, "The Reappearing Vanishing American," *Museum News* 59, no. 2 (1980): 44–51; George P. Horse Capture, "From the Reservation to the Smithsonian via Alcatraz," *American Indian Culture and Research Journal* 18, no. 4 (1994): 135–49; Beatrice Medicine, "The Anthropologist and American Indian Studies Programs," *The Indian Historian* 4, no. 1 (1971): 15–18, 63; Thomas Biolsi and Larry J. Zimmerman, *Indians and Anthropologists* (Tucson: University of Arizona Press, 1997). Broader critiques include Philip Deloria, *Playing Indian* (New Haven CT: Yale University Press, 1998); Rayna Green, "The Indian in Popular American Culture," in *The Handbook of North American Indians IV*,

ed. W. Washburn (Washington DC: Smithsonian Institution Press, 1988); Christopher Jocks, "Spirituality for Sale: Sacred Knowledge in the Consumer Age," *American Indian Quarterly* 20, no. 3 (1996): 415–31. On establishing independent tribal institutions, see Nancy Fuller and Suzanne Fabricius, "Tribal Museums," in *Native America in the Twentieth Century: An Encyclopedia* (New York: Garland Publishing, 1994), 655–57. On collaborative representational projects, see Ruth Phillips, "Introduction to Community Collaboration in Exhibitions: Toward a Dialogic Paradigm," in *Museums and Source Communities: A Routledge Reader*, ed. Laura Peers and Alison K. Brown (London: Routledge, 2003), 155–70.

13. Patricia Pierce Erikson, "Encounters in the Nation's Attic: Native American Community Museums/Cultural Centers, the Smithsonian Institution, and the Politics of Knowledge Making" (PhD diss., University of California, Davis, 1996).

14. Sharon Macdonald and Gordon Fyfe, eds., *Theorizing Museums: Representing Identity and Diversity in a Changing World* (Oxford: Blackwell, 1996).

15. Patricia Pierce Erikson with Janine Bowechop, "Forging Indigenous Methodologies on Cape Flattery: The Makah Museum as a Center of Collaborative Research," *American Indian Quarterly* 29, nos. 1–2 (2005): 263–73; Patricia Erikson, "Trends in Image and Design: Reflections on 25 Years of a Tribal Museum Era," in *Histories of Anthropology Annual*, vol. 1, ed. Regna Darnell and Frederic W. Gleach (Lincoln: University of Nebraska Press, 2005), 271–86.

16. Eilean Hooper-Greenhill, "The Museum in the Disciplinary Society," in *Museum Studies in Material Culture*, ed. S. M. Pearce (London: Leicester University Press, 1989), 61–72; James Clifford, "Museums as Contact Zones," in *Routes: Travel and Translation in the Late Twentieth Century* (Cambridge MA: Harvard University Press, 1997).

17. Curtis Hinsley, "Collecting Cultures and Cultures of Collecting: The Lure of the American Southwest, 1880–1915," *Museum Anthropology* 16, no. 1 (1992):12–20; Krech and Hail, *Collecting Native America*.

18. Clifford, "Museums as Contact Zones," 192–93.

19. Donna Haraway, *Primate Visions: Gender, Race, and Nature in the World of Modern Science* (New York: Routledge, 1989), 26–58; Benedict Anderson, *Imagined Communities: Reflections on the Origin and Spread of Nationalism* (London: Verso, 1991).

20. Mary Louise Pratt, *Imperial Eyes: Travel Writing and Transculturation* (New York: Routledge, 1992).

21. Hooper-Greenhill, "The Museum in the Disciplinary Society," 61–72.

22. Michael Ames, "Museums, the Public and Anthropology: A Study in the Anthropology of Anthropology," in *Ranchi Anthropology Series*, vol. 9, ed. L. P. Vidyarthi (Vancouver: University of British Columbia Press, 1986).

23. Ivan Karp, "On Civil Society and Social Identity," in *Museums and Communities: The Politics of Public Culture*, ed. I. Karp, C. M. Kreamer, and S. D. Lavine (Washington DC: Smithsonian Institution Press, 1992), 19–33.

24. Karp, "On Civil Society," 12.

25. Richard Hill, chairman of the North American Indian Museum Association, to Gene Bahlen [sic], curator of exhibits, Museum of Natural History, March 11, 1981, Box 17, SIA ACC 90-077, Office of Museum Program (OMP) Records.

26. Douglas H. Ubelaker to Richard S. Fiske, March 25, 1981, Box 17, SIA ACC 90-077, OMP Records.

27. Adrienne Kaeppler, chair, Department of Anthropology, to Secretary Robert McC. Adams, June 13 1985, William Merrill personal archives.

28. National Congress of American Indians, Susan Shown Harjo, executive director, to Robert McCormick Adams, secretary, Smithsonian Institution, December 16, 1986, Rayna Green personal archives.

29. John C. Ewers to NMNH director Frank H. Talbot, April 25, 1989, William Fitzhugh personal archives.

30. Proposal, personal files of William Merrill.

31. This description was based in conversations with both William Merrill and Joallyn Archambault, as well as the original proposal and vision statement materials, which they provided me.

32. Smithsonian Secretary Robert McCormick Adams, *Joint Hearing before the Select Committee on Indian Affairs and Committee on Rules and Administration, United States Senate, National American Indian Museum Act (Part I)* (Washington DC: U.S. Government Printing Office, 1987), 73.

33. See, for example, Jake Henshaw, "Burial Remains: Indians Urge Smithsonian to Turn Over Collections," *Argus Leader* (Sioux Falls SD), February 2, 1986, 7D.

34. Patricia Zell, interview by author, Washington DC, 1995; Senator Daniel Inouye, *Joint Hearing before the Select Committee on Indian Affairs and Committee on Rules and Administration, United States Senate, National American Indian Museum Act (Part I)* (Washington DC: U.S. Government Printing Office, 1987), 2.

35. Zell interview.

36. Robert McCormick Adams to U.S. Representative Bill Green, July 23, 1987, William Fitzhugh personal archives; Secretary Emeritus S. Dillon Ripley, *Joint Hearing before the Select Committee on Indian Affairs and Committee on Rules*

and Administration, United States Senate, National American Indian Museum Act (Part I) (Washington DC: U.S. Government Printing Office, 1987, 122.

37. William Grimes, "The Indian Museum's Last Stand," *New York Times Magazine,* November 27, 1988, 76.

38. Ives Goddard to curators, Department of Anthropology, May 11, 1987, memo regarding NMAI bill draft of May 4, 1987, William Merrill personal archives.

39. Secretary Robert McCormick Adams, Joint Hearing before the Select Committee on Indian Affairs and Committee on Rules and Administration, U.S. Senate, National Museum of American Indian Act (Part I), 1987, 15–29.

40. Adrienne Kaeppler to Secretary Adams, May 20, 1987, William Merrill personal archives.

41. Jack F. Trope and Walter R. Echo-Hawk, "The Native American Graves Protection and Repatriation Act: Background and Legislative History," *Arizona State Law Journal* 24, no. 1 (1992): appendix.

42. Trope and Echo-Hawk, "The Native American Graves Protection and Repatriation Act," 58.

43. Betsy Gehman, "The First Americans," *Promenade* (1994): 73.

44. Oren Lyons, *Joint Hearing before the Select Committee on Indian Affairs and Committee on Rules and Administration, United States Senate, National American Indian Museum Act (Part I)* (Washington DC: U.S. Government Printing Office, 1987), 79.

45. Donald Ortner to Robert Adams, April 18, 1991, letter regarding concerns of the departmental Americanists, William Fitzhugh personal archives.

46. Frank Talbot to Secretary Adams, April 29, 1991, letter regarding Indianists memo to secretary, William Fitzhugh personal archives.

47. Senate of Scientists Council to Secretary Adams, May 7, 1991, memo regarding National Museum of the American Indian policy statement, Herman Viola personal archives.

48. Richard Hill, interview by author, Washington DC, 1995.

49. Arapaho woman, ca. 1930, reprinted in *Creation's Journey: Native American Identity and Belief* (Washington DC: Smithsonian Institution and the National Museum of the American Indian, 1994), 35.

50. William Sturtevant, "The Meaning of Native American Art," in *The Arts of the North American Indian: Native Traditions in Evolution,* ed. Edwin Wade (New York: Hudson Hill Press, Philbrook Art Center, 1986), 23–44.

51. NMAI director W. Richard West Jr., press conference at the opening of the George Gustav Heye Center of the American Indian, October 25, 1994, Box 5, SIA ACC 04-170, NMAI.

52. Clara Sue Kidwell, "Introduction," in *All Roads Are Good: Native Voices on Life and Culture* (Washington DC: Smithsonian Institution Press, 1994), 14.

53. Kidwell, "Introduction," 15.

54. Susan Billy, "So the Spirit Can Move Freely," in *All Roads Are Good: Native Voices on Life and Culture*, 198, 206.

55. Randy Kraft, "Museum Doesn't Live Up: Huge Building Misnomer for New Indian Museum," *New Mexican* (Albuquerque), December 11, 1994.

56. Amy Gamerman, "New Indian Museum Opens with Preachy Show," *Wall Street Journal*, November 3, 1994.

57. Holland Cotter, "New Museum Celebrates Indian Voices," *New York Times*, October 28, 1994.

58. Hulleah J. Tsinhnahjinnie, *Photographic Memoirs of an Aboriginal Savant*, Nov. 13–Dec. 22, 1994, exhibition catalogue (Davis CA: C. N. Gorman Museum, Native American Studies Department, UC Davis, 1994).

3. Concourse and Periphery

Planning the National Museum of the American Indian

Judith Ostrowitz

Well Past Planning

The National Museum of the American Indian (NMAI) opened its doors to the public on September 21, 2004, with all of the fanfare that this high-point in its history as an institution prescribed. Although the building itself was pronounced complete on that day, planning processes for the museum must be considered ongoing, as the nature of this institution continues to be defined and developed. That being said, the earliest part of this process, initiated when the NMAI was established as a bureau of the Smithsonian Institution on November 28, 1989, must be considered as an historic passage.[1]

It was during those first years that new and unusual processes of design programming had to result in concrete directives that would generate finite forms. The three to four years of early consultation meetings among Native representatives from far-flung Indigenous groups that live, not only in North America, but all over the Western hemisphere, together with some non-Native specialists and representatives, were the most influential. The meetings were organized to determine what were called "commonalities" in the traditions and conceptual approaches of these very diverse communities, who were obliged to establish desiderata for a new phenomenon, a national museum made to represent Native American people to an international audience, said to be delineated on the basis of their own authority. The resulting institution is also meant to serve these various consulting populations of Indigenous people who have a critical interest in the disposition of the museum's collections. They have a large stake as well in the dynamism of this institution, in its potential to both preserve and re-create a public history and a sphere of influence for Native America. The development process initiated by their discussions was directed at first to inform design strategies for the museum building on the mall in Washington DC, the Cultural Resource Center (CRC) in nearby Suitland, Maryland, and some of the programs that animate the activities in these two locations as well as those implemented at the very first public venue of this institution, the George Gustave Heye Center in Lower Manhattan.

In this essay, I concentrate on the enormity of their task, the development of the architectural program as well as ideas generated very early on for appropriate exhibition and operations strategies. Because these conceptualizations have since become explicit with the opening of the museum on the Mall, I also trace relationships between ideals and reality through observations on final forms. Analysis of the early critical and public reception of the museum indicates that additional explication of the process of planning itself would provide a somewhat mystified audience with essential guidance.

Concourse and Periphery

Focusing on the voluminous documents that record much of these planning processes and speaking with some of the great number of individuals involved in these exchanges have been a bit like watching someone sculpt smoke. As Rina Swentzell from Santa Clara Pueblo, architect, PhD in American studies, representative and "transcending co-facilitator" for the NMAI consultation process said, "What came up was respect for water, earth, elders, one another, the spirit in each one, future generations, knowledge, life. How do we take the notion of respect for water, for example, and begin to think about how it might work in the museum itself?"[2] The manipulation of water, the very embodiment of the quality of mutability, functions as the most apt metaphor for the task undertaken by this broad constituency: to extract solid form from a thousand different stories or streams of consciousness and resolve that it would be representative of the American Indian.

The composition of the NMAI planning documents should not be underestimated as a key source to understand the sway that this new institution was meant to have. The formidable work and written products of these cultural activists for the NMAI may be associated with the sort of "impossible unity" that Homi K. Bhabha (1990) had claimed for images or "narratives" of nations, their origins justified by the primordial and steeped in heroic pasts. By the 1990s, previous notions of national unity became sufficiently complicated by processes of globalization and the exigencies of locality as to call for the type of structuring and redefining narratives that Bhabha referred to. In many ways, these processes summarize the task that the NMAI had set for itself, in its fierce and optimistically conceived insistence on considerable rewriting, in this case from the "periphery." The self-identification of criteria and qualities necessary for group membership developed over these few short years were meant to be concretized by "texts" and, by implication, through the very process of authorship itself. Characteristic of scholarly thought in this same period and apt for the NMAI project, Arjun Appadurai (1996) named similar resources for identity construction as the garnering of a "constitutive imaginary." Such acts are to be understood as full of potential for community making, the harnessing of words and images for the shaping of nations, particularly as deployed beyond their own borders. They are meant to enable greater sovereignty, making new "centers" and problematizing the former identification of marginal narratives.[3]

Under scrutiny, the collaborative acts of imagination and authorship for the NMAI disclosed in these documents can be shown to have established an extraordinary degree of generalization as appropriate for its public address. In fact, it is possible to theorize that no single one of the very many participating Indigenous communities was served as a discrete entity by this project. However, some good arguments can be made for a certain deference shown the "host community," identified as the nearby representatives of the Piscataway-Conoy group.[4] In a sense, the specificity accorded to the sovereignty of this particular Native nation may summarize, but only as a concept, the one true commonality established in the course of this staggering research project. All of the Native groups confirm as a part of ongoing practice the suitability of the controlling interest of Indigenous nations in their own, legitimate territory. Ironically, however, there has been significant culture loss through the exigencies of history for the Piscataway-Conoy. For this and other reasons, their traditions could be referred to by the NMAI only in a very abstract manner. However, their geographic proximity to the project was repeatedly affirmed as significant in the related texts, so that this nod to territoriality was implemented for the development of the museum, not as form but as an element of *process*. In fact, one would be hard-pressed to name any group-specific sources for the physical appearance of the NMAI buildings as *product*.[5] Some of the permanent installations planned for the NMAI did indeed highlight the traditions of particular groups as representative, but this is yet another process that suggests that audiences extrapolate from the concrete to imagine more general qualities of Native life. As I will show, repeated disjunction between new processes of conceptualization and the various media that ultimately informs audiences about the NMAI has resulted in great challenges for the success and credibility of the museum.

The buildings, as the NMAI planned them, are extremely broad in reference. For the creation of its global platform, this institution did not intend to present itself as a confluence of peripheral localities, for instance, a conglomeration of tipi and longhouse forms, no matter how neatly the traditional features of these could have been joined by a clever postmodern architect. Instead, the Mall museum was to be composed of gracefully stacked, undulating ribbons of limestone, meant to evoke cliffs of that material, carved away by wind and time. To many it may be more reminiscent of the circulating bands or horizontal registers of the Guggenheim Museum in New York, the Canadian Museum of Civilization in Hull, Quebec, or many other world-class institutions. The exhibitions and outreach programs, shaped by the same consultants' texts, also embraced progression and addressed the globe. They planned to make use of the most up- to-date technologies known to cyberspace to enable future generations of Native people to take care of their traditional business in private, but at the same time, prepared for the placement of Native nations as players in a worldwide sphere, in a commanding position.

As the ethicist and philosopher Enrique Dussel (1998) has suggested, there is an equation between the advent of modernity itself and the production of statements that universalized internal, European cultural phenomena as more than causal, as absolute in terms of position. As the self-designated "*center* of the 'world-system,'" argues Dussel, Europe relied upon taking up Amerindia and its colonization as its *periphery* in its process of definition.[6] Now, in the capital of the United States, installed on this nation's common ground, Indigenous groups have developed the intention to describe themselves as vital and integrated, not just conjoined according to the indexing criteria and perceptions of outsiders. Therefore, a more substantial entity has been suggested, charging an international audience to redress the former consignment of Native people as an ordered collection of groups, identified by colonial process, to marginalization. This strategy required substantial concourse and results in the current exigency to place most intertribal differences somewhat beyond the public purview, in relatively unexplored locations. It was devised to extend some access to planetary dialogue to those who had languished, when considered to be more diverse, at the periphery of modernism.

National identities the world over are obviously in great flux. It is abundantly clear that the public announcement of subnational regional status and antiquated charm does not admit participation at what functions as the "center." Key principles, useful metaphrases, and empowering technologies were therefore thought more effective in the context of the NMAI's project. Its establishing literature described the ambitions of the Mall museum: "This building competes with monuments of the world. It must be compatible, in that setting, as the monument to Native Americans."[7] And, as Anne Trowbridge, architect for Venturi, Scott Brown and Associates, Inc., a Philadelphia firm significantly involved with this planning process mused, "It seemed to work for the purposes of the museum to give the impression of a singular Indian culture."[8] This strategically conceived unity, first related in text, was meant to be inscribed in form for the NMAI project.

The Way of the People

The collection that is the nucleus of this institution originated with the Museum of the American Indian, George Heye Foundation in New York and was assembled under the auspices of collector George Gustave Heye (1874–1957) through expeditions and outright purchases that he funded early in the twentieth century from Native North, Central, and South America.[9] The museum meant to house his treasure trove opened in 1922 in the complex called Audubon Terrace at 155th and Broadway, a bit off the beaten track in New York. The exhibits were installed in a manner that would today be considered antiquated and jam-packed, and by the 1980s the cases became musty and sorely in need of update. A Research Center on Bruckner Boulevard in the Bronx was used for storage and the conservation of the collections, where the shelves had become closely stacked with almost one million objects that could hardly be attended to or studied properly. Also in financial crisis by this time, the desire for up-to-date museum representation was far overshadowed by the museum's growing inability to afford sufficient care for these valuable pieces. However, transition to national status for this collection was a bit circuitous. Interested parties came to vie for these long-neglected treasures. And, as a part of its own ultimately successful bid for the collection, the Smithsonian Institution was required to meet another great challenge of the period, by accelerating its development of acceptable repatriation policy.[10]

The first ten years following the establishing legislation were devoted, for the most part, to the development of conception and process. True to the Native requirement for legitimacy as established by local, aboriginal inhabitants, wide-ranging plans were made to hold regional meetings for Native consultation in selected locations throughout the territory to be represented. However, in this case the entire Western hemisphere was implicated as appropriate territory on the basis of the museum's holdings. Therefore, early sessions were organized to hear proposed requirements for this institution from selected representatives of a great many local populations.[11] Beginning in 1990, some meetings were scheduled in Oklahoma and Oregon, but the thirteen sessions held between May and November 1991 should be considered especially influential; these were held in places ranging from Washington DC, to Santa Fe and Albuquerque, New Mexico; Philadelphia, Pennsylvania; and Anchorage, Alaska. The voices heard at those venues were recorded and summarized to produce the first of three volumes of architectural programming documents, *The Way of the People*, the essential texts of this endeavor, published in November 1991.[12]

The NMAI continued with its formal consultation process well beyond this date.[13] Later sessions affected decisions as well, but these did not become a part of the Way of the People volume that functioned as the conceptual guide for both design and operation. In fact, this first phase of master facilities programming for both the Mall museum and the Cultural Resource Center in Suitland offered no specific formal solutions, architectural renderings, or floor plans. It was an outline of the project and a set of goals explicated for the architects and designers who would later carry these concepts out in form.[14]

Although the NMAI made sweeping efforts to consult far and wide and distribute representation evenly to create these documents, prominent and active community members who are accustomed to stepping forward for similar projects always play a larger role. More important, the roles of museum professionals, lead architects, and various other influential specialists should not be minimized in this undertaking, even when the egalitarian ideal to include the broadest range of Native representatives possible is highlighted in the supporting literature.[15] For instance, the architectural firm Venturi, Scott Brown and Associates was selected to play a pivotal role in this process. They were hired to record the flow of dialogue and also to effect a certain level of analysis with the material. Venturi architect Anne Trowbridge was the actual "hand that held the pencil" (in fact, a tape recorder) at the consultation sessions. She then transcribed tapes as initial "meeting minutes" that, to begin with, listed the comments of participants. She also maintained a separate column on each page of the minutes to extract items that she considered essential from the "streams of consciousness" that predominated at many of these gatherings. These reminders were a first step in the translation of laymen's terms and free-form statements into specific suggestions meant to inform the design process. For instance, a researcher who participated on May 30, 1991, commented, as was typical, in an ideational manner: "Research projects and methods and exhibitions should acknowledge that Indian people are not object oriented—focus on a holistic picture built around people who made objects." This resulted in a note in Trowbridge's column that reads, "Provide gallery spaces for exhibitions that could be multisensory environments rather than purely visual displays of objects in neutral settings."[16]

Douglas Cardinal Architects, PC, formerly of Washington DC, together with Gedde Brecher Qualls Cunningham Architects of Philadelphia were originally contracted as lead architects for this building on the Mall. They were not retained through the entire design and construction process, resulting in some adjustments to Cardinal's original design, but not eliminating the powerful effect of his ideas on the processes and most of the design solutions carried out there.[17] This architect, alternately identified as Blackfoot or Métis in the literature about him, is a Canadian of mixed ancestry; his mother was French, German, and Mohawk and his father was of Blackfoot, French, and Ojibwa descent. Consistent with the NMAI agenda, he calls his own manner of working a "consensual approach" to design.[18] He has conducted his own consultation processes for earlier projects and did so again to prepare for some stages of the design of the Mall museum. In February 1995 he held two sessions, one called a "vision session" and the other an "imaging session" or "design workshop," both conducted in Washington. While these sessions were said to initiate the design process, it should be kept in mind that many visual features of the building—its basic shapes—were already in place when he first presented himself as an architectural candidate to the NMAI. He had already read *The Way of the People* when he made his first Plexiglas model of the building as a part of his proposal. He describes the model making, saying he "sketched it as a spirit" and concedes that the final form of the building emerged as quite close to that of this first sketch.[19]

Meetings defined as "consultations" have been a part of earlier Native American projects. They have been thought of as the necessary inclusion of selected representatives, particularly for the development of exhibitions of Indigenous art at some museums. However, until this planning period, these individuals were rarely the sole or ultimate authorities for projects.[20] The NMAI claims a dramatic departure from typical consultation practices because of the significant difference in scale and level of ascendancy for selected Native spokespersons. Similar procedures now operate on a subnational level in relation to a general increase in commissions initiated by Native American clients for public architectural projects as well. This shift in agency should now be understood as a requirement for a "new consultation" phenomenon, particularly for museum architecture.

The New Native American Architecture:
An Emerging Genre

Planning processes that are meant to meet the requirements established by Indigenous clientele are now a prerequisite in a range of architectural projects, an increasing number of which have been initiated since the early 1990s. Many, but not all of these, have been led by Native American architects. It has now become clear that when serious consultation with local Native communities is carried out, some characteristic design criteria are identified. This suggests the emergence of a new genre, but one that is more conceptual than specifically formal, as clients usually refer to "qualities" that are considered appropriate by American Indians. Less frequently do they suggest specific forms. Significant variation is possible because architects are usually encouraged to interpret these qualities with any number of new materials and up- to-date architectural applications are highly appreciated by most of these groups.

Foremost among these delineated qualities is the repeated claim by most Native American spokespeople that they enjoy a special or privileged relationship with nature, as well as an accompanying responsibility for stewardship of the land, a concept that they wish to have expressed architecturally—for example, through the smooth integration of indoor and outdoor spaces, the citation of natural forms, textures, and colors. Not surprisingly, the "commonalities" that emerged in the course of consultation processes for the NMAI were also developed in great part from the desire to regard cues from nature, Indigenous habitats, and phenomena that result from the change of seasons and related visible occurrences in the sky.

Other Native American architectural projects, carried out in the early 1990s, almost simultaneously with the planning processes for the NMAI, included an additional proviso that would not be seen in Washington DC. For these, architects were also encouraged to translate, in creative variation, shapes that could be recovered from the building traditions of local Native clients, or to generalize to some extent from those of their immediate neighbors in cases where more specific examples were not available because of local culture loss. The lack of such an historical directive at the NMAI is reflective of its mandate to always remain broad in reference. This may provide additional freedom of expression, but it is also a more generalizing process. It precluded even the remote recycling of longhouse forms or even some references to the rectangular, barrel-roofed houses of old Piscataway villages in the appearance of its buildings.[21]

Dialogues between architects and Native American constituencies that consistently result in preferences like these (and others that will be described below) are now becoming common. It is difficult to pinpoint the inception of these requisite processes and the resulting common concepts for Native American architecture. It is interesting, however, that in 1989 the National Commission on American Indian, Alaskan Native, and Native Hawaiian Housing was established by the Housing and Urban Development Reform Act, which resolved to research more culturally appropriate housing requirements for Native American domestic architecture than those that had been applied before. This could be situated as a starting point for a transfer of design authority, or at least for greater design advice originating from Native American sources. A process of consultation was also considered indispensable by the American Indian Council of Architects and Engineers (AICAE), a nonprofit corporation that was established as far back as 1976. Interestingly, Louis Weller (Caddo/Cherokee) and David Sloan (Navajo), both architects who were active in the design process for the Cultural Resource Center of the NMAI, had been members of the AICAE Design Team.[22] It was not until 1994, however, that their work resulted in the publication of a guide for Native American domestic architecture in the form of a booklet titled *Our Home: A Design Guide for Indian Housing*, with information said to have been gleaned from a series of consultations or regional workshops that were held on the Plains, in the Southwest, on the Northwest Coast, and in Juneau, Alaska, for both Arctic and Subarctic participants. *The Way of the People* was first published in 1991, so certain ideas about procedure and resulting concepts about Native American form may be said to have been developed in tandem by these teams.

In examining the AICAE findings, it should be noted that their consultation meetings inserted knowledge about architectural tradition as a criteria from the very start with slide presentations of precontact- and early postcontact-style houses projected on each occasion. Although their published guide announces at the outset that each tribe or Indian group has its own distinct traditions and that it is important to avoid architectural generalization, nonetheless, some unifying criteria for proper Native housing are decribed. For instance, as might be expected, influential parties were encouraged to gain a special knowledge of patterns in nature and to establish harmony with the land. The AICAE publication also mentions the preference of many Native groups for eastern orientation of their buildings, a criterion that emerged as vital for the NMAI as well.

Smell was also said to be an integral part of the "experience of place" in Native American architecture. This sense is also brought up time and again in The Way of the People. An NMAI consultation participant expounded, "One should be able to smell sage, wood, fish, cedar. A giant scratch and sniff!"[23] This parallels comments in the AICAE guide, particularly the note that Native residents of the proposed homes would enjoy the smell of woodsmoke from cooking areas.[24]

Louis Weller, active for the NMAI projects as well as a member of the AICAE team, of Weller Architects, PC, in Albuquerque, New Mexico, a firm established in 1980 and in large part occupied with "Indian projects," has also noticed the development of convergent or some generally recognized "Native values" and the recollection of traditional qualities known from historical documents and oral histories that emerge repeatedly when Native people are significantly involved with planning processes.[25] Some are related to the citation of historical form. As an example, Weller himself has chosen forms based on the roofs of hogans or traditional buildings in designing a health center for the Navajo tribe in northwestern New Mexico. The curvilinear shapes of some kivas as well as configurations said to recall stacked adobe were combined for the Taos-Picuris Pueblo Health Center in Taos, New Mexico, that he designed. Weller also cites David Sloan of David N. Sloan and Associates in Albuquerque, and his associate in the AICAE project, who built a shopping center in Crown Point, New Mexico with wood beams called *vigas* that protrude from walls of local stone. The structure is meant to evoke the nearby Anasazi ruins of Chaco Canyon. The end walls are made of split-faced block, and inset designs were modeled after warp and weft patterns seen in rugs made by Navajo people. Many of these quasi-traditional forms are adapted to suit modern sensibilities. For instance, the Museum of the Southern Ute in southwestern Colorado was designed by Sloan in collaboration with Donald Stastny, AIA (non-Native). The central space is covered with a dramatic glass structure that is supposed to resemble the smoke holes of tipis.[26]

Johnpaul Jones (Choctaw/Cherokee) of Jones & Jones, architects and landscape architects of Seattle, Washington, makes similar references that may be conceived as strategic take-offs on architectural history. He designed the Longhouse Cultural Education Center for Evergreen State College in Olympia and the Makah De'aht Elders' Center in Neah Bay, Washington, both in reference to longhouses or the plank houses of the Northwest Coast region. These are situated to face the beach as were their historical antecedents.[27]

Similarly, Susan Rodriguez (non-Native) of Polshek & Partners, the firm largely responsible for the design of the CRC in Suitland and ultimately for the final stages of the NMAI Mall museum design preparation, claims historical precedent for the Museum and Research Center for the Mashantucket Pequot tribe in Ledyard, Connecticut. Polshek & Partners designed the building in 1993 with tribal interaction, although surviving members of this nation have suffered the loss of a great deal of traditional knowledge. Rodriguez suggests that, in the absence of authoritative elders or oral histories that tribal members might quote, the building is "a physical manifestation of the extensive research undertaken by the tribal anthropologist and archaeologist over the last fifteen years." Somehow, a formal vocabulary that stands for the Pequot nation was developed from the information recovered by these specialists, concepts about traditional regard for solar orientation, the significance of the cardinal directions, and the specifics of the landscape. Also, a fort excavated in Mystic, Connecticut, the site of a massacre in 1637, provided a basic design format for the Mashantucket Pequot Museum building: two interlocking semicircles. An impressive steel enclosure that defines a Great Hall is also said to be "basket-like" because its structure was informed by wigwam technology. A steel network is integrated with glass as an enormous curtain wall that faces north to the woods; this is meant to be related to the desired state of unity with nature discussed for all of these architectural projects. Other forms on the front of the building were suggested by wampum belt designs, and woven baskets are said to have inspired hand railings.[28]

Finally, an influential project affected by Native American consultation in the early 1990s is the highly regarded Museum at Warm Springs, designed for the Confederated Tribes of the Warm Springs Reservation of Oregon by Stastny and Burke, a non-Native firm. This firm hosted a week-long charette at Warm Springs, although they were not given specific, formal directives by the tribes. They also set up an office on the reservation toward the end of the design process, inviting comments from the community.[29] The resulting complex is meant to loosely resemble a Plains tipi encampment.[30] Three metallic roof peaks are meant to symbolize the tribes of the Warm Springs Reservation, and the cylindrical entrance of the museum, made of volcanic stone, is informed by the shape of a drum. The central meeting place that borders on an amphitheater is built as a "circle within a circle." Circular forms emerge repeatedly in these projects and, as we shall see, at the NMAI. At Warm Springs, sculptural stanchions mark the four cardinal directions (another appearance of the desired directional symbolism). Impressive columns and struts in the lobby are said by Stastny to be "stylized remembrances of the cottonwoods on the site," (Weller 1996) referencing the historical landscape. We hear of basketry as representative and inspirational, but perhaps interpreted in a somewhat generic fashion, here informing the stepped and crisscross patterning on the exterior brickwork.[31]

It is important to observe the continuing involvement and overlapping interests of selected players in many of these projects. Polshek has been a lead architect at the NMAI and also for the Mashantucket Pequot. In turn, there was an effective Pequot presence during consultation for the NMAI, and this Native nation has made a very significant financial contribution to the NMAI project.[32] Tuscarora architect Ken Rhyne, who carries out what he calls "cultural values workshops" for his projects, was instrumental in the interior design plans developed for the CRC. This was an indispensable part of the development of Rhyne's design for the Catawba Indian Nation's new Seven Feathers Cultural Complex in Rock Hill, South Carolina.[33] Louis Weller, David Sloan and Johnpaul Jones were NMAI consultants as well. Weller and Sloan are members of the Native American Design Collaborative, which participated in the design and development of the CRC project. No wonder, as Weller has also observed, processes like these engender a significant amount of intertribal borrowings.[34] Going forward, some of the devices invented by these influential architects will undoubtedly affect future notions of appropriate Native American form as well, particularly in collaborative projects. These may come to represent a baseline that future consultants will build on.

Principles, Paraphrases, and Commonalities

Nature, history, directional symbolism, circularity— to an extent, all of the concepts that emerged to inform these examples of new Native American architecture are highly plastic and open to interpretation because they are abstractions; they are "principle-based." None of them actually requires the true replication of precontact or early postcontact buildings. The NMAI must surely be understood and evaluated against other contemporary Native projects and, as I specify below, it parallels their development processes and reproduces and even exemplifies the principles found operative in their design solutions. However, the NMAI supersedes all of these other examples in the level of abstraction with which these commonly derived principles have been expressed.

Carol Herselle Krinsky, an architectural historian who has published a volume on contemporary Native American architecture, has applied the term "paraphrase" to refer to creative translations that take cues from traditional forms but are freely interpreted in modern materials and adjusted according to contemporary sensibilities.[35] I wish to expand on this definition to discuss formal solutions to design problems that are so abstract that they need not be based on historical form at all. These are not even paraphrases; they are *principles* that originate with the situation of design authority, at least ideally, with Native American constituencies. Those constituencies may now, in the absence of traceable, linear histories, be more broadly defined than ever before. Form then becomes infinitely flexible, as long as it can be traced to some aboriginal agency. This is now legitimately practiced, for instance, when cross-tribal borrowing augments the data available to groups whose history is poorly documented. It is de rigueur when an architectural client is the Indigenous population of the entire Western hemisphere. The NMAI's Board of Trustees Handbook is explicit on this issue of the ascendancy of agency over the required use of existing design solutions. This text announces that the "NMAI is conceptually and ideologically a new kind of institution; its creation is in a process of user intensive self-definition."[36]

As noted earlier, chief among the new commonalities arrived at through intensive Native self-definition has been this decree to incorporate "a sense of place," a special relationship to the land and the entity now called "nature" in all of these buildings and without doubt in the NMAI project. As *The Way of the People* narrative interprets this mandate, with some understatement, "The distinctions between indoors and outdoors may be blurred in places."[37] This injunction should be closely examined. In doing so, it is interesting to refer to Shepard Krech III's work *The Ecological Indian: Myth and History* (1999) because Krech explores the origin of ideas about the long-standing and agreed upon relationship with nature and more recently, the global belief in an inherent Native American environmental awareness. This is yet another work that emerged in the 1990s that foregrounds the strategic positioning of selected text and image as effective for the constitution of new group identity consistent with goals for social change. Krech investigates the history of these concepts about environment and addresses the possibility that they may, at least in part, have been constructed at first for the Euro-American mind.

Such theories are contested among Native and non-Native critics alike because of the authority ascribed to the group who "originates" such concepts. However, one may usefully interrogate this issue to evaluate by whom and for what purposes (not when) these ideas about nature and ecology have been applied as a component in the process of self-identification for Native Americans. Krech, for instance, supplies a provocative history that may serve as a model. He claims that Temagami Ojibwa Chief Aleck Paul in 1915 "could co-opt the language and imagery of private property and conservation to score points against outsiders who threatened." Krech suggests a Temagami Ojibwa strategy to appropriate non-Native concepts and perhaps even texts, in this case those written by the anthropologist Frank Speck and Indian Affairs employee Armand Tessier, as a means of adding authority to their claims.[38] Many Native spokespeople have made similar and effective assertions in support of their own superior relationship to the land since that time.

These are critical questions to amplify, particularly in relation to these crucial years of consultation on the self-defined nature of Indian commonality and its inscription by the NMAI project in documents meant to engender form. As Krech has said, from a critical perspective, "The Noble Indian/Ecological Indian distorts culture. It masks cultural diversity . . . Moreover, because it has entered the realm of common sense and as received wisdom it is perceived as a fundamental truth, it may also serve to deflect any desire to fathom or confront the evidence for relationships between Indians and the environment."[39] In other words, it denies specificity of case or generalizes the data, perhaps enough to prevent sufficient empirical evaluation. However, there are important purposes for these appropriations of "noble" status from Euro-American literary and social science sources that may override the necessity to better establish correct chronology or historical continuity for this idea about a special relationship with the land. The enshrinement in popular thought of the bond between Native people and nature may foster a positive public image in a contemporary Western world concerned with environmental issues. The larger population that maintains its own romantic sympathy with wilderness persists in associating this affinity with the first inhabitants of the North American continent. Perhaps more importantly, it may be related to that same nod to territoriality that the entire consultation process made to the Piscataway-Conoy. These ideas about nature may be wisely amplified and enlarged to express sovereignty on a very grand scale, by virtue of this special priority and access of Native people to the landscape of their country. It may even support larger ideas of nationhood that are useful in individual community efforts to regain control of important resources, perhaps even in land claims. These proprietary concepts may be strategic in Washington DC and may someday be applied on a global basis. The specific historical origins of these concepts may become a secondary question in relation to more pressing concerns with new general principles that serve the needs of contemporary communities who redefine themselves with aspirations for effective global interactions.

There were other "principles," selected and expressed as commonalities at the NMAI meetings. Many, but not all, who spoke up cited the importance of the circle in Native architecture and in related cultural phenomena and suggested that it be used as a defining structure in the buildings and explicated as a cosmogram. At an early Santa Fe consultation, one participant reminded the group, "The circle is the most universal and dominant. It is the shape of kivas and ceremonial spaces for Pueblos and Hopi. The circle is also important to whites—all their regulations have us going round and round!"[40]

More specific advice on the design of the (CRC) building was sought from a variety of Native American design professionals at a charette, also held in Santa Fe New Mexico in March 1993, run by the Native American Design Collaborative (NADC) and attended by representatives from the NMAI, the Smithsonian, and Polshek & Partners. In all, eighty to ninety Native American architects, engineers, and some cultural historians convened in a gymnasium, and they too discussed the importance of "circularity."[41] Consensus on this topic was elicited at this meeting by the display of a device called "The Cultural Analysis Matrix." This was a set of charts assembled from graphic representations of essentialized Native American imagery, gleaned from nature and from architectural history. Architect Louis Weller observed, "It was very important that a single particular tribal group or region not appear to dominate the matrix nor be selected to represent a consensus of Indian people of the western hemisphere." Instead, he claimed, "the matrix allowed the designers to compare attributes cross-culturally and discover a 'common ground,' recurring over time, geography, and culture that could be reflected in a cohesive design, drawing upon the universal commonalities of all Native cultures."[42] Cohesiveness, in this context and elsewhere in this project, seems to have been delineated on the basis of the majority experience. It is obvious that traditional style longhouses of the Northeast and the rectangular architecture of Northwest Coast groups are exceptions to the principle of circularity.

The Matrix included many circular and spiral forms derived from nature. There were pictures of chambered nautilus shells, pine cones, butterfly wings, and spiders' webs alongside such culturally generated forms as cone-shaped tipis, medicine circles, and circular dances. This pastiche is said to have been instrumental in producing the most outstanding visual feature of the CRC building, its dramatic radial steel roof structure that may be conceived of as a spiral, an expression of circular movement. At the center of this spiral or nautilus-like form is the large glass skylight that illuminates the round entrance lobby. A circular clearing in the woods, to be used for ceremonial purposes, was also envisioned during the charette process; this the CRC's "intertribal space," where it is possible for about thirty people to gather to sing, dance, or offer prayers.[43]

Some, but not all of the groups consulted also believe that it is important to orient the entrance of a Native American building toward the east, where the sun rises. Furthermore, many required that all of the cardinal directions be marked in some manner, but one was not specified. The first introduction of the audience to this institution at the entrance of the building was also emphasized as a defining process. It would be necessary to convey "a sense of welcome." Visitors should feel as though they are entering a home, or certainly a special place, but little consensus was reached on how this might be carried out. A way was sought to introduce the conventions and pleasures of Indian hospitality and to orient and encourage visitors and their children to enter in the proper spirit of this precinct. Finally, it was expressed across the board that the NMAI was now to become the caretaker of a vast collection of artifacts that must be handled according to diverse criteria originating from the traditional practices for the maintenance of such objects among these diverse groups. The 800,000 items that are to remain in the research and storage facility must be housed and handled properly; this means that, in some cases, they are to be treated as though they were living entities.

These stated requirements were interpreted by the invention of form and operating strategies as I summarize below. As the NMAI is well aware, "They illustrate a wide range of recommendations for the design, and even if they are not literally incorporated into the architecture, they should serve to inspire and encourage thoughtful and creative solutions."[44] Early on, Lloyd Kiva New (Cherokee) situated any imagined formal solutions in high spirits. Possibly they will be less than ideal, but he reminded his colleagues that they would all be based upon the ironclad mandate for proper process at the NMAI: "We will probably come out with the daddy of stereotypy regarding who American Indians are and what they stand for, but at least it can be a more or less updated version—espoused by Indians themselves."[45]

The Mall Museum

The museum on the Mall in Washington, constructed on the basis of the deployment of texts like those described earlier, is situated on a wedge-shaped lot of 4.3 acres. Its strategic location has been lost on no one. It is built right next to the ever popular Air and Space Museum and across the way from the prestigious National Gallery. The main entrance, on the east side as recommended for symbolic reasons, is also near the National Botanical Garden. Most important of all, the museum's proximity to the U.S. Capitol Building in the very last open space on the Mall places it in visual dialogue with the United States, "nation to nations," if you will. When fully mature, the elaborately planned landscape design will probably make for some opposition in this dialogue, more so than the structure of the building itself, although it is a bit more flowing and organic than the usual deference to classicism displayed by most other buildings on the Mall.[46] The stalks of corn, exuberant grasses and a return of some part of the land around the building to wetland promises to be a striking alternative to the formal and sober landscape that has, until now, been the established norm for the expanse that functions as the flat and grassy front lawn of the Capitol. In keeping with the stated desire to honor the integrity of place, particularly from what is known of its aboriginal form, Johnpaul Jones reminded his colleagues at a 1995 meeting in Phoenix, "The site has memory. In the past a stream ran across the site through forests and wetlands." At this meeting, the central role of ethnobotanist Donna House (Navajo/Oneida) emerged as well. She created a slide presentation, something of a pastiche of landscapes that varied from desert to rainforest, emphasizing the importance of water, rocks and even rock art in Indian belief. Her vision was expansive. Wetlands, plants, insects, and animals were included in the realm of nature that she asked participants to imagine, encouraging them to remember that all living things are interrelated. Again, nets were cast as broadly as possible for the NMAI, here including almost every conceivable ecosystem, as well as a complete set of specific regional qualities that should be cited. For the site design, House delineated hardwood forests to the north, wetlands on the east side, and meadows and grasslands on the south side. References to riverine environments may appear in the future as well. She suggested that someday the roof of the Mall Museum may even be thought of as the top of a mountain and may be another place for additional "micro-habitats." [47]

The "orientation experience," also suggested by consultation, is believed to be connected to this reconstructed landscape and is meant to serve multiple purposes. It is supposed to help distracted tourists and rowdy children to cool down and get their bearings and was supposed to be clearly keyed to observation of the habitats and interaction with the signs of nature displayed there. A sense of welcome is meant to be substantively conveyed at this entrance point, in a manner that was idealized as equal parts ambience conveyed by flowing water and the instructive plantings, live entertainment or demonstrations to be staged on an adjacent outdoor performance circle, perhaps some contact with real people (ambassadorial representatives) and other experiences that have yet to be fully realized. Then, on to the experience of the building itself where visitors are to be "sheltered" by the cantilevered upper floors that are also meant to reflect the welcoming nature of the museum itself. [48]

Douglas Cardinal, the original lead architect for this building, is best known for his design of the Canadian Museum of Civilization in Hull, Quebec and for an early work, a building for St. Mary's Church in Red Deer, Alberta, the town where he grew up. Both of these and all of Cardinal's buildings are based upon the flowing lines and sculptural curves that have become his signature. Cardinal traces his interest in these organic qualities to his regard for the landscape. [49] Accordingly, the limestone building, the undulating structure that Cardinal designed for the NMAI site, is said to recall the effects of geological processes, expressed in a series of stacked, curvilinear bands.

I would like to suggest that this architectural iconography, although it may indeed appear cliff-like, may also present some references to the function of this institution in its role as a formidable participant on a worldwide stage, perhaps unconsciously on the part of the architect. As suggested at the beginning of this essay, these curved registers may be compared with those of other museum buildings of international stature, for instance older projects like Frank Lloyd Wright's Guggenheim Museum in Manhattan, made of circular bands which has become an icon for the creative housing of contemporary art. Interestingly, Cardinal's admiration of Wright has been cited in published accounts of his biography and career.[50] Note as well that the stacked band, even though rectilinear, is a device known from the structure of the Whitney Museum, another established cultural icon, also in New York. These institutions are outstanding among many, but they are not new. A bit more recently, a great deal of excitement was generated by the construction of the Guggenheim Museum in Bilbao, Spain, designed by the architect Frank Gehry. In Bilbao, however, the curvilinear bands that I am proposing as signs of the new and the global in international museum architecture are actually set free. They are made of metal and wriggle forth, unbound by set registers. Animated metal bands have also been proposed by Gehry for several museum and performing arts facilities, including an even newer Guggenheim building that was at one point proposed for New York City.

Other museums, even those that are physically distant from urban centers, may also be lobbying for worldwide status through the banded façades they present to visitors. Among several examples that might be mentioned, the University of Alaska Museum of the North in Fairbanks has constructed a new art gallery wing designed by architect Joan Soranno and the GDM/HGA design team that seems a bit like an ice house or igloo traveling at warp speed. It too sports curvilinear bands, announcing its intention of addressing a global audience. Perhaps in Washington DC, Cardinal's serpentine elements clamor as well for the world stage.

The domed vault of the NMAI building grew from the many references to circular form that were so powerfully voiced as essentially "Indian" in the course of consultation, although at least one consultant did speak out, pointing out that this principle is not quite ubiquitous: "Don't generalize from one tribe's architecture. For Northwest Coast people, the rectangle is the main shape of rooms and buildings."[51] In the end, opportunities to express conceptual unity in terms of circular form at the NMAI were too useful and aesthetically provocative to ignore as a principle and too difficult to avoid when specified by so many at the Santa Fe charette and elsewhere for The Way of the People text. The outdoor dance circle has been mentioned and the accompanying water features parallel curvilinear paths. Upon entering the building, visitors are introduced to a large multifunctional space, the main circular area of the building housed under the dome that the NMAI has named the "Potomac." This is a word said to come from the language of the Piscataway-Conoy group, the geographic hosts of the NMAI, and it means something very like "a place where rivers and people come together and where the goods are brought in."[52] It was conceived as the main gathering space of the museum, certainly round, and the first and last space that a visitor would encounter. This is supposed to function as a multipurpose, multisensory environment for the concourse of visitors, performers, shoppers and diners who were originally meant to experience these functions in an integrated manner. Another, more formal theater space coexists with what planners had hoped would become a flowing "flat floor performance area" in this grand hall where opportunities to demonstrate aspects of Native life including cooking, dance, and craft production would be simultaneous. Idealized as an integrated "Indian village," these activities would be linked in a kind of Gesamtkunstwerk.[53] Some manner of representing the individuality of tribes was hoped for in the Potomac space as well, but as a very minor subtext. Suggestions included the addition of representative graphic elements, such as flags, designs carved into the floor, tribal seals, or the display of earth or perhaps other building materials brought from the lands occupied by each group. There was discussion of signs to be imprinted upon a granite seat wall that would run around the perimeter of the building. Whatever form these signs take as the museum develops, it is important to note that they will be applied, not made integral to the architecture of the Mall museum.[54]

Electing for Abstraction

Signs of individuality were not to be central in the public address at the NMAI and this was foretold most clearly in a text composed at the 1995 "vision session," conceived of and hosted by Douglas Cardinal. Discussion at this gathering was directed to the composition of a "vision statement" that introduces its authors as the "people from the four directions, across the mountains, the plains, and the oceans." The poetic language of the statement, prepared in draft by Cardinal and his colleague Satish Rao, is telling. "After four days, we speak as one nation: The importance of ancestors, the elements of nature, knowledge of duality and the need for balance and harmony" were cited.[55] It seemed to summarize the session well enough because participant Pauline Hillaire pronounced the document to be "perfect," and it was generally accepted by most of the other participants. Native philosophers approved statements such as, "When we become one with all the forces of creation, we are given the marvelous gift of creativity because we are one with creation and the Creator."[56] Their mission was expressed as spiritually informed, but the extreme difficulty of producing a unified statement from such diverse traditional sources is undeniable: "We will not attempt to duplicate the natural forms of the Creator, nor each individual expression that grew out of the lands that each of our nations inhabit. Here it will be our common voice that shapes this home we will create on the Mall: . . . We understand the power of symbols, which are an expression of our people. We know that we are masters of abstracting our interpretation of our Creator's handiwork."[57]

This statement is extraordinary as an explicit dispensation for generalization, here called "common voice" and "abstraction," as the prerogative and even the special ability of Native people. The making of symbols is noted as part of the traditional repertoire that links the creativity of the vision-making process with ancient practice. However, these authors were careful to say that there is no necessity to repeat individual architectural traditions, to reproduce specific historical form.

In addition to the written statement, Cardinal and his colleagues produced a visual aid to these processes of abstraction that cites the consultations and extracts some of the essential points from the "consensual approach," or the dynamics of process itself. Native approaches to discussion were distilled as symbols and expressed in form. The result was a chart created by Cardinal and his staff titled "Bringing Visions into Reality," with some images of people engaged in discussion in circular format. For instance, one group convenes in a tipi, and there is a photographic detail of what looks like the interior of a rounded wigwam. Other references to form derived from the dynamics of the discussion process are included in this visual tool. For instance, above the image of a ceremonial pipe, a caption reads, "Keep your word straight as the stem," associating rectitude with linear form.

In the absence of greater specificity, some may argue that non-Natives as well, long-informed by popular culture phenomena about the supposed inherent qualities of Native America—its ties to nature, its tipis and circular dances at powwows, and some of its works of art and stories—might well have arrived at similar design solutions for the public representation of Indigenous nationhood. It is significant that this was not the case, that non-Natives were not the most visible spokespeople for these themes. Older presentations of aboriginal people as pedagogical objects now demand correctives in the form of explicit assertions of authorship and resulting narratives that suggest coevality, in this case the contemporary vital presence of Native Americans in worldwide dialogues.[58] However, in a setting designed to express this high degree of commonality, often in abstract form, knowledge of the laborious development of contemporary narrative has so far been minimized, to the detriment of the widespread understanding of this key shift in agency that constitutes the true subject of the NMAI project.

A version of the Plexiglas model that Cardinal had "sketched as a spirit" is now corporeal and available for interpretation by the public. In the freezing cold weather of the museum's first winter (2005), substantial crowds gathered, waiting their turn to enter. It was then received as a great public attraction and simultaneously, it was the subject of quite serious criticism among members of the press and, anecdotally, among scholars. In many ways, their objections were related to the challenges discussed earlier: the attempt to delineate broad principles derived from the concerns of Native constituents and consultants, those meant to be explicated in a fairly general manner, through the use of abstraction.[59]

Although several writers admired the architectural expression of the delineated principles or "commonalities" discussed during the planning process, they were disappointed by the manner in which these same general concepts informed the exhibitions. For example, Paul Richards of the *Washington Post* commended the building, but had his high hopes dashed when he stepped inside. "Its exhibits are disheartening, their installations misproportioned, here too sparse and there too cramped . . . things both new and ancient, beautiful and not, all stirred decoratively together in no important order that the viewer can discern."[60] Edward Rothstein of the New York Times thought the design of the building itself "hints at what might have been, a collection of surpassing and aesthetic cultural value," although he did cite some imperfections that have diminished the ultimate power of the architecture since Cardinal's departure. For example, the northern Mall-facing façade has been significantly simplified. Much more importantly, the transfer of agency to the authority of Native curators resulted in the insistence upon a somewhat unified and therefore simplified Native perspective and this seemed gravely insufficient to Rothstein. "It is not a matter of whose voice is heard," he complained. "It is a matter of detail, qualification, nuance and context. It is a matter of scholarship."[61]

Most objections were similar, centering on the relative lack of specificity in excessively concept-driven exhibition strategies. Critics had expected to encounter more Western style scholarship, the authoritative voice of academically trained curators, and more of the particulars of history. They certainly expected to see more of the treasured works of art from the renowned collection of George Heye. Instead, a very new and different type of public platform was constructed for this project by the authors of *The Way of the People* planning documents. Planners had framed their instructions on the basis of the historic shift to Native authority made by this institution. Designers and curators took their cues from the "commonalities" that were considered useful on the basis of this mandate.

Many, although not all, of the commonalities or principle-based abstractions that were developed to inform the design and thematic orientation of the NMAI mall museum did indeed materialize in Washington. Architecturally, one may trace the textured limestone exterior, working waterfalls, and landscaped presentations of "grandfather rocks" and Indigenous plants to the explicit desire to quote nature. Interior and exterior spaces are not blurred, although the entrance lobby includes a number of related devices including a special prism to allow light to enter, but the galleries are quite insulated from the outside world. Circularity is first apparent in the outdoor Welcome Plaza that is inscribed with symbols for the astronomical conditions that existed in 1989 on the day the institution was established by law. As mentioned, the Potomac area, also circular in form, is the first interior space that visitors encounter; it does function as the museum's center, although the flurry of dance, demonstration, and activity that was promised for this space did not materialize during the first season. The Potomac is literally the base of the museum's atrium-like core. It is encircled on ground level by a copper screen with basketry-like features and this circularity is echoed by the swirling, balconied floors above it and the huge stepped dome with an oculus at its apex. In fact, the entire experience of the interior of the museum is characterized by the curvilinear traffic pattern that walls and halls dictate.

As conceptualized early on, the main entrance of the museum faces east. Stones mark all four cardinal directions as a part of the landscaping scheme, but it is not yet possible to identify the correspondence of immature plantings with the ecosystems that were planned in association with directional orientation. The Potomac circle itself is divided into four quadrants by fine lines in reference to the cosmological model that was cited so frequently. However, information about directional symbolism is not completely apparent for observation by the average visitor as a part of the architectural experience, although as described below, ideas about the cardinal directions were mentioned repeatedly in the inaugural exhibitions.[62] In reference to the idea of territorial priority, informational pamphlets suggested a relationship between the landscaping around the museum and the natural environment of the Chesapeake Bay region. No direct reference to the host group, the Piscataway-Conoy, who were singled out for special attention during the planning process, was evident.

As suggested ealier, the long history of similar precepts and sensibilities for non-Native architecture—from the interior of the Roman Pantheon to the circular balconied ramps of the Guggenheim Museum in New York; from Frank Lloyd Wright's cantilevered Fallingwater to Noguchi's preoccupation with the arrangement of stones in space—presaged the acceptance and admiration of non-Natives for the NMAI building. This sympathy and appreciation of form is not, however, a result of identical sources for the conceptualization of ideal architecture, but to some extent is coincidental. The Pantheon, for example, was an architectural expression, at least in part, of the worship of Olympian gods and not of the cosmological concerns of Aboriginal Americans. Wright's "organic architecture" was in some ways a response to the surfeit of ornament in the designs of his predecessors, quite different from the concern at the NMAI to summarize the philosophies of traditional Native cultures. In other words, contemporary Euro-Americans are very likely to arrive at the museum equipped with an aesthetic sensibility in common with that of the NMAI architectural team, but not in reference to an identical history of ideas or design strategies. There is little perception of the key issues of authorship available from the observation of the architecture itself.

The first exhibitions and some of the interior spaces were another story. The greater leap taken by NMAI curators, their clear concern with concept over the display of specific works of art, is not congruent with the format of most non-Native museums, and it was not received with the enthusiasm that the architecture elicited.[63] To a large extent, curators relied on the potential influence of photography, film, and other new media (as promised) instead of the tried and true fascination of outsiders with objects made by Native American hands, replete with historical information in text form. The modes of display that were finally worked out for the interior of the museum were not completely spelled out during the phases of the planning process. However, there were many suggestions put forward and it is important to detect their influence.

The NMAI experience is introduced by a multimedia presentation called *Who We Are* shown every fifteen minutes in the Lelawi Theater, also a circular space. If visitors head straight for the theater, the show is effective as a part of the orientation that was suggested by *The Way of the People* consultants, an idea that did not play out clearly in architectural form at the entrance of the museum. However, in *Who We Are* the great diversity of Native experience in different regions and according to the cultural specifics of particular Native groups is present and produced as an "eye dazzler." Filmed images of eagles fly above. Later, the domed ceiling becomes the surface of water where a kayak floats above visitors' heads, suggesting that they are now under water. Scenes from diverse Native lives are projected on textiles at eye level, and a central, altar-like stone transforms from ice to fire. After this, however, visitors emerge hungry for art and greater explanation. However, as stipulated in *The Way of the People*, the inaugural exhibitions were definitely not object oriented although there were almost eight thousand objects on view. The ideas put forward in the "permanent installations" are much more prominently presented than the pottery, beaded garments, and driftwood masks themselves. Recall the instructions of early consultants to use a holistic approach and a variety of media to avoid excessive focus on the art objects. Where a multiplicity of objects do appear, in the undulating walls of guns, goldwork, figures, and arrowheads, there is little emphasis on the significance of any individual piece.

After the advanced media of the *Who We Are* film, visitors encounter the Our Universes section; it is at this juncture that the new exhibition strategies take them by surprise. Here they must grasp and greatly appreciate the concepts outlined during the planning process for the transfer of authority to Native hands or they will certainly be lost. It is at this point that visitors must understand the significance of the photographs and biographies of the "community curators" in each section to see the importance of the eight idiosyncratic presentations of worldview that are positioned around the perimeter of the space. Mannequins dressed in traditional clothing, refugees from antique dioramas, are placed next to television monitors where living elders, speaking all the way from Indian Country, earnestly narrate their own stories of culture change. In the Lakota section, for instance, viewers are told that "all is related," and this is illustrated by the painted Lone Dog Winter Count (ca. 1870) in proximity to contemporary items of clothing and a handmade quilt. Hupa community curators also selected an unusual combination of films, diorama figures, objects, and texts to explain the ceremonial dances that "keep life in balance." If viewers understand the sea change in agency that operates here they may accept these unpredictable combinations of objects and media. They may tolerate the cramped quarters assigned to each community group. Similarly, if they are completely fascinated by Native people who speak for themselves at last, they will bear with the erratic traffic patterns. However, one visitor suggested the experience of most by asking, "How do you know where you've been and where you are going?"

There are micro-identities on view in these booth-like spaces, illustrated by the idiosyncratic choices made by the community curators. Ironically, at the same time, similar general themes about seasonal cycles and directional symbolism are reiterated in each of the presentations. It is unlikely that outsiders register enough nuance or difference among them. There is a genuine effort here to empower these small groups of individuals who wish to tell their own stories, but this is largely subverted by the repeated, unifying themes. And, at the center of the "Our Universes" exhibit, extremely diverse objects—a mask from Bella Bella, a Cree beaded vest, a Winnebago bandolier, a Mohawk pincushion, and a Zuni pot, for example—are brought together simply because they all include star imagery.

The next section, called Our Peoples is addressed to the historical identities of eight more communities. Here, and in the next section, called Our Lives, there are slightly larger, circular spaces for community presentations, although there is still some disorientation. One man called to his companion, "There's a lot of curlicues here so let's stick together." Each group is again introduced with the prominent display of photographs and printed biographies of community curators. Each of them has gathered a pastiche of oral histories, written treaties, and letters. Their ideas about their own histories are elaborated with the addition of still images, texts, and videos.

In the common area that runs through the center of the Our Peoples space, dramatic statements are made about the nature of history itself and the calamitous effects of contact in the Americas. An unnamed actor strides about and challenges received truths on video monitors that are interspersed with reproductions of paintings by George Catlin, portraits that have preserved the identities of specific Native people since the 1830s. Names of Native groups, some that have survived, others that have not, are projected on one wall. Provocative statements are printed on the curving glass walls that enclose a multiplicity of objects that serve here as props, as elements of theater, not as individual works of art or items of material culture. "The Americas 1491" is inscribed in proximity to many stone and ceramic figures in reference to the diversity of experiences and art traditions of the first inhabitants. Works of art made of gold are associated with corn, the power of the sun, and are identified as "the Prize" pursued by Spanish invaders. These pieces, as well as weapons, crucifix-

es, and Bibles, have not been delineated with specific historical information. At the center of the exhibition hall an enigmatic multiscreen video
installation reiterates the same themes. These in turn surround an unex-
plained exhibition case housing a textile representation of the four colors
and four directions. This is not the only piece in the museum that blurs the
line between installation art and museum display. This is potentially an
interesting approach that is relatively honest about the subjective nature
of museum representation, although there is much work to be done before
such innovations are fully comprehensible to the public. The participation
of artist-curators Truman Lowe (Ho-Chunk), Jolene Rickard (Tuscarora),
Gerald McMaster (Plains Cree), and the author and critic Paul Chaat Smith
(Comanche) are no doubt the source of these initial explorations.

Similar in format, the third permanent installation on the floor below
called Our Lives, is meant to suggest the complexity of contemporary
Native identities. The curving wall of photographed faces is effective in
complicating ideas about Native American appearance. The issues of
museum representation, participation in modernity, and the incongru-
ities of blood quantum as a measure of identity are brought out in this
section through the reproduction of works of art such as James Luna's
(Luiseño) *Artifact Piece* and Hulleah Tsinahjinnie's (Seminole/Muskogee/
Diné) critique of the Arts and Crafts Act of 1990. Again, recently made
works of art supplement more straightforward displays to educate NMAI
visitors. However, in this section, the most compelling information about
the disputed nature of contemporary Indian identity is presented within the community-made displays. Many viewers may know something
about Mohawk ironworkers and comprehend the necessity of snowmobiles as a part of twenty-first century life in Igloolik, but the combination
of Chicago Urban Indian organizations that affiliated to describe some of
the complexities of their experiences may come as more of a surprise.

Although the NMAI went to great lengths to argue for the wide range
of difference among contemporary Native American individuals, in
fact their planning and curatorial processes necessitated the selection

of a limited number of representative voices and defining themes. One may point to the initial selections and evaluate them as a small sampling. This was, of course, unavoidable and other groups will have their chance. However, it is important to recognize that the directives established at the original regional meetings of the 1990s had, by necessity, to be received and applied by administrators in an uneven manner. Not surprisingly, there are some regional consultants who now wonder how their own early contributions were finally made use of. The anthropologist Gloria Cranmer Webster (Kwak'wakawakw), for example, attended meetings in Vancouver in May 1993 together with other representatives from Alaska, British Columbia, and Washington State, all of whom have been involved with museums and cultural centers in their communities. Webster reports, "There was good discussion, as I remember, but we never heard from NMAI again."[64]

Another important point about the differential access of Native representatives to the curatorial process at the NMAI has been raised by guest co-curator Jolene Rickard. She was brought into this process in 2002 to work on the Our Peoples and Our Lives sections. Like Webster and others, Rickard has been engaged in discussions about the museological representation of Native people her entire professional life. She has noted that the NMAI made the participation of the first groups of community curators central to their exhibition design processes with some interesting results, although with a certain amount of simplification or "unified voice." The complexity of the Our Lives section may be considered an exception. However, Rickard wonders how thoroughly the voices and nuanced approaches of other potential contributors may ever be heard. Will it be possible for significant contributions to be made by more highly trained visual historians or, for that matter, by those few individuals who are uniquely qualified to explain the particulars of traditional Indigenous philosophies?[65] Of course, some information is not intended for the consumption of outsiders. Even so, there may be a great deal more to come in future representations.

Twenty-four groups were foregrounded for the initial presentations of the NMAI and a great many more were involved in conceptualization. What was most compelling about their efforts was this process itself, rather than the initial products that accompanied their concourse in the U.S. capital. The years of dialogue are just hinted at in the architecture, the exhibitions, and the content of some accompanying literature. For instance, a Smithsonian publication called *Spirit of a Native Place* (2004) is sold in the gift shops, it outlines some of the design and planning processes. The complex acts of Native self-definition that took place during the consultation meetings resulted in initial decisions about a proper public address. Active participants hammered out guidelines for what is present in the museum; just as important, these authorities decided what to hold back. The full process of planning would have been difficult to convey; however, this is actually what marks the inauguration of the NMAI as historic. Native American arbitration of design and exhibition planning as a process is central to the significance of the NMAI.

In those instances that indicate common aesthetics or parallel conceptual imperatives familiar to non-Native visitors—for instance, in the quotation of nature for architectural form, the organizational and artistic effects of circular space, the importance of specific environments for the identification of regional groups—outsiders experience comprehension and satisfaction. When newly devised strategies for the empowerment of tiny groups of individuals who hold sway in communities thousands of miles away result in unaccustomed formats, a sense of disorientation, and even a certain lack of sophistication about the possibilities of contemporary museum display, non-Natives become critical. They are also confused and disappointed when they are not granted access to as many works of art as they wish to see.

Visitors may not completely understand just how thoroughly the directives that guided the production of this museum have departed from those of the institutions that they are more familiar with. They have some inkling of the principles and processes that have operated and continue to be carried out at the NMAI, but they have a great deal to gain by knowing even more about them. Most visitors, critics, and art professionals will be pleased to see future exhibitions that reflect the depth of the NMAI's collection or the artistic merit of works on loan from other institutions. Many would also be enthusiastic about less familiar exhibition strategies and artistic and didactic devices if they were more completely aware of the history and significance of *The Way of the People* as well as future developments that affect strategies for the intervention of Native people in worldwide dialogues. Some would undoubtedly remain critical of the idea of process itself as sufficient for the definition of the museum.

However the museum proceeds, the aboriginal facility with abstraction and generalization identified and lauded by the NMAI authors in text, and ultimately in form, is sure to become standardized to some extent in any number of new undertakings. It may function in tandem with the development of greater dialogic processes with other institutions and the ascendancy of activists who wish to participate with full-fledged national status. As Walter Dasheno of Santa Clara Pueblo said at one of the early NMAI meetings, "We need to build on the premise of what role we play in the total of human life, worldwide as Indian people—how we want to present ourselves."[66] Following this choice, it has been their tactic to choose concourse and the useful abstractions that are meant to facilitate it. Participants selected a public platform that emphasizes an appearance of unity and a larger voice in the hope of greater consequence. In Washington DC, certainly understood as a place of global dialogue, representatives for the National Museum of the American Indian would do well to become more explicit about the processes of engaged, ardent participation that resulted in the production of these forms.

Notes

1. The legislation that established the National Museum of the American Indian and mandated the construction on the mall in Washington DC and of the Cultural Resource Center in Suitland, Maryland, as well as the establishment of the Heye Center in New York City, is Public Law 101–185.

It was sponsored by Representative Ben Nighthorse Campbell of Colorado and Sen. Daniel Inouye of Hawaii and signed by Pres. George Bush on November 28, 1989. This law established the NMAI as a bureau within the Smithsonian Institution, provided for the transfer of the George Heye collection from New York and for funding outreach programs to Native communities and to establish repatriation requirements. This legislation also required the Smithsonian to implement repatriation of Native American and Hawaiian human remains and associated funerary objects.

2. "Meeting Minutes, Santa Fe Consultation," NMAI/SI, July 15–16, 1991, 1.
3. From the ephemeral "will to be united" postulated by Ernest Renan in his seminal discourse in the last decade of the nineteenth century in Homi K. Bhabha, ed., Nation and Narration (London: Roultedge, 1990), 8–22, to Benedict Anderson's Imagined Communities (London: Verso, 1983), insights on the production and reproduction of "imagined communities," as well the authors referred to here, constructed public identities have been identified as a great deal more than ephemeral, as inextricably linked to issues of sovereignty.
4. At the time of European contact, Algonquian-speaking tribes were residents of the area that became known as Maryland. Christian Feest writes that "All tribes in Southern Maryland with the possible exception of the Pautuxets, were part of the Conoy group, so called by their Iroquoian name to differentiate between the larger group and its leading tribe, the Piscataway." Christian Feest, "Nanticoke and Neighboring Tribes," in Handbook of North American Indians, Northeast, Vol. 15 (Washington DC: Smithsonian Institution), 240. There is an unfortunate lack of information recorded about the history and cultures of the Indians of seventeenth century Maryland although scholars suggest that agriculture may have been a greater source of subsistence for the Piscataway than for some of their neighbors. The late seventeenth century saw the beginning of several migrations for the Conoy groups that continued throughout the eighteenth century. Although they remained neutral during the French and Indian War, the Nanticokes and Conoys were aligned with the British during the American Revolution and there was a period of sojourn in Niagara. A series of migrations affected the cohesiveness of these groups. Although many Conoy left Maryland, some remained and were officially classified for a time as "free Negroes." It was not until the 1880s, when some identified themselves as "Wesorts" that they were recognized again as Indians on official documents. In 1974, a group incorporated as Piscataways under state law (Feest 240–52).
5. I will refer later on in this text to the possibility of individualized iconography that may someday be applied in these buildings.

6. Enrique Dussel, "Beyond Eurocentrism: The World-System and the Limits of Modernity," in *The Cultures of Globalization*, ed. Frederic Jameson and Masao Miyoshi (Durham: Duke University Press, 1998), 3–31.

7. *The Way of the People: National Museum of the American Indian*, Smithsonian Institution Office of Design and Construction, Master Facilities Programming Phase 1. Revised Draft Report, (Philadelphia: Venturi, Scott Brown and Associates, Inc., November 22, 1991), 16.

8. Anne Trowbridge, telephone interview, March 24, 1998.

9. Douglas Cole, *Captured Heritage: The Scramble for Northwest Coast Artifacts* (Seattle: University of Washington Press, 1985), 216–17.

10. In the late 1980s Sen. Daniel Inouye of Hawaii was Chairman of the Senate Committee on Indian Affairs. The first priority of this group was a national museum policy that would acknowledge Native American religious and burial rights, requiring the return of human remains and cultural property from federally-assisted museums and collections in the United States. Inouye, together with Representative Ben Nighthorse Campbell of Colorado, Morris K. Udall of Arizona and others were dedicated to achieving some progress on these repatriation issues. However, the Museum of the American Indian's problems required immediate attention. If the attention of the museum world, the public, and legislators could not be called to the plight of the museum, it was possible that the collection would gradually be auctioned off and dispersed. There was some talk about its transfer to the American Museum of Natural History in New York, but nothing came of this. In a stunning gesture, Ross Perot offered to build his own museum and move the whole collection to Dallas, Texas. This suggestion generated the sought-after attention and soon interested parties expressed proprietary interest. Some New York politicians made statements about maintaining the collection on behalf of the city and state, but the Smithsonian Institution made a better case for the status of the collection as a matter of national importance.

Projected costs for the new 254,000 gross square feet museum building were estimated early on at about $110 million. As a part of the establishing legislation, Congress directed the Smithsonian Institution to raise one third of this amount from non-federal sources. Initial fundraising goals for construction as well as ongoing educational and outreach programs were already met in September of 1996. See Suzan Shown Harjo "NMAI: A Promise America is Keeping," *Native Peoples Magazines* 9, no. 3 (Spring 1996): 28–34. The present repatriation policy for the National Museum of the American Indian is the return upon request of human remains, funerary objects, communally owned Native property, ceremonial and religious objects transferred to or acquired by the museum illegally to Indian tribes or individuals with tribal or cultural affiliation. "Background Fact Sheet: National Museum of the American Indian," *Smithsonian Institution News*, January 1997.

11. It is useful to include the NMAI Mission Statement here in order to highlight this mandate to communicate with this enormous constituency of Indigenous peoples. "The National Museum of the American Indian shall recognize and affirm to Native communities and the non-Native public the historical and contemporary culture and cultural achievements of the Natives of the entire Western Hemisphere by advancing—in consultation, collaboration and cooperation with Natives—knowledge and understanding of Native cultures, including art, history and language, and by recognizing the museum's special responsibility through innovative public programming, research and collections, to protect, support and enhance the development, maintenance, and perpetuation of Native culture and community." "Background Fact Sheet: National Museum of the American Indian," *Smithsonian Institution News*, May 1996, 1.

In addition, the establishing legislation included a "special rule" that "At least 12 of the 23 members [of the Board of Trustees] appointed under paragraph (1)(C) shall be Indians. (Public Law 101-185—November 28, 1989. 103 Stat.1339). It provided as well for "Indian Museum Management Fellowships," for "stipend support for Indians for training in museum development and management." (103 Stat.1343) Put succinctly, Congress mandated that Indians comprise a majority of the outside members of the governing Board of Trustees and that it "make available curatorial and other learning opportunities for Indians." W. Richard West Jr., *Museum Anthropology* 17, no. 1 (February 1993): 6.

12. This volume was directed to various readers—both Native and non-Native architects, designers, planners, and government officials— and is something of a synopsis, or abridgement of volumes 2 and 3 that are dedicated, respectively, to the CRC and Mall Museum buildings and were meant for a more technical readership. The second and third volumes were used for calculating storage space, systems, and for surveys by civil engineers about the site.

13. The NMAI's director, W. Richard West Jr. (Southern Cheyenne) and his staff determined the invitees to the consultation meetings and prepared and distributed background material. Often, slide presentations about the

nature of the new institution were made and explanatory boards or flip charts were used as well to set out the proposed museum's basic mission. Meetings were moderated with the assistance of co-facilitators selected from the local communities who might address their own constituencies more effectively. In some cases, one or more of three "transcending co-facilitators," Native people who had been selected to shepherd along the consultation process, were present as well. These were George Horse Capture (A'ani Gros Ventre), Rina Swentzell (Santa Clara Pueblo), and Rick Hill (Tuscarora). They also took part in the planning and evaluation of meetings.

From January of 1992 through September of 1995, meetings to establish regional tribal concerns as well as to gather specific input on specialized issues (for instance, the traditional care and handling of Native American objects, repatriation, education, and design) were held in Riverside, California; Sacramento, California, New York City; Washington DC; Billings, Montana; Atlanta, Georgia; Vancouver BC; Rapid City, South Dakota; Tucson Arizona, Santa Fe, New Mexico; St. Paul, Minnesota; Phoenix, Arizona; and Olympia, Washington.

Staff and Consultation meetings that informed volumes 2 and 3 of *The Way of the People* took place almost two years later because of additional research and interviews with various technical and Smithsonian staff which were necessary in order to develop the non-cultural program requirements. The results were standards and requirements for building systems such as structure, environmental control, fire protection, security, collections housing, libraries, site constraints, etc. Taking these requirements and refining them into a program that fit the budget was a process that required several iterations and considerable time. Justin Estoque, electronic mail message, February 4, 1998.

In 1995, follow-up meetings or design iterations were held for the review of plans to date in Washington DC; Santa Fe, New Mexico; Phoenix, Arizona; and St. Paul, Minnesota. Douglas Cardinal (Metis/Blackfoot), the architect who originally designed the Mall Museum building, organized his own consultation sessions that he called a "Vision Session" and an "Imaging Session" in February 1995. These were held in Washington DC and are described in greater detail further on in this essay. James Volkert projected that the consultations and other sessions that would inform the exhibitions planned for the NMAI would continue through at least 2000. Telephone communication, April 10, 2000.

14. Venturi, Scott Brown, and Associates, *The Way of the People* 1, 57.

15. See also Judith Ostrowitz, *Privileging the Past: Reconstructing History in North-west Coast Art* (Seattle: University of Washington Press, 1999), 139–48, for related discussion about influential representatives from Native communities in museum and other projects.

16. NMAI/SI, "Meeting Minutes," *Researchers' Consultations*, May 30, 1991, 7.

17. At the end of January 1998 a decision was made to terminate the Smithsonian/NMAI's contract with Douglas Cardinal and GBQC. The situation was said to be caused by the relationship between the two firms, to procedural delays and contractual disagreements. First, Stewart Polshek & Partners and Tobey and Davis were hired to conduct a peer review of the project. The Smithsonian then hired these two firms, as well as four other design firms with Native American principals, to complete the project. The Smithsonian's own architect also worked on the plans.

   Then, in April of 1999, the Commission of Fine Arts rejected the Smithsonian's completion of the design because it did not follow the design concept developed by Mr. Cardinal. The commission's major objection was related to a column that had been placed in the design to support an overhang that had been a free-standing cantilevered structure in Cardinal's original version. In June, the Smithsonian again revised the plans which were then approved. Duane Blue Spruce, telephone interviews, February 4 and April 7 1998; "Federal Panel Approves Indian Museum on Mall," *The New York Times*, June 18, 1999; "Museum of the Indian Drops Its Designer," *The New York Times*, April 4, 1998, B11, B13.

18. "National Museum of the American Indian: Mall Museum Core Design Team and Native Advisors Biographies," *Smithsonian Institution News*, May 1996, 1.

19. Douglas Cardinal, personal interview, January 22, 1998.

20. Early exhibition projects that included some Native advisors in their processes of development were *Chiefly Feasts: The Enduring Kwakiutl Potlatch* at the American Museum of Natural History (1991) and *A Time of Gathering: Native Heritage in Washington State* at the Thomas Burke Museum (1989). Some Native people were also asked to consult for the exhibition called *Objects of Myth and Memory: Native American Art* at the Brooklyn Museum (1991).

21. Feest, *Nanticoke and Neighboring Tribes*, 244.

22. The AICAE project was funded and encouraged by the Design Arts Program of the National Endowment for the Arts, the Office of Indian Housing of the U.S. Department of Housing and Urban Development, and the Solar Energy Research Institute of the U.S. Department of Energy.

23. Meeting minutes, Alaska Regional Consultation, NMAI/SI, November 4–5, 1991, 11.

24. American Indian Council of Architects and Engineers, *Our Home: A Design Guide for Indian Housing* (Washington DC: National Endowment for the Arts, Design Arts Program, 1994).

25. Louis L. Weller, "Contemporary Native American Architecture," *European Review of Native American Studies* 10.1 (1996): 1–11.

26. Weller, "Contemporary Native American Architecture."

27. Weller, "Contemporary Native American Architecture," 5.

28. Susan Rodriguez, personal interview, June 23, 1998.

29. Jon Krakauer, "AD Travels: The Museum at Warm Springs, A Tribute to the Native American Spirit in Oregon," *Architectural Digest* (October 1993): 94–100.

30. Weller, "Contemporary Native American Architecture," 5.

31. Carol Herselle Krinsky, *Contemporary Native American Architecture: Cultural Regeneration and Creativity* (New York: Oxford University Press, 1996), 87.

32. Duane Blue Spruce, telephone interview, January 4, 1998.

33. Janet L. Rumble, "Keeping the Faith," *Metropolis* (September 1997): 111.

34. Weller, "Contemporary Native American Architecture."

35. Krinsky, *Contemporary Native American Architecture*, 81–117.

36. *Board of Trustees Handbook* 1, "Introduction and Executive Summary," 5.

37. *The Way of the People* 1, 85.

38. Shepard Krech III, *The Ecological Indian, Myth and History* (New York: W. W. Norton, 1999), 196–97.

39. Krech, *The Ecological Indian*, 197.

40. Smithsonian Institution/ National Museum of the American Indian, *Meeting Minutes*, Santa Fe Consultation, July 15–16, 1991, 12.

41. Duane Blue Spruce, telephone interview, January 8, 1998.

42. Weller, "Contemporary Native American Architecture," 9.

43. Duane Blue Spruce, personal interview, January 20, 1998.

44. *The Way of the People* 1, 16.

45. Smithsonian Institution, Lloyd Kiva New to Elaine Heumann Gurian, Consultation notes, May 6, 1991.

46. Documents prepared for the Board of Trustees acknowledge that "The Mall is a National Historic Landmark, and the NMAI facility must, by law, be reviewed by the Commission of Fine Arts, the National Capital Planning Commission, the District of Columbia Historic Preservation Review Office, and the Advisory Council on Historic Preservation. Their charge during the review process will be to insure that the architectural design of the new facility helps to realize the original intent of L'Enfant's plan for the Mall and contributes to its architectural character." This refers to the con-

cept for the mall sketched by Pierre Charles L'Enfant, a part of the McMillan Plan and the City Beautiful Movement. *The Way of the People* 3, 2.7).

47. July 10 Meeting, Concept Studies Conference Report of September 9, 1995, Task, 4.

48. "Backgrounder: Design of the National Museum of the American Indian," *Smithsonian Institution News*, May 16, 1996, 2.

49. George F. MacDonald and Stephen Alsford, *A Museum for the Global Village: The Canadian Museum of Civilization* (Hull, Quebec: Canadian Museum of Civilization, 1989), 12–16.

50. "A Warrior Architect Wrestles His Demons," *The New York Times*, October 24, 1996, C1, C10.

51. *The Way of the People* 1, 19.

52. *The Way of the People* 1, 9.

53. Smithsonian Institution, National Museum of the American Indian-Mall Museum, Phase 4.2, Concept Studies Conference Report of July 10, 1995. Task 4.2.10a: Consultation 1—Washington DC, *Meeting Minutes*, 3.

54. *The Way of the People* 1, 17; Duane Blue Spruce, personal interview, January 2, 1998; "20 Needs for the Museum," NMAI Technology Consultation, NMAI, September 9–10, 1991, 1.

55. Smithsonian Institution/ National Museum of the American Indian, GBQC Architects in Association with Douglas J. Cardinal Architects, Ltd., draft of *Pre-Design Submission, Volume I, Mall Museum*, March 3, 1995, 2–10, 2–33.

56. Pre-Design Submission, vol. 1, Mall Museum, 2–11.

57. Pre-Design Submission, vol. 1, Mall Museum, 2–12 to 2–13.

58. Bhabha, Nation and Narration, 302.

59. For a discussion of the criticism of the NMAI that appeared shortly after the opening of the museum see Janet C. Berlo and Aldona Jonaitis, "'Indian Country' on Washington's Mall—The National Museum of the American Indian: A Review Essay," *Museum Anthropology* 28, no. 2 (2005): 17–30.

60. "Shards of Many Untold Stories," *The Washington Post* September 21, 2002, C1.

61. "Museum with an American Indian Voice," *The New York Times*, September 21, 2004, E1, E5.

62. A references to the stone markers is made in print, in a pamphlet available at the information desk called "General Information."

63. The exception is the first exhibition in the Changing Exhibitions" space called *Native Modernism: The Art of George Morrison and Allan Houser*. This exhibition has been well received, particularly because of its thoughtful layout of objects that speak for themselves, yet they have also been illu-

minated through the inclusion of informative label copy and excellent videotapes.

64. Gloria Cranmer Webster, electronic communication, February 1, 2005.
65. Jolene Rickard, telephone communication, January 24, 2005.
66. Walter Dasheno, Smithsonian Institution/National Museum of the American Indian, *Meeting Minutes*, July 15–16, 1991.

Conversation 2
Indigenous Methodology
and Community Collaboration

4. Critical Reflections on the Our Peoples Exhibit

A Curator's Perspective

Paul Chaat Smith

The well-known Texas cattleman, Charles Goodnight, related that a Comanche shield he once procured was stuffed with the pages of a complete history of Rome.

—Christopher Bentley, "The Comanche Shield,
Symbol of Identity"

I decided to open my discussion with an image of words, maybe not surprising since I make my living with words. I found these in a book about three years ago, and I made sure to have them taped to the walls of the various cubicles I've worked in ever since. For me, they were a piece of found history, a prophecy telling me the task I had been assigned was perhaps not completely impossible. Because if a single Comanche shield could hold the history of Rome, then perhaps a single Comanche, with the right comrades, could tell an even bigger story, maybe the biggest untold story of all.

I am the newest curator at the National Museum of the American Indian (NMAI, and work on the Our Peoples exhibit precedes my arrival by many years. It takes a small village—of curators, carpenters, researchers, and electricians— to create an exhibition. In the space of this essay, I must leave out much of the history of this exhibit, but my curatorial team studied closely earlier incarnations of this exhibit, and I want to acknowledge and thank the many who came before me. They include framers like Dave

Warren, and later Bruce Bernstein, Craig Howe, and Harvey Markowitz. Curators Cecile Ganteaume, Carmen Arellano, and Ramiro Matos have been key to this project for years.

The Our Peoples gallery is really nine exhibits. Eight are collaborative ventures between the NMAI curators and people from Indian communities across the hemisphere. The ninth, constituting roughly half of the gallery space, tells this big untold story. I am going to talk about the curatorial team's goals, successes, and failures for that exhibit. There are no unimportant exhibits in this building, and in my view there are also no total failures, or complete successes. However, this piece of real estate, in the clumsy language of museums bureaucracy known as the "NMAI-curated section of Our Peoples," but one that I am going to call the Big Story, or sometimes Evidence, is in my opinion the raison d'être for the existence of the museum itself.

Awarding Indians the last open space on the National Mall was a profound act that showed the American government and its people wanted Indians to be part of a national conversation, to finally talk, seriously, and at the highest levels, about things we had never really talked about before. Let's be clear: you don't get a new museum right next to the Capitol itself for making excellent jewelry, or for having stories and songs, or religious beliefs you wish to share with the world. You get the last open space on the National Mall because the country's decided, in the mysterious ways nations decide such matters, that it's time, at last, to speak about the hard things, the painful things, the unspeakable things.

The National Museum of the American Indian project rests on a set of exquisite contradictions. The federal government has not always been a friend of Indian people. In fact, the United States for much of its history has targeted Indians for removal and physical destruction. We also aren't too crazy about museums, and of all the museums in the world we probably like the Smithsonian the least. And did I mention our museum is about all Indians throughout the Western hemisphere, from the beginning of time up to the present? Actually I think we're also supposed to be experts on the future too. The museum is much more than the exhibits: it is public programs, books and CDs, the landscape, the ducks, the water and rocks. Our floor staff and cultural interpreters are, in a way, really part of the exhibits. And in the building itself, the café and gift shops are as much a part of the experience as the exhibits are. In fact, exhibits make up only about 30 percent of the space inside the museum.

I was assigned to this project in January 2002. Although much work had been done on the larger narratives of Indian history, the museum leadership believed no viable exhibit had emerged. I was given the authority to hire one outside person, and that choice was easy. Dr. Jolene K. Rickard is a Tuscarora artist and scholar who is also, in the opinion of many, the most talented Indian curator in the United States. Jolene curated two groundbreaking exhibitions in the 1990s that challenged conventional Iroquois thinking: In the Shadow of the Eagle, and Across Borders, Beadwork in Iroquois Life. She also worked as a creative director on Madison Avenue during the 1980s, and I knew that experience would prove valuable to the project. We had been colleagues for years but had not collaborated on a project before. We did, however, have shared assumptions that allowed work to move quickly. The first shared assumption was that most shared assumptions are wrong. Our practice is grounded in deep skepticism. We relentlessly interrogate everything, including each other. If she tells me the sun will rise in the East tomorrow morning, I'll probably call the observatory in Greenwich to see if her story checks out.

Jolene believes that an exhibition should present something that has never been done before and not repackage knowledge that already exists. It should use objects to provide an experience you cannot have any other way. She believes it should generate controversy, questions, discussion, and, yes, argument. She also believes there is no safe space inside the museum: the museum is always part of the larger social forces in the world. For red people, that space is highly problematic. We focused early on how to make the exhibit one where the anthropological gaze—previously one that showed Indians on display, trapped in an ideological prison—would be returned by Indian people. She also believes a great exhibit should be both visually and intellectually challenging. Oh, and they should also be drop-dead beautiful.

The other person there from the beginning was my boss, Dr. Ann McMullen. She has always been key in this project and oversaw both the work Jolene and I did as well as the eight community spaces.

I wrote a statement of intent for the exhibit in February 2002. Though we had little time, and not so much money either, we did not lack for ambition. Here's an excerpt:

What really happened?

For the Americas, this question has never been satisfactorily answered. The usual replies are punch lines and cartoons, amnesia and denial, or not quite believable tales of paradise and conquest, generals and natives. It is not a question serious adults ask out loud, since asking it is proof of naïveté or bad manners, yet it preoccupies Americans—North and South—all the same. The continent is filled with Indian-named streets and rivers, corporations and sports teams, and mountains and cities. This untold past is everywhere, in the landscape and the air we breathe, and it's not even past, and we all know it. Confusingly, millions of Indians are still here too, living all over the place: in cities, jungles, suburbs, in the shadow of pyramids and shopping malls. Everywhere you look, there it is, asking the same question few ask but everyone still wonders about. What really happened, and why?

We conclude the answer is

The biggest story never told: the rise and fall and rise of the Americas, the ways America changed Europe, Africa and Asia, and how Europe changed America, a story featuring Indians as actors on the world stage and not merely victims. It is a story of changing worlds and how people managed that change in often surprising, ingenious ways . . . [of] the greatest mass human extinction in history, and the countless ways Indians survived and triumphed in the face of adversity. It is a story where Indians are partners in global markets, savvy diplomats, and eager consumers of new technology. It brings into focus a hemisphere that before contact was outrageously diverse, deliciously complex, endlessly fascinating, and one that would become only more so with every passing century.

It is a story with Indians at the center but also, by definition, relevant to every visitor, whose identity and personal history is shaped by those events. We argue understanding this hemisphere and your place in it is impossible with-

out investigating the centrality of the Indian experience. We argue it changed everything, it changed you. Further, we advise visitors that just about everything you know about this story is wrong. That goes for red people too.

We will privilege beautiful stories and objects and ruthlessly edit out the mediocre ones. This story is so extraordinary, so important, so different from what people expect and think, and yet at the same time precisely what our visitors, especially our Indian visitors, are hoping for: finally, to learn a bit about what really did happen.

We're going to tell them. To do so this must become the most exciting, the most controversial, the most moving and talked about exhibition in Washington. The United States Holocaust Memorial Museum currently holds that position, and we pay them our highest compliment by declaring today our ambition to put them in second place.

Okay, so that looks pretty silly right now. I wrote those words not out of delirious ambition, but because I believed the story demanded such an exhibition. I'll say more about this later.

As I would be reminded hundreds of times during the following months by Jolene and others, a museum exhibition is a visual experience, and people don't go to museums to read essays by Paul Chaat Smith. I did some research and it turned out that, tragically, this was the case.

So Jolene presented her vision for Evidence in April 2002. She said the physical space must reflect the exhibit's central idea that history changes and is a matter of perspective. And it must look contemporary, and begin the process we'd started to name as gently destabilizing the space for visitors. She referenced the sculptor Richard Serra and suggested his curving, disorienting walls offered a way for the exhibit to become experiential. By then our designers, Verena Pierik and Lynn Emi Kawaratani, were on board, and they embraced and improved these concepts.

The crucial early decisions about content repositioned the exhibit so that all visitors, Indians, non-Indians, tourists from Beijing, would be challenged. Our central message was this: Contact was the biggest thing ever, the most profound and momentous event in recorded human history. It created the world we know today. It places Indians, and the Indian experience, at the very center of world history.

Now there are a lot of problems with that message. It's counterintuitive, even though it's factually sound and is not disputed by scholars and historians. But it is so different from how most people understand Indians that it feels like it can't be true. If there really were as many people in the Americas as lived in Europe, why wasn't I taught that in school?

The problem isn't that it's controversial. It's something else, what psychologists call cognitive dissonance. Cognitive dissonance: defined as a psychological conflict resulting from incongruous beliefs and attitudes held simultaneously. That's what happens when you tell visitors of wealth Europeans had never imagined.

This becomes extremely problematic when designing an exhibit for a mainstream audience, because museums traditionally are not about challenging visitors' most deeply held beliefs. Some people, both Indian and non-Indian, believed the museum could merely act as tape recorder and bring back the unfiltered truth of Indian history, philosophy, and contemporary life. That didn't match the vibrant, disputatious Indian world Jolene and I knew. And you're always up against what I've come to regard as the great cosmic joke about Indians: we're portrayed as simple, even cartoon-like, and the terrible truth is that our lives and history and philosophies are absurdly complicated.

We believe there is always a filter.

Jolene and I also believe the Indian world is vast, so complicated, so endlessly surprising, that no one could possibly claim to know more than a small piece of it.

For direction we closely studied two projects: the Vietnam Veterans Memorial and the Holocaust Memorial Museum. The first teaches that this work is more art than science, and insight in the human condition and the human heart is more valuable than a million visitor surveys. There is probably not a single Vietnam vet who, if asked, would have described the appropriate memorial for their service as a slab of black granite adorned with nothing more than names. It would have sounded cold and sterile to nearly all of them. Yet history shows that is precisely, exactly, what they wanted. Maya Lin's genius insight made those walls the most beloved memorial in Washington. She knew how to understand what people wanted, and not just listen to what people said.

The second taught us the value of understatement, the importance of using real artifacts, and, most important, the rewards of respecting the intelligence of viewers. The Holocaust Memorial Museum breaks every museum rule about how long text labels can be, or how educated visitors in Washington's museums are, and has defied expectations by creating a massive audience of people willing to spend half a day, even an entire day, reading labels that are more than seventy-five words long. The creators of the permanent exhibit at the Holocaust Museum gambled that the conventional wisdom was wrong and that millions of people craved deep knowledge about the Holocaust, and not superficial treatment. I always believed, and still believe, that the NMAI has the same kind of potential audience out there, an audience of readers, people who want depth beyond what seventy-five-word labels can deliver.

And I deeply respected a singular part of the Holocaust Museum exhibit, and that is the one that happens the night before at home, when out-of-town visitors are debating whether they are up for a visit to the Holocaust Museum. I'm sure many of you have had that experience. I have friends here who love museums and to this day think they are not ready. That is an extraordinary achievement that is also completely appropriate for a Holocaust Museum.

The NMAI was never meant to be a holocaust museum. Yet it was also determined to portray this part of our history. When I think today about the failure of the Big Story to even come close to that kind of emotional power, I believe one reason is the mandate to tell the darkest of stories right next to exhibits that are celebrating life. Elie Wiesel famously spoke of the Holocaust as "the kingdom of night" and resisted all attempts to find silver linings. Curators initially opposed giving much attention to interventions like that of Oskar Schindler, because however noble his rescues were, they had no impact on the Nazi machine. How different would the permanent exhibit at the Holocaust Museum have been if relegated to a single floor, or even two floors, alongside other exhibits that focused on the bright side of that era, or if the museum was not about the Holocaust but instead about Jewish life? The relentlessness of the permanent exhibit is perhaps its greatest strength.

Now let me talk about the biggest story never told. It begins with a single word: EVIDENCE. We imagined the exhibit as a beautiful excavation site, where history is buried, lost, and found. The first installation, a blast of white, like a fresh layer of snow on a frozen lake, reveals objects beneath the surface. We are telling visitors several things here: what you see depends on where you look, things change, and this Indian history museum is going to look nothing like an Indian history museum is supposed to.

The second installation is called 1491, a teeming convention of contrarians, figurines, lots of whom don't look especially Indian. They are from all over and made of stone, wood, silver, jade. A label describes the Americas as half the world and Americans as numbering in the tens of millions. "Their world is ancient and modern, and forever changing, with memories from the beginning of everything. The figures standing before you knew this world. Many spent centuries underground, until farmers, tomb raiders, road builders and archeologists brought them to light. Like their human descendants, they are survivors of a buried past." The key ideas here are ancient, always changing, tens of millions of people, and incredible diversity. This is the first time we use something called "repetition with difference": 250 objects that are similar but completely distinct from one another. This allowed us to get at the complexity of the Indian experience without reducing it to a few generalities.

Past 1491, you find a wall of gold. Why gold? We chose wealth and dispossession as the central organizing principle of the exhibit. We wanted to present visitors with a new and unsettling idea of precontact America as a rich place. We describe late fifteenth-century Europe as a place where there was a shortage of gold and silver for money, and Peru's Cuzco as a place where gold was used on the side of buildings, and a garden where the dirt itself was made of gold. We don't say this was typical in 1491, and are careful not to say life in the Inca Empire was better than life in northern California. We focus on wealth, power, and abundance. In less than a dozen labels we show how Spanish businessmen seized that gold by kidnapping the Incan leader Atahualpa. And how that gold made Spain the superpower of Europe and the largest empire since the days of Julius Caesar. And how perhaps 20 million died not from disease but as a direct result of the greatest transfer of wealth in history.

The curving s wall that began with the people of 1491 ends with a column of fire and a quote from Eduardo Galeano. Nobody has written better about the Big Story than Galeano. Across from the gold is a free-standing installation called *Ocean*, which tells visitors our thesis: that contact between the world's two halves was the most profound event in human history and changed everything. On the other side of *Ocean* is a wall that tells the story of two invasions: Seventeen Ships, named for the number of craft in Columbus's second voyage to the Americas, and Infinite Thousands, about the unprecedented biological catastrophe that forever shaped the way colonialism would function in this hemisphere. In this section, we say this: "The explosion of death was one of the greatest tragedies in human history because it was unintended and unavoidable, and even inevitable. What happened in its wake was not."

In this section we wanted our visitors, particularly our Indian visitors, to reflect on events we have no direct memory of. In North America our disease narratives go back only to the nineteenth century. As terrible as those events were, they were nothing like the pandemics that destroyed up to 90 percent of the Native population.

Then we offer a room full of George Catlin masterpieces, each one numbered and crammed together.

There is also a portrait of George Gustav Heye, and here we tell the creation story of the NMAI. Without Heye's obsession to collect Indian things in vast quantities, there is no National Museum of the American Indian.

Here we most directly reverse the gaze, and present the tools of the collector for observation and study.

A video, shot in this building, at our research facility a few miles away in Suitland, and also in the National Arboretum, puts our cards on the table. We tell visitors that although the past never changes, the way we understand it changes all the time. We say that all histories have agendas, including ours.

Floyd Favel Starr, a noted Plains Cree playwright, walks through columns that, believe it or not, once held up the East Portico of the U.S. Capitol. Every president from Andrew Jackson through Dwight Eisenhower walked through them, which were removed in the late 1950s. Elegiac and beautiful, this location was suggested by our friends at Interface Media Group.

Things change.

In the center of the gallery, we created three walls we named, perhaps unimaginatively, *The Storm*. We kept asking ourselves, what are the forces that confronted Indian people across the hemisphere, and concluded pretty much everyone was familiar with firearms, Christianity, and the power of governments not our own. Labels describe these forces as making us Indians, giving us shared experiences that those people back in 1491 never had. Inside the walls, another media piece describes the biggest of storms, the hurricane, as a force that creates and destroys, and as a teacher. In the closest thing to a joke we could come up with in this dark exhibit, Floyd Favel Starr asks if there's anything more Indian than a Winchester rifle, except maybe a horse. At the very center of a hurricane is the eye, in this case an extraordinary work of conceptual art by Edward Poitras.

Evidence seeks to upend one of the most enduring beliefs about Indian people: that we fear change, and are only really Indian as long as we don't change, or don't change very much. Evidence argues that we love change, have always changed, and that change is key to our survival.

Okay, so there you have it: Evidence. Creating this exhibit was unbelievably difficult, much harder than writing a book, which practically killed me, and I feel extraordinarily fortunate to have been part of it. The exhibit is massively imperfect, yet it achieves many of the goals we set. I am very grateful to have had the chance to work on this project, and particularly want to thank Lynn Emi Kawaratani and Verena Pierik, the two finest designers on the East Coast.

I also want to address a few other issues. Like the labels on each installation. My relatives loved it, but having my name plastered on label after label is really embarrassing. As a professional writer, it's like signing each paragraph. It also misrepresents authorship. I mean, really, what do you think is more important to know: who imagined the gold wall, or who wrote the labels? Who spoke the fifty words on the wall of a tribal exhibit, or who chose those fifty words out of fifty thousand to put in the exhibit? This is something the curatorial department is looking at now, and perhaps we'll find more accurate ways to let visitors know who created the exhibits.

As everyone knows, the opening was a fantastic success. The procession drew eighty thousand people, the building has been a hit, and we just had our millionth visitor. The exhibits, however, have taken a beating in the press. People say, Paul, what's it like reading those reviews that describe your exhibit as a public service announcement, or homogenized pap? I tell them, you know what, truthfully, it's not so great. When Herb Rosen and I decided to end the *Making History* video by exhorting visitors to reflect on our exhibit, encounter it, and argue with it, who knew the press would be so obedient? If only we'd changed the last three words to "Write gushing reviews." Anyway, I thought nearly all of the reviews made valid points, and many were painfully on target.

However, I would like to take this opportunity to correct a few factual mistakes. For example, The *Denver Post* reported in November that in this museum "American Indians hold all the key leadership positions." Actually, in the countless meetings about this project over the past three and a half years, I was usually one of just a couple of Indians, and quite often the only Indian in the room. Our splendid director, W. Richard West, and his splendid special assistant, Gerald McMaster, are both reds, and they had final authority over the exhibit content. But for those concerned that a large pack of dour, nonhegemonic Indian nonscholars have taken over a Smithsonian museum, I can assure them no such thing has happened. Indians are a minority at the Indian museum, and are especially a minority on the content and exhibit side of things. We are nothing to be afraid of, just a thin red line of government workers surrounded mostly by white folks who are also government workers (and often some of the nicest people you'd ever meet), making our way as best we can.

My hope for the museum is that in this next chapter we become both more ambitious and more humble. As far as the white folks are concerned, I think this biggest of all stories should attract the sharpest minds from all over the planet, and the color of their skin matters not at all. Expertise, scholarship, experience, creative thinking is what counts. My closest intellectual partner inside the museum has been Ann McMullen, and last time I checked she was beige. I also know that telling stories of Indian America is a challenging task, and though it's possible that someone, either Indian or not, could fly into some Indian community for a few weeks with no expertise, scholarship, or experience and come back with something worthwhile, it is pretty unlikely. World-class exhibitions require world-class scholars and designers and thinkers, and being world-class has always been this museum's destiny.

Jack Valenti, boss of the Motion Picture Association of America, was asked once why there are so many bad movies. He said it's because in this country, we make five hundred movies a year, and we don't have enough talent to make five hundred good movies. Making exhibits, I think, is not so different. It requires talent, skill, and luck. We never came close to dethroning the Holocaust Museum, but we're just getting started.

In the beginning of this essay, I discussed the museum as a site of a national conversation. We are the very beginning of that conversation, and like any difficult conversation, it can be rough going, especially at first. Let's keep arguing, because at least it means we're talking. And of course by now you know I'm talking also about arguments among Indians, not just those boring arguments between Indians and cowboys. But we'll get better at this, because we have to. I mean, it's not like anyone's going anywhere, right?

I'm going to close with the exhibition's last label. It's called *All My Relations.*

> Entire nations perished in the wave of death that swept the Americas. Even their names are lost to us. We cannot tell you where they lived, what they believed, or what they dreamed. Their experiences are buried and unknowable. Like much of Indian history, we have only fragments.
>
> This wall lists the names of our relatives who are still here, with those of ancestors who vanished without a trace. The list will always be incomplete, ruptured, and fragmented. It can never be whole.
>
> Nine of ten perished. One in ten survived. All Indians alive today are here because our ancestors used intelligence, skill, planning, strategy and sacrifice. They didn't fear change; they embraced it. They survived because they fought for change on our terms.
>
> Their past lives in our present. As descendents of the one in ten who wake up in the 21st century, we share an inheritance of grief, loss, hope, and immense wealth. The brilliant achievements of our ancestors make us accountable for how we move in the world today. Their lessons instruct us, and make us responsible for remembering everything, especially those things we never knew.

5. Collaborative Exhibit Development at the Smithsonian's National Museum of the American Indian

Cynthia Chavez Lamar

In September 2004, the Smithsonian's National Museum of the American Indian (NMAI) opened on the National Mall in Washington DC. As expected, enormous fanfare and celebration ensued, particularly by those Native communities represented in the exhibitions. Our Lives: Contemporary Life and Identities, one of the four inaugural exhibitions, focuses on the identities of Native peoples in the Western hemisphere at a local and global level. As part of Our Lives, representatives from eight Native communities, from as far north as Igloolik, Nunavut, and to the south in Carib Territory, Dominica, Caribbean, collaborated with NMAI staff to create smaller exhibits within Our Lives highlighting their communal identity.[1] This was significant for these communities because this was the first time a large institution asked them to engage in self-representation as curatorial partners. As part of this request, communities established committees that served as the primary collaborators with the NMAI. They came to be known as community curators.[2]

Negotiations over power, authority, and, inevitably, Native voice edged to the forefront of our experience as NMAI staff and Native community members forged a path of collaborative exhibit development.[3] This was not necessarily a new experience for everyone involved, but the high stakes—this exhibit was to mark a significant moment in the history of museums and in the representation of Native peoples in exhibitions—

and the fact that I, a Native curator, was working with eight dissimilar Native communities resulted in unique outcomes and situations along our collective journey.

An Invitation and a Guarded Response

It all began in January 2001, when I started meeting with the designated leadership from each of the eight communities. The NMAI considered it extremely important to respect the sovereignty of the Native tribes and nations we collaborated with; therefore, a certain protocol was adhered to in contacting the communities. A letter from Executive Director W. Richard West went to each of the tribal councils or other recognized leadership body, which introduced me as the curator and indicated my future contact with them. I then made contact with the community and established a date to visit and meet with the leadership.[4] Not surprisingly, every group I met agreed to work with the NMAI on Our Lives.[5] Nevertheless, some community members were wary of our invitation, taking a "wait and see" attitude, and others clearly expected to be disappointed. Eventually I also realized that, due to my identity as American Indian, I was given much more benefit of the doubt than a non-Native would have received.[6]

In my professional and personal opinion, establishing trust was paramount to the success of the endeavor, which proved difficult at times, especially when decisions were made at an NMAI upper management level that had to be conveyed by me to the co-curators. Essentially, everything I communicated to them became my word, and I had to be extra careful about what I said. Carol Dunstan notes the potential trust issues that can arise when working with community members on collaborative exhibits:

> Trust was a major issue that we all had to deal with. There was really no reason that the community participants should trust the museum staff and students at all. They only had our word that this exhibit was going to reflect well on their communities, and that they would feel proud having been part

of the process. We were asking them to loan the precious items that they had brought with them from home, to open their lives to us, and to discuss their problems and concerns with us. What they would receive in return was not readily discernable.[7]

I offered each of the communities only the opportunity to represent their community at a national venue. Beyond the physical exhibit, I was not in a position to promise anything more. Many times, I felt I vacillated on various questions asked by the co-curators because the answers involved discussions or decisions by NMAI management. Being perceived as wishy-washy did not help establish trust. For example, early on one of the more consistent inquiries from the co-curators was whether their exhibit could travel to their community. This would have been preferred by the NMAI, but budget constraints and poor planning eventually did not allow for this.[8] In the end, what helped me build trust was that I was as straightforward with them about what I knew and did not know regarding every aspect of the exhibit's development.

Establishing Parameters for Better or Worse

After each of the communities established a group for me to work with, I begin my first meeting with the co-curators discussing the parameters of the exhibit. Although I did not want to dictate the content of their exhibits, I considered it important to provide a framework for their discussions, otherwise I believed it would be difficult to pare down the content. I told each group of co-curators that their exhibit in Our Lives should not solely be:

A history of the community

A sanitized, tourist advertisement for the community

A treatise about the traditional or cultural practices of the community.

In retrospect, I failed to understand how these parameters would shape the eventual outcome of the exhibit's content despite how general I tried to make them. However, parameters seemed crucial given the expedited timeframe and limited budget of Our Lives.[9] NMAI, quite rightly, also did not want curators entering the collaborations without a clear overall exhibit concept and methodology for guiding the work.

The co-curators knew this exhibit was about contemporary Native identities in general and understood NMAI wanted to present a 21st century representation of Native peoples. I wished to achieve honest, complex representations of each community not recognizing the dynamics at play that would inhibit such a representation particularly in trying to capture the challenges facing Native tribes and nations in the 21st century. In our meetings the co-curators told many stories, both past and present, which explicated a complex, transitional, and maturing community identity. I listened to assertive, strong Kahnawákeró:non women tell of their roles in their community and how they helped shape an education system establishing Mohawk values and beliefs in the foreground. These stories inevitably transitioned into discussions about the spiritual divide in the community because the school systems were originally Western religious based. Another time, I witnessed proud Kalinago men and women of mixed heritage speaking forcefully about their identity and what it meant to be Kalinago. Their declarations led to testimonies about the prejudice they experienced in their community for not "looking" Kalinago. These frank, difficult representations of the communities proved prohibitive to include in the exhibit for various reasons. Considered sensitive topics by some of the co-curators, they felt the inclusion might be perceived as "airing dirty laundry." Others thought there were other more important subjects to present to the public. From a curatorial perspective, some of these issues did not fit contextually within the exhibit's messages and to include them would have appeared unseemly considering the mixed feelings of the co-curators.

As an example, in many of our initial meetings the Yakamas spoke of crucial issues concerning the youth and continuance of cultural traditions of their Nation. Once I presented exhibit concepts and themes back to the Yakama curators, they realized I listened to what they said because the issues they openly discussed in our meetings were being considered part of the exhibit content. At that point they decided these issues were not for public consumption and told me not to include them. This was an important turning point for them and me as well. They recognized they directed the exhibit content development, and I realized as a museum curator that decisions were not always up to the NMAI even though some topics might make for intriguing exhibit text and insight into Native identity. I knew it was not within my authority or conscience to include sensitive information because of the trust I had established with the community curators. Such realization reminded me of what one of the Yakama curators said at our first meeting: "[W]e as a people, . . . the Yakamas, we have to decide how much we can tell and how much. . . . we [don't] tell. There are certain things we can't talk about." Even at the very beginning, the co-curators were cognizant of their limitations in sharing information with a visiting public. They had enormous burdens to carry for they were chosen to speak on behalf of their entire communities. The choices they made and words they spoke were going to be on display for the world, more importantly, for their community to see and eventually judge. Acutely aware of their positioning, many of the co-curators' choices were weighted against this reality which is why some of the harsher truths of their communities' existence did not make it into the final exhibition.

Some communities such as the Kalinago of Carib Territory in Dominica wanted to include information on the challenges their people faced, but within the context of their efforts at cultural revitalization and self-determination. As such, even as visitors read about their economic and educational hardships, they also sense a strong proclamation of cultural identity. The strongest identity statement the Kalinago chose to make in their exhibit concerned their name: How did they want to be known by those visiting the NMAI? For centuries and in the preponderance of literature, the Kalinago have been known as the Carib, but this was not the name of their ancestors. Today, they want to be known as Kalinago, a name that was recorded in 1642 as what they called themselves in their language. As one Kalinago person stated: "For me I am not Carib. I'm not black. I'm not white. I'm a Kalinago."[10]

Each of the community exhibits emphasizes pride and revitalization of culture and/or language. Looking back at the parameters established at the beginning of the process, I am not surprised that most of the content of the community exhibits resulted in forward-looking concepts. It was a team effort based on consensus, and most groups worked toward achieving a balance between history, cultural traditions, and pride.

Outlines, Bubble Diagrams, and Exhibit Content

Organizing and consolidating all the information shared by the co-curators into a tangible format identifying exhibit messages and themes that were understandable and usable for them proved challenging. I and other NMAI staff met with each group of community curators four to eight times to develop and refine the exhibit content.[11] Initially, the information I presented back to them took the form of an outline, which they reviewed and revised. This method proved useful for only a couple of meetings, and then the co-curators experienced some frustration because they had difficulty imagining how this information helped organize their exhibit. Many requested visuals to help them understand the conceptual structure of the exhibit floor, which also helped the designers determine how much importance to place on the various themes of the exhibits. The bubble diagrams greatly helped everyone comprehend the relation of the themes to the main messages and also aided the designers in the physical layout of the content. As part of the process, the designers asked the co-curators to assign percentages to each of the themes; these were later used to determine space allocations in the design.

Throughout the content development process refinements and editing of material occurred since we used the main messages to determine whether the content supported the premise of the exhibits. This proved extremely useful in helping the community curators see how visitors might get confused or overwhelmed with information if we strayed into areas not relevant to the main message.[12] I continually heard co-curators remind one another of the parameters I set forth at our first meeting, especially when they felt someone was delving too deep into history. It certainly helped to provide an initial framework for developing the content and also a preliminary schedule for the overall exhibit development, even if both changed as we progressed.[13]

Alterations in scheduling and methodology were inevitable due to the dynamic and expedited nature of the Our Lives exhibit development. When the other inaugural exhibits, Our Peoples and Our Universes, reached certain milestones in the exhibit development, such as draft design, this was presented to the community curators for a review and approval so the work could proceed. This collaborative curation methodology was termed the "five-phase process" at the NMAI. The five phases were:

1. Meeting with the leadership body to present invitation to participate in exhibit
2. Fieldwork, including meetings with community curators and research for content development
3. Draft content and design presentation to community curators for their suggested revisions
4. Revised exhibit content and design presentation to community curators for further review and comment
5. Presentation of final content and design to community curators

One aspect of this particular methodology that changed as Our Lives moved forward was the concept of "final approval." Final approval was implemented at the various milestones related to exhibit development, as indicated in phases 3, 4, and 5. The co-curators were asked for approval on the milestones before the NMAI moved to the next phase. Our Lives did not strictly adhere to this five-phase methodology but used it as a framework and utilized the idea of approval as a fundamental value of the collaborative exhibit development process. In other words, I involved the co-curators in as much of the decision making as possible (this was not limited to the final approval phases), despite the physical and technological distance between us. Back- and-forth review of materials by co-curators, which most of them received by e-mail or fax to review independently or as a group, occurred often. This proved essential to maintaining the integral involvement of the community curators. They were listened to and treated as partners despite the distance.[14] E-mail greatly helped maintain communication, especially over long distances, but it could never compete with face- to-face contact. Working side by side in their communities helped establish camaraderie. Jacinte, Arlen, Kanatakta, Garnette, Susan, to name only a few, were my colleagues and some, my friends. Others, removed from the experience for one reason or another, had more of an advisory role.[15]

Trying to Put Aside the Personal

I struggled to maintain a professional distance from the co-curators and communities. I served as lead curator on Our Lives not completely understanding the magnitude of what it meant to represent Native peoples at the NMAI's historic opening. I actually believed it would be easier because I was also Native, but I overlooked the obvious fact that in accepting this project I essentially positioned myself between the NMAI and the Native communities. Throughout the project I was, at the same time, a San Felipe Pueblo/Hopi/Tewa/Navajo woman and an NMAI curator. Needless to say, my commitment to the project was often tested, as was my loyalty to the NMAI. As a Native person at the NMAI, I occasionally felt anxiety and disappointment over how budget, time, and upper management priorities conflicted with the needs and desires of the community curators. At the same time, I felt dismay over the limited availability of some co-curators to the project due to lack of interest and commitment, but also due to their multiple project, committee, job, and family responsibilities.[16]

Despite my internal conflicts, I believe the eight communities I helped represent in Our Lives benefited from having a novice Native woman curator positioned to speak on their behalf to NMAI staff. In turn, the NMAI benefited from having me represent the museum to the communities. Who better to send out to each of these eight communities than a young (at the time) Native curator without a chip on her shoulder? Growing up in San Felipe Pueblo, New Mexico, I entered the communities similar to the way I am when at home: I listened, showed respect for the unfamiliar, and knew when to become unobtrusive. I approached this experience with humility, naïveté, and honesty and let the community curators know that we had to figure out together how to get this accomplished. In this way, I suppose I leveled the playing field so that the NMAI was not presented or perceived as the experts in the collaboration, except that we knew the technicalities of putting an exhibit together.

And at the NMAI, who better to represent the eight communities' position to staff than a young Native curator without a chip on her shoulder, whose Indianness was not in their face? Often, I had to convey the co-curators' perspectives and positions in meetings with exhibit designers, project managers, educators, conservators, and assistant directors. I could not speak as a San Felipe Pueblo/Hopi/Tewa/Navajo woman, but as a museum professional whose authority came from the consent and knowledge granted me by the co-curators. The fact that I am Native and have a PhD went largely unrecognized because I was primarily viewed as a conduit to the communities.[17] At times I became amused at my position; while I felt I had little authority as an individual NMAI curator, I seemed to hold great authority if I began my sentences by saying "The community curators said . . ." This was common language usage when we developed the inaugural exhibits; unfortunately, such phrasing had the potential to cause anxiety among NMAI staff because they were not sure if they could meet those expectations and knew that negotiations would be in order. Tensions among NMAI staff and co-curators occurred throughout the experience for reasons having to do with authority, deadlines, perspectives, and priorities.

Decisions and Divisions

Eventually, the label "community curators" became the source of discussion among some NMAI staff.[18] By historic definition, the term "curator" typically connotes a level of expertise, knowledge and research background, and, most important, authority: the authority to represent a body of knowledge in an exhibition. Some at the NMAI believed the designation "community curators" overly gratuitous because the co-curators were not directly involved in every aspect of the exhibit's daily development, as were those of us who worked at the NMAI. No one questioned the community curators' level of cultural knowledge and expertise; rather, it was their capacity to function as curators, considering what we have known curators to typically be. I believe this doubt was directly related to the possibility that some felt threatened by the designation, as in some way it lessened the authority of the NMAI curatorial staff. "Why have curators if the NMAI can rely on Native peoples in communities to function in that capacity?" was a question considered by some. As such, NMAI curators of the inaugural exhibitions who collaborated with Native communities often became recognized more as facilitators than curators, which denied their agency in the decision-making process. One of our responsibilities was to function as facilitators, but we also had to make many day- to-day decisions in the absence of the community curators.

Decision making reflected the complicated dynamics of the project. I recognized that power and authority were at play, with the NMAI having all the power yet the community curators seemingly granted all the authority to make decisions, but only when the NMAI presented them with the opportunity (the five-phase process of approval). This is not a criticism of the NMAI, only a revelation of the realities of collaborating with numerous individuals in different states and countries over a four-year period. Logistically, the co-curators could not be involved in every single decision made about the exhibit because they were not full-time staff or located in Washington, DC. E-mail and phone discussions became essential to contacting community curators with questions I felt could be answered only by them.[19]

Whose "Voice" Is It?

The NMAI wanted to make it clear that Native peoples were directly involved in the exhibit development. This resulted in what was termed "Native voice," which appears often in the rhetoric and media of the NMAI. The tangible method for conveying Native voice in the exhibit took the form of exhibit labels identified by an author. However, having all of the exhibit labels signed by the supposed author of the text hid the "translative editorial processes of exhibition design [script writing, media development, educational programming, and public relations]."[20] When one walks through Our Universes, Our Peoples, and Our Lives, most exhibit labels are signed by individual NMAI staff, individual community members, or the co-curators as a group, for example, the Yakama curators. In some instances, signing labels appears absurd when you see one individual's name listed multiple times for short exhibit labels. Although they are a commendable effort and alternative to typical museum labels, I believe the intention of authored labels should have been explained to reveal the collaborative nature of the script writing.

A few years later, it is plainly evident to me that the inaugural exhibitions did a poor job at revealing the collaborative nature of the inaugural exhibits' development.[21] I base this opinion on the reviews published after the opening and my discussions with individuals who have visited the NMAI. I remember walking through the Our Lives gallery during the Smithsonian employee soft opening and hearing a man remark while standing in the Campo Band of Kumeyaay Indians exhibit that this was not "real scholarship." He said, "This is just what the Indians have told them." Despite this comment's blatant privileging of Western forms of knowledge and scholarship, such critiques alert me to the fact that, as an NMAI curator, I took for granted visitors' lack of background of the collaborative exhibit development process and the mission of the NMAI. How are visitors to know that the exhibits were more than direct quotes, without any interpretation, from Native peoples? Reviewer Philip Kennicott at the Washington Post noted this need for transparency of process and knowledge in the inaugural exhibits:

The new museum on the Mall, its leaders say, is a resolute effort to step out-side the objectifying habits of anthropology and all the other disciplines with mainstream museum credentials. But it is also a museum with a very broad mandate, devoted to native cultures from Peru to the Hudson Bay, which means its curators will eventually have to work with peoples ever more remote from American cultural life. When they do, they may find themselves hav-ing to explain the whole concept, the purpose of the museum, [and] the kinds of objects that other groups have contributed.[22]

It may be that in the NMAI's well-intentioned quest to further democ-ratize and decolonize the process by which exhibits about Native peo-ples get developed we made it appear that the "Natives spoke, we listened and wrote it down for visitors to read," which was far from actual reali-ty. Personally I find it astounding and commendable that the NMAI col-laborated with twenty-four Native communities in its inaugural exhibi-tions, yet this fact is rarely noted by reviewers or visitors because the final product, the exhibition, becomes the tangible reference point for criti-cism and commentary. Nowhere in any of the exhibits is the process of collaborative curation provided ample label copy.

Too Much "Expertise"

As expected in a collaborative exhibit with a variety of participants, differ-ences of opinion arose over co-curators' choices about what was impor-tant to include and how it was translated into connecting themes within the exhibit and eventually the exhibit text.[23] The divergences between co-curators' priorities and the NMAI's while creating Our Lives had much to do with perceived museum visitor experience, comprehension, and attention span.[24] Particular exhibit topics and eventually the text were challenged by some staff throughout the development because they felt visitors would not understand or that they would be bored by too much explanation. Complex, interconnected beliefs, traditions, histories, and spiritualities often became compartmentalized and simplified as they transformed into physical spaces in the exhibit design and text. Often, media in the form of first-person interviews or interactives became the vehicle to transmit information considered too complex or uninteresting as a text panel.

In developing Our Lives, we used the tools available to any major institution creating an exhibit. We resisted thinking innovatively because the risk of delaying the schedule or going over budget seemed too great. Consequently, the tools used to develop the exhibit remained static, resulting in exhibition ideas constrained by conventionality. As Christina Kreps stated in the special issue of *Museum Anthropology* on Indigenous curation, "We may come to see how professional curatorial practices, regarded as 'natural' and 'logical,' are cultural constructs and products of our own museum culture."[25] In working with co-curators, most of whom were not museum professionals, ideas were suggested that could have challenged conventional approaches to museology, but they did not make it onto the exhibit floor. Nonconventional ideas seemed to be the victims of budget, time, and museum professionals who wanted to stick with what they thought worked well in exhibits. Early in my visits to Chicago, one co-curator told me he would have liked to see their exhibit without words—maybe sound, but no words. Of course, that did not happen.

Other community curators from the very first visit also had conceptual ideas regarding their exhibits. At Yakama Nation, a tribal council member stated that he did not want to see Yakama represented as only beautiful things in cases: "We don't want to just show our pretty things." He wanted more of his community's truths to be known and elaborated with this short anecdote: "Arnold Schwarzenegger came here one year. . . . He flew in [by] helicopter, [and] he asked me, 'The Yakama people never lost a war?' . . . He knew that. He read that somewhere. That's the kind of thing people should hear [in the exhibit]." The fact the Yakama have never lost a war is in the Our Lives exhibit; it represents an important facet of their experience and is one way they represent their Yakama identity. However, I think the Yakama exhibit, like the others, did fall short by not telling more truths such as this. This is the unfortunate nature of exhibits, with their physical and conceptual parameters: the community curators had to prioritize themes and ideas, and always within the framing device of their exhibit's main message. Some topics just did not fit, or their importance diminished because they became a sentence within larger thematic concepts.[26] Nevertheless, these community exhibits did resound with the voices of the co-curators and other community members. As Linda Tuhiwai Smith writes in her seminal text, *Decolonizing Methodologies*, "Representation is a project of indigenous artists, writers, poets, film makers and others who attempt to express indigenous spirit, experience or world view. Representation of indigenous peoples by indigenous peoples is about countering the dominant society's image of indigenous peoples, their lifestyles, and belief systems."[27]

Consensus and Compromise

The community curators spoke as one voice in the final exhibit, although in the content development meetings disagreement and differing opinions occurred. One of the Chicago curators had a museum background and often looked critically at how his group could represent their community's contemporary identity. His ideas often conflicted with his group's perspectives. He wanted to problematize urban Indian identity in the exhibit, not only celebrate the unity they shared as Native peoples. The discussions among the Chicago urban Indian curators illustrated that Native peoples may also resort to positive stereotypes to represent their cultures, communities, and identities because these are readily identifiable as "Indian" or they provide an idealized vision of their identity. All of the co-curators struggled with how to represent themselves to others. While they wanted to be honest, they also realized they did not necessarily want to be negative or bare their souls.

At the 2005 American Association of Museums annual meeting that same Chicago co-curator reflected on the collaborative exhibit development experience: "Objectifying culture is something Indians do too." He noted that the entire experience instigated, for the first time, a community discussion about pan-Indian identity in Chicago and how pan-Indianism has the potential to dilute or neutralize the specific tribal identities existing in the city. However, this discussion did not make its way into the final exhibit. Their common history became the foundation to organize their exhibit, and they also wanted to celebrate their community, not highlight its internal conflicts. The five-phase exhibit development process focused on consensus among the co-curators and it competed against having diverse or conflicting opinions and perspectives. Of course, such viewpoints would have been ideal in an exhibit about Native identity.[28] In the end, I believe that Chicago co-curator felt the Chicago exhibit in Our Lives diminished tribal-specific voices. The community curators worked together to arrive at consensus, which ultimately meant compromise. They also did not want to present conflicting messages in their exhibit.

Power, Authority, and Ownership

An article in *Museum Anthropology* by Miriam Kahn, "Not Really Pacific Voices: Politics of Representation in Collaborative Museum Exhibits," asks an important question that is certainly relevant five years later: "Does the shift from curatorial authority to community involvement, and the addition of diverse, multiple, indigenous voices, address and resolve the issues of representation that were raised by the museum critiques [of earlier years]?"[29] In my opinion, community involvement further complicates issues of representation because the roles of all the players are not as simple as the dichotomies earlier museum critiques suggest: Native/community and non-Native/museum. Additionally, trying to balance Native and non-Native perspectives with mere numbers doesn't avoid issues of power and authority. As Michael Ames has stated, "If the purpose of allowing many voices to be represented in an exhibition is to move towards a greater degree of equality between an institution and the peoples it represents, then more drastic measures are required than simply balancing non-Native curators with Native consultants, like counterpoising so many cowboys and Indians."[30]

Ownership in collaborative projects may be even more important than issues of power and authority. The more important question is how to achieve a feeling of ownership in collaborative projects with Native peoples.[31] In Our Lives, community curators did not feel complete ownership of the final exhibition. They felt empowered during the process of determining the exhibition content; however, as the exhibit underwent the design process, their involvement was curtailed and they understood it was the NMAI's turn to take over. To date, the NMAI still remains at the center of the dialogue despite efforts to offset this, and I believe it is because the agency still originates with the NMAI: the NMAI approached communities to collaborate with, rather than the community coming to the NMAI. Agency and commitment must begin with the community and its representatives for the project to be considered a true partnership. Otherwise, the museum drives the endeavor and the community will rarely ask for anything in return.

Several of the Our Lives communities saw their involvement as an opportunity to establish a long-term relationship with the NMAI, which is important for any institution to consider when working with community groups. In their important book *Museums and Source Communities*, Peers and Brown also note this need: "Though many relationships begin with a specific project . . . community expectations are that such projects are vehicles to developing long-term relationships, while museums may assume their responsibilities are over when the project ends. Project teams need to give thought to what happens once the exhibition opens or the initial project concludes."[32]

To date, the Métis of Saint-Laurent continue to pursue various opportunities with the NMAI gift shops, provide objects for rotation in their exhibit, and attend training provided by the Community and Constituent Services Department. I recently heard from one co-curator who, after much persistence, managed to get the Mitsitam Café of the NMAI to include saskatoons in one of their menu items. This will contribute to the economic development of Saint-Laurent because they will sell the preserved saskatoons to the café. Regrettably it takes much determination and persistence on the part of Native peoples to make such situations happen, but they are certainly possible.

NMAI Postscript

I recently visited the NMAI and viewed the Listening to the Ancestors exhibit, which is also a collaboration with Native communities. Eleven Northwest Coast communities participated in its development. Unlike the inaugural exhibits, Listening to the Ancestors positions upfront its co-curation process with Native communities.[33] The introductory text reads:

> In this exhibition, representatives from 11 Native communities along the North Pacific Coast share their perspectives on more than 400 ceremonial and everyday objects that connect them to their lands, customs, and ancestors. Their words reveal the deeper meaning that lives within the objects, as well as the enduring lifeways of which they are a part.
>
> The Native representatives visited the National Museum of the American Indian to select objects for the exhibition. Reunited with pieces long-separated from their homelands, the community representatives were able to listen anew to their ancestors. Tour the gallery to find out what they heard, and learn how the Native peoples of the North Pacific Coast balance time-honored values in the modern world.

Visitors see this exhibit label at the entrance and another at the exit further explaining the co-curatorial process.[34] Particularly interesting is the exhibit's exit, where much more insight into the collaborative process is provided. A series of photographs are shown along with personal statements from the various NMAI staff who were involved in the exhibit's development. This provides visitors a more tangible connection to how the exhibit came to be, but more important, it highlights the work with Native communities that the NMAI endeavors to accomplish. It also establishes the shared authority among those involved, recognizing protocols, diverse expertise, and holders of cultural and traditional knowledge.

It appears that the NMAI has taken to heart some of the earlier critiques launched by reviewers who did not understand the collaborative process at work in this institution. This is an important new direction for the museum to follow: to make more transparent the complex process of community collaboration.

Notes

1. The communities included the Campo Band of Kumeyaay Indians (California), the urban Indian community of Chicago, Yakama Nation (Washington State), Igloolik (Nunavut, Canada), Kahnawake (Quebec, Canada), Métis from Saint-Laurent (Manitoba, Canada), Kalinago from Carib Territory (Dominica, Caribbean), and the Pamunkey Tribe (Virginia).
2. I also refer to them as co-curators.
3. In my opinion, the NMAI did not engage in anything new or particularly groundbreaking in its collaborative exhibit development. However, I believe the scale (the number of Native communities, the time frame, and the venue) resulted in interesting and new approaches to shared curation.
4. Another approach for the NMAI included establishing contact with a scholar or anthropologist who worked in or for the community to be invited. The NMAI curator met with the scholar first so the curator could obtain background information on the community and determine the best method for working with them. I used this approach with the Métis from Saint-Laurent and a South American community (the work with this community did not proceed). This proved useful if the scholar was amenable to assisting initially and then being involved on an as needed basis. The scholar had to realize we viewed the community members as the experts regarding their culture and history, and the scholar was essentially a preliminary consultant. In every instance, the NMAI and I wanted to avoid creating a situation in which the scholar spoke for the community.
5. Each community recognized the prestige and notoriety that accompanied collaborating with the NMAI on an exhibit showcasing their culture. In accepting, they relinquished some of their curatorial authority to fit within the parameters established by the museum. The communities acknowledged that it was in their best interests to participate in the project, and the NMAI did have the best intentions, despite how the whole endeavor actually transpired due to various problems and issues encountered along the way. Native peoples have long analyzed situations to determine the best approach and decision to make. This goes for anything they do, whether

a multimillion-dollar economic development project or a museum exhibition at the NMAI.

6. Before I met with the communities I was advised of the possible distrust I might encounter due to being a museum employee and being perceived as a representative of the federal government.

7. Carol Dunstan, "Fostering Symbiosis: A Collaborative Exhibit at the California State University Sacramento Museum of Anthropology," *Museum Anthropology* 22, no. 3 (1999): 55–56.

8. The co-curators and I eventually discussed how parts of their exhibit might be returned since the NMAI had in its possession the media footage, photographs, and graphic files for the existing exhibit, along with additional footage and photos that were not used.

9. At the time I was hired by the NMAI, the Our Lives exhibit lacked a lead curator and was behind in its development.

10. Kalinago community meeting, Carib Territory, Dominica, January 17, 2002.

11. These visits did not include those for media and other related requests by the co-curators for visits.

12. This corresponds with my previous comment about the exclusion of certain topics.

13. I felt it was important to be as transparent as possible concerning expectations and limitations because that helped to establish a mutually trustful and respectful relationship.

14. There were times when the NMAI could not make the changes the communities wanted or suggested, but this was always explained to them, which they appreciated and which provided them with greater insight into the intricacies involved in exhibit development.

15. Curators, researchers, and fieldworkers working in communities develop various relationships with community members. Ann Lane Hedlund characterized individual Navajo weavers according to their level of engagement with the project as informants, consultants, or partners: "In the largest sense, some weavers became my teachers, I was their student and sometimes apprentice. Others remained more distant informants, or slightly more engaged consultants." "Speaking *for* or *about* Others? Evolving Ethnological Perspectives," *Museum Anthropology* 18, no. 3 (1994): 37. The level of engagement by all Native people involved in Our Lives development did determine their characterization. I could not force people to be involved more than they wanted to be. Their participation required work and commitment on the project in addition to their full-time obligations as employees, mothers, and fathers.

16. As the NMAI left the selection of the co-curators to the communities, a number of those asked to participate had high-profile roles in the community, which ensured they would have limited availability. Each co-curator was compensated for their participation in the meetings, and the NMAI also entered into contracts with some co-curators who served as field-workers and researchers to follow up on tasks that NMAI staff could not do. I would have liked to have contract fieldworkers or researchers in each community because this proved a successful way to accomplish tasks that would have to be done long-distance by NMAI staff, who were coordinating efforts among eight communities.

17. This corresponds with the presumption that NMAI curators functioned more as facilitators, as will be discussed later.

18. This discussion arose primarily during the script writing and editing process because all exhibit labels had to be signed (i.e., authored) to indicate who was speaking. This was the NMAI's attempt at transparent authorship as a way to distinguish the museum from exhibits whose authority and authorship remain unknown to visitors. It became difficult to determine whose name should appear on some labels because the co-curators, script editor, and I were all involved in the scripting of labels. However, due to the level of co-curators' involvement in the process, the NMAI wanted their names or group name identified on labels.

19. Due to the perceived pressure NMAI staff felt about the 2004 opening, instances occurred when some staff wanted decisions made immediately. At times I succumbed to the demand; at other times I successfully deflected it so I could contact the co-curators for their decision.

20 Hedlund, "Speaking *for* or *about* Others?," 34.

21. I take responsibility for the exhibition's lack of explanation regarding the collaborative process. I did not push the need for transparency during the script writing process.

22. Philip Kennicott, "A Particular Kind of Truth," *Washington Post*, September 19, 2004, R02.

23. In this paragraph I reference the content development phase, but disagreement over co-curators' choices also occurred during the design development stage.

24. As a public institution representing Native peoples of the Western hemisphere, the NMAI will always be in a compromised position in terms of its ability to balance its major constituencies (i.e., Native peoples and the visiting public). The NMAI is unlike tribal museums, which can make it their mission to address tribal needs and priorities.

25. Christina Kreps, "Introduction: Indigenous Curation," *Museum Anthropology* 22, no. 1: 3.

26. As an example, the consequences of the allotment of Yakama lands are referenced on the label of a graphic of Yakama's current landholdings, where it will undoubtedly be overlooked

27. Linda Tuhiwai Smith, *Decolonizing Methodologies: Research and Indigenous Peoples* (London: Zen Books, 1999), 151.

28. Differing views from community members were accomplished only in a Kahnawake media interactive. The interactive was based on the concept of the Nosy News Thug in their local newspaper, in which various Kahnawákeró:non are asked questions and provide different responses.

29. Miriam Kahn, "Not Really Pacific Voices: Politics of Representation in Collaborative Museum Exhibits," *Museum Anthropology* 24, no. 1 (2000): 70.

30. Michael M. Ames, "The Politics of Difference: Other Voices in a Not Yet Post-Colonial World," *Museum Anthropology* 18, no. 3 (1994): 15.

31. Our Lives remains in Washington, DC, with no plans to travel. However, some of the communities represented would be interested in the possibility of having some aspect of the exhibit in their communities.

32. Laura Peers and Alison Brown, eds., *Museums and Source Communities: A Routledge Reader* (New York: Routledge, 2003), 9.

33. As a critique, however, Listening to the Ancestors does not deviate from a prescribed method of working with communities in that objects were the basis or framework for the dialogue with community representatives. Frankly, having something to look at and talk about becomes a framing device, which makes the work somewhat easier. I say this as a curator who worked with eight Native communities, only one of which had substantial collection holdings at the NMAI (Yakama Nation). For the most part we began our dialogue speaking about ideas and trying to develop a concept (main message) and framing devices (themes); objects would then complement these ideas. Consequently, in Our Lives many of the objects used are not exquisite, one-of-a-kind collection items but part of their everyday lives (e.g., brochures, sports memorabilia, powwow ephemera).

34. I managed to include such personal statements in the introductory panels of all the Our Lives community exhibits. However, these were limited to three to four sentences.

6. The Making of *Who We Are*, Now Showing at the National Museum of the American Indian Lelawi Theater

Beverly R. Singer

Introduction and Significance

Who We Are is among the exhibitions that premiered in September 2004 during the opening of the Smithsonian National Museum of the American Indian (NMAI) in Washington DC. It is a multimedia-formatted film being shown in the distinctive circular Lelawi Theater located on the fourth floor of the museum. "Lelawi," a Lenape (Delaware) word for "in the middle," is an appropriate name for the gathering space as the film is an introduction for museum visitors to visually tour Native America and her people in the twenty-first century.

This essay describes my participation as associate producer for *Who We Are* and provides some context for many of the decisions that were made in producing the film. I also take some of the responsibility for the film's errors and omissions.

The completed film was contracted to Batwin and Robin Productions, Inc. by the National Museum of the American Indian in full consultation and with final approval of its content made by NMAI executive management and curators. B+R Productions is a consummate, in vogue, multimedia production company based in New York City that was founded by Robin Sylvestri and Linda Batwin. Batwin served as principal (director), and Elle Kamihira, a B+R staff member, served as producer; the remainder of the production team contracted by B+R included Charles Davis, director of photography, and Gregory Coyes, script writer; I was the associate producer. The executive producers, Karen Fort and Jim Volkert, represented the NMAI executive staff; the lead NMAI curatorial staff included Deputy Assistant to Collections Dr. Gerald McMaster; and curator Dr. Ann Mullen advised the project throughout. Museum staff member Machel Monenerkit served as production supervisor, coordinating schedules between Batwin and Robin and the museum exhibit development teams. Andrew Merriell, another museum exhibition designer on contract with the NMAI, also participated in helpful ways during the pre-production phase of planning the film.

By the time I joined the project several decisions had already been made by NMAI executive and curatorial staff. They and contract museum exhibition designers had made plans for a stylized theater in which to showcase a short film about Native America. The idea of preparing museum visitors is not new; however. *Who We Are* was designed to be shown as a multisensory experience, incorporating a variety of surfaces on which images are projected. The theater is a circular space with a domed ceiling, and object cases that highlight the museum's collections are placed right in the seating area. The decision to keep the film's length under ten minutes and the general themes concerning Indigenous peoples' ties to their land and their language, religion, traditional subsistence, and self-expression were in place prior to my joining the project. The NMAI had a very clear line of exhibition authority; Jim Volkert, who had a key role in all early museum exhibition decisions, stepped down from his leadership position in 2001 to take on other NMAI duties and was replaced by his deputy assistant, Karen Fort. All final approvals for each exhibition always came directly from Rick West, NMAI's director.

Having researched and studied Native American images for many years and visited museums and cultural centers featuring Native people, I knew it was important to keep in mind the Indigenous community perspective. That perspective often was lacking in other films shown in other museums, owing in part to their being produced by non-Native filmmakers who are not familiar with nor comfortable in the community about whom they are telling a story. The NMAI staff remained directly involved in the project throughout, which in the end significantly reduced any setbacks that could have occurred (i.e., they could have rejected our final film). There were scores of teleconferences about the project between Washington, DC, New York, and New Mexico, where I am based. These exchanges, along with massive e-mail correspondence, facilitated this project's being completed by committee. Although I had not worked on such a large-scale project before, it was not as daunting a task as one would think because everyone involved was working toward the goal of seeing the National Museum of the American Indian become a reality. It was a bureaucratic process, but because my contract was with Batwin and Robin as a creative specialist and a bridge to the Native community, I saw my role as the peoples' advocate, not the museum's representative.

In all honesty I think the various intended outcomes for the multimedia film to "introduce," "orient," "sensitize," "gather diverse people together to hear and see modern Native people express themselves," and "provide a base from which visitors could experience the reality of Native America" were surpassed. The production is not perfect, nor is the theater viewing space perfect; depending on where one is seated one may miss seeing all the action going on above and around the room when the object cases light up. The production is far too short, and there is practically no time to absorb the mechanics of what we the filmmakers tried to envision and expose audiences to. What one will experience watching *Who We Are* is a feeling of hope and celebration that Indigenous America is not dead but very much alive in the land and her people, who, in spite of all attempts to deprive us of our ways of living, are fully sentient beings with a purpose: to pass on the ways of our ancestors and live out our days protecting what remains of our older belief and knowledge systems.

Developing Words into Images

My participation began in early 2001 after being selected as associate producer by Batwin and Robin Productions. Initial face- to-face meetings between B+R and NMAI staff were accompanied by extensive telephone conferences regarding key decisions concerning the Indigenous themes for the film. From the outset, all were agreed that the film had to present contemporary stories that emphasized the resilience and survival of Native peoples in the face of ongoing struggles to retain their ancestral rights to land, spirituality, and subsistence practices. One of the early issues confronting us was the question of Indigenous languages. At least two months of discussion concerned the necessity of including a separate theme regarding Indigenous language survival and renewed attention to language loss. I provided extensive background and materials, including several films and videos featuring Indigenous language programs and statistical materials about current Indigenous language use by Native peoples. Among the language programs I referred to B+R for review was the Punana Leo Hawaiian immersion programs. The NMAI opted to integrate as much as possible Indigenous languages throughout the film rather than have a separate language segment. Another early decision involved the elimination of a segment addressing boarding or residential school education of Indigenous peoples, as it did not reflect the present-day portrait we set out to highlight. It was also clear that we should emphasize the traditional knowledge that older generations continue to share with their young. The process of negotiating themes and topics also took into consideration the Smithsonian Institution's position in the overall planning process.

A particular example arose as a concern about the Washington State Makah's passing on of traditional knowledge and practices involving whaling. In initial discussions, the NMAI was determined to avoid overly controversial or contested issues involving Indigenous communities. In hindsight, Barrow, Alaska, was an excellent choice for documenting the long-standing traditional whaling practiced by the Inuit, who helped to establish the International Whaling Commission early in the twentieth century.

Six themes were selected: (1) the opening greeting; (2) Indigenous peoples' relationship with the earth or homelands; (3) beliefs associated with spirituality; (4) learning from and practice of traditional knowledge related to subsistence lifeways; (5) a demonstration of Native nationhood as the right to be self-governing; and (6) the conclusion, a montage of self-expression acknowledging Indigenous accomplishment in the arts, firefighting, dance, music, literature, sports, and other professions.

Greg Coyes, a Métis filmmaker and writer, was contracted to provide a script outline and sketches focusing on the various themes to give us a sense of how the film would flow between story segments. I was assigned to research potential communities and individuals to be featured in the film stories that would go into the script we planned to submit to the NMAI by the end of 2001. During the preproduction phase, several field visits were made to potential filming locations; among the most memorable for me was to Barrow, Alaska, to collect research for the story on Inuit whaling. Other research trips were timely, such as our trip to Bear Butte, where we attended a gathering of medicine and traditional pipe carriers meeting in South Dakota. They were discussing their right to practice their vision questing at Bear Butte, a right threatened by tourism and developers around the butte, a site revered by Indigenous peoples but within the homelands of the Cheyenne, Lakota, Dakota, and Nakota. A particularly unique opportunity to research Oklahoma tribes yielded our decision to focus on the Muscogee Creek Nation's sovereignty and government. We visited the Osage Nation headquarters in Pawhuska and the Comanche Nation in Lawton and met with the leaders of each, and in many cases with cultural preservation officers. Perhaps the deciding factor favoring the Muscogee Creek was the enthusiasm and passion with which they told us their story of how they reestablished their tribal government after being relocated to Oklahoma Territory following the Trail of Tears from Alabama and Georgia in the 1830s.

It needs to be said that my role in contacting various communities to schedule field visits in the preproduction phase of the project was most informative, as it was NMAI policy to work directly with the official representative body of any Indigenous or reservation community. Letters of introduction followed by several phone calls often led to the desired outcome of scheduling field site visits to discuss our interest in the community as a potential film location for the NMAI's "orientation film to Native America."

From the start of my participation to the end of my work on this project, it was always referred to as the "preparation theater" film. Museum planners viewed the "prep theater" as the gathering place to prepare visitors to shed their preconceived ideas of "Indians" by immersing them in a full-bodied experience of contemporary Indigenous life.

In November 2001, we (the B+R team) made a PowerPoint presentation to the NMAI of the full script, with visual samples of how the film would play in the prep theater. Rick West, the NMAI's director, received a private screening of our final script proposal and in his most efficient style indicated his confidence in our work. Pending a complete review of the script, B+R would be considered for producing the film by submitting their bid along with other production companies, according to Smithsonian (U.S. government) policy.

Batwin and Robin Productions received the NMAI contract to produce the film in 2003. A year had passed since the script had been prepared, and in January 2003 my role as associate producer was reactivated, and I began making contact with each community where we planned to film on location and collect interviews. The intensity of jump-starting production also meant that a director of photography with underwater film skills had to be found, as we were now planning to film a whale hunt in Barrow.

Indigenous filmmakers were sought for the position of director of photography, but none had underwater filming expertise or the range of production experience and equipment required to shoot digital beta video and 35mm film. Charles "Chuck" Davis was hired as director of photography, along with his long-time assistant Hector Ortega, who devised a fish-eye lens for shooting images for the theater dome. Indigenous filmmakers based in the communities where we planned to film were commissioned to collect additional footage for the project; in most cases, they also served as location managers during our field location filming, and local production assistance was also provided at each location. One of the issues the NMAI had to grapple with was the ownership rights to commissioned footage taken by community filmmakers. The issue was resolved by allowing the filmmakers to retain their rights to footage that did not end up in the film.

We began our location filming in Barrow, Alaska, and our first test was the weather. As Percy Nusingingwa says in the film, "It's really quite something to live out here on the ice for nine months out of the year." Barrow is one of the largest Inuit villages, with about four thousand residents who live on the edge of the Artic Ocean. The selection of Barrow for filming was strongly recommended by Jim Volkert of the NMAI executive staff, who had recently visited Barrow. It was an excellent choice for the production, and the entire community of whalers and whaling wives welcomed our interest in filming their ages old dependence on whaling as a traditional source of food. Whale meat cannot be sold commercially, and so it remains a staple of the Inuit diet in spite of the fact that prepackaged frozen beef and chicken are flown into Barrow from the south and sold in the local supermarkets. The Inuit prefer their traditional seal, whale, and caribou.

Two separate filming location trips were made owing to seasonal inaccessibility. The first filming trip to Barrow was in late April 2003. We had received the heartbreaking news that the Whaling Captains Association had denied our application as well as all requests for permission to film whaling crews in the water during whaling season. Their decision was based on their concern for safety, as the ice depths along the Artic coast where the whaling camps are set up have decreased due to the overall warming trends in the Artic. However, we were allowed to visit one of the whaling camps where one of the crews had killed a bowhead whale. The excitement of the news traveled quickly throughout the community, and we were able to film the whale meat being transported back to the village by gas-powered snowmobiles (which the Inuit call "snow machines"). Our production coordinator in Barrow was a young videographer named John Nusingingwa. His assistance was invaluable to the filming in Barrow, and we were able to use his footage for scenes that we could not film, including close-ups of the whale being butchered and women sewing the sealskins used to make a sealskin boat.

The second location filming trip to Barrow was taken by Kamihira, Davis, and Ortega, at which time they were able to film underwater and collect much needed images to complement the above-water footage. One of the incredible stories that was shared with us but that did not fit into the NMAI film was told to us by John Nusingingwa about his father, Percy, who refused to follow the "outsider" rules imposed on the Inuit's whale hunting. Apparently Percy killed a whale out of the officially sanctioned hunting season and was fined and sent to jail for breaking the rules; he said he did so to prove that the Inuit had the right to hunt in their traditional seasons and thereby suffered the consequences to make his stand.

Our next filming site was at Pipestone, Minnesota, in May 2003. Pipestone is the location of one of the first sites to be quarried for the red clay hardened stone used by Indigenous people to carve into pipes. The quarry was considered a place of peace among those who traveled there to collect the stone considered sacred for pipe making. The quarry is under the jurisdiction of the National Park Service, which manages the park where Native people continue to quarry the stone and make pipes for both commercial and ceremonial purposes. In our initial film research trips we had met with and decided to feature a young Dakota man named Travis Erickson, who grew up quarrying at the site with his family and is a pipe maker. His unassuming approach to his work and life allowed the film to examine a more personal statement of spirituality; as he explains in the film, his life's purpose is to continue quarry pipestone to make pipes.

From Pipestone we traveled west to South Dakota to interview two brothers, Alan and Wilbur Flying By, from the Standing Rock Reservation. Alan was our host, though we were not able to include his personal and sometimes controversial work involving horse therapy to keep youth in his community involved in positive activities. The Flying Bys gave us extraordinary interview footage about their knowledge of Lakota beliefs taught to them by their father, who had professionally recorded many of his stories in songs. We left the Standing Rock Reservation and traveled to the Black Hills, where we received permission to film the buffalo herd, after which we relocated to Bear Butte State Park, where we interviewed individual Lakota about the significance of Bear Butte. In preparing for this section, many individuals were suggested as good spokespeople, and I drove from Rapid City to the community of Kyle on the Pine Ridge Reservation, some ninety miles each way, to pick up one of our interviewees and return him home in one day. The following day we drove back to Pine Ridge to film at KILI Radio Station, located near Wounded Knee.

A key lesson I learned in this process of establishing contacts with individual Native people concerns their understanding and perception of what filmmakers want from them and then securing written permission to use their images. In trying to establish the significance of Bear Butte as a sacred site for Indigenous peoples, it would have been inappropriate and not essential for us to have filmed any part of a ceremony or ritual practice to make the point in the film that certain spaces are considered spiritual because of the rituals Indigenous people conduct or honor there. It was always my intention to allow the people to speak their truth and share their beliefs about the value of particular places so as to respect their wish to keep those places protected.

The primary production crew—Elle Kamihira, Chuck Davis, Hector

Ortega, and I—left the Black Hills and traveled to Vancouver, British Columbia. Our next film location was Haida Gwaii, also known as the Queen Charlotte Islands, located about an hour and half off the coast of Vancouver. This location was chosen to present the people born from the ocean, the Haida Nation. We were fortunate to visit a natural wonder and cultural treasure when we flew to the southern tip of the island and filmed on location at Gwaii Haanas, a protected area that epitomizes the rugged beauty and ecological character of the Pacific Coast. It contains thousands of years of Haida culture, including hundred-year-old mortuary totem poles that remain standing in the ancestral Haida village of SGang Gwaay Llnagaay, named a World Heritage Site by UNESCO in 1981. Haida Gwaii Watchmen are individual members of the Haida Nation who serve as cultural emissaries and preservation officers at the site. The title of the film *Who We Are* was inspired by the voice of Roberta, one of the Watchmen, who says, "Haida Gwaii is who I am." Film viewers see images of sea lions, white waves hitting rocks, blue skies, and sea kelp dancing on the ocean waters. We also filmed at Masset and Skidegate, two contemporary Haida communities located on the Queen Charlotte Islands. I interviewed Haida Nation President Gujaaw, who is heard in the film saying, "We're not living out an ancient fantasy." The present-day lives of Haida require commitment to remaining on the island and protecting what remains of their seafaring lifeways. Additional Haida communities are located on Prince of Wales Island and in southeast Alaska.

Our production coordinators at Haida Gwaii were Maryann Jones (Haida) and Jeff Bear (Mi'kmaq). The production schedule required numerous set-ups and permission processes, which they facilitated to a degree; however, I sought direct permission from one of the totem carvers to film a totem he had carved in the 1980s, in addition to the clan family for whom the totem was commissioned, whose approval we also needed. It seemed the smaller the detail in matters of protocol throughout filming this project, the greater the cooperation.

The location filming continued in Oklahoma, where our production

coordinators Lily Shangreaux (Lakota) and Dan Bigbee (Comanche) awaited our arrival. The story we traveled to film in Oklahoma was the history of
self-government of the Muscogee Creek Nation. The filming in Oklahoma
was easier on the production team overall, with the Muscogee Creek Nation
well prepared in advance of our visit. I had made two research trips pri-
or to filming and received complete cooperation. The staff of the Creek
Council House Museum in the township of Okmulgee, Oklahoma, was
especially forthcoming with assistance during our location filming. Joyce
Bear, cultural preservation officer for the Nation, was instrumental in providing the background of the Muscogee Creek and in the film speaks eloquently about their history as ancestors of the Mississippian mound culture that flourished tens of thousands of years ago. The Muscogee Creek
story, and the stories of all the Native nations relocated to Oklahoma, are
profound indicators of the determination of Indigenous people to rebuild
themselves after great losses and to name their new towns after their
original homeland towns which were stolen from them. Okmulgee is
only one example; it was named for the original Creek village and mound
site of Ocmulgee, located near Macon, Georgia. It should be noted that
Joyce Bear and the Muscogee Creek Nation Cultural Preservation Office
in Oklahoma collaborate for interpretation and with projects sponsored
by the Ocmulgee National Monument operated by the U.S. National Park
Service in Georgia.

Two additional filming locations were to the Hopi Reservation in Arizona
and Mexico City. The locations were as different as night and day: one in
the middle of desert mesas, with sometimes only the clouds to commune
with, and one in Mexico City, with its millions of people and activity twenty-four hours a day. Victor Masayesva Jr. (Hopi) served as our production
coordinator, and with permission from the Hopi Cultural Preservation
Office we filmed at the Sipaulovi Village on the Second Mesa at Hopi and
interviewed Harlan Nakala, First Mesa *kikmongwi* (village leader), and his
assistant, Ron Lewis. The visit to Hopi provided much needed grounding
for the production. The quality of life at Hopi is effectively presented in

the footage provided by Masayesva of a family working together during the planting and harvesting of their subsistence corn.

Filming on location in Mexico City involved high security, required by our production coordinator, who regularly works for Hollywood productions. Her advice and counsel were useful, although the crew were mildly tickled to have been each assigned a bodyguard the entire day we filmed in the Zocalo of Mexico City. The highlight of filming in Mexico was at the pyramids of Teotihuacan, located outside of the city. We received permission to film after the park closed, which gave our small crew the entire run of the place. We remained at Teotihuacan until close to midnight. I walked down the Avenue of the Dead in the night and climbed the Pyramid of the Moon by myself late in the afternoon to see the 360-degree view of the surrounding mountains, which are the same shape as the pyramids. What was most apparent to me was the absence of any spiritual energy, as though the ancients had cleansed the place prior to leaving. I interviewed an Indigenous educator of Papantla heritage and learned that the Indigenous of Mexico are typically more concerned with the daily struggle to survive. So much of their amazing ancestral civilization and history have been co-opted for profit from tourism, and so little of the real Indigenous history is documented, which is why he is working to promote Indigenous language programs among his people in the Mexican State of Veracruz, where he is from and where he plans to return one day.

I did not travel to the other two filming locations of Kejimkujik National Park in Nova Scotia, in the homeland of the Mi'kmaq, and Lake Titicaca, homeland of the Aymara in Bolivia. The funds were dwindling at this point in the production schedule, and there were no full interviews to conduct. Key footage of the land and environments was the main reason for filming at these locations.

This extraordinary production was very expensive. I do not know the cost of the entire film production. The quality of the finished film speaks to the expertise and planning by the production teams at the NMAI and Batwin and Robin Productions. In my opinion, it is a well-crafted, visually impressive model that allows the voice of the land, her people, and the sanctity of life to breathe and share our Indigenous wealth. It is my hope that those who travel to Washington, DC will stop by the National Museum of the American Indian and experience Indigenous America, now showing in the Lelawi Theater.

Concluding a Project

As one enters the darkened theater, it is not immediately apparent how thoroughly the theater has been designed to make the viewing of the film a more engaging experience. The seating is relatively low to the floor, and the seats are stone bench tiers in a circle, directing the gaze to the center space. In the center are four plain tapestry panels hanging at eye level on four posts. The ceiling is a forty-foot dome filled with deep blue light. Also in the theater are object cases placed within the seating area that light up objects chosen by the curators from the communities appearing the film. The theater has seating for up to 125 but remains intimate.

The theater space was designed with "the spirit in the details" well in advance of the film production as such. When I began work on planning the film with B+R Productions early in 2001, we based the film on the design, which called for multiple projection spaces: the domed ceiling, the four center screens, and underneath the screens a transparent rock shape on which additional images are projected. Métis fiddling was selected as the welcome music for the Lelawi Theater. I suggested and would have preferred the quiet picking of a guitar solo by Keith Secola from his INDN Cars debut recording of "Wassonade."

The theater goes black and a heartbeat begins as the rock becomes illuminated. On the center screens appears the horizon along a mesa in which lightning strikes. Just as thunder cuts to rain droplets on the ground, a male voice begins speaking in English and is followed by Indigenous tongues saying, "Mother Earth rolls and turns towards the sun, the waters flow, life force connecting us all. Let us bring our minds together to give thanks to all these gifts that nurture us and sustain us. Let us bring our minds together as we acknowledge our connection to all life. Let us bring our minds together to greet each other as human beings."

As I watched the production with an audience during the museum's opening week celebration in September 2004, all the energies that went into creating it—the tables of schedules, the view of over twenty whales as I flew from Queen Charlotte City to Skedans at the southern tip of Haida Gwaii, my conversations with people such as Percy Nusingingwa in Barrow—came through in this exhibition that breathes a life force originating from Native people everywhere.

Conversation 3
Interpretations and Response

7. Gym Shoes, Maps, and Passports, Oh My!

Creating Community or Creating Chaos at the National Museum of the American Indian?

Elizabeth Archuleta

> For those of you accustomed to a structure that moves from point A to point B to point C, this presentation may be somewhat difficult to follow because the structure of Pueblo expression resembles something like a spider's web—with many little threads radiating from a center, criss-crossing each other. As with the web, the structure will emerge as it is made and you must simply listen and trust, as the Pueblo people do, that meaning will be made.
>
> —Leslie Marmon Silko

To better understand a perspective or worldview that is different from ours, we should step outside of our lives and enter the lives of people or groups who are different from us. Literature allows us to do this, because writers create for their readers worlds within texts. Yet literature is not completely imaginative. Writers are born into families and communities with whom they have interacted and from whom they have learned about the world, meaning that writers' works express opinions, beliefs, and values that can reflect worldviews and experiences different from ours. American Indian literature is popular for what it can teach mainstream Americans about groups of people often little known to them, and like literature, museums are places where mainstream Americans have learned about American Indians. In fact, museums resemble literature in many ways. First, museum displays are texts that allow us to "read" about different groups, such as the Indigenous peoples represented in the National Museum of the American Indian (NMAI). Second, like literature, museums have often perpetuated American Indian imagery and stereotypes that justify American Indians' disadvantages. Museums have also perpetuated histories that ignore the violence of conquest and that have converted theft and violence into a heroic narrative of struggle to tame the wilderness.[1] Like literature, the NMAI displays have the potential to touch something in us and give us something with which to connect, which is why we can "read," analyze, and interpret responses to the museum as well as its exhibits and displays using the tools of rhetorical and literary analysis. As with a work of literature, we can question, interpret, and challenge the meaning of museum displays, because they present imaginative worlds "written" both visually and textually within a particular time and place, recording curators' opinions, beliefs, and values. Finally, literature as well as museums such as the NMAI, dedicated to the voices and memories of subjugated or marginalized groups and their experiences offer perspectives and versions of history that vary from the dominant culture. Indigenous peoples' memories and oral histories in the NMAI displays are records of events that challenge dominant history by disputing or contesting the official version of events.

Because the NMAI, like American Indian literature, challenges official history, it represents a social, historical, and political world outside the "text." It creates arguments about the world in which Indigenous peoples have lived and continue to live. Just as authors do, NMAI museum curators make claims about the "truth" of the world, and their claims are based on personal experiences, including encounters with families, community leaders, and government authorities. American Indian authors and NMAI curators form connections between the texts they "write," the world around them, and external conditions. Because NMAI narratives contain stories mostly unfamiliar to mainstream Americans, the stories they do tell teach us about American Indians' subjugated knowledge. The dominant culture has suppressed American Indians' knowledge because it often questions and challenges the legitimacy of the United

States, but it typically does so in ways that are hard to detect, especially if one is unused to "reading" or hearing the voices of American Indians. Because all texts are open to various interpretations, one needs to construct meaning even if one is "reading" American Indians or museum displays, and this essay begins by analyzing non-Indian interpretations of American Indians as well as the NMAI. Several strategies exist for disqualifying subjugated knowledge, and I highlight some of these strategies that are evident in newspaper reports and two museum reviews about the First Americans Festival and the museum's grand opening. I end by offering another interpretation by an Indigenous scholar, myself, who found very different meanings in the NMAI as "text" through a reading of several items: beaded sneakers, information on a Kuna Yala mapping project, the Yakama Nation's Land Enterprise and Closed Area, Central America's Indigenous peoples, and a Haudenosaunee passport.

A Non-Indian "Reading" of American Indians

One strategy the dominant culture has used to disqualify Indigenous knowledge is to question the authenticity of the community that remembers. The use of this strategy becomes evident in reports about Indigenous peoples attending a celebration that accompanied the NMAI's grand opening. For the September 2004 First Americans Festival, *Washington Post* journalists attempted to convey what they observed when thousands of Indigenous peoples converged on the Mall of the nation's capital to celebrate the museum's grand opening. Newspaper articles on the First Americans Festival tended to be positive, undoubtedly because "real" Indians in bright colors, beads, buckskin, and feathers delighted reporters.[2] Nevertheless, journalists mulled over items seemingly out of place. For instance, Hank Stuever expressed his surprise at seeing an Indian in full regalia with a cell phone, describing the image as "almost anachronistic."[3] The image amused Stuever, a response he rationalized by referring to his preconceived, stereotypical notions about Indians: "A non-Indian couldn't be blamed for delighting in the banal details that make today's

Indians seem less mythological and quite real." Stuever's response illustrates the distinctive associations non-Indians have attached to "Indians," transforming them into unreal mythological objects whose lives have remained static and untainted by the modern world and technology. Indian families pushing high-end strollers, drinking Pepsi, and not appearing "classically Indian" entertained a reporter who had expected to experience cultural difference in romantic and mythological terms. When he experienced something vastly different from this, he appeared to question whether Indians carrying cell phones or pushing strollers were really "authentic" Indians.

Washington Post Reviews of the NMAI

While coverage of the First Americans Festival tended to be congenial, two Washington Post reviews on the museum, which opened in conjunction with the festival, were more hostile and angry. An analysis of the discourse both reviews contain highlights beliefs that unite them across an ideological spectrum and allows us to better understand the reviewers' choice of words as they describe what they see and how they depict Indians and the museum. Deconstructing their language hints at the general public's expectation of national museums, which the reviewers imply should be (a) repositories for objects that experts have identified as culturally significant and displayed in an unbiased manner, (b) visual representations of other cultures with labels and factual information that allow objects to "speak for themselves," or (c) exhibits that educate the public through "scientifically" accurate displays constructed by art historians or anthropologists. Their language also points to the public's expectation of Indigenous peoples. Analyzing the reviewers' language tells us more about non-Indians and why many tend to more easily accept mythological and less real images and interpretations that are familiar, easy to understand, and, most of all, noncontroversial than they do real Indians. As a marketplace of ideas and public discourse, the NMAI became, for two reviewers, a "symbolic battleground for underlying questions of community, citizenship, and identity . . . defined by entrenched 'us-versus-them' positions."[4]

In addition to strategies that disqualify Indigenous knowledge by questioning the authenticity of the community that remembers, other strategies include dismissing memories that appear tainted by politics and undercutting the legitimacy of its knowledge claims. Chon Noriega argues that "minority" issues remain marginalized rather than perceived "as an integral part of national categories and debates," making Indigenous peoples' concerns and problems appear "as an unsettling set of outside demands." A majority of the dominant culture wants national museums to be homogeneous and noncontroversial entities rather than places where various groups might use space differently, cater to different audiences, or exhibit alternative aesthetic positions.[5] Noriega contends that the public debates museums generate remain disputes between "us" and "them," and the hostile reviews of the NMAI resemble the fictive statement he creates to illuminate opinions on one side of the debate: "The barbarians are at the gate with their multicultural demand. We must tolerate their necessary inclusion, but at the same time their work is different—it is politically correct, identity-oriented, and, as an aesthetic matter, merely illustrative. In some ways, it is not really art as we have come to know art, . . . and, hence, it is work that cannot sustain a close reading."

Marc Fisher and Paul Richard from the Washington Post position themselves as gatekeepers against the "barbarians" who are waiting to invade "our" institutions of knowledge and confuse "our" notions of what national museums and American Indians should be.

While some form of interpretation in museums always takes place, whether through instructive labels, gallery handouts, catalogues, recorded tours, docent talks, lectures, films, and symposia, NMAI community curators took a different approach, an Indigenous approach to educating the public. Yet, rather than take the time to learn about the way Indigenous peoples disseminate knowledge, Fisher and Richard expressed irritation or frustration at the cognitive dissonance they experienced once inside the museum. Their discomfort led them to rely on another strategy designed to disqualify Indigenous knowledge, undercutting the legitimacy of its knowledge claims. Fisher complained that the NMAI's appeal was, for him, only "skin deep."[6] He described the museum as "an exercise in intellectual timidity and a sorry abrogation of the Smithsonian's obligation to explore America's history and culture," not considering that Indigenous peoples have typically been left out of this history and culture. He warns potential visitors that, once inside, they will be inundated with "repetitive stories of survival" and "of how tribal customs and rituals are nourished today," all of which he describes as "a painfully narrow prism through which to view American Indians" in museums. Fisher expected to see displays that depicted "the clash between foreign colonists and the native people they found here." He wanted the exhibits "to trace Indians' evolution from centuries of life alone on this land to their place in reservations and among the rest of us today." In other words, Fisher wanted stories from American Indians' "pre-history" that have already been told, ad nauseam, by museums as well as history textbooks and popular culture. He wanted a familiar story, the story of colonists who overpowered and then claimed and took over Indians' land, situated them on reservations, and set aside a place for them "among the rest of us." He wanted his Indians to remain uncomplicated and unfettered by celebrations of survival that beg the question for museum-goers: Why are survival stories cause for celebration when Indians, even those on reservations, continue to live "among the rest of us" in the United States? What Fisher did not see is that many NMAI exhibits did present the story he wanted, but they did so in a way he did not comprehend.

Fisher again relies on the strategy that dismisses memories that appear politically tainted when he admonishes the Smithsonian for "let[ting] the Indians present themselves as they wish to be seen," hinting at an irresponsible decision that led to what he deems was the NMAI's failure to provide visitors with the tools they need to "judge the Indians' version of their story." According to Fisher, Indians are not qualified to create comprehensible museum displays. He positions the Smithsonian as an institution filled with authority figures whose expertise surpasses that of the Indians, who presumably lack the skills or knowledge to represent themselves in a coherent or even appealing manner. Rather, he implies, someone else could have better presented "the Indians" than the Indians presented themselves. His use of "they" and "us" signals the distinction he makes between Indians and non-Indians; he believes the latter have more authority or knowledge to interpret and display Indians in a way that will allow museum-goers to better judge "their" stories against "ours," as if exhibits in the NMAI are competing against stories other museums tell. Fisher concludes, "The museum feels like a trade show in which each group of Indians gets space to sell its founding myth and favorite anecdotes of survival. Each room is a sales booth of its own, separate, out of context, gathered in a museum that adds to the balkanization of a society that seems ever more ashamed of the unity and purpose that sustained it over two centuries."

While many Indigenous communities have used the marketplace to help maintain their heritage, Fisher connects the NMAI communities to capitalism in a way that sullies and devalues how each represents itself and what they choose to display. He suggests that their exhibits are selling problematic creations, which he is not willing to "buy." What he wanted to see were depictions of homogeneous "Indian" communities whose stories meld into, privilege, and center the larger story of the United States and its Indians from popular culture and Western knowledge. His charge of balkanization points to his narrow view of the American Indian, defining "American" as synonymous with the United States and ignoring Indigenous peoples in Canada, Mexico, Central America, and South America with distinct cultures and histories. The museum does not present just one nation's "founding myth" or "anecdote of survival." Rather, it allots the multiple Indigenous groups of the Americas a separate space to tell their own stories in their own way. This obviously irritated Fisher, who wanted a display of "United States Indians," speaking in one voice and with one purpose and reflecting an uncontentious history from the past two hundred years. What he wanted was a museum with exhibits that make the United States its core of influence and center of experience.

Another biased yet more hostile *Washington Post* review came from Paul Richard, who brought similar expectations to his assessment of the NMAI and Indians, but unlike Fisher, Richard moves from critiquing the NMAI to engaging in a diatribe over Indian identity.[7] Richard's review began by criticizing curators for exhibits he found confusing, unclearly marked, and seemingly contradictory. He compares his failure to understand the exhibits with the Puritans' failure to make sense of the Indians they encountered nearly four hundred years ago. Like the Puritans who felt stymied, confused, and unable to "explain" or account for the Indians, Richard also feels baffled and unable to understand the Indians he encountered in the museum. His professed ignorance and confusion demonstrate how little some have learned about the peoples whose lands they now occupy. As a result of his bewilderment, Richard cautions potential visitors, "The new museum . . . is better from the outside than it is from the in," a statement hinting at the way he apparently "knows" Indians, which is superficially. Richard's anger puzzled me and left me wondering how my perception of the museum would differ. When I attended the museum later that day, I attempted to make sense of his review by contrasting his descriptions, opinions, and questions with my own observations.

Annoyed that the museum's Indians elude classification, Richard employs the same strategies Fisher uses to disqualify Indigenous knowledge: he questions the authenticity of the communities that remember, he dismisses memories that appear tainted by "politics," and he undercuts the legitimacy of Indigenous peoples' knowledge claims. Richard begins by charging curators with presenting an anomalous claim to museumgoers: "Indians are all different; overarching Indianness makes them all alike." Exasperated at this perceived inconsistency, he angrily asks and then answers his own rhetorical question: "Well, which is it? The museum can't make up its mind." Indigenous peoples are all different, but their experience makes them alike in many ways. Their shared experiences connect them historically, cognitively, and spiritually in ways that resist uncomplicated classification or codification by appearance, blood quantum, or CDIB number.

Yet, just as Stuever seemingly wants Indians to remain familiar, untouched by time and without cell phones or strollers, Richard also wants his Indians easily identified and uncomplicated. He asks, "What is this Indianness? Well, according to your CDIB (Certificate of Degree of Indian Blood issued by the Bureau of Indian Affairs), it comes with your genes; you inherit it. A thousand cultures share it. Indianness exists in people now alive and those dead 12,000 years. It is ineffably mysterious. No one can describe it except in generalities."

He acknowledges Indigenous peoples' diversity represented in the museum, but he refuses to accept that Indianness also encompasses heritage, history, and experience, all of which contribute to a larger and more contemporary sense of self. The apparent incongruity between a historical, biological, and contemporary Indian identity leads Richard to conceive of Indianness in superficial ways: "Indianness is not just vague. It also is so elastic you can stretch it to cover Inuit walrus hunters, Mohawk skyscraper constructors, public-information specialists, plumed Aztec kings, Mississippi mound-builders, political activists, filmmakers, Navajo codetalkers, surfing Hawaiians, art professors, bus drivers and all the other individuals that the Indian Museum claims to represent."

Richard's offhand rejection of all these individuals as Indian is his way of exercising rhetorical power and domination over what it means to be Indigenous. When someone takes on the position of defining another group of people, he or she is attempting to exercise control over them. Those with the power to represent, deliberately or unconsciously "reinvent" people to better serve their own needs. Richard's images of American Indians are a case in point. His descriptions and protestations about who is or is not Indian reveal as much about him and the dominant culture's intellectual and political landscape as they reveal about American Indians.

For NMAI curators, Indianness is more than blood and politics; it is about being human, which means one is respectful, exercises responsibility, and believes in reciprocity, among a host of other values. Indigenous peoples see themselves as distinct, and many exercise that uniqueness in creative ways. Mohawk construction workers celebrate their Indianness when they adorn their hardhats with traditional turtle and buffalo images or with images from popular culture, such as Betty Boop.[8] Rejecting the idea that Indian identity is fluid enough to encompass "Inuit walrus hunters, Mohawk skyscraper constructors, public-information specialists, plumed Aztec kings, Mississippi mound-builders, political activists, filmmakers, Navajo code-talkers, surfing Hawaiians, art professors, [and] bus drivers," Richard proclaims, "I don't buy it. To be accepted officially as a Nez Perce, according to Title Six, the Enrollment Ordinance, you need at least one-fourth Nez Perce blood. What about the other three-quarters?" For Richard, "real" Indians include only those from federally recognized tribes or those who have received "your CDIB" card, as he calls it. He bases Indianness strictly on blood quantum, which grossly simplifies the complexities of Indigenous identity.

Richard's reaction to Indian identity and notions of Indianness demonstrates the complicated task of distinguishing between the legal, biological, and cultural definitions Indians use to understand who they are as peoples who belong to distinct and unique tribal nations. Not aware of these complexities, Richard sarcastically charges Indians with equating blood, culture, and identity as he does: "The notion that one's spirit, one's values, one's identity, arrives automatically with whatever blood-percentage defines you as an Indian smacks too much of octoroons and pass laws in South Africa and sewn-on Stars of David." Clearly, Richard's confusion about Indianness carries across many issues (from NMAI exhibits to blood quantum) and undoubtedly stems from an ignorance that leads to a misreading of the museum and the communities that created the exhibits. I agree with Richard that most of the exhibits resist easy classification, but the displays reflect an overarching Indigenous perspective that he failed to see.

An Indigenous Reading of the NMAI

After reading Fisher's and Richards's reviews, I was surprised at what I found in my visit to the museum. I saw Indigenous "self-portraits" that both mediate popular stereotypes, such as those held by these journalists, as well as images that respond to the general tendency to imagine Indians always at the periphery (yes, Indians do use cell phones and high-end strollers and drink soda). But more significantly, I saw museum exhibits presenting multiple stories structured like the spider web that Silko uses in the epigraph to explain the process of Pueblo storytelling. Rather than structure the exhibits in a way that guides visitors and "teaches" them about Indians, leading them from point A to point B to point C, museum curators structured their displays like the "many little threads" of a spider web, each strand adding to the larger picture, radiating out from the center that is the NMAI. This method of organization requires visitors to set aside notions they previously held about museums and Indians, "listen" to the stories being told in the exhibits, and trust that meaning will be made if they become involved as participants in the storytelling process.

Indigenous peoples throughout the world are connected through shared histories and understandings, so instead of creating objective models of reality displayed for the public's edification, many twentieth-century museums are creating space as forums for debating the past and giving voice to the historically silenced. Nevertheless, having grown accustomed to museums' authoritative role in defining perception, Fisher and Richard expect to remain passive observers at the NMAI rather than active participants, engaging in the process of reading and interpreting museum exhibits. They entered the NMAI expecting curators to have displayed and interpreted the exhibits for the public. Fisher criticizes the museum for failing to offer "any science or sociological theories" that would clarify what he saw. In similar fashion, Richard proclaims the exhibits to be "disheartening" due to unbalanced installations that lack explanation or theories similar to those that Fisher had desired. Moreover, Richard encounters and describes exhibits that appear chaotic and space that is either too sparse or too cramped and filled with a mixture of "totem poles and T-shirts, headdresses and masks, toys and woven baskets, projectile points and gym shoes," which he describes as "all stirred decoratively together in no important order that the viewer can discern." In his description of individual items, it becomes clear that Richard fails to appreciate that the key to comprehending the larger story contained within this seemingly random collection lies in the visitor's ability to connect the individual stories in each display by understanding their relationship across all of the exhibits.

The NMAI's decision to challenge traditional museum modes of exhibition is political, because the outcome confronts stereotypes created by museums and other knowledge-producing institutions. More often than not, Indigenous peoples have not recognized themselves in traditional museum exhibits because the displays have overlooked or concealed their realities, experiences, and worldviews. The NMAI should be read as a testament to Indians' ability to adapt and change yet remain true to the core values of their respective nations. Achieving museological liberation and working against established structures, practices, and images by substituting them with Indigenous models is a decision that has the potential to destabilize and dislocate a majority audience, as evidenced by Fisher's and Richard's responses. Had he looked more closely, Richard would have seen that even the artwork to which he refers disparagingly as "gym shoes" contains multiple stories rather than stereotypes or romantic images of Kiowa peoples. When read as a whole, the NMAI's larger claim, as evidenced in individual exhibits such as the beaded sneakers, the Kuna Yala's mapping project, the Yakama Nation's

Land Enterprise and Closed Area, and the Haudenosaunee's passport, is that Indigenous communities are heirs to their peoples' historical memories. Moreover, their exhibits establish their communities' historical and cultural continuity.

Teri Greeves's Beaded Sneakers

Because stereotypes and romantic or mythological imagery obscure the reality of Indigenous peoples' lives, NMAI curators had the courage and vision to transform the strictures that Western museums have established and situate Indigenous stories in exhibits that intermingle their experiences of cultural persistence and change. The gym shoes narrate such a story of change and adaptation. As she explains it, Kiowa artist Teri Greeves tells stories through beaded sneakers in order to educate others about the history and values of her people and to bring balance into the world.[9] Her beaded sneakers, including those entitled *We Gave Two Horses for Our Son, Gourd Dance*, and *Grandma and Grandpa Raised Me at Warm Valley*, celebrate and honor significant events as well as Kiowa traditions and peoples. The red beaded sneakers in the NMAI exhibit celebrate children. The text that accompanies the shoes explains, "Traditionally Aw-Day (Favorite Children) lead the Kiowa Black Legging Society into the dance arena as preparation for tribal leadership." Greeves beaded an image of her son onto this pair of shoes to celebrate his presence as a favorite child who will one day assume a leadership role among his people.

Not only does she celebrate her family and community through her artwork, but Greeves's sneakers also challenge several popular assumptions about Indians. First, she challenges the notion that history can be passed down only through words, through oral histories or written text. Next, she challenges the notion that Indians have abandoned older ways of communicating. Greeves shares Kiowa history one bead at a time in images she creates rather than words she writes or speaks; her work resembles stories contained in pictographs. By incorporating larger histories beaded onto high-top sneakers, Greeves's work echoes Lee

Marmon's photo *White Man's Moccasins*, both of which challenge traditional images of Indians in moccasins. Like Marmon, Greeves self-consciously adapts the traditional to the contemporary, claiming a difference
between whites and Indians who wear sneakers; Greeves's beading on
the shoes illustrates this difference visually and ideologically. By beading
sneakers rather than moccasins, she signals American Indians' contact
with the West and their adoption of Western material culture, which challenges images of mythological or unreal Indians.[10] Altogether, Greeves's
beaded stories challenge the tendency to privilege text as well as Indians
untouched by time. Nevertheless, Richard refused to "hear" or "read"
her pictographic narrative when he singled out the presence of her artwork for criticism. Unfortunately, Richard interpreted everything he saw
as a hodgepodge of items unclearly marked and incoherently displayed.
Consequently, he did not "listen" well enough to make meaning out of
the stories embedded in items such as sneakers. Neither did he understand how the stories in the shoes connect with other communities' stories of historical and cultural continuity.

Reading NMAI exhibits is similar to the practice of reading and interpreting texts; readers are free to construct meaning out of the various
stories the museum tells. Storytelling is integral to Indigenous culture
and a method used to educate one's children and one's community. In her
multigenre text titled *Storyteller*, Silko claims that all of the stories need
to be told before one can create a sense of self or community because stories tell individuals who they are. Therefore, she includes in her book the
letters, photographs, family stories, oral traditions, anecdotes, gossip,
jokes, poems, and legends that make up the patchwork collection of her
family's life and their connections to land and community.[11] Resembling
this Pueblo web of stories is the NMAI's larger web of Indigenous narratives created from a patchwork or combination of texts, including totem
poles, T-shirts, woven baskets, and, yes, even gym shoes.

For political reasons, many Indigenous artists encode their work with
additional meaning through the stories inherent in their art, leaving

the task of interpretation to the viewer. Before viewers can unravel an object's political significance, however, they must first understand that Indigenous stories sometimes contain an absence that is always present, inviting the "listener" in. For example, Greeves encodes her sneakers with histories and political connotations that give the shoes added meaning, but her audience must read between the lines. They must be responsible for uncovering the histories or narratives left untold, such as the history of the Kiowa Black Legging Society represented in Greeves's beaded sneakers. Kimberly Blaeser advises listeners or readers of Indigenous stories that they have both a response-ability and a responsibility to the telling, because the story is made by storyteller and audience together.[12] The result of creating a story together, of taking responsibility for meaning making, is that there is no "truth" or ending to the story, because listeners constantly re-create and remake the stories in order to add their own truths based on their own experiences and perspectives. The narrator in Betty Louise Bell's novel *Faces in the Moon* describes this process of meaning making in Indigenous cultures: "They heard, and they taught me to hear, the truth in things not said. They listened, and they taught me to listen in the space between words."[13] The narrator learns how to listen for the unspoken and the unarticulated. She does not expect anyone to explain the story; she understands that she must make meaning for herself. By saying less rather than more, the museum's exhibits require the same kind of active participation or response-ability from their audience. Finally, the exhibits require patience to understand things not said. They require the "listener" to pull meaning out of what might appear to be blank spaces. In addition to demonstrating through their displays that their communities are heirs to historical memories as well as establishing their communities' historical and cultural continuity, NMAI curators' exhibits resemble Indigenous storytelling traditions and literary techniques in a most significant way: the exhibits tell stories that are meant to effect change, pointing to Indigenous claims that storytelling is not just for entertainment.[14] Greeves's sneakers, along with the exhibits discussed below, all speak to Indigenous peoples' survival, adaptation, ingenuity, and victory over tremendous odds while maintaining and celebrating their sense of Indianness through material culture, land, capitalism, and markers of identity.

Mapping the Comarca Kuna Yala

Space is never neutral, nor is it ever merely a backdrop in which people live out their lives; space is literally filled with ideologies and politics. For example, the District of Columbia is a city dominated by marble and granite and neoclassical styles that are reminiscent of the United States' transplanted European heritage and reminders of a government that has tried desperately to assimilate Indians and transform them into "white," unraced Americans. The NMAI's presence in space largely occupied by the federal government challenges this heritage and history and asserts Indigenous peoples' survival. Although it was built in the last available space on the National Mall, the museum now occupies the first place on the Mall facing the Capitol. For Richard, however, the politics of unnamed space is unobservable and therefore meaningless, even after an NMAI placard claims and politicizes space by naming and defining it: "Native space is land— and something more. Native space is a way of feeling, thinking, and acting. Even away from our ancestral lands, we carry our Native space with us. All of the Americas is Native space, but in the course of 500 years most of us have been displaced. Even today, indigenous people continue to be uprooted from ancestral homelands."[15]

The placard identifies the Americas not as American, Canadian, Mexican, or South American but as Native. Jolene Rickard's and Gabrielle Tayac's inscription of space is double-edged. They inscribe Native space as land that contains emotion and thought and action. But more important, they present a truth that remains unspoken: "All of the Americas is Native space." By "reading" and identifying space in the Americas as Native and space as land, Rickard and Tayac's placard embodies a historical claim. It asserts territorial possession, proclaiming what Indigenous peoples have always known: that the Americas are and will always be Indigenous Country in spite of removals, relocations, and displacements, and even in spite of being the last group invited to occupy space on the National Mall.

Other museum items that silently challenge non-Indigenous assumptions about space appear in political documents such as the Kunas' map of their homeland, the Comarca Kuna Yala. Text that accompanies the map places in historical and global context what museum-goers see: the ongoing colonization of the world's Indigenous peoples. The NMAI curators share with museum-goers some of the numerous threats that the Kunas and their homelands now face, because they "do not possess documents proving their ownership."[16] These threats include the invasion of Kuna Yala by loggers, cattle ranchers, land developers, and landless settlers from overcrowded and already developed provinces. The Pan-American Highway's scheduled completion represents another threat. In Central America, the Kunas occupy Panama's Darién region, which contains the largest section of intact rain forest. Although the region became a designated buffer zone in the 1970s, protecting the U.S. cattle industry from the hoof- and-mouth disease endemic to Colombia, it also remains the only uncompleted section of the Pan-American Highway.[17] Due to the ever-present cloud cover, maps of this region are based only on approximations.[18] Therefore, it is highly likely that engineers hired to complete the highway would have to thoroughly explore and map the region before construction can begin. The absences contained in Western maps are the histories of colonization, and outsider attempts to map the Kuna Yala would create and expand these silences.

Like space, maps are not neutral documents that contain facts and figures but images that are represented in histories, ideologies, and politics. In the past, colonial regimes named, organized, constructed, and controlled space and place through the imperialist practice of mapmaking. Maps are virtual realities that represent for the colonizers permanent and visible markers of conquest, domination, the triumph of civilization, and the subjugation of nature. Maps are also myths designed to conceal Indigenous ways of knowing and connecting with their homelands.

When the Kunas began the project of mapping their homeland, they were, at the same time, unmapping colonial space by removing these visible markers that colonial and settler societies have used to define themselves and legitimate their ongoing occupation. These markers have concealed for colonizers Kuna ways of knowing and identifying Comarca Kuna Yala. Colonial maps erased an Indigenous presence when they substituted Kuna markers with representations of their own world. In *Race, Space, and the Law*, Sherene Razack claims that although mapping enabled colonizers to legally claim and possess lands they came upon, the Indigenous act of unmapping undermines "the idea of white settler innocence (the notion that European settlers merely settled and developed the land) and . . . uncover[s] the ideologies and practices of conquest and domination."[19] The Kunas' mapping project challenges the denial of their presence on Western maps. The Kunas' map includes sites important to their traditional way of life, and their mapping project ensures that the "real" names and land use patterns for the geographic landscape include those places where they hunt, fish, cut firewood, gather medicinal plants, and pick fruit.[20] The Kuna names replace those that have been given only recently, after colonization. Ironically, the map's accuracy and detail have encouraged the Instituto Geográfico to use it to update official Republic of Panama maps.

The Kunas' Western mapmaking techniques combined with their own complex cultural cartographies signify a conscious reclamation of space in the creation of a political document that blends the traditional (their accumulated geographic knowledge) with the contemporary (the science of mapping and the legalities of ownership). The map embodies both a historical claim and a geographic assertion, transforming it into something resembling Rickard and Tayac's placard: the map asserts territorial possession. Moreover, it makes a property claim by formally delineating and authenticating Comarca Kuna Yala. In an interview, Marc

Chapin, from the Center for the Support of Native Lands, observes that the Kunas' map represents their effort to "work within the political system and through the courts of law" to legitimize their land claim. This was their reason for creating the map in the first place, so the Kunas' inclusion in the NMAI retells a story of the ongoing struggles and efforts to protect Indigenous lands. Their inclusion also signals an awareness among Indigenous peoples that struggles at the local level also occur at the global level.

The shared experience of land struggles that help define "Indianness" connects many of the museum's narratives. Other stories that echo threats to the Kunas' land as well as their reclamation of land include exhibits with stories of the Central American diaspora, Clause 231, and the Yakamas' Closed Area. The museum defines "diaspora" as displacement from one's ancestral homeland, the space where one's identity formed. Even though the 1980s civil wars displaced close to one million Indigenous people in Central America, these groups transplanted their traditions to their new homes, taking their Native spaces with them. Many of these displaced groups have ended up in the United States, but most still long to return home. While diasporas have displaced some from their lands, Western legal systems have rendered others incapable of making decisions about lands they still occupy. Brazil is one such example. Since 1934, Brazil's Constitution presumably protects and preserves for Indigenous peoples the lands they occupy. Clause 231, paragraph 1 of Brazil's 1988 Constitution defines occupation as "lands traditionally occupied by the Indians and inhabited by them on a permanent basis, used for their production activities, essential for the conservation of the environmental resources necessary for their well-being and those necessary for their physical and cultural reproduction, in accordance with their uses, customs and traditions."[21]

In spite of this outwardly liberal policy, Brazil's Civil Code "puts indigenous peoples in the same category as minors—persons 'relatively incapable of exercising certain rights.'"[22] The NMAI publicizes the struggles of Indigenous peoples in Panama, Central America, and Brazil to protect, preserve, and remain in their homelands, rendering their stories visible in a space of power, the U. S. Capitol.

The Yakama Nation Land Enterprise and Closed Area

Land struggles closer to home include Washington State's Yakama Nation, who tell a story of successful nation building. One of their NMAI display cases includes a bottle of Broken Spear pickled asparagus, a box of Chief Yakama apples, a baseball cap, a timber industry catalogue, and pictures of a warehouse and fruit orchard. At first glance they might appear to be products from the thousands of businesses that exploit Indian imagery to sell their wares, but the placards tell a different story. At a time when non-Indians believe casinos to be the only money-making venture on reservations, the Yakamas' products dispel this stereotype. In 1950, the Yakama Nation Land Enterprise was created as an institution to offset the crisis of land loss. The Enterprise is an institutional vehicle that oversees the management, control, and promotion of land repurchase and development on behalf of the Yakama Nation. In addition to increasing the reservation's land base by tens of thousands of acres, the Enterprise has also contributed to the development of agriculture, timber, and tourism industries. Moreover, in addition to selling "pears to Del Monte Corporation and Monson Fruit," the Enterprise also "developed three Yakama Nation Apple labels, and popularized its Broken Spear Pickled Asparagus," and has successfully marketed its products overseas as well. As a result of its success here and abroad, the Enterprise now "purchases between three and six million dollars worth of land every year," incorporating it into their current land base.[23]

Alongside successful nation-building efforts are efforts to preserve documents that signify a powerful claim to space and place that defines and embodies Yakama culture and identity. Clearly exhibiting pride in their economic achievements, the Yakamas also include items that serve as reminders of times very different from today, such as the original pages of an 1855 treaty that formed fourteen tribes and bands into the Yakama Nation. Indigenous peoples regard treaties as sacred documents not to be violated, a sentiment voiced in a quote from community member Carol Craig: "Back in the '60s, some non-tribal people would wonder, 'Why are Yakama people talking about these antiquated pieces of paper? They don't mean anything.' But those people didn't realize the rights the treaty guaranteed us. These rights have been reaffirmed in several different court cases over the years."

The "antiquated pieces of paper" of which Craig speaks not only represent rights, they also represent land and lives lost to westward expansion and colonialism and so are made sacred by the blood of people who sacrificed their lives to protect and preserve community and homeland. Affirming this sacred connection to land is the Closed Area, a protected and restricted land area, which forms another part of the Yakamas' NMAI exhibit. The Closed Area remains sacred because it is strictly controlled and "accessible only to tribal members, their immediate family members, and select outsiders." Created in 1954 and comprising 807,000 mostly forested acres, the Closed Area is described in the words of community member Lehigh John as a place where Yakama people can go and "pick up a piece of dirt and run it through their fingers and say, 'This is Yakama land that no one can take away from us.'" The Kuna Yala, Central America's Indigenous peoples, and the Yakamas tell just a few of the stories about land lost and land regained, interlinking a web of stories in the museum and creating shared histories that contribute to a collective sense of "Indianness."

A Haudenosaunee Passport and the
International Lacrosse Federation

Another museum item that contests received notions of legally demarcated space is the Haudenosaunee passport, whose mere existence signals a refusal to defer to the border or Western notions of citizenship by identifying Kahnawa'kehrónon as citizens of the Iroquois Confederacy.[24] The

Haudenosaunee do not define their national status in U.S. or Canadian terms. They define themselves through the Gayanashagowa, the Great Law of Peace, and the Guswentah, the Two Row Wampum, the latter being an agreement with the Dutch colonists that the Haudenosaunee have honored since the seventeenth century.[25] The Haudenosaunee interpret the wampum belt thus:

> You say that you are our Father and I am your son. We say, We will not be like Father and Son, but like Brothers. This wampum belt confirms our words. These two rows will symbolize two paths or two vessels, traveling down the same river together. One, a birch bark canoe, will be for the Indian People, their laws, their customs and their ways. The other, a ship, will be for the white people and their laws, their customs and their ways. We shall each travel the river together, side by side, but in our boat. Neither of us will make compulsory laws or interfere in the internal affairs of the other. Neither of us will try to steer the other's vessel. The agreement has been kept by the Iroquois to this date. Passports are formal documents issued by national governments to their citizens, which allow for travel abroad as well as exit and reentry into the country.[26]

The Mohawks' refusal to defer to a border diminishes the authority or legal status of an "objective" boundary or imaginary line defined and enforced by the United States and Canada. It is the Gayanashagowa and the Guswentah that define and embody the boundaries of Haudenosaunee culture, lands, and identity, and this claim extends both historically and geographically.

As a legal document, the passport also challenges Canadian and U.S. legal claims that would attempt to diminish the sovereign status of nations that make up the Iroquois Confederacy. In 1794 the Jay Treaty recognized the Haudenosaunee people's right to move freely across Canadian and U.S. borders. Nevertheless, in the twentieth century, the United States challenged this right when they arrested Paul Kanento Diabo for working in the United States. The Mohawks' NMAI exhibit includes a statement about this event, asserting that Diabo "sued the U.S., claiming his arrest violated his rights as a citizen of the Mohawk Nation under the Jay

Treaty," and concludes with the statement, "In *Diabo v. McCandless* (1927), a U.S. court ruled in his favor." The Mohawk Nation occupies a space that refuses to become "American" or "Canadian," that refuses to cross over into a status other than Mohawk. In 2001, the Mohawks' pride in maintaining and protecting their sovereign status for almost four hundred years is expressed by Laura Norton, a community member quoted in the exhibit: "In this community, we've never recognized the border. We're here because we've always been here, and we will always be here. These countries developed around us, and we kept moving back and forth across the border." Like Greeves's beaded sneakers and the Kuna's map, the Haudenosaunee passport evolved out of an oral tradition, this one contained within a wampum belt; the passport is an extension of that tradition.

Many American Indians perceive their communities as maintaining dual citizenship: they see themselves as citizens of their tribal nation as well as citizens of the United States. The exception to this is the Haudenosaunee, who have exercised their sovereignty by refusing to acknowledge U.S. or Canadian citizenship and national and international boundaries. Like the Kunas' map, the Haudenosaunee passport throws off the mantle of colonialism by disregarding what Lauren Berlant calls the "national symbolic," or the "official story about what the nation means, and how it works."[27] As the accepted version of a nation's identity, the national symbolic controls collective memory by excluding countermemories; yet the Jay Treaty, *Diabo v. McCandless*, and the Haudenosaunee passport challenge the Canadian and U.S. national symbolic. The passport also challenges Canadian and U.S. myths of national identity and sovereignty because other countries recognize the Haudenosaunees' status as a sovereign nation, evidenced by their membership in the International Lacrosse Federation, which officially welcomed the Iroquois Nationals Lacrosse Team. When the team travels outside their nation's boundaries, they carry their Haudenosaunee passports, not U.S. or Canadian passports.[28] The museum's inclusion of the Haudenosaunee passport helps visitors to understand how tribal nations continue to preserve items significant to their traditions; at the same time, the passport reflects how their lives have changed and evolved. Contained within the passport is knowledge that Indigenous peoples' lives cannot be viewed in a vacuum or in isolation from the institutions and events that have shaped them.

Conclusion

The stories told across generations interweave individual and tribal experiences to create a shared sense of Indianness, but the NMAI's negative reviews raise questions about whether a largely uninformed public understood what museum curators had worked hard to create. Because museum curators were made up of community members, it was impossible for the museum to create any kind of unified picture whose goal was to teach museum-goers about the world's Indigenous peoples. Is it the job of the NMAI to educate the ignorant, or should the museum cater to an Indigenous audience? Although it tried to do both, the goal of educating a public uninformed about the world's Indigenous peoples is too monumental a task to ask of one museum, so it is the responsibility of "readers" to take what they see and engage in their own research to learn more. This is the active exchange that takes place in Indigenous storytelling, about which Blaeser speaks in terms of response-ability. The NMAI curators appear to have wanted to invoke a sense of response-ability in their audience, making the exhibits a participatory story rather than one handed out to passive listeners. I took it upon myself to find out more about all of the exhibits discussed in this essay, because even as an Indigenous person I cannot know all the stories of struggle and victory that exist. I do not think it is the task of any museum to spoon-feed information to an audience. Museums should offer enough information that sparks our curiosity, invoking in us a sense of response-ability.

The spider creates a web strand by strand, so its beauty is not evident until the end, when the pattern materializes. Often this pattern does not become apparent until we look at each strand individually, add to the web, and add our own knowledge through our own research and active involvement. The storyteller's talent becomes apparent when the story maintains or strengthens community, and as museum-goers, we are all storytellers who must contribute. Indigenous stories have a purpose beyond entertainment; they record the details of daily existence little known beyond stereotypes and reinforced by popular culture, and they make visible the cross-fertilization that has taken place among and between Indigenous and non-Indigenous peoples. The NMAI's stories attempt to effect change, to abolish stereotypes and create lines of communication by initiating dialogue and reinforcing a sense of community even when the issues and items community curators have chosen to exhibit appear divisive, chaotic, or complex. Stories maintain a history, and the NMAI exhibits capture histories that include the United States as just one frame of reference in a more complex reality that encompasses Indigenous peoples' lives. It is our job to fit ourselves within this larger story, not wait to be told where we fit in.

Notes

1. Examples of museum displays representing histories that were ignored and sanitized or that generated controversy include the Smithsonian's Enola Gay exhibit, the National Museum of American Art's West as America exhibit, the re-creation of a slave auction at Colonial Williamsburg, various controversies surrounding the Columbus quincentenary, and tensions connected with the creation of and exhibits included in the United States Holocaust Memorial Museum.

   The Last Act, a planned exhibit at the Smithsonian's National Air and Space Museum, was to feature elements of the Enola Gay, the aircraft that dropped the atomic bomb on Hiroshima in 1945. The exhibit created a storm of controversy, as historians and veterans clashed over whether the historical or commemorative voice should predominate. The exhibit opened in modified form. The labels for The West as America: Re-interpreting Images of the Frontier, 1820-1920, at the Smithsonian's National Museum of American Art asserted new interpretations for works of art from the period of westward expansion, chiefly related to the victims of Manifest Destiny. The reenactment of an eighteenth-century slave auction at Colonial

Williamsburg, developed in response to criticism that interpretive programs there sanitized slavery, brought angry protests from the Virginia NAACP, charging that the auction was a sideshow used as entertainment. The protests were withdrawn, but the auction was discontinued. Controversy around the Florida Museum of Natural History's First Encounters, a Columbus quincentennial exhibit, centered on the negative impact that the arrival of the Europeans had on the Native American population. Protesters splashed blood on the sails of a ship reproduction. Faces of Sorrow at the United States Holocaust Memorial Museum, an exhibit of photographs that portrayed the effects of "ethnic cleansing" in the former Yugoslavia, was charged with being anti-Serbian. The controversy questioned the museum's decision to address contemporary as well as historical issues. See Australian Museum Online for a timeline of museum controversies on "Exhibitions as Contested Sites Research Project," http://amonline.net.au/amarc/contested/timeline.htm, accessed June 13, 2006.

2. "On the Mall, 'A Feast for the Eyes,'" *Washington Post*, September 22, 2004, A19; available at *Washington Post* online, http://www.washingtonpost.com/wp-dyn/articles/A39919-2004Sep21.html.

3. For photo and story, see Hank Stuever, "A Family Reunion: Opening Day on the Mall Brings Traditions into the Light of Today," *Washington Post*, September 22, 2004, C01, available at *Washington Post* online, http://www.washingtonpost.com/wp-dyn/articles/A39980-2004Sep21.html.

4. Chon Noriega, "On Museum Row: Aesthetics and the Politics of Exhibition," *Daedalus* 128, no. 3 (1999): 5.

5. This and all subsequent references from Noriega, "On Museum Row," 5-6.

6. This and all subsequent references from Marc Fisher, "Indian Museum's Appeal, Sadly, Only Skin-Deep," *Washington Post* online, http://www.washingtonpost.com/wp-dyn/articles/A36831-2004Sep20.html.

7. This and all subsequent references from Paul Richard, "Shards of Many Untold Stories: In Place of Unity, a Melange of Unconnected Objects," *Washington Post* online, http://www.washingtonpost.com/wp-dyn/articles/A36886-2004Sep20.html.

8. To see the hardhat, go to *Washington Post* online, http://www.washingtonpost.com/wp-dyn/articles/A36886-2004Sep20.html.

9. Teri Greeves, School of American Research, http://www.sarweb.org/iarc/dobkin/greeves03.htm.

10. Laura Addison, Capital City Arts Initiative, http://www.arts-initiative.org/live/neighbors/essays/laura_addison.html.

11. Leslie Marmon Silko, *Storyteller* (New York: Arcade Publishing, 1981).
12. Kimberly M. Blaeser, "Writing Voices Speaking: Native Authors and an Oral Aesthetic," in *Talking on the Page: Editing Aboriginal Oral Texts*, ed. Laura J. Murray and Keren D. Rice (Toronto: University of Toronto Press, 1999), 54.
13. Betty Louise Bell, *Faces in the Moon* (Norman: University of Oklahoma Press, 1994), 56-57.
14. Leslie Marmon Silko, *Ceremony* (New York: Viking, 1977), 2.
15. Jolene Rickard, guest curator, and Gabrielle Tayac, NMAI, 2004.
16. Kuna Yala exhibit, NMAI, 2004.
17. Mac Chapin, "Indigenous Land Use Mapping in Central American," *Yale School of Forestry and Environmental Studies*, Bulletin 98, pp. 197-98, http://www.yale.edu/environment/publications/bulletin/098pdfs/98chapin.pdf.
18. Chapin, "Indigenous Land Use," 200.
19. Sherene Razack, "Introduction," in *Race, Space, and the Law: Unmapping a White Settler Society*, ed. Sherene Razack (Toronto: Between the Lives, 2002), 5.
20. Chapin, "Indigenous Land Use" 199.
21. Brazil's Ministry of External Relations, http://www.mre.gov.br/cdbrasil/itamaraty/web/ingles/polsoc/pindig/legislac/c1988/art231/index.htm?.
22. Rickard and Tayac, NMAI guest curators.
23. "Yakama Nation Land Enterprise," Honoring Nations: 2002 honoree, The Harvard Project on American Indian Economic Development, http://www.ksg.harvard.edu/hpaied/hn/hn_2002_land.htm.
24. The Haudenosaunee, also known as the Iroquois Confederacy or Six Nations, comprise the Mohawk, Oneida, Onondaga, Cayuga, Seneca, and Tuscarora nations.
25. Information on the Haudenosaunee taken from the Haudenosaunee official website, http://sixnations.buffnet.net/Great_Law_of_Peace/.
26. http://sixnations.buffnet.net/Lessons_from_History/?article=2.
27. Lauren Berlant, *The Anatomy of a National Fantasy* (Chicago: University of Chicago Press, 1991), 11.
28. Honoring Nations: 2002 honoree: Iroquois Nationals Lacrosse, The Harvard Project on American Indian Economic Development, http://www.ksg.harvard.edu/hpaied/hn/hn_2002_lacrosse.htm.

8. "Indian Country" on the National Mall

The Mainstream Press versus the National Museum of the American Indian

Aldona Jonaitis and Janet Catherine Berlo

> For the most part, aboriginal museums probably have no interest in producing for the general public the kinds of object-focused exhibitions that non-native museums produce about aboriginal cultures. The tasteful lighting of objects, which for Western society is culture—beautiful baskets, spoons, and clothing items, for example—illuminate far more about Euro-Canadian aesthetics and values than they do about the cultural views of the people who made the objects. Such an exhibition within an aboriginal world view completely ignores the basic values and cultural principles that the object represents.
> —Deborah Doxtator, "The Implications of Canadian Nationalism for Aboriginal Cultural Authority"[1]

The National Museum of the American Indian (NMAI) opened on September 21, 2004. On that brilliant and warm Washington day, about twenty-five thousand Native people from Alaska, Hawaii, Chile, and many places in between marched in full regalia on the Mall. They celebrated the endurance of their diverse cultures and the opening of the long-awaited national museum dedicated to, and for the most part curated and directed by, Native peoples themselves. That same day, both the New York Times and the Washington Post ran reviews that were overwhelmingly negative, conveying a sense of disappointment, and even outrage. The contrast between the joy clearly manifested by the hemisphere's First Nations and the sometimes vituperative reactions to their museum by two of the most important newspapers in the country could not have been more striking.[2]

The *New York Times* decried the "studious avoidance of scholarship" behind the exhibits, the emphasis on a "warm earthy mysticism with comforting homilies behind every façade," and pronounced the museum "a self-celebratory romance."[3] The *Washington Post* pronounced its exhibits "disheartening," lacking "the glue of thought," and "a blur."[4] One of the first rules of writing a book review is to address the book that was written, and not the book one thinks the author *should* have written. The same holds true for museum reviews. As one of us (Berlo), who did not attend the opening, commented after spending just two hours in the NMAI, "This is *not* the museum that I read about in the newspapers."[5] We wondered why the reviewers seemed unwilling actually to evaluate the museum that was presented to them, choosing instead to bemoan that the museum they wanted to attend was not in evidence.

Equally striking is the apparent ignorance of the past several decades of museum critiques, a literature that has inspired many attempts to repair the damage caused by more than a century of colonialist representations of Aboriginal people. The "new museology" (which is by no means new any more) has subjected museums to intense scrutiny. Instead of uncritically accepting as "the truth" what institutions placed before their visitors, we are now more apt to question the unspoken messages behind seemingly objective representations. We now understand that neither the objects on display nor their interpretations are ever value-free, but implicitly express subjective points of view about issues such as politics, class and racial distinctions, and embodied historical and philosophical values. When it came to representing aboriginal people, museums have been forced to rethink the long unexamined trope of the "disappearing primitive." Native people complained, sometimes acerbically, about the tendency of museums to "museumify" them by putting their heritage into glass cases, communicating that Indian culture was a thing of the past and that contemporary Native people (having lost their traditions) were of no interest.[6] Moreover, North American Natives, like so many Indigenous people, resented the decades of anthropologist "experts" explaining their "traditional" cultures in books, exhibits, and the media—while ignoring their own contemporary explanations as inauthentic.

In the 1970s, Native Americans, like other marginalized groups, began demanding more equal treatment. One of many complaints they had was that anthropology, as well as the museums informed by anthropology, misrepresented Native cultures by denying them history, refusing to recognize the existence of contemporary Native culture and asserting an authoritative expertise in which non-Native explained Native culture. Responding to paradigmatic changes in anthropology, museums in the last quarter of the twentieth century began to rethink their exhibits and began demonstrating the ongoing vitality of contemporary Native life. As anthropologists strove to rid their discipline of its unintentional colonialist biases by equalizing their relationships with those they studied,[7] museums began bringing those represented into the process of creating their representations. In the late 1970s, Michael Ames, director of the Museum of Anthropology at the University of British Columbia, was one of the first to urge museums to become more democratized and to shed their colonialist mentalities by welcoming Native people into exhibit development.[8] Soon thereafter, panels on the topic of bringing "the Native voice" into museums began appearing at professional meetings of organizations such as the American Association of Museums and the American Anthropological Association. Today, it is virtually unthinkable for a museum to create an exhibit about Native people without including Native people themselves in the planning and curatorial process.

This, of course, is one reason the NMAI is so important. As Judith Ostrowitz describes in her essay on the extensive consultations that went into its creation, staff listened to large numbers of North and South American Native people describe what they wanted their museum to be.[9] There was considerable agreement among these varied groups: the museum should highlight the vitality of contemporary Native life, presenting objects not as isolated masterworks but as inseparable from life; moreover, museums should privilege the voices of Native people rather than non-Native "experts." They also did not want to dwell on the history of extermination and discrimination but instead to look positively toward the future. Ironically, it is precisely the transformation of these concepts into exhibits at the newest museum on the Mall in Washington that has infuriated so many critics.

In this essay, we discuss the NMAI in terms of contemporary museum theory and practice, particularly but not exclusively as they relate to representations of Aboriginal people. Curiously, the solipsistic reviews it received in the national press, as well as in a variety of Internet journals, actually serve to highlight the innovations presented within the walls of the NMAI. Indeed, had the reviewers devoted some time to a study of recent museological literature—which exists in abundance[10]—they would have realized that this new institution embodies new thinking about museums. With just a small measure of self-reflection, they may even have understood how deeply and unreflexively they had imposed outmoded and colonialist values upon an innovative project. This is not to say that the NMAI has no flaws, but we believe that this museum should be praised for taking risks and not being like other museums. Perhaps even more important, it should be lauded for responding to what the Indians who were consulted want—something that has never happened so completely in so large and important an institution.[11]

It is useful to state what this museum is not. It does not present a linear history of Native Americans. It does not provide in-depth anthropological displays about individual cultures, or even broad culture areas. It does not cover all the tribes of North and South America. Most important, it is not an art museum. Instead of the objective, anonymous third-person voice of the "expert," in this museum individuals tell their stories, some more fluently than others. The NMAI deliberately denies the grand narrative of Euro-American historical representation. In its place, the museum offers eloquent fragments of various realities, leaving to the history and anthropology museums the tasks of more conventional interpretations of Indian culture. For the most part (with one significant exception: the Native Modernism exhibit discussed below), it leaves to the art museums the lionization of individual artists and a scholarly exploration of their works.

The reviewers discussed in this essay clearly did not like this renegotiated identity of the American Indian. Instead, they appear to want the museum to present their notion of what "Indians" are: ecologically oriented, highly folkloric, and the victims of a painful past. In their criticisms, which can be classified into the categories of art, ethnography, history, identity, and guilt, such critics reveal their deep resistance to— and perhaps even the perceived threat to them of—the increasingly prevalent postcolonial episteme that underlies the entire NMAI project.

The Experience

The museum itself is architecturally striking. The original design, by the Canadian architect Douglas Cardinal (of Blackfoot, Métis, and German heritage), shares many features with his design for Canada's Museum of Civilization in Hull, Quebec, which opened in 1989.[12] The organic curves of the museum are a visual delight and a welcome interruption to the resolutely Euclidean geometry of most of the buildings on the Mall. Yet the undulating walls work surprisingly well with the sternly modernist East Wing of the National Gallery across the Mall and the adjacent National Air and Space Museum.

From the exterior, what impresses the most is the view as one walks from the L'Enfant Plaza metro station: the NMAI building begins to take form, and as it does, it gradually reveals the U.S. Capitol on the hill beyond. The juxtaposition of these two buildings calls to mind the vexed and often cruel relationship between the federal government and Native American tribes. The buildings appear to be in conversation about their past relationships and their present one. The power and elegance of the National Museum of the American Indian hints at a more egalitarian future—a meeting of equals. As Gyan Prakash argues, contemporary museums have the opportunity to undo past history and enact a new history in which Aboriginal people play a larger role;[13] the NMAI, in its privileged location, certainly is situated to do this.

Nevertheless, we must keep in mind curator and artist Jolene Rickard's statement that the presence of Native art in mainstream Canadian museums "represents simultaneously a colonizing act and a decolonizing act."[14] We can think of the NMAI's location from a similar perspective. Is the museum— and its Native American constituency—finally in a position of equality in relation to the dominant society, or does the closeness of the Capitol to the museum serve as yet another indication of the control the government still has over this country's Aboriginal people? Although we favor the first interpretation, one cannot assume that the presence of a Native museum signifies that a genuine era of parity has arrived.

The first sight of the museum interior is striking. As one enters, on the left is a Welcome Desk and a twenty-foot-long screen above it on which are projected scores of words meaning "welcome" in the indigenous languages of the Americas.[15] To enter the vast, open lobby, the visitor must walk around a curving, woven copper screen that partially encloses and demarcates a wooden-floored dance circle. The screen, which at its greatest height is over six feet, recalls Indigenous bark and wood splint architecture and basketry. The large-scale interlacing of sheets of copper (evocative of interlaced wooden slats) is sometimes interrupted by a delicate detail of spun copper and brass wire (evocative of twined basketry techniques). We searched in vain for a placard offering the artist's name, but there was none. It was a collaborative effort of the design team, though museum director Rick West credits Hopi weaver Ramona Sakiestewa for artistic leadership here.[16] It is one of the most elegant aspects of the museum's interior and, like many of its other features, a poetic merging of the contemporary with the traditional.

The Art of Experience

One can imagine the circular wooden-floored dance circle, or "Potomac," as it is called, resounding with drums and the circular movement of Native dancers. In early November 2004, this gathering place was the site for hands-on displays of a Native Hawaiian canoe and a Central Arctic kayak. Named with an Algonquian/Powhatan word for "where the goods are brought in," this space is conceptualized as "the very heart of the museum building, the sun of its universe."[17] In the center of the wooden dance floor is inset a small disk of red stone cut in an abstract fire design. Around the perimeter are low curved walls made of polished granite that serve as seating areas. This space was buzzing with activity the Sunday we were there. Nonetheless, it was a calm space, providing a point for restful contemplation.

More and more institutions today are accepting the philosophy, clearly articulated by Hilde Hein in her aptly titled *The Museum in Transition*, that for a museum to successfully attract and maintain a diverse audience it must change its focus from simply the presentation of objects to the production of experiences.[18] The NMAI offers the "total" museum experience, with a café and two gift shops in addition to the exhibits and performances and other public programs.[19] The Mitsitam Café is an experience in its own right; we can think of no other museum in which the cuisine supports the didactic program of the museum! Different stations provide Native-themed food from different regions. Examples include cedar-planked salmon from the Northwest Coast, quinoa salad and peanut soup from South America, buffalo chili from the Great Plains, pork pibil and chicken mole from Mexico, and maple-roasted turkey with wild rice salad from the Northern Woodlands. On both a Sunday and a Monday in November, the café was full. It will surely become one of the most popular places to dine in the Mall area.

All museums today depend on their gift shops for income, and the NMAI is no exception; two gift shops offer different kinds of goods. (Indeed, the Grand Opening press release boasted that the museum set a Smithsonian record, with more than one million dollars in sales at the two museum stores during the first week.)[20] On the second floor, the Roanoke Store sells the T-shirts, carrying bags, cards, toys, and books that museum visitors expect to find. An interesting touch is the Kwakwaka'wakw potlatch figure standing in the corner, next to shelves with woolen blankets. Here, store morphs into museum exhibit, but not inappropriately. Photographs of late nineteenth- and early twentieth-century potlatches illustrate the piles of woolen trade blankets chiefs distributed to their guests; here, reminiscent of such photos, the kind of figural sculpture often presented in a potlatch context stands next to piles of woolen blankets ready to be distributed to the buying public. On the ground floor, the Chesapeake is an expensive fine arts gallery featuring original artworks. These range from Yup'ik baskets and Dorothy Grant–designed clothing in Northwest Coast style to fine Pueblo pottery and jewelry. The hand-adzed cedar walls add to the elegance and beauty of the shop.

In her treatise on museums' transition from maintaining and interpreting objects to creating experiences, Hein points out that manufacturers of illusion such as theme parks and the media increasingly compete with museums for attention and attendance. Instead of stubbornly refusing to change, or enthusiastically accepting all the trappings of a theme park, Heim urges museums to maintain their standards while they create experiences: "Confronted with the observation that not all experiences are born equal and that some are more meritorious than others, museums must recast themselves responsibly together with their mission."[21] The NMAI has, for the most part, been responsible in its efforts at offering visitors a whole experience. Yet some reviewers attacked the results. They appear to understand neither the motivations behind nor the results of those efforts.

In the *Washington Post*, Paul Richard objects to the "fact" that the museum has more places to shop, gather, and eat than it has for art. First of all, this is simply not true. Second, virtually all museums, art or not, have income-producing activities, so why single out the NMAI? Third, this is, as all the museum publicity makes clear, not an art museum, although it contains and displays art. Instead of criticizing these choices made by the museum, one can celebrate its references to living cultures that prize their Native foods, cherish time spent in community, and appreciate the opportunity to make an income by selling their own creations. Richard also dismisses the authenticity of pots made for gift shop sale and the value of trading-post bracelets and beaded purses, thus demonstrating his own ignorance of the significance that so-called tourist art and intercultural commerce has long had for American Indians. Richard clings to an outmoded paradigm of the authentic and the unsullied—a hermetic world in which commerce plays no part.

There is so much to see and experience on the first floor, it is curious that another highly negative reviewer, Andrew Ferguson, writing for www.Bloomberg.com, states, "Having navigated the entire first floor . . . you still won't have seen a single museum exhibit"[22] He ignores the artistry of the woven copper fence, a fine Susan Point sculpture visibly situated in the lobby, several oversize Navajo textiles in cases on the way to the café, and an impressive totem pole by Nathan Jackson standing in the Chesapeake store. Ferguson apparently resents the presence of jewelry for sale at "$950 and up," and overlooks the fact that this store is an exhibit, elements of which a visitor can take home. He also objects to the price of lunch at the café; quality Native food made as well as that in Mitsitam does not come cheap. Experiencing such cuisine adds to the museum-goer's experience, and twenty dollars for a nutritious lunch is by no means exorbitant in Washington DC.

But more worrisome is Ferguson's blindness to the carvers, weavers, dancers, storytellers, poets, playwrights, singers, and educators who conduct family programs in the Potomac Atrium and the nearby Rasmusson Theater. Innumerable studies have proved that the most important and meaningful part of a museum visit is the visitor's interaction with a knowledgeable person—not an object. No longer can a museum succeed simply by placing beautiful things on its walls; visitors must have some way of personally having a meaningful encounter with those things. And, in a museum dedicated to Native Americans who have themselves urged the exhibit designers to go well beyond the pristinely displayed object, these first-floor performers, artists, and educators are certainly as central to the NMAI—if not more so—than the exhibits on the upper floors.

The first-time visitor to the NMAI is advised to watch a short film introducing contemporary Native life in the Lelawi Theater, an intimate circular space with banks of platform seating. This multimedia experience prefigures and encapsulates many aspects of the museum as a whole: the warm welcome by a Native host, the intimacy of the space, and most especially the sophisticated use of technology to convey traditional cultural mores. Above the central fire pit are video screens facing the four directions. Imagery on the main screens is augmented by imagery projected onto the sky dome. This is done very effectively, whether it is a panorama of the flags of many Indian nations or the shadowy images of Native dancers.

The video opens with a prayer and then seamlessly moves through short clips of contemporary Native cultural experience on the Northwest Coast, in the Pueblos, among the Nahua of Central Mexico and the Aymara of Bolivia, as well as the Lakota, Iñupiat, and Muscogee. The film ends with the familiar rousing refrain "This Is Indian Country" from "Stomp Dance (Unity),"[23] while a cavalcade of images of contemporary Native people from all walks of life—athletes, scientists, dancers, artists—are projected. We found this film and its multimedia environment both effective and affecting. And the processional music is a stirring aural reinforcement of the message conveyed visually in the rest of the museum:

> *Together we dance*
> *All the first nations*
> *There's no chance*
> *We're ever gonna give up*
> *Beating hearts, beating hearts*
> *Come as one, come as one*
> *This is Indian country*
> *This is Indian Country.*

Objects and Their Artistry

Windows on the Collection are small exhibits appearing on every floor
in the halls that overlook the rotunda. They survey the museum's vast
holdings. These display cases serve as a kind of visible storage, presenting a panoply of objects and materials. Their arrangements are artistic, and their contents perhaps intentionally designed to jar the visitor.
For example, the largest case on the fourth floor displays animal imagery of all sorts. Older sculptures of birds, mammals, and sea creatures
appear alongside witty contemporary works, such as Larry Beck's version of a Yup'ik mask made of rubber tire treads and metal tools, and Jim
Schopper's *Walrus Loves Baby Clams* mask. Recently made ivory carvings
challenge the common distinction between so-called authentic fine art
and commodity (a distinction that may be passé in the academic world
but that still holds sway among much of the general public). These objects
are not themselves labeled, but before each case is a touch screen, where
small images provide access to detailed views and brief labels.

Timothy Noah, of the online publication *Slate*, interprets the NMAI's
message that Native groups do all they can to keep their culture alive as
"the museum . . . willing into being an unchanging continuum between
past and present that doesn't really exist."[24] According to him, the museum's premise is that Native peoples live the same way now as they did
in the sixteenth century; by way of contradiction, he points to American
Indians Web-surfing and shopping in Wal-Mart. How Noah got this idea
is curious, because the museum has numerous references to the effects
of globalization on contemporary Native life, from masks made of tires
and Indian Barbie dolls to the Denver Pow Wow's display of bumper stick-
ers, a plastic cup, and a jean jacket bearing the powwow logo.

Not surprisingly, such exhibits of objects of daily life (some of them of
commercial manufacture) offend other critics, as in Ferguson's dismiss-
al of the Pow Wow exhibit's "banality." Noah complains that fine pieces
are interspersed with kitsch. Since their first encounters with foreign-
ers, Native Americans have created artifacts out of materials originating

within the dominant culture but which they transformed into expressions of Indian identity. Moreover, these are legitimate artifacts of contemporary life. Some may object to a world in which Barbie dolls play so large a role among little girls, but they cannot make the appeal of those dolls for both non-Native and Native children go away, nor pretend that Barbie dolls in Indian clothing are not important affirmations of identity to some Native girls. The critics seem to object to the presence of such "kitsch" in a museum that should have higher aesthetic standards. But this is a museum of Native American culture and life, and not, as we have already stated, an art museum. Moreover, some adventuresome art museums have been challenging distinctions between "high" and "low" art, elite and popular culture, and embracing the values not of art history and its tradition of connoisseurship but of the relatively new discipline of visual studies.[25] Exhibits such as the Denver Pow Wow and Indian Barbies might very well find a welcome reception in art museums that demonstrate the broad range of visual communication in the contemporary world. More than a decade ago, Andreas Huyssen confidently claimed that the "quality argument" had collapsed with the great expansion of what is considered a "legitimate museal project," and that the blurring of high and low art contributes to the "falling of the walls of the museum."[26] The NMAI's critics evidently are unaware of this.

Several critics lament the fact that only eight thousand of some eight hundred thousand Heye Foundation objects are on display.[27] Ferguson compares the large number of contemporary items he calls "bric-a-brac" to the dearth of the museum's treasures on exhibit. And he complains that those on exhibit are improperly interpreted, with no information given as to what the objects mean, why some things are together, and why they are on exhibit in the first place. He acknowledges that computer screens do give some information on the individual pieces, but not enough to satisfy his interests, concluding, "The museum stubbornly refuses to impose any recognizable standard of scholarship, or even value, on the items in the galleries."

Had he spent some time studying the case of peace medals, to cite just one example, he could have read an informative text about how their meaning changed with settlement. Medals appear in cases underneath a collage of medal-wearing Indians from several centuries; even the museum's director is pictured. As in all the museum's text panels, the author is identified. We applaud this strategy of identifying individual curatorial voices. It is an important step in dispelling the ponderously authoritative yet anonymous voice of "truth" that still presides in most museums. And, like all curators who understand the behavior of visitors (most of whom read only a small number of lines in any label), the NMAI curators include only what they judge to be the most important ideas about the objects on display.

Returning to Noah's criticisms about the amount of information on the touch screens, it is worthwhile mentioning that the typical art museum labels of individual paintings simply list the artist, date, and donor—a good deal less than the information provided on the touch screens. Yet we doubt that any art museum would be reprimanded for flawed scholarship because of such labels. Why impose a different standard on the NMAI?

The Nature of Multivocal Scholarship

Several themes pervade the criticisms of the NMAI: a lack of scholarship, an unwillingness to present history in a coherent fashion, the inconsistency that results from a large number of curators, and a disregard for the value of the object. In the academic world, essentialism and grand narratives are viewed with suspicion, yet many in the nonacademic world continue to embrace such paradigms. The objections raised by the NMAI's critics all appear to accept uncritically that there are *correct* ways to exhibit objects, *correct* methods of historical presentation, *correct* types of scholarship. And for them, the NMAI fails to adhere to proper, conventional museum procedures and thus is itself a failure.

The critics not only have strong opinions about what the NMAI should be, but also retain atavistic attitudes toward Native culture and history and their public presentation. Rothstein of the *New York Times* objects to what he sees as inadequate research, especially, in his words, "since American Indians largely had no written languages, and since so much trauma had decimated the tribes, the need for scholarship and analysis of secondary sources is all the more critical." True as such a seemingly objective statement may be, it adheres to the prejudice, seen most clearly in some Canadian land claims court decisions, that oral history is fictitious. He goes on to almost mockingly describe the ten most crucial moments in Tohono O'odham history (listed in one of the community galleries), which include the birds teaching humans to call for rain and a 2000 "desert walk for health." Rothstein seems unaware that in their present circumstances, a group's cosmological origins are often just as important as addressing the serious health problems that plague so many contemporary Native communities.

A subtext within these complaints about lack of scholarship involves the prevalence of community curation at the NMAI. Andrew Ferguson snidely comments, "Almost all the exhibits have been designed by native peoples themselves, with a minimum of curatorial oversight, and it shows." Paul Richard of the *Washington Post* decries the lack of systematic, consistent, and scholarly substance, in part because there were "too many cooks. The eye should have been offered a feast of many courses. Instead, it's served a stew." According to Edward Rothstein, "The notion that tribal voices 'should be heard' becomes a problem when the selected voices have so little to say." One particularly objectionable exhibit for them is Our Universes, curated by Emil Her Many Horses (Oglala) along with a team of community curators. The central introductory area presents Native stories of creation and cosmology, as well as art objects with cosmological imagery. This is expanded by eight "pods" or small community-curated galleries which present the distinctive artifacts and cosmological ideas of eight Native groups: Santa Clara Pueblo, Anishinaabe, Lakota, Quechua (Peru), Hupa, Q'eq'chi' Maya (Guatemala), Mapuche

(Chile), and Yup'ik. At the entrance to the pod, photographs and biographies of community curators contribute to the personal experience. More important, such biographical information adds to the understanding that information does not exist in a vacuum but is presented by particular people with particular points of view, be they museum curators or community members. As in other exhibits, good use is made of touch screens that offer further information on artifacts.

The individual sections in Our Universes do vary considerably in their substance and information, which is not surprising, considering that each one was curated by a community group. But the fact remains that for the first time on the National Mall, a museum listened to community views on how they wanted to be portrayed. These stories may not tell the coherent master narrative about American Indian culture, but they do tell a great deal about what community groups think is important about their representations. Whether or not one ultimately finds such expressions useful or illuminating, there is a postcolonial imperative to listen and try to understand them, something the critics apparently refused to do.

Historical Scholarship

Several reviewers condemned what they felt was the absence of solid historical scholarship at the NMAI. Andrew Ferguson accuses the museum of simply ignoring the past. Marc Fisher, another *Washington Post* columnist, complains that there is no story about the painful consequences of the colonial encounter and the path Indians took from owning the land to settling in reservations. For him, the NMAI is "an exercise in intellectual timidity and a sorry abrogation of the Smithsonian's obligation to explore America's history and culture."[28] But who tells history? Only the non-Native academic "experts"? And what are historical documents? Should they be limited solely to materials written by missionaries, travelers, professional scholars?

We strongly disagree with Fisher's perspective; history plays a large role in some galleries, but perhaps not in a familiar manner. Our Peoples: Giving Voice to Our Histories combines artistic presentation of objects that tell a compelling story with the more intimate first-person accounts, again of eight chosen communities. The central open space is dedicated to telling a Native version of contact. It was curated by Paul Chaat Smith (Comanche writer and critic), Ann McMullen (NMAI staff member), and Jolene Rickard (Tuscarora artist and scholar). As Smith so cogently argued in a lecture on the museum:

> Awarding Indians the last open space on the National Mall was a profound act that showed the American government and its people wanted Indians to be part of a national conversation, to finally talk, seriously, and at the highest levels, about things we had never really talked about before. Let's be clear: you don't get a new museum right next to the Capitol itself for making excellent jewelry, or for having stories and songs, or religious beliefs you wish to share with the world. You get the last open space on the National Mall because the country's decided, in the mysterious ways nations decide such matters, that it's time at last to speak about the hard things, the painful things, the unspeakable things.[29]

This is the exhibit that focuses principally on the painful things, and it does so with considerable visual and textual eloquence. Amid seventeen images of nineteenth-century Indian portraits by Catlin, the Plains Cree playwright Floyd Favel Starr is himself a "talking head" within a frame, as he narrates a video entitled Making History. This provides an effective and startling merging of past and present, old media and new. He reminds us, "All histories have a history themselves, and one is incomplete without the other." This exhibit introduces Native counternarratives to the Eurocentric versions of history that we have all been taught. It offers a powerful visual experience, more like an artist's installation than a didactic display. Indeed, artist Jolene Rickard was responsible for the concept behind its visual eloquence. A long sinuous Plexiglas wall curves its way through the gallery. The viewer walks along it, confronted by hundreds of artifacts. The experience is like being hit by a tidal wave of objects embodying the changes wrought by contact.

The time before Columbus is represented by a large installation of ceramic and stone figures that offer the myriad human faces of the precontact world. The late prehistoric and initial contact period is represented by scores of Indigenous gold objects. All of these were drawn from the Heye Foundation's vast holdings of nearly a million objects. To us, this installation seems a better use of them than yet another display of "Costa Rican Gold" or "Tlatilco Figurines" ordered by the tired standards of nineteenth-century anthropological classification (region, tribe, artifact type, etc.). Idea and artistry are the motivating factors here, not Linnaean classificatory schemes that Indian people have found so fossilizing.

The overwhelming military might of the conquerors is demonstrated first by swords and daggers, which begin to be interspersed with the gold, followed by a cavalcade of more than one hundred examples of firearms, from early arquebuses to Colt revolvers, Remington rifles, and even semi-automatic weapons like those used against Native peoples of El Salvador and Guatemala in recent decades. A large panel entitled Invasion offers compelling quotes from North and South America about the consequences of the diseases that decimated Indigenous populations. God's Work: Churches as Instruments of Dispossession and Resilience presents a visually stunning wall of Bibles—over one hundred of them in English, French, German, and a host of Indigenous languages. Bibles hand-bound and hand- tooled and with quilled, beaded, and feathered covers are vivid examples of the incorporation of these texts into Native worldviews. Having just recovered from the weight of all those swords and firearms, the visitor is assaulted by these weapons of a spiritual and ideological invasion, whose consequences were perhaps even more grave than the military invasion. To us, this was the eloquent, elegant, and elegiac core of the museum experience, and we won't soon forget its impact.

Jolene Rickard's aim was to provide an experiential engagement with history through the museum's substantial collections. "The objects are more powerful than anything we can say," she observed in answer to our questions about the genesis of this installation:

I referenced Richard Serra's curvilinear torqued sculptures as having the appropriate sensibility. [The wall] is reminiscent of land formations, grand in scale, and would create a modestly destabilizing experience for the visitor. I feel that the meta-narrative of how America imagines Natives is so entrenched that the mere presentation of any object or thought needed to be carefully articulated through a de-romanticized and very contemporary lens.[30]

Rickard worked closely with designers Lynn Emi Kawaratani and Verena Pierik to achieve her aims, which included, in her words, "boldly working with the collections as if they were the colors on an artist's palette." Moreover, she related, "It wasn't about the history of each one of these objects individually, rather it is about the overall history told by their assemblage. This installation created for me an indigenous context. We can not go in and tease out their multiple histories, but wasn't the objective the presentation of this material from a Native perspective? I tried to reframe the content to make that point."

Further encouragement for viewers to consider history "not as a single definitive immutable work, but as a collection of subjective tellings"[31] is found in the eight community galleries in Our Peoples. They include the Seminole of Florida, the Tapirapé of Brazil, the Kiowa of Oklahoma, the Tohono O'odham of Arizona, the Eastern Band of the Cherokee of North Carolina, the Nahua of central Mexico, the Ka'apor of Brazil, and the Huichol of western Mexico (here called the Wixarika).

Native Identity

Who created the ethnic category "Indian" anyway? Invaders, governments, educators, and so many others—all of them non-Native. Following the principle that small groups have less power than large ones, it was in the dominant society's best interest to maintain strong tribal distinctions. Now, many seem troubled by signs of a positive unity among the diverse groups of Native Americans.[32] Another of the reviewers' objections to the NMAI is what some view as its homogenization of Native Americans. Rothstein grumbles that there are so many Indian tribes that needed to be taken into account that the museum "filter[ed] away detail

... and minimize[ed] differences." He claims that every group, and every idea, is presented as equal. His examples are from the Our Universes section, leading us to wonder if he visited the intellectually compelling and complex gallery Our Lives: Contemporary Life and Identities, which takes up half of the third floor. The gallery focuses on how Native people not only live in a land where they are minorities, but also function in a globalized world. In some ways this gallery's design blends that of the two upstairs exhibits.

The central area of Our Lives, curated by Jolene Rickard and Gabrielle Tayac, is devoted to the complexities of Native identities and how they can be maintained today. It asks the ever-compelling question Who is Native? Ways of "measuring" Indianness—blood quantum, appearance, federal recognition, and documentation—challenge the visitor. The wall text asks, "What is Native?," and responds, "It's not just your blood" but in your head, heart, thoughts. The exhibit Hard Choices also brings the visitor's attention to the kinds of internal tribal disputes that occur when income sources conflict with traditional values, such as disagreements on the value of casinos to Native communities. This, more than any other exhibit, would benefit from a clear introductory label that succinctly states what this interesting gallery is all about, for one needs to spend considerable time figuring out the connecting threads of these various exhibits. The typical museum visitor, unaware of many of the issues this gallery raises, would find an orientation of considerable value.

Surrounding this core are smaller displays on eight tribes and Native communities. This section challenges the visitor's preconceptions about Indians by presenting a variety of groups, some well-known, such as the Inuit and Iroquois, some less well known, at least in the United States. One section on the Métis of Canada introduces this hybrid yet state-recognized group, another features the Carib Kalinago, a tiny group who survived in the Caribbean, and there is even an "all tribes nation": Chicago's thousands of urban Indians. This gallery successfully carries out one of the NMAI's goals: to convey the variety of Native American peoples, from those living a subsistence lifestyle to urban dwellers. The reality and diversity of contemporary Indian life is vibrantly transmitted in these displays, community-curated under the guidance of Cynthia Chavez and Ann McMullen. They complement similar community exhibits in Our Peoples and Our Universes.

Our Lives contains several nice design touches. On the introductory panel to the Igloolik Eskimos is an arrangement of stacked glass blocks that allude to the *inuksuk*, a pile of stones in abstract human shape that marks trails, direction, or the site of a food cache. In the middle of the Métis exhibit sits a large tank-like vehicle, a Bombardier used for ice fishing. Most visitors to an Indian museum might expect exhibits on subsistence and travel to show birch bark canoes or beaded arrow quivers. This jarring Bombardier forcefully confronts visitors with the message that Native culture does not adhere to their expectations, which are too often informed by false stereotypes.

In the Kahnawake section are some real steel girders of the type erected by the famed Mohawk "high steel" ironworkers. Marc Fisher is particularly incensed at this section, which refuses to give any scientific or sociological reasons for the Mohawks' ability to do this work. He treats as uselessly self-evident the words of Kyle Karonhiaktatie Beauvois that "a lot of people think Mohawks aren't afraid of heights; that's not true. We have as much fear as the next guy. The difference is that we deal with it better." What Fisher does not realize is that this comment about how group values influence behavior is a clear and understandable expression of how culture operates: not from an anthropological, academic perspective, but a personal one.

Art and Identity

The themes of art and contemporary Native identity at the NMAI converge in the reviews of the special exhibit installed for the opening. Native Modernism, on the third floor, provided a first-rate art historical examination of the work of George Morrison (Chippewa, 1919–2000) and Allan

Houser (Apache, 1914–1994), two of the most important Native artists of the mid- to late twentieth century. While this exhibit was not part of the long-term installation, the fact that it was chosen as one of the inaugural exhibits points to its importance. It sent an important signal that exhibits at the NMAI would be heterogeneous, diverse, and varied. For that reason, we consider it here as a key part of the inaugural message of the museum.

For those seeking a familiar art museum experience, Native Modernism, with its elegant design and spacious layout, was a welcome visual relief from the permanent installations, all of which were densely packed with texts and objects. Curated by Truman Lowe (Ho-Chunk, himself a well-known artist who serves as curator of contemporary art at the NMAI), the exhibit carefully surveys Morrison's abstract expressionist paintings of the 1950s and 1960s and his meticulous wood collages of the 1970s and 1980s, as well as Houser's naturalistic drawings of nudes and other Indian subjects and his monumental sculptural works that distill those naturalistic figures into semi-abstract forms.

In terms of both its style and substance, this exhibit would be at home in any art museum in the country. To us, this is precisely the point of its inclusion. We enjoyed watching the encounters that many museum-goers had with this exhibit, for some who might eagerly visit an "Indian museum" might not necessarily venture into a modern art museum and seek out large marble nudes or abstract assemblages. This perhaps unexpected encounter with classically modern art added to the pedagogical aims of the museum, with its implicit endorsement that this, too, is Indian experience: abstract art, Fulbright and Guggenheim grants, a professorship at Rhode Island School of Design, and the awarding of the National Medal of Arts. The accompanying catalogue takes its place with other recent and forthcoming works that consider the variety of Indigenous modernisms, most of them still unrecognized by canonical modernism.[33] Yet mainstream critics were vexed at the familiar art museum approach as much as they were disturbed by the rest of the museum. Paul Richard wrote a

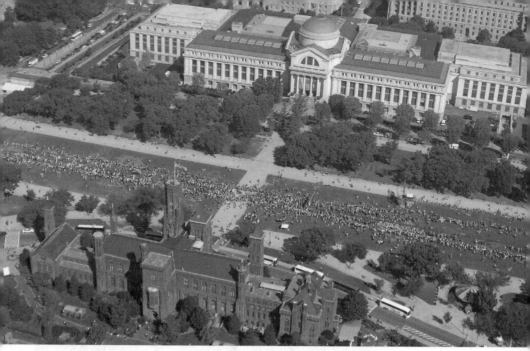

1. Opening-day procession on the National Mall in Washington DC. Image no. 2004-53058. All photos courtesy National Museum of the American Indian, Smithsonian Institution.

2. View of east entrance of the National Museum of the American Indian on the National Mall. Photo by Leonda Levchuk (Navajo), NMAI.

3. The east-facing main entrance of the National Museum of the American Indian at dawn. © Judy Davis/Hoachlander Davis Photography.

4. Interior of the Potomac room with domed ceiling.

5. Windows on Collection exhibit. Photo by William Larrimore, NMAI.
Image no. 120704WOC4th fl 47.

6. Sioux Bible and hymnals with beaded and porcupine quill–embroidered covers,
North and South Dakota, ca. 1900. Photo by Walter Larrimore. Image no. 236809 multi-A.
Beaded sneakers by Teri Greeves, featured in the Our Lives exhibit. Image no. 263325A.

7. Interior of the Our Universes exhibit, featuring the
Pueblo of Santa Clara in New Mexico. Photo by Walter Larrimore, NMAI.

8. Interior of the Our Universes exhibit, featuring the Hupa.
Image no. 091205WLOU07!. Photo by Walter Larrimore, NMAI.

9. Wall of gold objects in the Our Peoples exhibit. Photo by Leonda Levchuk (Navajo), NMAI.

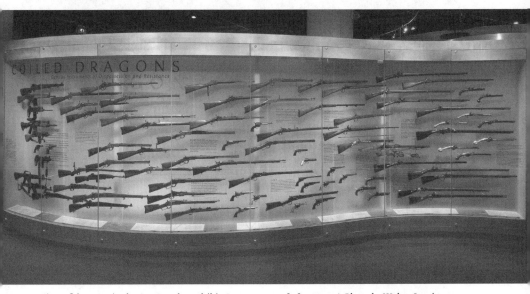

10. View of the guns in the Our Peoples exhibit. Image no. 012606WLOP09!. Photo by Walter Larrimore, NMAI.

11. Case of Bibles in the Our Peoples exhibit. Image no. 120004KFMALLOP013.
Photo by Katherine Fogden, NMAI.

12. Treaty case in the Our Peoples exhibit. The guns, Bibles, and treaties are part of the Storm installation.
Image no. 012606WLOP01!. Photo by Walter Larrimore, NMAI.

13. Storm installation in the Our Peoples exhibit. Image no. 012606WLOP07!.
Photo by Walter Larrimore, NMAI.

14. Interior of the Our Peoples exhibit, featuring the Tohono O'odham.
Image no. 012606WLOP21!. Photo by Walter Larrimore, NMAI.

15. Interior of the Our Peoples exhibit, featuring the Wixarika. Image no. 120004KFMALLOP007. Photo by Katherine Fogden, NMAI.

16. "Hard Choices" display focusing on tribal gaming issues in the Our Lives exhibit. Image no. 090105WLOLI2!. Photo by Walter Larrimore, NMAI.

17. Interior of the Our Lives exhibit, featuring the Campo band of Kumeyaay Indians. Image no. 090105WLOL08!. Photo by Walter Larrimore, NMAI.

18. Interior of the Our Lives exhibit, focusing on the Yakama Nation. Image no. 090105WLOL21!. Photo by Walter Larrimore.

19. Native Modernism, a temporary exhibit at the National Museum of the American Indian featuring the work of George Morrison and Allan Houser, opened September 24, 2004. Image no. 090904MEA-005.Photo by Ernest Amoroso.

20. Image of Allan Houser in the Native Modernism exhibit. Image no. 090805KFMALL019. Photo by Katherine Fogden.

separate review of Native Modernism for the *Washington Post*.[34] He compliments it as "the best looking and the least amorphous" of the inaugural exhibits, but goes on to complain, "This really isn't a show about Indianness. It's a show about 20th century art." As he chronicles for his readers the acceptance of these artists into the white, mainstream, modernist art world, Richard seems to imply that because the Morrison paintings on display "take your thoughts not just to Lake Superior but also to Cape Cod and Antibes" and the Houser sculptures "send your mind to France, not just to Santa Fe," this work does not belong in an Indian museum. But the point of the exhibit (beyond the basic art historical interest in exploring the full range and depth of two important twentieth-century artists) is that Indian art is cosmopolitan. In some cases, twentieth-century Native art did face Europe as much as it faced the shores of Lake Superior and the deserts of New Mexico.

Ken Ringle, another reviewer (who describes himself as a retired cultural critic from the *Washington Post*), writing for the *Weekly Standard* in Vancouver, is similarly dismissive of Native Modernism. "Much of this gorgeous material unquestionably deserves exhibit somewhere—maybe in the National Gallery of Art," he writes.[35] These comments reveal how deeply an essentialist notion of "American Indianness" is entrenched even in the psyches of those who are supposed to be open-minded, as they serve as cultural critics and interpreters for cosmopolitan audiences.

Why All This Criticism?

On October 8, 2004, the online version of the well-known Native-run newspaper *Indian Country* carried a front-page story entitled "National Museum of the American Indian Reviews: Ceremonies Were Nice but Critics Pan Content."[36] It described the negativity of the newspaper and online journal reviews discussed in this essay, with very little analysis other than judging the quality of the reviews, from high in Rothstein and Richard to low in Fisher. In conclusion, it suggests that Richard West "faces his biggest challenge in applying tangible experience and a synthesizing intelligence to make sense of the museum's voluminous content of American Indian historical and cultural realities." *Indian Country* does not ask the question we pose here: Why have reviewers attacked the museum so severely— and many times, as we have indicated here, judged the museum so harshly, to the point of accusing the NMAI of not doing things it actually does do?

By refusing to present its multivalenced stories in the expected fashion, the NMAI has been subject to reductive criticism in the nation's newspapers of record. Many of these criticisms are, as we have pointed out, unfair. Perhaps the museum made a tactical error in its preopening publicity; it positioned itself as the conveyor of Indigenous knowledge that stood in opposition to anthropological knowledge. In fact, much perfectly "legitimate" research informed many of the exhibits, so this supposed opposition is not, in fact, entirely accurate. The museum did, however, raise the hackles of those ready to challenge the exhibits as intellectually impoverished, perhaps without pausing to reflect that somewhat different intellectual paradigms were operative here.

Both Ferguson and Noah dislike the museum's enthusiastic promotion of contemporary cultural vitality. For Ferguson, the exhibits on Indian life today "giv[e] off an unmistakable air of ethnic boosterism." Noah charges the museum with the "boosterish message that Native cultural is as vibrant today as it ever was." James Clifford, in his essay on several Native exhibits in Alaska, investigates the concept of "heritage," a conscious construction on the part of Indigenous people to present their culture to both themselves and outsiders as it relates not only to the past, but also to place (which is, of course, often contested), to the powers of the local, regional, and national governments, and even of the globalized world.[37] He makes a strong case for the benefits to Native people of what he calls heritage work: "For indigenous people, long marginalized or made to disappear, physically and ideologically, to say 'We exist' . . . is a powerful political act. . . . Heritage work, to the extent that it selectively preserves and updates cultural traditions and relations to place, can be part of a social process that strengthens indigenous claims to deep roots— to a status beyond that of another minority or local interest group."[38]

This sounds eminently reasonable; why then, do the critics find the entire project so infuriating? Perhaps because it represents an exclusivity that denies some voices? Michael Ames's "Declaration of Exhibition Rights" would include a group's sovereign right to represent themselves, their history, and their heritage as they see fit.[39] The NMAI certainly has manifested these rights. However, Ames continues in his discussion of museum representation by pointing out that "contact between peoples is a universal occurrence that may best be described from multiple perspectives." Thus, some critics of the NMAI would be pleased to see exhibits from the point of view of conventional—that is, of the dominant society's—history. (In fact, a number of non-Natives work on the curatorial staff of the NMAI, and their knowledge is reflected in the exhibits.) Indeed, there are many exhibits in museums around the country that depict Indians in that fashion; there seems no need for the NMAI to do the same. Furthermore, on the Mall are two other major museums, the National Museum of Natural History and the National Museum of American History, which should present Native culture in a way that complements the NMAI's perspective. The fact that they don't is a shame. The NMNH has an extensive collection of Native objects. Curator JoAllyn Archambault (a Standing Rock Sioux with a PhD in anthropology from Berkeley) was midway through the planning process for totally revamping the outmoded North American Indian Hall at the NMNH in the early 1990s, with much input from Native scholars such as Tlingit anthropologist Rosita Worl and Lakota artist and scholar Arthur Amiotte, when her budget was cut and the project canceled. Former Smithsonian secretary Robert McCormick Adams was quoted as saying that it was impossible to ask Congress to fund two substantial Indian projects at the same time.[40]

Andreas Huyssen applauds the way that the entrance of previously marginalized groups into the museum world has restructured the concept of the past as well as the nature of the present. Apparently, this can be threatening to conservative critics still lodged safely within the intellectual domain of modernism that privileges the strong subject and considers only a linear passage of time: "Some within the fortress of modernity will experience these changes as a threat, as dangerous and identity-eroding invasions. Others will welcome them as small but important steps toward a more genuinely heteronational culture, one that no longer feels the need to homogenize and is learning how to live pragmatically with real difference."[41]

At the end of this passage Huyssen notes, "We are far from that." Certainly, the critics of the NMAI have demonstrated how very far *some* are from this goal.

The Mall as "Indian Country": Native Autonomy and Interpretive Strategies

In his introduction to *Creation's Journey*, the first volume to come out of the NMAI's Heye Center in lower Manhattan, Seneca scholar and museum professional Tom Hill wrote about his own journey as one who "yearned to penetrate the haze of past museum practices and public attitudes that had accumulated around the objects over time, and to ask new questions about them." He pondered the ways Native curators might "construct new cultural paradigms for the 21st century."[42]

If there is anything we have learned from the past twenty years' worth of literature on museum representation, it is that dissatisfaction with the old paradigms has been pandemic among forward-thinking art historians, anthropologists, and museum professionals, as well as Native peoples and others who have felt disenfranchised by the old paradigms.[43] Yet as Bruce Ferguson wrote in a now-classic essay, "Exhibition Rhetorics":

> *The surprise, of course, given the multiplicity of forms of art, is how few genres of exhibitions there actually are and how few are animated differently from one another. The labyrinth of possible utterances from multiple voices and*

complex cultures seems to remain unsearched and unresearched. Repetition of genres and figures remain systematically patterned and structurally repetitious. But if other authentic classes, races, and formerly marginalized voices are committedly introduced, the exhibition form may produce unexpected flourishes, new sub-genres, new sites of speech. New dimensions of the signifying field may expand the play of exhibitions, and thus expand the possibility of serious achievements.[44]

Oddly, the general public, rather than the journalists who chronicle museum exhibitions, seems open to the new utterances and new sites of speech that have arisen on the Mall in Washington. And new utterances they are. This is "Indian country," as the processional song in the Lelawi Theater proclaims. As Director Rick West has explained on numerous occasions, "This is the museum *different*."

On the days we visited, the museum was a joyful place of intercultural encounter. We watched tourists of all ages and ethnicities avidly taking in every visual, aural, spatial, and culinary message the museum offered. We heard people speaking various European, Asian, and African languages to each other and to their children as they examined everything on display. We also saw many more Native American faces than one usually sees in one place in the nation's capital. Clearly people are coming from everywhere to see and hear what Native Americans have to say and show about their cultures. Almost everyone we eavesdropped on seemed absorbed and delighted by their experience. We met a young university student who was writing a paper on the museum for her anthropology class; when asked what she thought, she described how other museums objectify their artifacts, whereas here, she felt real people were talking to her about themselves. She found this gratifying and more appealing than the more familiar museological mode.

An impressive team of Native writers and artists have contributed to what we judge to be an intellectually serious and visually pleasurable experience. It is noteworthy that so many artists of considerable stature were deeply involved in the development of these exhibits, among them Gerald McMaster, Jolene Rickard, Ramona Sakiestewa, and Truman Lowe. Their artistry is evident throughout the museum, from the curving wall of figurines, gold, guns, and Bibles, to the woven copper fence in the lobby, to the grace of the Native Modernism installation. This visual eloquence is sometimes muffled by the cacophony of the accompanying texts, but this is a problem that will be worked out as the museum refines and modifies its exhibits over the next several years.

In most senses, those inhabiting a multimillion-dollar museum built on the last space on the Mall in Washington can no longer be considered marginalized. They have arrived at "the center." Yet we believe our colleagues at the NMAI have proudly embraced a particular sort of marginality, one articulated by the "museum *different*," by "Indian Country." The African American cultural critic bell hooks has identified the power inherent in a marginality that is deliberately chosen, that is about articulation rather than exclusion:

> I make a definite distinction between that marginality which is imposed by oppressive structures and that marginality one chooses as a site of resistance—as a location of radical openness and possibility. This site of resistance is continually formed in that segregated culture of opposition that is our critical response to domination. We come to this space through suffering and pain, through struggle. We know struggle to be that which pleasures, delights, and fulfills desire. We are transformed, individually, collectively, as we make radical creative space which affirms and sustains our subjectivity, which gives us a new location from which to articulate our sense of the world.[45]

hooks's words are consonant with the aims of the new NMAI. "This is an intervention," she proclaims.

> I am speaking from a place in the margin where I am different, where I see things differently. I am talking about what I see. This is an intervention. A message from that space in the margin that is a site of creativity and power, that inclusive space where we recover ourselves, where we move in solidarity to erase the category colonizer/colonized. Marginality is a site of resistance. Enter that space. Let us meet there. Enter that space.[46]

"This is Indian Country," the extraordinary curvilinear, limestone building on the Mall in Washington proclaims, through its form as well as its contents. "Let us meet there. Enter that space." This Indian Country on the Mall is the place to discover the new, postcolonial paradigms emerging in transdisciplinary practices such as cultural studies and visual studies (as well as in the traditional disciplines of anthropology, art history, and history)—not just in North and South America, but worldwide.

Should you enter the NMAI, your views on what constitutes Indian Country will be transformed.

Notes

1. Deborah Doxtator, "The Implications of Canadian Nationalism for Aboriginal Cultural Authority," in *Curatorship: Indigenous Perspectives in Post-Colonial Societies: Proceedings*, Mercury Series, Directorate 8 (Victoria: Canadian Museum of Civilization, the Commonwealth Association of Museums, and the University of Victoria, 1996), 64.

2. This essay is a substantially revised version of Janet Berlo and Aldona Jonaitis, "'Indian Country' on Washington's Mall—The National Museum of the American Indian: A Review Essay," *Museum Anthropology* 28, no. 2 (2005): 17–30. We are grateful to Amy Lonetree for inviting us to take part in this volume of essays.

3. Edward Rothstein, "Museum with an American Indian Voice," *New York Times*, September 21, 2004, Weekend section, 1, 5.

4. Paul Richard, "Shards of Many Untold Stories: In Place of Unity, a Melange of Unconnected Objects," *Washington Post*, September 21, 2004, C1.

5. Our review is based on three visits to the museum: Jonaitis's attendance at the opening, our joint visit on November 7, 2004, and Berlo's return visit on November 8, as well as our study of the press releases and publications released to coincide with the opening.

6. Two especially good books on this topic, both out of Canada, are *Curatorship* and Lynda Jessup with Shannon Bagg, eds., *On Aboriginal Representation in the Gallery* (Hull, Quebec: Canadian Museum of Civilization, 2002).

7. Such means included dialogic endeavors, such as those advocated by Dennis Tedlock and others. See, for example, Dennis Tedlock, "The Analogical Tradition and the Emergence of a Dialogical Anthropology," *Journal of Anthropological Research* 35 (1979): 387–400, and Dennis Tedlock and Bruce Manheim, eds., *The Dialogic Emergence of Culture* (Urbana: University of Illinois Press, 1995).

8. Michael Ames, "Applied Anthropology in Our Backyards," *Practicing Anthro-*

pology 2, no. 1 (1979):7, 23–24. For a collection of essays that address museums and Native people, see Ames's *Cannibal Tours and Glass Boxes: The Anthropology of Museums* (Vancouver: University of British Columbia Press, 1992).

9. Judith Ostrowitz, "Concourse and Periphery: Planning the National Museum of the American Indian," this volume.

10. See, for example, Gail Anderson, ed., *Reinventing the Museum* (Walnut Creek CA: Altamira Press, 2004); Reesa Greenberg, Bruce Ferguson, and Sandy Nairne, *Thinking about Exhibitions* (New York: Routledge, 1996); Eilean Hooper-Greenhill, *Museums and the Shaping of Knowledge* (London: Routledge, 1992); Flora Kaplan, ed., *Museums and the Making of "Ourselves": The Role of Objects in National Identity* (London: Leicester University Press, 1994); Ivan Karp and Steven Lavine, eds., *Exhibiting Cultures: The Poetics and Politics of Museum Displays* (Washington DC: Smithsonian Institution Press, 1991); Laura Peers and Alison Brown, eds., *Museums and Source Communities: A Routledge Reader* (New York: Routledge, 2003); Moira Simpson, *Making Representations: Museums in the Post-Colonial Era*, revised ed. (New York: Routledge, 2001). For a huge compendium of reprinted essays, see Donald Preziosi and Claire Farago, eds., *Grasping the World: The Idea of the Museum* (London: Ashgate Press, 2004). For critiques focused principally on Native American representation in museums, see Aldona Jonaitis, "First Nations and Art Museums" in Jessup and Bagg, *On Aboriginal Representation*, 17–26. Janet Berlo and Ruth Phillips, "'Our (Museum) World Turned Upside Down': Re-presenting Native American Arts," *Art Bulletin* 77, no. 1 (1995): 6–10, reprinted in Donald Preziosi and Farago, eds., *Grasping the World*, 708–18; Ruth Phillips, "Community Collaboration in Exhibitions: Toward a Dialogic Paradigm. Introduction," in Peers and Brown, *Museums and Source Communities*, 153–70; Ruth Phillips, "Show Times: De-celebrating the Canadian Nation, De-colonizing the Canadian Museum, 1967–92," in Darryl McIntyre and Kirsten Wehner, eds., *Negotiating Histories: National Museums Conference Proceedings* (Canberra: National Museum of Australia, 2001), 85–103; Miriam Clavir, *Preserving What Is Valued: Museums, Conservation, and First Nations* (Vancouver: University British Columbia Press, 2002); James Clifford, "Museums as Contact Zones," in *Routes: Travel and Translation in the Late Twentieth Century* (Cambridge ma: Harvard University Press, 1997), 189–219; Gloria Jean Frank, "That's My Dinner on Display: A First Nations Reflection on Museum Culture," *BC Studies* 125/126 (Spring/Summer 2000): 163–78.

11. Of course, many museums now bring in Native consultants and curators to help create exhibits of Native culture. In the forefront of this trend was

the University of British Columbia Museum of Anthropology, under the direction of Michael Ames in the 1970s and 1980s. Other important early collaborative efforts include the Burke Museum's 1989 exhibit A Time of Gathering: Native Heritage in Washington State, curated by Robin Wright. See Robin Wright, ed., *A Time of Gathering: Native Heritage in Washington State* (Seattle: The Burke Museum and the University of Washington Press, 1991). See also Aldona Jonaitis's exhibit, Chiefly Feasts, at the American Museum of Natural History in New York in 1992, with extensive collaboration of Kwakwaka'wakw people, and its catalogue, *Chiefly Feasts: The Enduring Kwakiutl Potlatch* (Seattle: University of Washington Press, 1992). For an assessment of the collaborative techniques used in Jonaitis's exhibit, see Janet Berlo and Ruth Phillips, "Vitalizing the Things of the Past: Museum Representations of Native North American Art in the 1990's," *Museum Anthropology* 16, no. 1 (1992): 29–43. Many others have followed. For an insightful overview of community collaboration in exhibits of Alaskan Native art of the past two decades, see James Clifford, "Looking Several Ways: Anthropology and Native Heritage in Alaska," *Current Anthropology* 4, no. 1 (2004): pp. 5–30. The NMAI, however, as a large national museum, has been developed with far more community involvement than any other of which we are aware.

12. Cardinal was apparently fired from the NMAI project in 1998; the best way to express the difficult gestation of the building's design is simply to quote from the museum's own press release, for surely this statement was as carefully negotiated as the opening credits of a Hollywood movie:

> *The museum's conceptual designers are Canadian architect Douglas Cardinal (Blackfoot) with* GBQC *Architects of Philadelphia and architect Johnpaul Jones (Cherokee/Chocktaw); Ramona Sakiestewa (Hopi) and Donna House (Navajo/Oneida) also served as design consultants. Following the conceptual design work, the project was further developed by the architectural firm of Jones and Jones of Seattle and SmithGroup of Washington,* DC *in association with Lou Weller (Caddo) and the Native American Design Collaborative; Polshek Partnership Architects of New York City; and* EDAW *Inc., landscape architects in Alexandria, Virginia." (*NMAI *Building Features Backgrounder, Office of Public Affairs, press release, September 2004, p. 1)*

13. Gyan Prakesh, "Museum Matters," in *Museum Studies*, ed. Bettina Messias Carbonell (Oxford: Blackwell, 2004), 208.

14. Jolene Rickard, "After Essay—Indigenous Is the Local," in Jessup and Bagg, *On Aboriginal Representation*, 115.

15. But on a day with large crowds queuing for the bag search and the walk through the metal detectors (a feature of all Smithsonian museums now), one simply does not notice the Welcome Wall.

16. Rick West, personal communication, November 7, 2004. We discovered the director on a Sunday afternoon, undercover in blue jeans and a work shirt rather than his usual impeccable suit, strolling through the museum and listening to the comments of the crowds, to learn firsthand the effectiveness of the displays.

17. James Volkert, Linda Martin, and Amy Pickworth, *National Museum of the American Indian: Map and Guide* (London: Scala Publishers in association with the National Museum of the American Indian, 2004), 34.

18. Hilde S. Hein, *The Museum in Transition* (Washington DC: Smithsonian Books, 2000).

19. Whereas purists might lament such "commercialization" of the museum, less than adequate funding levels necessitate inclusion of income-producing elements in museum design. Moreover, there is no question that visitors enjoy these activities.

20. "Facts and Figures from the Grand Opening of the Smithsonian's National Museum of the American Indian," press release, NMAI Office of Public Affairs, October, 2004, p. 1.

21. Hein, *The Museum in Transition*, 16.

22. Andrew Ferguson, "New American Indian Museum Misses the Mark," www.Bloomberg.com, October 5, 2004.

23. Familiar to some because of Bob Dylan's collaboration with The Band, this song is by Robbie Robertson and his Red Road Ensemble. Its full lyrics can be found at http://www.sing365.com.

24. Timothy Noah, "The National Museum of Ben Nighthorse Campbell," *Slate*, September 29, 2004, www.slate.com/id/2107140.

25. See, for example, Michael Ann Holly, Norman Bryson, and Keith Moxie, eds., *Visual Culture: Images of Interpretation* (Middletown CT: Wesleyan University Press, 1994); Nicholas Mirzoeff, *The Visual Culture Reader* (New York: Routledge, 2002); Margaret Dikovitskaya, *Visual Culture: The Study of the Visual after the Cultural Turn* (Cambridge MA: MIT Press, 2005). Moreover, contemporary artists have been in the forefront of this reexamination of the art museum and the creative reuse of artifactual history. See, for example, Lisa Corrin, ed., *Mining the Museum: An Installation by Fred Wilson* (New York: New Press, 1994); Jim Drobnick and Jennifer Fisher, eds., *Museopathy* (Kingston, Ontario: Agnes Etherington Art Centre, 2002); Laura S. Heon, ed., *Yankee Remix: Artists Take on New England* (North Adams

MA: MASS MoCa, 2003.

26. Andreas Huyssen, *Twilight Memories: Marking Time in a Culture of Amnesia* (New York: Routledge, 1995), 22. See also Douglas Crimp, *On the Museum's Ruins* (Cambridge MA: MIT Press, 1995).

27. Although the appearance of just 1 percent of so enormous a collection is not unreasonable, it would be interesting to compare this figure with the percentage of items on exhibit at the Smithsonian's National Museum of Natural History. For the origin of the vast Heye collection, see Clara Sue Kidwell, "Every Last Dishcloth: The Prodigious Collecting of George Gustav Heye," in *Collecting Native America*, ed. Shepard Krech and Barbara Hall (Washington DC: Smithsonian Institution Press, 1999), 232–57.

28. Marc Fisher, "Indian Museum's Appeal, Sadly, Only Skin Deep," *Washington Post*, September 21, 2004, B1.

29. We are grateful to Paul Chaat Smith for providing us with a copy of this lecture, delivered as part of the Monthly Curator Series at NMAI, March 4, 2005, and reprinted in this volume as "Critical Reflections on the Our Peoples Exhibit: A Curator's Perspective."

30. All quotes are from a personal communication from Rickard to J. C. Berlo, March 9, 2005.

31. Volkert et al., *National Museum of the American Indian, Map and Guide*, 50.

32. Judith Ostrowitz points out how such unification serves the NMAI's political goals.

33. Truman Lowe, ed., *Native Modernism: The Art of George Morrison and Allen Houser* (Washington DC: Smithsonian Institution in association with the University of Washington Press, 2004). See also W. Jackson Rushing, *Allan Houser: An American Master* (New York: Harry N. Abrams, 2004), and Bill Anthes, *Native Moderns* (Durham NC: Duke University Press, 2006), which features case studies of George Morrison and others.

34. Paul Richard, "Explorers of the New: Two Modernists Who Are Also Indian," *Washington Post*, September 19, 2004, R2.

35. Ken Ringle, "Where's Tonto? You Won't Find Out at the New Indian Museum," *Weekly Standard* (Vancouver), 10, no. 27 (April 4, 2005).

36. www.indiancountry.com/content.cfm?id=1096409661.

37. Clifford, "Looking Several Ways."

38. Clifford, "Looking Several Ways." 9.

39. Michael Ames, "Retrospective: Reflections on Some Common Themes Arising Out of Diversity," in *Curatorship*, 211.

40. Bob Thompson, "Spirit Lodge," *Washington Post*, August 2, 2004, C1.

41. Huyssen, *Twilight Memories*, 28.

42. Tom Hill, "Introduction: A Backward Glimpse through the Museum Door," in *Creation's Journey: Native American Identity and Belief*, ed. Tom Hill and Richard W. Hill Sr. (New York: National Museum of the American Indian, 1994), 14, 19.

43. The literature on this topic is, of course, enormous; we assume familiarity with that literature on the part of the readers of this volume and will not reiterate its familiar critiques here.

44. Bruce Ferguson, "Exhibition Rhetorics: Material Speech and Utter Sense," in Greenberg et al., *Thinking about Exhibitions*, 184.

45. bell hooks, "Choosing the Margin as a Space of Radical Openness," in *Yearning: Race, Gender, and Cultural Politics* (Boston: South End Press, 1990), 153.

46. hooks, "Choosing the Margin," 152.

9. What Are Our Expectations Telling Us?

Encounters with the
National Museum of the American Indian

Gwyneira Isaac

I had two vastly dissimilar encounters with the inaugural exhibits at the National Museum of the American Indian (NMAI) in Washington DC during its celebratory opening in September 2004. My first encounter was at the reception for museum staff, consultants, and their families, where I was accompanied by a group of anthropologists and museologists who were animated with anticipation for what they hoped would be a landmark series of exhibits and a turning point in Native American museology. As a group of people whose lives are clearly defined by museums, we were at home analyzing the architecture and displays. During our critique, however, we discovered that a number of features confounded us and thwarted our understanding of the goals of the exhibits, providing stimulating discussions and an immense amount of intellectual and critical fodder for future examination and research.

My second visit was with an enthusiastic colleague who accompanied me in the small hours of the morning on the first day the museum was made accessible to the public. The museum stayed open through the night to accommodate the large groups of visitors who had flocked to this new and significantly visible personality on the Mall. On this occasion, I found the museum to be a welcoming beacon alight in the otherwise still night, the entrance dome pulsating with singing and the galleries alive with hundreds of families enjoying a midnight adventure. During this second visit, we spent less time analyzing the exhibits and more on conferring about the palpable sense of a shared public experience and the performance of history here in Washington. This late-night journey through the museum was so markedly different from my first encounter two days earlier that I felt compelled to write not only on the exhibits themselves, but on what we bring to them as visitors. I wanted to explore how the stories museums tell us are not just presented in the exhibits; their social meanings are created by the intersection of curators, audiences, media, and scholars who publicize, frame, and ultimately layer varied interpretations of the exhibits. While curators may aim to communicate particular meanings, we need to develop a framework for understanding how exhibits are experienced that allows for the co-construction of meaning between curators and their audiences. To further complicate things, all of these players may identify with or use different knowledge systems and approaches to knowledge, therefore requiring a nuanced framework that recognizes how these systems differ or overlap.

The opening of the NMAI also offers an unprecedented opportunity to look at how Native Americans have chosen to tell their stories in a national venue and to consider how museum experiences are performances of history, where audiences play a crucial role in determining how these histories create meaning at a broader social level. The aim of this essay is to move beyond issues of representation and to address how museum meanings are made on the ground in ongoing encounters between displays and the ideational worlds their audiences bring with them into the museum space. In particular, I explore how contrasting expectations about exhibits can serve as an interpretive strategy to identify coexisting, but distinctly different, approaches to knowledge that operate within the museum space. My explorations are based on four different encounters with the NMAI. The initial two encounters are visits to the museum itself, and the following two are experiences with the museum through newspaper articles and discussions. To give an interesting twist to James Clifford's travel diary of four Northwest Coast museums, I have written this as a personal reflection on four encounters with the same museum, showing the open-ended and fluid nature of histories and the ongoing processes we use to make sense of contrasting expectations, experiences, and knowledge systems.[1]

In effect, I am considering where the locus of meaning in museum exhibits is situated. Is it in the exhibit itself, or in the mind of the viewer? An analogous and appropriate framework for examining the construction of meaning comes from the interpretation of photography.[2] Although a deceptively simple medium that materializes an index of reality, photographs require a complex framework of interrogation in order for us to wholly grasp our relationship with these man-made simulacra of the world, and how our perceptions of the world are, in turn, determined by photographs themselves. Photographs can also be seen as agents of change, transforming our perception of the passage of time and change itself and therefore our ideas about reality.[3] We now consider the locus of meaning within photographs to be between the creator, the world, and the viewer in the dynamic process of the co-construction of meaning. Elizabeth Edwards's work on our assumptions about photographs and their use in exhibits helps us to consider the extent to which we can interpret the co-construction of meaning that takes place between viewer and museum displays.[4] She argues that there is a "nexus of genre, expectancy and performance" that is "used within the exhibit context to generate a preferred reading of the exhibition or specific objects within it."[5] The implication is that expectations about particular genres may be created as a tacit concordance between the perspectives of the curators and the public.[6] This process results in what I refer to here as "genres of expectancy," which are preferred ways of doing things and which are easily recognized by an intended audience. I use the concept of genres of expectancy to examine the different approaches to knowledge and how these may determine the co-construction of meaning between curators and audiences at the NMAI.

While reviewing this essay, colleagues asked me two questions about genres of expectancy that I want to address at this point. First, are the genres determined by the curators' preferences or by the expectations held by their audience? I have specifically chosen the term "genre" to refer to an arena in which there are shared assumptions about the ways of doing things, in the same way "style" may be understood as a shared aesthetic. In acknowledging the diversity of perspectives, we know it is impossible for curators to meet the needs of all members of their audience; however, genres of expectancy can be used to identify the groups created where the expectations of audience members and curators overlap. Second, are genres of expectation acted out by the curator in anticipation of how exhibits are read by a specific audience? Genres of expectancy do reflect how curators choose target audiences and anticipate how they will interpret an exhibit. More important, however, genres of expectancy are not just preferred ways of doing things; they are also preferred ways of seeing the world, and are therefore linked to the particular system or systems of knowledge adhered to by the curator and his or her audience. I have chosen the term "expectancy" because it implies a mental state that brings together judgments of past, present, and future performances of someone or something. Thus the study of expectations allows us to look at the layering of meanings within a temporal context.

Although we may agree on accepted and recognized genres of expectancy, we must also consider that the meaning or interpretation of an exhibit may not be so easily controlled or limited. It has already been established that a dissonance of intended meanings can occur between curators and their audiences, as in the case of the controversial exhibit Into the Heart of Africa at the Royal Ontario Museum.[7] In this exhibit curators used nineteenth-century posters originally designed as propaganda that depicted European colonialism as a beneficent patriarchal society. The curators' intent had been to alert audiences to the power of racist social ideology to determine public policies. These posters in their contemporary Canadian context, however, aroused suspicion and anger from visitors who thought that they were displayed with the intention of supporting racist ideology. Similarly, there have been conflicts over the particular versions of history that should be communicated by an exhibit, as seen in the *Enola Gay* controversy at the Smithsonian.[8] Through these experiences, the idea of a new museology with alternative practices was developed, such as multivocal exhibits and community collaborations, which were designed to counteract the problems raised by conflicting ideas about authority.[9] In the ongoing critique of museums, we have continually asked who has the authority to tell history. Often conflicts arise in which the different portrayals of cultural viewpoints or the perspectives of different social classes collide uncomfortably within the museum space. The problem is perceived to be an issue of representation that can be somewhat solved by creating exhibits that incorporate multiple perspectives.[10] Alternatively, it can also be solved through the development of displays or tribal museums that are founded and operated by the cultures themselves in a move toward self-representation.[11] By incorporating reflexive methods and community collaborations, curators imagine that they can co-construct meanings in exhibits before these displays are encountered by the public. Although this is not a consciously articulated perspective, I would argue that curators are aiming to incorporate their target audiences' viewpoints into the exhibits as a means of encouraging visitors to identify with the displays, thus making them participants rather than observers. This approach, however, does not take into account how people do not merely translate exhibits using different perspectives on history, but adhere to different knowledge systems. The resulting interpretations are also based on audiences' expectations about varied approaches to knowledge.

In the case of the NMAI, curators openly argued that they wanted to privilege Native Americans, and therefore this particular target audience would determine the manner in which the exhibits communicate and are interpreted. Native Americans, however, do not adhere to a simple, singular genre of expectancy for the interpretation of museums exhibits. Some want to move away from anthropologically informed models; some expect a conventional, if not "traditional," museum. We need to uncover a complex range of contrasting expectations about museums in order to understand how the NMAI adheres to or creates new genres of expectancy. Although a detailed exploration of the broad range of expectations is beyond the scope of this essay, I focus on the mix of different approaches to knowledge from which new genres of expectancy now stem.

I am always drawn to thinking about the relationship between personal and collective histories, and in particular the processes we use to locate ourselves in collective narratives. How do we identify with the historical narratives we find in exhibits and museums? In this particular analysis of historical narrative at the NMAI, it is important to explain the origins of my interest in museums and how this journey has led me to look at the different approaches to knowledge. My research currently focuses on the A:shiwi A:wan Museum and Heritage Center in the Pueblo of Zuni and how this public institution mediates Euro-American and Zuni approaches to knowledge. In the early 1990s I met members of the Zuni Religious Advisory Team who were visiting the Peabody Museum at Harvard University as part of the consulting process for the repatriation of an Ahayuda, the Zuni War God. During this visit I learned that photographs of Zunis from the past century that were housed at the National Anthropological Archives had been duplicated and sent to the Zuni Museum. This duplicate collection provided a remarkable opportunity to examine how the same objects were curated in two different cultural contexts: within a local community museum, the A:shiwi A:wan Museum and Heritage Center in Zuni, and in a national context at the Smithsonian Institution.

Between 1996 and 1998 I conducted eighteen months of fieldwork in the Pueblo of Zuni, largely based at the A:shiwi A:wan Museum, during which time I learned of the complex origins of the museum and its relationship with the community. Knowledge in Zuni is compartmentalized into a complex series of esoteric religious societies, medicine lodges, and clans.[12] No individual has access to all of these societies, and esoteric knowledge is the responsibility of specific individuals, who maintain it for the larger group. Expectations about the transmission of knowledge privilege transfer through oral tradition and initiation into esoteric religious societies. As a result, the Zuni museum faced the challenge of mediating Euro-American and Zuni knowledge systems and defining what is permitted as public knowledge, both for uninitiated Zunis and for non-Zuni visitors. From my experiences in Zuni, I was forced to think about different systems of knowledge and how these may coexist and, at times, operate independently from each other within a single institution such as the A:shiwi A:wan Museum.[13] My analysis of the NMAI is a continuation of this research, drawing from experiences in Zuni and applying them to a broader examination of how different but concurrent systems of knowledge may operate at a national level.

Although the approaches to knowledge that are at play at the NMAI are numerous, I want to tease out two particular systems that I see as codeterminants in shaping both shared meanings and the underlying tensions present in the museum. The first of these two approaches is the concept of comprehensive knowledge, namely, the idea that knowledge "is singular, not plural, global and not local, that all knowledges ... ultimately turn out to be concordant in one great system of knowledge."[14] Although this concept of knowledge harkens back to Enlightenment philosophies and nineteenth-century ideas about the stability of scientific data, it is still extremely influential within current ideational and organizational schemas. The second concept is belief in the plurality of knowledges and knowledge systems, heralded by the critiques of the grand narratives of history and anthropology as well as in sociology and the study of the complex construction of different social realities.[15] Although this schema of the plurality of knowledges can accommodate the concept of comprehensive knowledge as one particular system among many, the ideas that structure notions about comprehensive knowledge negate the possibility of many independent systems functioning according to different organizational categories and logic.

My first encounter with the NMAI was framed within a very specific critical discourse on museums. Within this largely academic discourse and, as I explore here, genre of expectancy, we develop and interpret exhibits by looking for themes that provide coherence and an organizational framework, as well as question how these themes are used to communicate information to the public. The central concerns are the message of the exhibit and whether it is communicated successfully. However, we need to ask, What are some of the criteria used within the critical academic discourse to determine if an exhibit is successful? In this realm, we tend to have assumptions about the scholarly objectives of any project, and we critique exhibits on whether they reveal in-depth research and, more specifically, if they add new dimensions to the discipline in which the curator is seen to participate. I say "we" to specifically refer to those involved in the academic critique of museums, thus locating myself and my assumptions within this particular interpretation of museums. Critiques also center around how the exhibit engages with particular discourses, including the style of narrative and if it is based on a singular authority or multiple voices. We question how the curator determines the relationship between objects and texts and if he or she intended the objects to speak for themselves or to be contextualized or anchored by a text. Over the past two centuries, museologists, historians, and anthropologists have developed models not only of how museum exhibits should operate but also how they should be interpreted.[16]

To avoid oversimplifying the processes that go into the critique of exhibits, I want to provide an example that not only is from my personal experience but also offers a broader perspective on the evaluation of museum exhibits. When I first started my joint position as an assistant professor and museum director, I had numerous debates with colleagues, department chairs, and deans about the appraisal of exhibits in the tenure process. These discussions were informative because they helped me reach a more nuanced view of the relationship between academia and museums. Some argued that a book would be more highly regarded than an exhibit; others suggested that exhibits were important, but that they must travel nationally in order to be considered public dissemination of research. Many suggested that I needed to prove that the exhibit had been peer-reviewed, to show that the knowledge displayed was acceptable to a specialist audience. Although people presented different ideas about how to evaluate exhibits, all agreed that an exhibit should have an accompanying publication to show in-depth research and how this contributed to the discipline. This particular "reading" of exhibits privileged textual over visual dissemination of knowledge, a point also made by Ruth Phillips, who argues that some view exhibits as "essentially ephemeral, performative, and 'soft,'" versus knowledge in the academy, "the home of the book," where knowledge is "essentially permanent, objectifiable and 'hard.'"[17]

As I explored the NMAI with my colleagues on September 21, I was acutely aware of the expectations that we shared stemming from this academic discourse on museums. Our first impression was awe at the magnitude of the NMAI project: the building, the media, and the political parading. During this first encounter, however, I never quite felt at home. Trying to understand the museum was like fiddling with the tuning dial on a radio and picking up only sound bites and static while looking for a clear signal. The grand entrance hall is breathtaking, with its soaring domed roof and undulating walls, but the ground level of this space is partitioned awkwardly, creating jarring barriers to the circular rotunda. Above is an architectural analogy of the universe, but on the ground is a fractured and disjointed maze of barricades. Similarly, in the hallways between galleries are rolling, wave-like walls juxtaposed with mundane corporate carpet. This reading of the building paralleled my interpretation of the museum as a whole, as a universe made up of dissonant parts. I was also intrigued by the decision not to have a starting point for the museum and no clear distinction on how one should travel through the galleries. Should one travel from the top down, or from the ground up?

The museum is made up of four floors of galleries, cafés, theaters, and stores. At the ground level is the grand entrance hall, which is flanked by the Chesapeake Museum Store and the Mitsitam Café, which means "Let's eat" in the language of the Piscataway and Delaware peoples. Opposite the café is the large main theater space used to show films and hold live performances. On the second floor there are staff offices and the Roanoke Museum Store, which overlooks the rotunda. Above these, on the third floor, are two large exhibit spaces that showcase Our Lives: Contemporary Life and Identities, which explores the historic and contemporary forces that shape modern Native life, as well as a changing exhibit space that is currently showing Native Modernism: The Art of George Morrison and Allan Houser. There are two more permanent exhibits on the fourth floor: Our Universes: Traditional Knowledge Shapes Our World looks at Native American philosophy and the relationship between humankind and the natural world, and Our Peoples: Giving Voice to Our Histories presents Native Americans telling their own histories. Also on the fourth floor is the Lelawi Theater, which seats 120 and shows a thirteen-minute presentation on contemporary Native life. On both the third and fourth floors are glass cases referred to as Window on Collections: Many Hands, Many Voices that have typologically organized objects from the NMAI collections. The inaugural Windows included categories such as beadwork, dolls, jars, peace medals, lithics, and baskets.

After our initial tour of the museum, my colleagues and I decided to join up again to hear everyone's thoughts on the exhibits. The first part of our conversation focused on the exhibit Our Lives, as we felt it was so dense with text that it would overwhelm the general public. It was also pointed out that there was not a clear organizational structure or guiding narrative and that the decision to have a multitude of voices was taken to the extremes of this particular museological practice, so that the messages of the exhibit were scattered, disparate, and unguided. The unstructured approach to moving the visitor through the museum was mirrored in the lack of an overarching narrative in the majority of the exhibits. We also discussed the glass cases in the corridors Window on Collections and our surprise that, though they were assembled according to basic themes such as beadwork or dolls, there were no labels or identification of the objects themselves. The only source of information was provided on computer screens perched on podiums in front of the cases; thus any curiosity about an object required the viewer to draw away from the object itself and look into the virtual world of info-technology. This lack of labels appeared to go against any accepted museological principles concerning the educational purposes of museums. We concluded that knowledge in this space was seen by the curators as not transmitted through text, but transferred visually and to be predicated on aesthetic judgments alone.

A window case on arrowheads became the focal point of our conversation. This display consisted of a dramatic and beautiful arrangement of lithics, where a multitude of arrowheads were oriented in such a way as to make a swirling pattern that moved like a river, eddying, floating, and sweeping across a neutral background. There was no information in this case on the tools, no cultural or geographic regions of origin listed, and no accompanying dates indicating when they were made. Although this lack of information confounded my colleagues, they were more concerned with the fact that the display resembled, if not mimicked, the decorative conventions of amateur collectors and their cabinets of curiosity of the nineteenth century. These cabinets were a tradition much criticized by Native Americans for their inability to demonstrate the values attributed to these tools by their creators. It is a display technique reevaluated in the 1920s by museologists and anthropologists, such as Franz Boas, who eventually developed new methods such as the diorama in order to contextualize objects by evaluating them according to use and social context rather than aesthetic values.

The exhibit everyone seemed more comfortable with was Native Modernism: The Art of George Morrison and Allan Houser. Many would consider this the most conventional of the four inaugural exhibits. Not only does it follow Morrison and Houser according to the chronology of their development as artists, but there is also a single curatorial voice that guides the visitor through the exhibit. The development of each artist is explored according to his life, as well as the influences of various art movements and their contribution to the field. This exhibit style resonated with us as a familiar arena in which the intellectual architecture contextualizes the work within a larger body of knowledge. Our knowledge of this genre was also played out in our ability to understand directly the relationships between objects and texts as presented in the exhibit. While the spotlights focused on the objects and gave them center stage, there were texts providing the information many museum-goers seek, such as biographical information and the date the art piece was made.

From my first encounter with the NMAI, I developed the view that the exhibits created an ambiguous museological realm that resulted from a mixture of expectations about comprehensive and plural knowledges. The titles of the main inaugural exhibits are very telling: the first three—Our Universes, Our Peoples, and Our Lives—are comfortable with their celebration of the plurality of knowledges. Clearly, Our Universes implies that there are not just different perspectives and voices, but that in fact there are a multitude of different knowledge systems. Interestingly, the only title of the four exhibits that is not in the plural and does not use a possessive pronoun is Native Modernism, and indeed this is the only exhibit that adheres to some of the accepted means of arranging knowledge within a singular and cohesive organizational structure. Moreover, the contrast in titles suggests that the museum values frameworks based on comprehensive knowledge as less useful in the process of establishing identity politics than those based on the plurality of knowledges. This is not to argue that this exhibit merely places art within the Western discourse on art, because it provides a layered portrayal of the role of Hauser and Morrison both in Native American and Euro-American terms. The curator, however, uses two protagonists, Hauser and Morrison, to get the audience to think about what it takes to transcend both national and international boundaries as artists and, more specifically, as artists drawing on and exploring their Native histories and identities. While many visitors may not be conversant in the history of art, Native Modernism allows people to discover the ways these artists explored art movements, thus both providing the individual artist's view of Native and non-Native worlds as well as relating these views to a cross-cultural social history. This exhibit demonstrates how ideas about comprehensive knowledge and plural knowledges inevitably coexist, but it finds a way to articulate the route through this terrain, showing how the work is both located within a singular body of knowledge on "art" as a Western category and also stems from and continues to circulate within specific Native systems of knowledge and meaning.

My second visit to the NMAI was so strikingly different from the first that it became instrumental in leading me to question the various factors that go into the interpretation of exhibits. Specifically, it raised my awareness of the need to distinguish between the interpretation and the experience of exhibits. My aim here is to provide a deeper understanding of how these approaches differ or overlap and how we relate to or position ourselves in the production of knowledge/s and the performances of public history. I would also argue that we do not interpret the meanings of exhibits only from the visit to the exhibit itself. Expectations created prior to experiencing an exhibit and discussions following our first encounter, as well as subsequent visits to the exhibit, merge to form a complex layering of experiences that determine how that exhibit will mean to us.

During this subsequent visit I concluded that this museum was indeed a complex creature with which I needed a second encounter to fully grasp its personality and eccentricities. You may be sure that the crowd of people visiting a museum at 2 in the morning is made up of dedicated museum-goers or event enthusiasts. At the entrance to the museum music reverberated around the rotunda and resonated throughout the building and staircases, bringing people together to face inward toward the central performance arena. On this visit, I attended an introductory film in the Lelawi Theater. Although I have subsequently discussed the positive aspects of the film with my colleagues, during my first encounter with it, I found the film to be an oddly romantic depiction of nameless tribes that created a blurred view of pan-Indian identity. The performance of the film, however, created a positive dynamic in the audience. Placing forty or so museum visitors in a circular screening room where they can see each other generates a not unimportant or unrecognized cohort of people that now share this experience.

At the entrance is a vast undulating glass wall that displays a constellation of gold artifacts and figurines from the Aztec, Mayan, and Olmec cultures of Mesoamerica. During my first visit to the museum, I had been confounded by the fact that none of these objects was labeled and so they formed a nebulous bundle of "things." On my second visit, however, I was struck by the fact that the purpose of the exhibit was not to inform the public on the intricacies of Mesoamerican arts and histories, but to overwhelm and dazzle us with the basic concept of "gold" as a valuable and desirable metal. This wall curves around into the exhibit space, leading into a wall display of weapons. In the course of my first encounter these were merely unidentified swords, rifles, and pistols of conquerors, but in this second viewing they confronted me in their sheer quantity and iconographic value as symbols of "power." Another wall is made up of Bibles translated into Native American languages, representing colonialism and assimilation, the ideology of the colonists. The curators, Paul Chaat Smith and Jolene Rickard, appeared to argue that the detailed dates and names of the invaders and their chronologies of victories may fade, but we still need to question how the vestiges of their ideology continue to hold a significant place of iconographical and ideological power.

Our Peoples wants to elicit an emotive response from its audience about the experience of being colonized. While this is not necessarily a new genre of exhibits, what makes it more complicated is that the curators are also engaging with postmodern discourse on the history of colonialism—a discourse that stems from the academic critique of how history is created, constructed, and controlled. At the beginning of the exhibit is a video performance with a narrator who refers to the process of "making history" and argues that "all histories have a history themselves, and one is incomplete without the other." This ideology is firmly within postmodern and postcolonial discourses on the reflexivity and plurality of histories. The narrator states that this gallery "offer[s] self-told histories." This first portion of Our Peoples is not about a collaboration of Native American communities per se; it is about responding to the preexisting European system of meaning and relocating Native voices in the discourses that reverse ideas about the colonized as victim. The exhibit exists not to give specific Native Americans a voice. It exists to argue that history itself is subjective and that the Native experience of colonization cannot be understood until the nature of the varied histories themselves is understood.

As a result, this exhibit compels us to consider how we view the various genres of expectancy associated with how history is performed in different cultural contexts. We are also thrown back onto our earlier exploration of comprehensive knowledge and plural knowledges, but now with the understanding that the manner in which we tell our history or histories relies on these systems. We therefore need to ask, Is history a cross-cultural category? Although genre-specific interpretations and performances of the past do not transcend cultural systems of meaning, all cultural systems have ways of telling about or performing the past. In "A Poetic for Histories," a chapter in his book *Performances*, Greg Dening portrays different Euro-American vernacular genres. This appreciation of the different performances of the past introduces the idea that all cultures have diverse vernacular genres for telling past experiences, as well as more specialist and privileged genres and practitioners.[18]

In Our Peoples Jolene Rickard and Smith do not want us to learn the details of Native American history, they want us to question our ethnocentric ideas about history itself. With its lack of labels and guidance, the exhibit is deceptively simple. Its purpose, however, is exceedingly intricate and challenges commonplace ideas about history as a singular and shared experience. What should we make of this new genre that confounds people who want labels and textual guidance? Is it designed to appeal to postmodernists wanting not only the deconstruction of the symbolic ideology of colonialism, but also the deconstruction of the museum as the authority of our history/histories? Although it could be argued that postmodernist ideology is the organizational schema that provides the guiding narrative, the construction of meaning here forms a complex process that merges comprehensive and plural notions of knowledge. This exhibit almost becomes a mediational space that encourages audiences to combine and separate, evaluate, and define these different knowledge systems. I am not arguing that this was necessarily the intent of the curators, as their focus was on portraying to visitors their ideas about interpretive frameworks based on the plurality of histories. Yet when Smith argues that there are alternative "self- told" histories, he automatically also acknowledges that there are metanarratives in the tradition of the comprehensive system of knowledge. As a result, the audience is faced, whether or not by curatorial intent, with the challenging experience of coming to terms with two different ways of looking at the world.

James Clifford proposes that certain processes exist in museums and exhibits within the negotiations between Native Americans and scholars and that "the complex, unfinished colonial entanglements of anthropology and Native communities are being undone and rewoven."[19] He identifies the key processes involved as the articulations, performances, and translations of identity and argues that these processes are useful "components of an analytic tool kit for understanding old/new indigenous formations."[20] He is focused on uncovering the politics of tradition through an analysis of the history of collaboration in the Arctic; however, his analytical tools (or processes) are not explained in terms of cross-cultural categories or in reference to, as Ruth Phillips points out, the different approaches to knowledge production. Phillips argues that "key aspects of traditional indigenous knowledge are fundamentally incompatible with Western traditions of knowledge production."[21] This exchange between Clifford and Phillips is useful in highlighting the need to find new frameworks to assess the production of knowledge through the confluence of or independently coexisting knowledge systems. With a framework based on genres of expectancy, we can ask how people are situating themselves within the public performance of history and how they use particular knowledge systems to validate and authenticate these histories. As I will now address, we need to recognize the manner in which individuals collect these experiences to internalize coexisting layers of meanings and continually engage with the relationships between different knowledge systems.

My third encounter with the NMAI was through the many reviews written about the museum in newspapers. I followed these closely to study how the media created meanings from the exhibits at the NMAI. I also asked what assumptions or genres of expectancy were being employed to critique exhibits. A handful of journalists who reviewed the NMAI scripted their articles around their disappointment of the lack of a singular guiding narrative, accusing the museum of being ahistorical. This particular critique originated from assumptions similar to those I addressed in my discussion on the academic and scientific genre of expectancy of contributions to a singular body of knowledge. For example, Marc Fisher of the *Washington Post* wrote, "The museum fails to give visitors the basic tools needed to ask good skeptical questions. There is not nearly enough fact or narrative to give us the foundation we need to judge the Indians' version of their story."[22] Paul Richard, also of the *Washington Post*, argued, "What's missing is the glue of thought that might connect one [object] to another. Instead one tends to see totem poles and T-shirts, headdresses and masks, toys and woven baskets, projectile points and gym shoes, things both new and ancient, beautiful and not, all stirred decoratively together in no important order that the viewer can discern."[23] Thus far, Euro-American scholars have largely constructed their ideas about history and culture, as well as collected data on these subjects, through organizational schemas that are, at least in the imaginations of the general public, vestiges of nineteenth-century beliefs in the idea of comprehensive knowledge. Fisher provides an example of this way of thinking in requesting a unified history in the NMAI, both for political and scholarly reasons: "American History is a thrilling and disturbing sway from conflict to consensus and back again. But the contours of the battle between division and coalition are too often lost in the way history is taught today. Now sadly, the Smithsonian, instead of synthesizing our stories, shirks its responsibility to give new generations of Americans the tools with which to ask the questions that could clear a path toward a more perfect union."

Journalists looking for traditional Euro-American historical chronologies or organizational schemas were disappointed in the exhibits. Edward Rothstein of the *New York Times* argued that the museum privileged multivocality and the diversity of viewpoints over an organized investigation of Native American culture and history: "The goal of making that museum answer to the needs, tastes and traditions of perhaps 600 diverse tribes . . . results in so many constituencies that the museum often ends up filtering away detail rather than displaying it."[24] Tiffany Jenkins from the *Independent Review* in London looked at the access policies and therefore the role of the museum in contributing to research agendas. She noted that some of the collections are restricted and may be viewed and studied only by members from the tribe where these objects originate. She argued that "what is lost at NMAI is that knowledge and truth does not come from our biology and background. We can all attempt to comprehend our shared pasts through investigation, inquiry and debate, regardless of where we were born and to whom."[25] Again, this particular perspective assumes that there are shared truths that can be ascertained through objective frameworks of inquiry and that these truths also come together to form a shared unifying history of humankind.

The journalists who wrote favorable reviews celebrated the museum's

opening as a stance against traditional scientific schemas and, in particular, the anthropological frameworks through which Native Americans
were viewed:

> For five centuries, others have tried to define these people labeled Indians, to
> categorize them, to put them in some kind of taxonomy, the way scientists
> describe beetles, birds or bison. Conquistadors had their say, and tobacco
> planters, and Pilgrims, and Founding Fathers, and missionaries, and Army
> generals, and finally all the ethnologists and anthropologists who in the 19th
> century emerged from universities and East Coast museums, taking the mea-
> sure of these native people— and perhaps bringing home some masks, pot-
> tery and human bones.[26]

This particular stance taken against anthropology could also be linked
to the perspectives of many Native American curators at the NMAI who
encouraged alternative modes to understanding history and culture. As
Clifford argues, "'The anthropologist'—broadly and sometimes stereo-
typically defined—has become a negative alter ego in contemporary indigenous discourse."[27] In the Washington Post, James Pepper Henry, the NMAI
deputy assistant director for cultural resources, was quoted as saying that
the NMAI would not follow conventional anthropological practices, as
"this is a venue for native peoples to tell their story. You are not going to
get the anthropological perspective."[28] Gerald McMaster, a deputy assistant director for the museum, argued, "Anthropology as a science is not
practiced here. . . . We look to the communities themselves as authorities about who they are."[29] Another reporter stated that museum leaders
argued that the NMAI was "a resolute effort to step outside the objectifying habits of anthropology and all the other disciplines with mainstream museum cred."[30]

A number of journalists also demonstrated how they believed anthropology still relies on antiquated ideas about comprehensive knowledge:
"Anthropologists roam from the present to the distant past, from the
Information Age to the Stone Age. They gobble up data, connect cultural dots, listen to exotic tongues and attempt to push their observa-

tions through some kind of scientific filter."[31] In this view, anthropology adheres to nineteenth-century ideas about the production and categorization of knowledge and has yet to accept the plurality of knowledges. Phillip Kennicott of the *Washington Post* argued that rather than "simply putting a sunny face on the kind of anthropology represented by Mead," the new museum "is a monument to Postmodernism— to a way of thinking that emphasizes multiple voices and playful forms of truth over the lazy acceptance of received wisdom, authority and scientific 'certainty.'"[32] These journalists broadened the critique of anthropology beyond colonial politics and the struggle for self-representation and tackled what they saw as the public's legitimate mistrust of science as an arbitrary form of authoritarianism.

The media's view of the NMAI shows the two perspectives that are central to my argument about the ways dissimilar systems of knowledge are negotiated in this museum. One group of journalists argued that the museum has failed to provide a systematic treatment of knowledge; another group suggested that the NMAI acknowledges the plurality of knowledges and is successful in giving Native Americans a voice. In each perspective, the genre of expectancy to which the journalists ascribe privileges either comprehensive knowledge or the plurality of knowledges as the accepted framework for the creation and interpretation of exhibits.

The apparent bifurcation of these two views, however, belies the nature of the world we live in and how these different ideas play out on the ground. Comprehensive and pluralistic views of knowledge have coexisted for at least half a century, and there are areas of ambiguity where both are used simultaneously and are part of the dynamic construction of meaning. As I illustrated in my discussion of the Houser and Morrison exhibit, these two approaches are, in some areas, a necessary part of understanding the exhibits at the NMAI. The production of new knowledges at the NMAI comes from the coexistence of and conflict between these two approaches. This process also creates irresolvable tensions in which both viewpoints are mutually dependent on each other for their interpretation in a public setting. In this particular case, the NMAI's stance against anthropology is valid as long as comprehensive or scientific knowledge is upheld by others and therefore sustains an ongoing dialogue.

We must note the assumptions made by journalists who portray anthropologists as the purveyors of comprehensive knowledge and Indians as the purveyors of postmodern and pluralist perspectives on knowledge. They fail to acknowledge that anthropology has been a central part of the critique of paradigms that relied on comprehensive knowledge. Similarly, not all Native Americans are arguing for paradigms based on multivocal and plural systems of knowledge; some are arguing for Native American voices to be included in the master narratives of history, thus legitimating both grand narratives and the plurality of knowledge. It is also worth clarifying that the journalistic view of the NMAI is not necessarily that of the general public, and much of what was considered in these reviews, such as the positive or negative role of anthropology, is not necessarily central to how members of the public interpret the exhibits at the museum.

To conclude, I want to relay a fourth encounter with the NMAI, which took place a month after my first two visits and my reading of the newspaper reviews. I had telephoned my uncle, Rhys Isaac, a historian of colonial America, to hear his views on the new museum. He responded to the museum's location at the right-hand shoulder of the Capitol by declaring it the public announcement of a new order of political representation in Washington: "The museum is concerned with manifesto and is a wonderful declaration" of the principles and objectives of contemporary Native Americans. He agreed that the museum openly experiments with alternative ways of telling history and eschews Euro-American categories in favor of new rhetorical modes. It proclaims that "there is not one way of knowing, or one way of telling history and that scientists do not have a monopoly on understanding Native American history and culture." He also referred to the "stream of artifacts" in the museum that were designed to be visually and textually fluid in order to develop this new genre for telling history, and as such, these exhibits were "sure to madden the archaeologists and delight the postmodernists."[33]

He and I also discussed the layering of ideologies, and I shared with him my argument about different but mutually dependent knowledge systems. Our conversation raised my awareness of how meaning is not merely co-constructed within and limited to an engagement between curator, visitor, and exhibit, but also needs to be seen as layers of coexisting meanings. An appropriate analogy would be the sediments of a riverbed, which can be seen simultaneously and diachronically when a profile section is cut and analyzed. The history of the river can be seen only either horizontally or vertically, because cutting a profile of one destroys the visibility and translation of the other. From above, however, each layer coexists and forms a complex undulating landscape, and it is this perspective with which we are most familiar. The underlying layers influence the shape as a whole, and all layers are contrasting, separate, and at the same time mutually dependent in shaping the riverbed. The different public meanings that have been produced by visitors to the NMAI are made up of the intersection of numerous knowledge systems, two of which I have highlighted here.

I also want to clarify that readers should not take away from this essay the idea that there is an agreed upon and purposeful coherence to the exhibits at the NMAI, thus suggesting that all curators and the museum as a whole worked together to form a specific message about Native American culture and history. Individual curators project specific themes, and some of these themes are shared among the various curators, but it is far more interesting to encounter a complex layering of meaning and perspectives in the museum.

What can we learn from four encounters with one institution? How do we interpret the palimpsest of encounters, each one with its own audience, script, and performance? Once layered, like the riverbed, these form complex landscapes that often bring together contradictory ideologies and beliefs. In her review of current models used to develop exhibits, Phillips points out that we cannot understand the meanings produced by exhibits at only one point in time, but must see them as products of ongoing processes: "Museum exhibits do not work in a moment, and the creators of exhibits usually find out only years later, if ever, about the new perspectives that were suddenly glimpsed by a local visitor, a tourist, or a school child during a visit to an exhibit . . . of the curiosity that was whetted, or of the small epiphanies that were sparked."[34]

As shown by the varied responses from the media, visitors to the NMAI are exposed to both comprehensive knowledge and plural knowledges in contexts outside of the museum. Yet many people are obviously perplexed by the existence of these different underlying principles within the museum environment itself and are ill equipped to reach an understanding of the interactive dynamics between these dissimilar systems. Although the interaction between knowledge systems is not discussed openly by museums, we must imagine that we are at the start of the creation of new genres of expectancy, where different but coexisting systems are mutually dependent in creating dialogues and meanings. In her exploration of museum models, Phillips asks, "Is the increasing acceptance of the collaborative paradigm . . . evidence that a pluralistic postcolonial ethos has established itself as ideology?"[35] I would argue that although the intercultural and collaborative paradigm may be partially accepted within museums, the public is not aware of how these collaborations also adjudicate diverse knowledge systems. Phillips makes the astute comment that museums need to communicate to their audiences the intellectual processes that are involved in producing exhibits. I would take this line of reasoning further by arguing that we need to convey in some way to the public the manner in which different systems of knowledge are negotiated and mediated through institutions such as museums. As I discovered through my four encounters with the NMAI, museum experiences and ideational exchanges help us internalize the engagement of different knowledge systems, which are continually at play in the world around us.

Notes

This essay is very much the direct result of discussions held with colleagues about the National Museum of the American Indian, and I would like to acknowledge here the ideas and contributions made by Amy Lonetree, Joshua Bell, Keith Kintigh, Elizabeth Edwards, and Roger Anyon. I also want to thank my students at Arizona State University, Ramsi Watkins, Kimberley Arth, and William Calvo, who challenged and developed further my theories on knowledge systems. Appreciation for the clarification of the thoughts communicated here must go to Sean Walsh, who untiringly helped me to say what it really is that I want to say.

1. James Clifford, "Four Northwest Coast Museums: Travel Reflections," in *Exhibiting Culture: The Poetics of Museum Display*, ed. Ivan Karp and Steven D. Lavine (Washington DC: Smithsonian Institution Press, 1991).

2. Roland Barthes, *Image, Music, Text* (London: Fontana Press, 1977); John Berger and Jean Mohr, *Another Way of Telling* (Cambridge, England: Granta Books, 1989); Elizabeth Edwards, *Raw Histories* (New York: Routledge, 2002).

3. Gwyneira Isaac, "Re-Observation and the Recognition of Change: The Photographs of Matilda Coxe Stevenson 1879–1915," *Journal of the Southwest*, in press.

4. Edwards, *Raw Histories*.

5. Elizabeth Edwards writes that the origin of this argument stems from Henrietta Lidchi's article "Exposing 'Others'? Photography in the Exhibition Context," in *Boletin de Antropologia Visual* 1, no. 1 (1997): 15–39.

6. Edwards, *Raw Histories*, 184.

7. Henrietta Riegel, "Into the Heart of Irony: Ethnographic Exhibitions and the Politics of Difference," in *Theorizing Museums: Representing Identity and Diversity in a Changing World*, ed. Sharon Macdonald and Gordon Fyfe (Oxford: Blackwell, 1996).

8. Thomas F. Gieryn, "Balancing Acts: Science, Enola Gay and History Wars at the Smithsonian", in *The Politics of Display*, ed. Sharon Macdonald (London: Routledge, 1996).

9. Peter Vergo, *The New Museology* (London: Reaktion Books, 1989); Ivan Karp and Steven D. Lavine, eds., *Exhibiting Cultures: The Poetics and Politics of Museum Display* (Washington DC: Smithsonian Institution Press, 1991).

10. Ivan Karp, Steven D. Lavine, and Catherine Kreamer, eds., *Museums and Communities: The Politics of Public Culture* (Washington DC: Smithsonian Institution Press, 1992).

11. Moira Simpson, *Making Representations: Museums in the Post-Colonial Era* (London: Routledge, 1996).

12. Matilda Coxe Stevenson, "The Zuni Indians: Their Mythology, Esoteric Fraternities and Religious Ceremonies," in *23rd Annual Report of the Bureau of American Ethnology for 1901–1902* (Washington DC: U.S. Government Printing Office, 1904); Fred Eggan, *Social Organisation of the Western Pueblos* (Chicago: University of Chicago Press, 1950); Alfred L. Kroeber, *Zuni Kin and Clans*, Anthropological Papers of the American Museum of Natural History, vol. 18, part 2, 1917.

13. Gwyneira Isaac, "The Museum as Mediator; A Case Study of the A:shiwi A:wan Museum and Heritage Center, Zuni, New Mexico" (D.Phil. diss., University of Oxford, 2002).

14. Thomas Richards, *The Imperial Archive: Knowledge and the Fantasy of Empire* (London: Verso, 1993), 7.

15. Peter Berger and Thomas Luckmann, *The Social Construction of Reality* (New York: Doubleday, 1966).

16. Didier Maleuvre, *Museum Memories: History, Technology, Art*, (Stanford: Stanford University Press, 1996).

17. Ruth Phillips, "'Reply' to James Clifford's 'Looking Several Ways: Anthropology and Native Heritage in Alaska,'" *Current Anthropology* 45, no. 1 (2004): 25.

18. Greg Dening, *Performances* (Chicago: University of Chicago Press, 1996).

19. James Clifford, "Looking Several Ways: Anthropology and Native Heritage in Alaska," *Current Anthropology* 45, no. 1 (2004): 6.

20. Clifford, "Looking Several Ways," 20.

21. Phillips, "Reply," 25.

22. Marc Fisher, "Indian Museum's Appeal, Sadly, Only Skin Deep," *Washington Post*, September 21, 2004.

23. Paul Richard, "Shards of Many Untold Stories: In Place of Unity, a Melange of Unconnected Objects," *Washington Post*, September 21, 2004.

24. Edward Rothstein, "Who Should Tell History: The Tribes or the Museums?," *New York Times*, December 21, 2003.

25. Tiffany Jenkins, "The Museum of Political Correctness," *Independent Review*, January 25, 2005.

26. Joel Achenbach, "Within These Walls, Science Yields to Stories," *Washington Post*, September 19, 2004.

27. Clifford, "Looking Several Ways," 5.

28. James Pepper Henry, cited in Achenbach, "Within These Walls."

29. Gerald McMaster, cited in Achenbach, "Within These Walls."

30. Phillip Kennicott, "A Particular Kind of Truth: As the Culture Wars Rage, a Rare Victory over Routes of Knowledge," *Washington Post*, September 19, 2004.

31. Achenback, "Within These Walls."

32. Kennicott, "A Particular Kind of Truth."

33. Rhys Isaac, personal communication with the author, October 30, 2004.

34. Ruth Phillips, "Community Collaboration in Exhibitions: Introduction," in *Museums and Source Communities*, ed. Laura Peers and Alison Brown (London: Routledge, 2003), 167.

35. Phillips, "Community Collaboration," 167.

10. No Sense of the Struggle

Creating a Context for Survivance at the
National Museum of the American Indian

Sonya Atalay

Museums, collecting, anthropology, and archaeology were developed within, and are deeply entrenched in, a Western epistemological framework and have histories that are strongly colonial in nature.[1] As with most contemporary fields of study, these areas of research and practice are fully steeped in Western ways of knowing, naming, ordering, analyzing, and understanding the world. Indigenous people, both outside and within the academy, along with a number of non-Indigenous scholars globally, have struggled long and hard to bring the Western and colonial nature of these fields to the foreground. They have worked to bring us to the place we are today, where such statements are acknowledged (by most scholars) and where those who want to continue working to change these disciplines in positive ways have a space to do so.

The National Museum of the American Indian (NMAI) is one of those spaces. The NMAI attempts to profoundly change the practice of museology and the role of Indigenous people in museums on a grand scale. In some ways it is successful in its mission, yet other areas leave room for improvement. This essay focuses on the latter, and in it I offer critiques of the exhibits on display during the museum's opening on September 21, 2004. Although the substance of this essay is primarily critique and suggestions for improvement of the NMAI's exhibits, I want to be clear in stating that my aim is ultimately to support the NMAI because I believe so strongly in its aims, mission, and efforts, and in the profound power it has to speak to so many people about us—our lives, our communities, our struggles, and our rights as Native people of sovereign nations. I strongly believe that along with the NMAI's gift of voice, which is the result of financial, political, and community support from Native people, the U.S. government, and private and corporate donors, the museum also carries a serious responsibility to (re)present our stories to its several million visitors each year, both U.S. citizens and an increasingly large global audience.

My perspective is as a Native person (Ojibwe) who has academic training and research experience in archaeology, heritage studies, and public anthropology. My research focuses on Indigenous archaeology and the ways Native people in North America, along with Indigenous and local people globally, have positively influenced and continue to change the discipline of archaeology. I am not a specialist in museums exclusively, but museums are a critical part of heritage studies, and I have thought deeply for many years about issues of Indigenous heritage—about our pasts and the role of the past in the present. I've strived to both critique Western archaeological and anthropological practices and to develop models in which to do things better, as I believe that for practices to move forward and improve, dialogue and critique are crucial first steps that must be followed by practical models and ideas for change.[2]

Critical engagement, critique, and suggestions for improved practice are prominent themes in much of my own research, which attempts to decolonize archaeology and make it a more ethical and socially just practice that benefits the Indigenous and local communities it studies. In its creation and execution, the NMAI shares some of the aims of Indigenous archaeology. The museum consulted and worked closely with Native communities from throughout North and South America, moving beyond standard contemporary museum practices on a grand scale to create a museum and a process of operation that listens intently to the voices and concerns of Indigenous people. In these efforts, the NMAI joins a growing number of smaller, tribal museums in allowing Native people the power to control their own representation and heritage. The NMAI attempts to create an ethical and socially just museum practice, one that benefits Native communities, while it also educates the wider American and global community about Native peoples.

The aims of the NMAI overlap in many ways with my own research goals; however, whereas my work will likely reach only a limited group of scholars, students, and nonacademic publics, the messages within the walls of the NMAI will reach a far larger audience. Thus the NMAI has the potential to engender substantial transformations in the way diverse publics think and feel about the Native people of this hemisphere. In its role as a public educator, the NMAI literally has the ability to touch and influence the hearts and minds of millions, the voting citizens of our country and others, who are increasingly asked to vote on issues that directly affect the daily lives of Native people, such as tribal gaming, land and water issues, and fishing and hunting legislation. Visitors to the NMAI include school board members who approve curricula and textbooks that teach about "Columbus discovering America in 1492"; they are the senators, judges, and government leaders who write and have the power to approve legislation, such as the proposed changes to the Native American Graves Protection and Repatriation Act (NAGPRA) and intellectual and cultural property rights law.[3] Important audiences for the NMAI also include many of our own Native children and grandchildren, from both reservation communities and urban areas. In my experience as an educator I've found that Native youth are keenly aware of contemporary Native American life. They know that we're still here, but they are often less knowledgeable about the experiences and struggles our ancestors endured to bring us to this point and of the battles and accomplishments of Native leaders of this century. These stories of struggle and adversity provide inspiration and encourage pride by building a context for understanding our ability to not only survive but thrive in the contemporary world.

In this essay, I continually emphasize the educational role of the NMAI, the messages it presents to multiple audiences, and the level at which it successfully engages those audiences. This is because, in walking through the exhibits on opening day, I constantly found myself thinking of exactly how much is at stake in the exhibit halls of the NMAI. Museums play a critical role in painting a picture of the people, communities, and cultures they portray; they create a resonant take-home message for visitors. In this way museums shape the public mind-set and have an effect on policy in this country and internationally. This is a particularly important role for the NMAI, as it attempts (and rightly so) to remove authority from museums that present Native people only through a Western, anthropological gaze.[4] As the NMAI claims to (re)present Native Americans in their own voices and perspectives, many will look to its exhibits as the authority on Native people, replacing traditional anthropological interpretations and representations of Native Americans.

In many ways, this marks a hard-won victory for the empowerment of Indigenous peoples to control, represent, and maintain sovereignty over their own cultural heritage. For several decades, amid struggles with archaeologists and anthropologists, Native people have reiterated the importance of the past in the present, and the connection of contemporary research and representations of our communities and heritage for the future well-being of our people.[5] In regaining control over our own heritage and having both the power and the opportunity to represent it on such a truly grand scale as a museum on the National Mall of the U.S. capital, it is critical that we remain cognizant of the effects that representations of our cultures, history, and heritage have on future generations. From this vantage point, the NMAI holds a tremendous responsibility to Native people, not only in the past and present, but also quite literally for future generations as well. It is with a profound respect for our ancestors and a deep concern for those of future generations that I examined carefully and have thought critically about the exhibits in the NMAI and write this essay.

The NMAI's Mission

As stated on the NMAI web site, the museum's mission is as follows:

> The National Museum of the American Indian shall recognize and affirm
> to Native communities and the non-Native public the historical and con-
> temporary culture and cultural achievements of the Natives of the Western
> Hemisphere by advancing—in consultation, collaboration, and cooperation
> with Natives—knowledge and understanding of Native cultures, including
> art, history, and language, and by recognizing the museum's special respon-
> sibility, through innovative public programming, research and collections,
> to protect, support, and enhance the development, maintenance, and perpet-
> uation of Native culture and community.[6]

In this mission statement, the NMAI clearly defines its audience as both
Native and non-Native publics. Through its exhibitions, the museum
aims to "recognize and affirm" both historical and contemporary Native
cultures, as well as "advanc[e]" knowledge and understanding of those
cultures, including the history and cultural achievements of Native peoples. Elsewhere, W. Richard West Jr., the museum's founding director,
points out that the NMAI is "the only national institution in the United
States whose exclusive mandate covers the entirety of the native cultures of this hemisphere."[7] This is quite an ambitious mission, and the
challenges inherent in attempting to cover the numerous and diverse
cultures living in such a large geographic area, over such a vast period
of time, were certainly substantial. There were numerous views to be
included and considered and myriad thoughts and desires to be accom-
modated, as both George Horse Capture and Duane Blue Spruce highlight when describing their experiences in the early consultation process with Native communities during the planning stages of the NMAI.[8]
Consultation took on many forms, including surveys, interviews, and
visits to Native communities throughout the hemisphere. The efforts to
incorporate this input productively and to then decide what the organizing principles and themes of the museum would be were certain to have
been quite challenging.

Although much of the organization of the display context in the museum was generated in consultation with Native people and communities, I am unclear on how the tone of the exhibits was determined. I use the word "tone" because I've found it difficult to find another word to express what I noticed repeatedly about the NMAI's exhibits. As I explored the galleries on opening day, I was powerfully struck and sadly disappointed by the lack of struggle portrayed in both the text and images present on the exhibition floor. Furthermore, I found that the messages about colonization and its devastating and continual effects on Native communities were benign. In the ways I detail more fully in the following paragraphs, there was a noticeable lack of hard-hitting critique of the process and effects of colonization in Native communities.

Agency and Victimization

Postcolonial theorists have pointed out that colonization is never simply a one-way process in which a victim is acted upon by a colonizing individual or force.[9] Binary and unidimensional representations of colonization are vastly oversimplified and remove the agency of the actors involved, particularly those portrayed as colonized "victims." Such complexity of interaction was certainly the case in the colonization of North America. Native people were not simply passive receivers of colonial actions; they actively resisted repeated attempts of cultural, spiritual, and physical genocide and simultaneously had profound effects and influence on colonial settler populations and governments.

Native agency and the ways Native people actively worked to create and change their lives and circumstances are presented repeatedly in the NMAI's Our Peoples exhibits. Aesthetically beautiful displays offer celebrations of accomplishments and agency of Native people—a goal that I support fully. However, the presentation of these accomplishments is hollow because the exhibits do not offer visitors the context of struggle necessary to appreciate these victories and the ultimate survival of Indigenous communities of North America as sovereign, self-determining nations. The NMAI's goal in presenting Native American history in such a way may have been to give power and agency to Native people and simultaneously to represent to an international audience Native accomplishments and ability to adapt and change in the contemporary world. However, the Our People exhibits do not do justice to nor adequately (re) present Native history; they fail to inform and educate the visitor by not effectively presenting information and experiences to appreciate and respect the continued existence of Native cultures. Certainly the agency of Native people, in the past and present, is critical to highlight in any telling of Native history, present, and future. However, we do not honor our ancestors and their struggles and sacrifices if we ignore or fail to tell the stories of extreme brutalization, struggle, and suffering that they endured and overcame. Agency is indisputably vital, and representing Native people as passive victims is not only damaging but inaccurate. However, in teaching and presenting the history of Native America, the choice is not one between binaries of active agent and passive victim. Native history can be skillfully presented in ways that demonstrate the horrors of colonization across this hemisphere yet portray the agency of courageous children, strong women, brave elders, and spirited leaders who struggled to resist the decimation of their worlds. Sadly, the NMAI missed opportunities to provide powerful, nuanced versions of Native American history that would have emotional resonance for visitors and add appreciably to their knowledge about Native life and experience.

Guns and Bibles

The Our Peoples gallery offers several examples of such missed opportunity. One of the focal points of that gallery is a large display of guns, all pointed in one direction, toward the display of gold in the adjacent panel. A portion of the text inside the gun case reads:

> *Why Guns? Guns are everywhere in the Native past. Like Christianity and foreign governments, they weave a thread of shared experience that links Native people across the hemisphere. Native desire to adopt new goods drove early encounters between Indians and Europeans. Indigenous people gave up some*

technologies—pottery, stone, knives, and leather clothing— and adopted brass kettles, metal tools, and eventually, guns. Europeans increased their manufacture capacity to meet the needs of the new American market. Native people made guns their own, using the new technology as they used all new technologies: to shape their lives and future.[10]

Such a reading of these weapons that were used to slaughter, rape, and maim our ancestors is upsetting and outrageous. It literally brought tears to my eyes to read it, as I thought about what the countless warriors, women, and children who were slaughtered by those very guns would have said in reading that text panel. Is the agency given to those ancestors by museum curators worth the massive loss in terms of impact and opportunity for knowledge and education? What do visitors gain from viewing that case? What message do they take away with them?

To be effective and to educate audiences, the guns need to be contextualized in a much different way. The curatorial staff must find a way to give the visitor a sense of the extreme terror inflicted by those guns and the creative and courageous efforts of Native people to use these weapons to protect their families, land, and communities. In a time when discussions of terrorism are rampant, these guns might have offered an appropriate and effective way to push back the clock of terrorism in the United States— to remind museum visitors that the first major act of terrorism on this land did not occur on September 11, 2001, and that acts of aggression and the infliction of mass casualties in this country did not begin at the bombing of Pearl Harbor. This would have been an excellent opportunity to educate several million people a year on the facts surrounding this country's foundation on acts of extreme terror, biological warfare, and genocide against civilian women and children.

Recently a T-shirt has become popular at powwows and in Native communities. The T-shirt has a photo of Geronimo and several other Native men holding guns, and the text reads, "Homeland Security: Fighting Terrorism since 1492." Colleen Lloyd (Tsa-la-gi/Tuscarora) created the Homeland Security T-shirt and sells it, along with other products carrying the same image and message, on her web site (www.westwind world.com).

This T-shirt effectively and simply communicates volumes about our history as Native people. It gives agency to the men pictured and demonstrates the ways they used a foreign object and, to use the words of the NMAI's guns text panel, "made it their own." It brings the past into the present, providing a historical context to contemporary events in a way that is humorous yet hard-hitting, powerful yet inoffensive. The T-shirt carries the tone of decolonization—a message that the NMAI is sorely lacking.

The NMAI's discussion of religion in the Our Peoples gallery is another example of missed opportunity. The religion case, located directly behind the guns case, contains a series of Bibles that were translated into Native languages. The text panel for this case reads, in part:

> Why BIBLES? Christianity weaves a thread of shared experience that links Native People across the hemisphere. Where ever Europeans went, they spread the gospel. This wall features more than 100 bibles, translated into nearly 75 indigenous languages. Such translation is a testament to the tireless efforts Christians have made to convert Indians since 1492. Today the majority of Native peoples call themselves Christian. It is a story not only of choice, but also of adaptation, destruction, resistance and survivance.[11]

As with the guns case, the desire to portray the agency of Native people is obvious, but it is made at the expense of utilizing this space to portray Christianity as a powerful agent of colonization, one that Native people fought harshly against. Although this text panel does briefly mention the destruction involved in Christianizing Native people, in viewing this display and reading the accompanying text one does not get a sense of the range of struggles that Native people endured to keep their own spiritual practices alive. The Ghost Dance, the slaughter at Wounded Knee, the illegality of the Sun Dance, and the great lengths Native people went to in order to preserve their traditional spiritual practices are not emphasized. Instead, as with the guns case, the curators chose to give a large space in the gallery to a group of objects that were not made by Native people but were used to control them. At the same time, the display minimizes the role (or reading) of the Bibles as artifacts of colonization.

Curatorial staff might have more appropriately chosen to display the translated Bibles in a way that recontextualized or reinterpreted them, making clear the intimate connections and multiple threads of action involved. Such threads include contemporary celebrations of the survival (indeed resurgence) of traditional Native spiritual knowledge and practices, dramatic efforts of Christians and the government to destroy or silence such knowledge, the creative and courageous routes taken by Native and non-Native people to preserve it, and the extreme misbalance of power embedded in all of this. Although the text panel mentions "adaptation, destruction, and survivance," it does not offer or effectively communicate a view that problematizes Christian leaders' attempts at spiritual genocide and the powerful impact of shame, language destruction, and fear that accompanied it. The irony of the Bibles and their translation into Native languages during the same period in which Native children were punished, even beaten, for speaking their language is another point left unexplored in the galleries of the NMAI.

There is disappointingly little in this display that problematizes for the visitor the inherent power relations involved in Christianizing Native people and the literal demonizing of traditional practices. Yet the gallery adjacent to this one, titled Our Universes, presents various forms of traditional Native American spiritual practices. However, the celebration of traditional knowledge displayed in the Our Universes gallery also lacks emphasis on the past struggles our ancestors endured to preserve spiritual practices for present and future generations.

Presenting paradoxes and agency in discussions of Christianity and Indigenous people may be challenging, but there are examples where it has been done in a large, national museum context. One such example is from the Australian Museum, the national museum in Sydney. In their discussion of the changing practices of the Australian Museum and its representations of Indigenous cultures, Jim Specht and Carolyn MacLulich mention the Pieces of Paradise exhibit of 1988, which presented cultures of the Pacific Islands. In their review of the Gogodala section of the exhibit, Specht and MacLulich note that it highlights the presentation of Indigenous resistance and cultural revivalist movements in reaction to the "oppressive practices of fundamentalist Christian groups."[12] Sadly, in dramatic contrast to the Australian Museum's focus on Indigenous struggles against oppressive religions, the NMAI chose not to highlight Native resistance. In presenting Native history in Our Peoples, the NMAI curators had ample opportunity to educate visitors about any of the multiple resistance efforts undertaken by Native people against the powerful forces of Christianization. Native agency and survivance could have been powerfully portrayed in that way, but instead curators made the choice to provide visitors with benign representations of guns, churches, and governments.

At the NMAI it is not only historical struggles that are benign, absent, or difficult for viewers to access due to lengthy text panels, but also more contemporary issues of confrontation, such as present-day battles and victories to repatriate our ancestors and the sacred objects lost during colonization. Highlighting this topic would have brought the struggle for spiritual sovereignty into the twenty-first century through an exhibit focused on the NAGPRA. This is particularly relevant for a national museum that will have a large non-Native audience, as the case of the Ancient One (Kennewick Man) has been widely reported in the mainstream media, making national newspaper headlines as well as the cover of Time and Newsweek magazines, and has even been featured in an episode of 60 Minutes.[13]

Furthermore, efforts in Indian country have been ongoing to amend and improve the NAGPRA legislation to address critical issues such as so-called unaffiliated remains and the very definition of "Native American" under the law.[14] Legislation to amend NAGPRA was recently introduced by former Senator Ben Nighthorse Campbell (R-Colorado), and such an exhibit at the NMAI could have played a critical role in helping Native communities educate both Native and non-Native publics about the importance of this legislation as a matter of human rights, religious freedom, and cultural property law.

Along these same lines, the museum might have developed a critical view of the process of collecting, display, and representation of Native objects, culture, and heritage. However, such critical engagement with and hard-hitting critique of Western intellectual traditions are sorely lacking. Closely related to these topics, and similarly lacking in the NMAI's exhibits, is any mention of cultural and intellectual property rights and a discussion of who has the right to control, utilize, and profit from Indigenous knowledge, symbols, images, and other areas of intangible heritage (for example, stories, songs, dances). All of these are crucial and relevant issues for Native people today that will continue to play an important role in our communities for generations, and each involves a strong intellectual tradition of Indigenous scholarship and leadership. Yet visitors to the NMAI will have no chance to engage with these issues and to take home with them ideas about the various Native perspectives relating to such critical topics.

Context for Survivance

My primary criticism of the displays at the NMAI is that they provide the visitor with no sense of the struggle that Native people faced as a result of European colonization. In the Our Peoples gallery, the NMAI introduces the important concept of "survivance." This is a term developed by Anishinabe scholar Gerald Vizenor. In defining the concept of survivance, Vizenor states, "Survivance . . . is more than survival, more than endurance or mere response; the stories of survivance are an active presence. . . . The native stories of survivance are successive and natural estates; survivance is an active repudiation of dominance, tragedy, and victimry."[15]

Vizenor goes on to discuss this concept, and throughout the book

Fugitive Poses: Native American Indian Scenes of Absence and Presence, he provides examples of what he refers to as, "stories of native survivance."[16] One of the powerful examples he provides is that of Dr. Charles Eastman. Eastman was living on Pine Ridge in South Dakota on December 29, 1890, when the Seventh Cavalry massacred ghost dancers and their families at Wounded Knee. In his writings, Eastman describes the massacre and his attempts to find and help any survivors. He writes, "Fully three miles from the scene of the massacre we found the body of a woman completely covered with a blanket of snow, and from this point on we found them scattered along as they had been relentlessly hunted down and slaughtered while fleeing for their lives."[17] Eastman goes on to describe the women, elderly, and children whom the Seventh Cavalry had ruthlessly maimed and slaughtered.

Vizenor describes the work that Eastman and his wife, Elaine Goodale, did as they lectured and wrote about "the horror at Wounded Knee." He explains the important work that Eastman did as a "name giver" and the central role such work played in helping Native people with land claims and cash settlements. Vizenor describes the writing and work of Eastman: "He encircled the horrors of that massacre in stories of native courage and survivance. That sense of presence, rather than absence or aversion, is natural reason and a source of native identities. The doctor enunciated his visions, memories, and totemic creations as an author. Clearly, his autobiographical stories are native survivance not victimry."[18]

It is my understanding from this and many other notable examples in Vizenor's work that the concept of survivance is not about avoiding or minimizing the horrors and tragedy of colonization. It includes agency and Native presence, but does not refuse stories of struggle, particularly those that create a context for understanding and appreciating the creative methods of resistance and survival in the face of such unimaginable turmoil. In my understanding of survivance, Native people are active, present agents whose humanity is emphasized as their responses to struggle are poignantly portrayed. Presenting the horror, injustice, and multifaceted aspects of Native peoples' struggles while simultaneously highlighting their active engagement in and resistance to such onslaughts is not to portray Native people as victims. One cannot appreciate and experience the power of Native survivance if the stories and memories of our histories are not placed in the context of struggle.

The museum specifically mentions and describes the concept of survivance on one of the text panels in the Our Peoples gallery:

> *Survivance: Native societies that survived the firestorm of Contact faced unique challenges. No two situations were the same, even for Native groups in the same area at the same time. But in nearly every case, Native people faced a contest for power and possessions that involved three forces—guns, churches, and governments. These forces shaped the lives of Indians who survived the massive rupture of the first century of Contact. By adopting the very tools that were used to change, control, and dispossess them, Native peoples reshaped their cultures and societies to keep them alive. This strategy has been called survivance.*[19]

I agree with the words of this text panel and am particularly pleased with the point made about diversity of challenges, even within the same community. The power of the tripartite forces of "guns, churches, and governments" is central to discussions of power relations between and among Natives and non-Natives. These are important aspects of Native survivance; however, at the NMAI, and in any museum or other telling of Native histories, there can be no stories of survivance without an understanding of extreme struggle and survival in the face of horrific circumstance. Comments by W. Rick West reflect the museum's choice to not focus on the hard-hitting stories of colonization. West told the *Washington Post*: "Here's what I want everyone to understand. As much and as important as that period of history is, it is at best only about 5 percent of the period we have been in this hemisphere. We do not want to make the National Museum of the American Indian into an Indian Holocaust Museum. . . . You have to go beyond the story of the tragedy and the travesty of the past 500 years. What we are talking about in the end is cultural survivance. We are still here."[20]

The message "We are still here" is indeed an important one, and it is one that is effectively and beautifully demonstrated in the NMAI's exhibits. However, as I've argued and demonstrated, the exhibits do not offer visitors the context to understand and appreciate Native survivance.

Controversies surrounding the importance of bringing Native people's voice and experience to bear in tellings of Indigenous history occur often in archaeology, my primary field of specialization. Native and non-Native archaeologists, particularly those who are engaged in Indigenous, public, and community archaeology, are exploring more effective methods of involving descendent communities and a range of stakeholders in archaeological research designs and practices and finding ways to make such work relevant and beneficial for Indigenous and local communities. Similarly, both Native and non-Native people involved in the area of Indigenous archaeology continually face the challenge of bringing Native voices to bear in the "peopling of the past" and in effective and ethical ways of including Native voices, collaborating with Native people, and making our work relevant in Native communities. Indigenous archaeologists have pointed out that archaeological research should not only focus on precontact periods, but must also contribute to decolonization by providing physical evidence of the process of colonization, the dramatic effects it had on our communities, and the changes and adaptations Native people made as a result. One of the important goals is to present the public with alternative views to the benign language and interpretations that mainstream archaeologists have used for periods of "culture contact." Yet how can we expect this of non-Native archaeologists, when the messages in the exhibits of the NMAI, which presumes to speak for Native people, do not themselves take on this challenge?

Public Audiences

Exhibitions are designed with audiences in mind, and those at the NMAI are no different. As highlighted earlier, the NMAI has consistently described its audiences as including both Native and non-Native visitors. The museum has also been explicit about the critical role of consultation and the importance of giving up authority and including Native voices on the exhibit floor. However, as Steven D. Lavine points out, "If exhibition makers are simple facilitators, they still have to decide which version of the past to articulate."[21] Making such decisions can be quite difficult, even when only addressing the needs of *one* community.[22] The challenges are compounded when the aim of the museum is to (re)present diverse cultural groups to a range of audiences, as is the ambitious mission of the NMAI.[23]

In his discussion of the growing industry of cultural tourism and the role that museums play in this area, Greg Richards points out the importance of anticipating and meeting the needs of the visitor. He also demonstrates what visitors expect and desire when they visit a museum: "People are increasingly looking for an 'experience' when they visit museums and other attractions," and their basic motivation is often to learn and experience new things. Richards's research from 1999 indicates that 70 percent of museum-going interviewees stated that learning was an "important motivation for their visit." This research indicates not only that people visit museums in search of being educated on some topic but also that they want to experience something and engage in a meaningful way with museum exhibits. Richards demonstrates why it is "increasingly important to provide a total visitor experience that satisfies not just the passive tourist gaze, but that engages the senses."[24] Therefore, the *experience* of the museum is critical, and its exhibits must have resonance for visitors if they are to provide new knowledge that visitors will actively incorporate into their previous understandings. Providing new knowledge to visitors is particularly important at the NMAI precisely because Native Americans have been so stereotyped and essentialized by people around the globe.

As both Constance Perin and Paulette M. McManus point out, museum professionals do not assume they have a unitary public, and they are increasingly attempting to reach visitors who will engage with the museum in very different ways. Some will browse the exhibits visually, others will read all the text carefully, and yet others will engage with the exhibits using a combination of reading and visual skills.[25] McManus points to the limited time that visitors spend engaging with museum exhibits and reading the text carefully. Her research on a large exhibition about cultural relativism indicated that visitors spent six minutes and thirty-five seconds in each gallery, with an average of four minutes and fifty seconds spent in front of the exhibits themselves. With this in mind, it is critical that written and visual communication effectively convey the intended messages and main themes of the exhibit.

Aside from the way visitors experience the exhibits and the time they spend engaging with the text and displays, visitors to the NMAI are quite diverse culturally. As discussed earlier, audiences to the NMAI are both Native and non-Native, and they also include a large non-American audience. Richards demonstrates the growing tendency of tourists to visit museums as part of their vacation travel.[26] Washington, DC is a major tourist attraction, and the National Mall is one of the city's primary tourist destinations. The NMAI will thus not only see millions of American tourists each year but will also benefit from the overall growth of the cultural tourism industry that will bring increasing numbers of foreign visitors through the doors of the museum. To effectively communicate a message to the "streakers" (those who quickly walk through and predominantly visually browse exhibits), the "strollers" (those who engage with displays for a longer period of time, exploring both visual and textual materials), and the "readers" (those who take more time and read all the text presented in an exhibit) requires sophisticated layering in museum displays and demands the attention of experienced curatorial staff with the highest level of expertise in museology practice.[27]

I strongly and emphatically agree that Native people from diverse backgrounds, communities, and experiences—women, elders, men, children, spiritual and political leaders, activists, and intellectuals from locations across the hemisphere—should all be consulted and involved in the creation of the NMAI's (re)presentations of Native cultures. Native stories and experiences must be clearly presented in a way that has an impact on and resonance with the audience, for there is so much at stake in these exhibits. Future generations will feel the direct effects of the impressions, lessons, and messages that visitors take home with them in their hearts and minds.

There is no doubt that the NMAI curatorial staff faced a great challenge in trying to effectively communicate messages and information to such a diverse public audience. Specht and MacLulich describe one such challenge in their work developing exhibits for the Indigenous Australians: Australia's First Peoples gallery in the Australian Museum in Sydney. They describe how focus groups and evaluations produced "widely divergent reactions": "Indigenous respondents felt that the exhibitions would not be sufficiently hard-hitting, whereas non-indigenous people said that it would be too confrontational."[28] This must have been an issue that the NMAI grappled with as well, perhaps even more so since, unlike the Australian Museum, the NMAI has a primary commitment to being a Native place and a mission to collaborate, consult, and cooperate with Native people. Even before accepting the position as director of the NMAI, W. Rick West had concerns about Native and non-Native audiences. In his essay in *Spirit of a Native Place: Building the National Museum of the American Indian*, he writes, "Before I accepted that honor, and challenge [as founding director of the museum], I asked myself not only how the museum could become a place where Native peoples could say who we are, but also whether the larger culture would be willing to accept such an institution. Clearly, I decided that it would."[29]

Although I appreciate the challenges expressed here, I argue that the primary concern of the NMAI should be with effectively presenting accurate portrayals of Native histories, regardless of whether the larger culture is "willing to accept" them. The NMAI must provide a context for visitors to experience the meaning of our survivance and all the painful, triumphant, inspiring, resistant, horrific truths encompassed in it—even though such portrayals are confrontational or difficult. In fact, I would argue that such presentations must be confrontational and challenge the visitor to experience Native histories in a way they unfortunately cannot find in the educational system of this country, in mainstream media portrayals of Native life, and in all the stereotyped messages and lessons of victimry and noble savagery incessantly present in mainstream American life. It is not only celebratory messages of our success and presence in the contemporary world that will touch visitors' spirits at the deeper, more personal level of their humanity, but also the day-to-day experiences of struggle and survivance. This does not mean that visitors must be hit over the head with stories of victimization and oppression. Shallow messages of victimry have been the mainstay of information presented to American and global audiences for centuries.

What is needed at the NMAI is collaborative museum exhibit design that incorporates the voice and views of Native communities to present real, heart-felt, complex histories and experiences that are not relegated to celebration while glossing over the hard-hitting realities that rob visitors of an entire range of emotions and limits their ability to connect, on a basic human level, to Native people. More than anything else, the NMAI must demonstrate to non-Native and Native audiences that we are not two-dimensional cut-outs of victimry or triumph; we are human, and, as do others , we have a range of stories to tell. Many of our stories are happy songs of revival and strength; others are sad or difficult and instructive of the shadows of colonization that still loom and continue to challenge our communities.

We, as Native peoples, have many stories to tell. We have a unique way of viewing the world; it is one that has been severely affected by colonization yet is ever changing and resilient. Bringing Native voices to the foreground to share these experiences and worldviews is a critical part of readjusting the power balance to ensure that Native people control their own heritage, representation, and histories. If we wish to share these experiences and histories with each other and a non-Native audience, hoping to foster and protect them and to raise awareness and respect for them, then we must take seriously the job of educating and the important role of effective communication in the exhibits of the NMAI. We must expect that the galleries will not only celebrate our presence but also value and honor the sense of struggle, as it is such struggle that provides a context for understanding and truly appreciating our survivance.

Notes

I would like to thank Amy Lonetree and Amanda Cobb for inviting me to partic-ipate in this edition, and many thanks to Sydney Martin for her careful read-ing and critique of an earlier draft of this essay. Both readers substantially improved this essay with their comments and suggestions. This research would not have been possible without the generous support of the University of Cali-fornia President's Postdoctoral Fellowship.

1. The terms "Western" and "Indigenous" are used throughout this essay to denote very broad, general groups of people and communities, each of which in itself encompasses a great deal of complexity and diversity of views. While I assume that the reader is aware of the categories that I refer to, I want to be clear that by using these broad categorizations in an attempt to present this argument from a general perspective, I do not intend to insinuate that either term refers to a monolithic, homogeneous group, with rigid and clearly defined epistemologies and worldviews, but rather each includes a great deal of diversity.

2. For examples of both critiques and models for a changed practice in archae-ology, see Sonya Atalay, "Domesticating Clay/Engaging with 'They': Ana-tolian Daily Practice with Clay and Public Archaeology for Indigenous Communities" (PhD diss., University of California, 2003); Sonya Atalay, "Gikinawaabi: Knowledge Production and Social Science Research from an Indigenous Perspective," paper presented at the Women's History Con-ference, Queens University, Belfast, Ireland, 2003; Sonya Atalay, "Multiple Voices for Many Ears in Indigenous Archaeological Practice," paper pre-sented at the Society for American Archaeology annual meetings, Mon-treal, Canada, 2004.

3. For more information on proposed changes to NAGPRA, see http://www .indianz.com/News/2004/004562.asp.

4. George Horse Capture, "The Way of the People," in *Spirit of a Native Place:*

Building the National Museum of the American Indian, ed. Duane Blue Spruce (Washington DC: National Geographic Society, 2004), 42–43.

5. The literature on this topic is now quite extensive, but some of the critical texts to consult are Thomas Biolsi and Larry J. Zimmerman, *Indians and Anthropologists: Vine Deloria, Jr., and the Critique of Anthropology* (Tucson: University of Arizona Press, 1997); Vine Deloria Jr., *Custer Died for Your Sins: An Indian Manifesto* (London: Macmillan, 1969); Devon A. Mihesuah, ed., *Repatriation Reader: Who Owns American Indian Remains?* (Lincoln: University of Nebraska Press, 2000); George P. Nicholas, "Seeking the End of Indigenous Archaeology," paper presented at the 5th World Archaeological Congress, Washington, DC, 2003; George P. Nicholas and Thomas D. Andrews, eds., *At a Crossroads: Archaeology and First Peoples in Canada* (Burnaby, British Columbia: Archaeology Press, 1997); James Riding-In, "Our Dead Are Never Forgotten: American Indian Struggles for Burial Rights and Protections," in *"They Made Us Many Promises": The American Indian Experience, 1524 to the Present*, ed. Philip Weeks (Wheeling IL: Harlan Davidson, 2002), 291–323; James Riding-In, "Repatriation: A Pawnee's Perspective," in *Repatriation Reader: Who Owns American Indian Remains?*, ed. Devon A. Mihesuah (Lincoln: University of Nebraska Press, 2000), 106–20; Linda Tuhiwai Smith, *Decolonizing Methodologies: Research and Indigenous Peoples* (London: St. Martin's Press, 1999).

6. The NMAI web site lists the museum's mission and can be accessed through this link: http://www.nmai.si.edu/subpage.cfm?subpage=press&second=mission.

7. W. Richard West Jr., foreword to *Creation's Journey: Native American Identity and Belief*, ed. Tom Hill and Richard W. Hill Sr. (Washington DC: Smithsonian Institution, 1994), 10.

8. Duane Blue Spruce, "Foreword: An Honor and a Privilege," in *Spirit of a Native Place*, 15–29; Horse Capture, "The Way of the People," in Blue Spruce, *Spirit of a Native Place*, 30–45.

9. Chris Gosden, *Archaeology and Colonialism* (Cambridge, England: Cambridge University Press, 2004); Robert J. C. Young, *Postcolonialism: An Historical Introduction* (Malden MA: Blackwell, 2001); Ania Loomba, *Colonialism/Postcolonialism* (London: Routledge, 1998).

10. This text is attributed to Paul Chaat Smith and Ann McMullen, NMAI, 2003.

11. This text is attributed to Gerald McMasters, NMAI, 2003.

12. Jim Specht and Carolyn MacLulich, "Changes and Challenges: The Australian Museum and Indigenous Communities," in *Archaeological Displays*

and the Public: Museology and Interpretation, ed. Paulette M. McManus (London: Archetype Publications, 2000), 39–63.

13. 60 Minutes, October 25, 1998; Sharon Begley and Andrew Murr, "The First Americans," Newsweek, April 26, 1999; Michael D. LeMonick, "Bones of Contention: Scientists and Native Americans Clash over a 9,300-Year-Old Man with Caucasoid Features," Time, October 14 1996; "The Lost Man," New Yorker, June 19, 1997.

14. For more information on proposed changes, see "Two Word Change to NAGPRA Pending in Senate," http://www.indianz.com/News/2004/004562.asp.

15. Gerald Vizenor, Fugitive Poses: Native American Indian Scenes of Absence and Presence (Lincoln: University of Nebraska Press, 1998), 15.

16. Vizenor, Fugitive Poses, 18.

17. Charles Eastman, From the Deep Woods to Civilization (Lincoln: University of Nebraska Press, 1977), 111; Charles Eastman, Indian Boyhood (Mineola NY: Dover, 1971).

18. Vizenor, Fugitive Poses, 18.

19. Paul Chaat Smith, NMAI, 2003.

20. Quoted in Joel Achenbach, "Within These Walls, Science Yields to Stories," Washington Post, September 19, 2004.

21. Steven D. Lavine, "Audience, Ownership, and Authority: Designing Relations between Museums and Communities," in Museums and Communities: The Politics of Public Culture, ed. Ivan Karp, Christine Mullen Kreamer, and Steven D. Lavine (Washington DC: Smithsonian Institution Press, 1992), 142.

22. For a discussion of this, see Lavine, "Audience, Ownership, and Authority." Also see the following for further discussion and examples: Gerald T. Conaty, "Glenbow's Blackfoot Gallery: Working towards Co-Existence," in Museums and Source Communities: A Routledge Reader, ed. Laura L. Peers and Alison K. Brown (New York: Routledge, 2003), 227–41; Nancy J. Fuller, "The Museum as a Vehicle for Community Empowerment: The Ak-Chin Indian Community Ecomuseum Project," in Karp et al., Museums and Communities, 327–65; Jane Peirson Jones, "The Colonial Legacy and the Community: The Gallery 33 Project," in Karp et al., Museums and Communities, 221–41; Stephanie Moser et al., "Transforming Archaeology through Practice: Strategies for Collaborative Archaeology and the Community Archaeology Project at Queseir, Egypt," in Peers and Brown, Museums and Source Communities, 208–26.

23. Lavine, "Audience, Ownership, and Authority," also discusses some of the

challenges. Karp, Kreamer, and Lavine, *Museums and Communities*; McManus, *Archaeological Displays*; Peers and Brown, *Museums and Source Communities*, each provide examples of museums that attempt to represent diverse Indigenous or local communities; each aims to reach Indigenous and non-Indigenous visitors from both national and international audiences.

24. Greg Richards, "Cultural Tourism," in McManus, *Archaeological Displays and the Public*, 2, 4, 8.

25. George F. Macdonald, "Change and Challenge: Museums in the Information Society," in Karp et al., *Museums and Communities*, 158–81; Constance Perin, "The Communicative Circle: Museums as Communities," in Karp et al., *Museums and Communities*, 182–220.

26. Richards, "Cultural Tourism."

27. For a description of these terms and a discussion of layering museum displays, see Perin, "The Communicative Circle."

28. Specht and MacLulich, "Changes and Challenges," 58.

29. W. Richard West Jr., "As Long as We Keep Dancing: A Brief Personal History," in Blue Spruce, *Spirit of a Native Place*, 54.

11. (Un)disturbing Exhibitions

Indigenous Historical Memory at the
National Museum of the American Indian

Myla Vicenti Carpio

I was recently in Washington DC to visit the National Museum of the American Indian (NMAI). In the city, I found myself amid some of the most beloved and well-known monuments and museums in the "nation's" capital. Every year, people flock to see these monuments to former leaders, to visit museums and gain a specific perspective on U.S. history. Most monuments act as conspicuous bookmarks in American history, embedding certain historical events, figures, or places in the nation's collective memory. Places such as the Washington Monument and Lincoln Memorial in DC and the Statue of Liberty in New York attract visitors from around the world to pay homage to these assumed great leaders and the freedoms they represent. However, when we look at monuments and museums, we must also understand the different meanings these monuments represent for multiple publics.

I arrived in the District of Columbia with a different perspective, one critical of the impacts of European and American imperialism on Indigenous peoples. As I visited different memorials, monuments, and museums there, I was struck by the patriotic and nationalistic rhetoric, all the while remembering the countless Indigenous lives lost or affected by this nation's expansion. I witnessed the different publics visiting monuments and bringing with them their own awareness or investment of that particular historical memory. When different publics traverse monuments or spaces, conflicting historical memories likewise intersect and reveal underlying tensions and conflicting interpretations about the past.

Caroline Chung Simpson in *An Absent Presence: Japanese Americans in Postwar American Culture, 1945–1960*, suggests that Japanese American identity and internment constituted an "absent presence" in post–World War II American society. Her work seeks to understand "how history and memory are negotiated when the need to remember an event challenges the ideals of democratic nationalism and the narrative unity of nation that historical discourses ostensibly provide."[1] The "absence" or deliberate exclusion of the "other's" history works to construct and reify the master narrative as does the utilization of a historical "presence" or inclusion that only benefits the dominant narrative. Indigenous history, I suggest, is situated as the "absent presence" in American history, deliberately erased or radically transformed to reinforce and maintain the master narrative. Its discursive inclusion, a retelling or distortion of Indigenous history, is designed to justify the colonizers' violence and exploitation of Indigenous peoples, lands, and resources. The processes of colonization have created this "absence" in the American historical memory, which shapes how Indigenous history, space, and place have been and continue to be renamed, redefined, and destroyed.

Museums, in particular, are educational tools used to create and perpetuate specific ideologies and historical memories. They have played a prominent role in defining the visibility of Indigenous peoples and cultures in American historical memory by creating exhibits of Indigenous peoples based on perceptions and views that benefit and justify American colonialism. As an elementary student, I learned about the damaging representations of Indigenous peoples in museum exhibitions during a class visit to the Denver Museum of Natural History. We viewed the museum's American Indian exhibit, which depicted Natives as scantily clad, uncivilized savages carrying spears and bows and arrows. This had an enormous impact on me. I knew where I came from and who I was, that we were not as they depicted—and I stood there as students, knowing I was Indigenous, looked at me, at the exhibit, and back at me. I cried from the hurt and humiliation I felt as some of the students laughed. My teacher was unsympathetic to my hurt and objections to such imagery. Through this experience, I gained firsthand knowledge of the tenuous relationships museums have with their publics, especially the Indigenous peoples of America.

As did the Denver Museum of Natural History of the 1970s, many museums dehumanize Indigenous peoples with their exhibits. These museums, private and public, teach "America" that Indigenous peoples are peoples of the past who never "progressed" forward. Dehumanizing exhibits of Indigenous peoples with and among animals dramatically contrast with those of Europeans and Americans, who are portrayed as making progress in the chronological narrative of human development and nation building. With many national and international museum visitors accustomed to envisioning Indigenous peoples in such contexts, the National Museum of the American Indian faces an enormous task: to shift the paradigm from Indigenous peoples as exhibition subjects, to educate the different publics visiting the museum about the Indigenous peoples of the Americas and, importantly, make Indigenous history "present."

It is clear from the video in the Our Peoples gallery that the NMAI curators understand the long history of misrepresentation. The video's narrator states, "We're viewed as saviors of the environment, barbarians, and Noble Savages, the lowest form of humanity. Sometimes all at once. Rarely are we seen as human beings. It's a dizzying spectrum of impressions deeply embedded, fiercely held, hard to dislodge. They've been fixed in our minds, by histories taught in classrooms, generation after generation."[2] The National Museum of the American Indian indeed has an ambitious goal in educating a largely ignorant public, and the opening statements seem to affirm the importance of historicizing European and American colonization and its impacts on Indigenous peoples. Its purpose seems clear: to inform, educate, and, from an Indigenous perspective, contradict what the American public has been taught. Yet, rather than fulfilling this imperative, the NMAI shies away from the challenge.

The opening images of the film presentation *Who We Are* in the Lelawi Theater, showing complexities in the peoples and cultures from around the country, begin to illustrate that Indigenous peoples are distinct peoples. Moreover, the Our Universes exhibit attempts to illustrate the multiplicity between Indigenous and Western European worldviews. The first panel that the visitor encounters upon entering this section states, "You'll discover how Native people understand their place in the universe and order their daily lives. Our philosophies of life come from our ancestors. They taught us to live in harmony with animals, plants, spirit world and the people around us. *In Our Universe, you'll encounter Native people from the Western Hemisphere who continue to express this wisdom in ceremonies, celebrations, language, arts, religions, and daily life.*"[3]

The emphasis (mine) focuses on those who "continue" these traditions. Some visitors clearly engaged with the exhibits in Our Universe; I overheard a woman saying, "I didn't realize how different each tribe was" after leaving the Anishinabe exhibit. This is important to the museum's mission to "celebrate the lifeways, languages, literature, history, and art of Native Americans," survival and "survivance."[4] However, the museum never tells us exactly how many nations existed and still exist in the United States, Canada, and Mexico, which is especially important when trying to express how they are surviving and from what.

The museum's strengths are evident in the beauty of the architecture and landscape and the exhibitions created by Indigenous communities. However, by not providing visitors with more context or information about what they are viewing, the museum perpetuates long-standing distortions of Indigenous peoples. These distortions were evident in the conversations and comments I overheard visitors make throughout the museum:

> "Yeah, we're here smoking a peace pipe."
> "I want to take you where they teach you to do Indian dances."

These visitors brought with them images of American Indians as performers of dances for tourists or making peace with the U.S. military, images that could remain intact after walking through the museum. In particular, one family's interpretation of the bronze statue by Edward Hlavka, *Allies in War, Partners in Peace*, 2004, a gift from the Oneida Nation, poignantly illustrates how the visiting public carries and maintains colonized conceptions of American Indians and the museum's failure to challenge these colonized conceptions.

Hlavka's statue is a powerful depiction of the relationship between the Oneida Nation and the newly formed United States during the American Revolution. The Oneidas helped to "sustain" the revolutionaries by supplying food and wartime alliances. The statue depicts Polly Anderson carrying a basket of corn, with the information plaque explaining that she taught the soldiers how to cook the corn. Oskanondonha is depicted in the role he played as an ally with the Americans. George Washington is shown holding a wampum belt of their agreement to not "interfere in the other's internal affairs." The three stand with the different clans of the Haudenosaunee at a white pine, the tree of peace, with weapons buried. The information plaque explains the statue with a brief discussion of the Peace Keeper and the tree of peace. The work emphasizes the Oneidas' relationship with the American revolutionaries and places Haudenosaunee understandings of peace and negotiation second. Moreover, the information plaque does not clarify how the United States not only did not adhere to the agreement, but went on to treat these "allies" as "conquered peoples," stealing their lands.

The visitors I watched never read this information and instead interpreted the cultural and historical intricacies based on their preconceived notions from textbook interpretations of European, American, and Indigenous relations.

> "What do you see?"
> "Yes, an Indian."
> "What is she carrying?"
> "Yes, that's corn."
> "Yes, that's a pilgrim wearing that hat."
> "What is this?"
> "Yes, it's Thanksgiving."

A parent asked her children these questions, and rather than walking away with a new or different understanding of a nation or international relations, the family imposed their colonial conception of Thanksgiving—the most dominant and perhaps the most romanticized image of Indigenous-colonial relations—onto this statue.

As an Indigenous visitor to the museum, I found that I became part of the spectacle. Because I possess phenotypical characteristics of an "Indian" (black hair, dark skin), many visitors halted their conversation when I walked into the exhibit areas or interrupted their conversation until they walked past me. I witnessed these reactions several times. It was as if my humanity disrupted their ability to observe Indigenous life and culture from a distance. Tellingly by their actions, many visitors were more comfortable encountering the artifacts than they were engaging with an Indigenous person other than museum cultural interpreters. Thus, the NMAI fails to disturb preconceived notions of history and the "dizzying spectrum of impressions" that the general public carries with them into the museum.[5]

In an interview with National Public Radio prior to the opening, W. Richard West Jr., the founding director, said he wanted visitors to get a "clear understanding, not just of tragedies, but a broader sweep of time and space of the first citizens of the Americas."[6] The lack of historical context, moreover, is presented as positive and progressive, with the museum's director proudly noting, "We are not retrospective. We live in the present and we look toward the future."[7] (Looking "to the future" does not explain why the museum continues to use the term "tribe" rather than "nation," which many Indigenous nations have now chosen to emphasize their sovereignty.) West tellingly noted that indigenous peoples' history spans twenty thousand years and that the worst of it has been 5 percent of that history.[8] This does not explain why the museum's chronology begins in 1491 in the Our Peoples gallery, focusing on tribal histories, misleading visitors to assume that Indigenous peoples came into existence only when they entered European consciousness. The NMAI devotes a majority of its exhibits to celebrating Indigenous peoples' survival of over five hundred years of violence and genocide. Clearly, the impact of colonization has had a much greater impact on our history that extends beyond those thousand years.

The 5 percent solution of minimizing the discussion of colonization, especially in a historical context, thus centers colonialism as the "absent presence" in the NMAI. Conspicuously absent from the museum's presentation is a clear critique of colonization and its impacts on Indigenous lifeways, religions, and cultures. Although sections in the museum mention colonialism and cultural interpreters mention colonization, a clear sense of who the colonizers are is lacking. As an absent presence, it does not disturb the preconceived notions of different publics and the American historical memory. Yet, while the exhibits' focus on survival illustrates the resiliency and continuation of Indigenous peoples, the lack of historical context begs the question, Survival from what?

Confronting colonization, according to the NMAI, interferes with the mission to celebrate the Native American survival and "survivance." It is precisely this ahistoricism that undermines the museum's mission. Historical context and critique play an important role in educating the general public about Indigenous history. If the museum is to change the paradigm by which the public perceives Indigenous peoples, providing a clear historical context is part of that educational process. It is imperative that Indigenous history from an Indigenous perspective be made "present" in our own communities and in the American historical record.

The absence of colonization and empire throughout the museum renders the actual presentation of colonialism most problematic. In the video *We Are the Evidence* colonialism is described as a "storm" comprised of three sides (exhibits): rifles, books and Bibles, and treaties. The exhibit situates Indigenous communities at the center of this colonial storm, the calm of the storm. With colonization placed as the absent presence, these exhibits lack a historical context that informs or explains the continuing impacts of colonization and ignores the continuing presence of colonization in our lives. Moreover, these exhibits do little to disturb colonial rhetoric, notions, and history of Indigenous peoples. Instead, they maintain Indigenous absence or fascination in the American historical memory.

That the curators had difficulty mapping colonization onto the museum's celebration of survivance is clear when one considers the physical arrangement of The Storm exhibit. Three cases, Guns, Books and Bibles, and Treaties, face outward, outside The Storm walls. The Storm represents the colonizer's destructive forces, and the walls fashion a sort of circular, enclosed, center space, the eye of the Storm. At the center sits a round glass case with red and black cloth containing rocks, a feather fan, a staff, seeds, and a cowboy hat. The curators provide no explanation for this cryptic symbol of a drum, but visitors standing in that space are surrounded by television monitors playing tornado and hurricane storm footage, with sounds of thunderstorms from the speakers above. The assumption is that it symbolizes the spirituality and culture of Indigenous peoples that have survived and withstood the storm. Although this exhibit does raise for consideration the enormous destruction and violence colonization wrought upon Indigenous peoples, the "calm of the storm" wrongly implies a minimal or unsustained effect. Furthermore, storms are produced not by humans but by nature. The tools of colonization—Bibles, books, distorted views of civilization, and treaties—appear suspended or floating in nearby cases, which might imply that humans did not have a hand in wielding these tools but that it was an inevitability for cultures to collide.

Although the Guns exhibit mentions that Europeans and Americans used the guns on Indigenous peoples, without a historical context many of these incidents seem like individual confrontations and not an ideologically driven campaign to eradicate Indigenous peoples. The Pepperbox panel, for instance, states, "Native women suffered abuse during the gold rush and Indians who intervened on their behalf were shot." Unfortunately, it appears as though women only suffered during the gold rush from greedy miners when, in fact, European and American colonizers systemically utilized violence against women and men in their colonization of Indigenous peoples, lands, and resources.

Guns had an enormous impact on Indigenous peoples through trade, war, and resistance, yet the display of these "historical" rifles plays into the general public's fascination with and image of Indians as warmongers and savages in western movies. The display highlights those firearms through the twentieth century that are infamous in American allure and memory, such as the "Sioux" (not Lakota, Dakota, or Nakota) and Geronimo and "Apaches." Rather than disrupt popular stereotypes of Indigenous peoples, this display seems to confirm the American mythology that the West, and its Indigenous inhabitants, had to be tamed and civilized.

The ambiguous wording of the Storm exhibit intentionally allows multiple readings. One panel explains that guns and Christianity "weave a thread of shared experience" among Indigenous peoples. While this is true, it is also true that Indigenous peoples shared the struggle to survive against the guns and Christianity wielded as weapons by the colonizing governments of Spain, France, England, and the United States. Europeans and Americans utilized guns and Christianity as weapons and in their rationale to invade, colonize, steal, and commit genocide on Indigenous peoples.

The books and Bibles on display are described as representing the "tireless efforts to convert indigenous peoples," overlooking the brutal impact and destruction Christianity and Western education has had on Indigenous peoples and maintaining colonization as the absent presence. Among the many unmentioned facts are how Franciscan priests used slave labor to build the churches and missions, and how they were complicit in the murders of Indigenous peoples, especially religious leaders. The statement that more than half of Indigenous peoples today are Christian demonstrates the extent of this storm, yet the museum omits any discussion about Indigenous religions in this context. Ignoring this fundamental aspect of Indigenous communities only further silences the voices of those who resisted and fought for our survival.

The final third of this trilogy, Treaties, again lacks the historical context that leaves visitors without an understanding of the extent of American legal incursion into Indigenous lives. The language used on the exhibit panels misleads visitors by focusing on treaties as markers of friendship between nations rather than legal agreements between sovereign nations. Without a discussion of imperialism and colonization, the public is left with little knowledge of how these treaties are colonizing tools, used to steal Indigenous lands and oppress Indigenous peoples on all levels of their societies. The exhibit emphasizes U.S. power over Indigenous peoples and offers little knowledge about the difficult decisions our leaders made or of the understanding of Indigenous nations' sovereign status.

The lack of comprehensible discussion about sovereignty, from an Indigenous perspective, does not disturb the general public's little understanding of Indigenous sovereignty, nor does it reinforce Indigenous self-determination (sovereignty). The Treaty of Ft. Harmar states, "The treaty *allowed* [emphasis added] the Wyandot, Delaware, Ottawa, Chippewa (Ojibwe), Potawatami, and Sauk Indians to hunt on the territory they ceded, but limited their commercial dealings to traders licensed by the U.S." What is sovereignty if another nation is *allowing* activities and their commerce? Treaties are another tool of the colonial process, destroying Indigenous claims to land and resources. Yet, the United States broke these treaties.

When I lecture in Intro" to American Indian Studies and Law, Policy and American Indians" it takes more than a few slides to get across the clear understanding of sovereignty for Indigenous peoples and how it is played out today. The text panels in the Treaty case do not illustrate the extent to which Indigenous lands were stolen, rights usurped, and true self-determination lost. The exhibits exclude discussion on how many of these treaties were, in fact, the result of coercive negotiations. Again, the lack of historical context limits the understanding of Indigenous nations today and why Indigenous peoples must continue fighting for fishing and hunting rights and access to land and constantly justify gaming as a sovereign right. The museum also does not clearly address its multiple publics. The primary public for the museum is the "American" public, those individuals who have mostly only heard the "American" history perspective. It is mostly this public that will come to the museum. What is absent only makes more conspicuously present the apologist mission of the NMAI that refuses to disrupt the mythologies of the noble and savage Indian.

After all, we still exist. The NMAI claims to celebrate our survivance while simultaneously ignoring whether it adequately addresses its Indigenous publics. With its opening exhibits the museum has squandered the opportunity to educate Indigenous peoples and provide leadership for long-lasting change by providing a much needed critical perspective of dominant historical narratives supported with facts, documents, and alternative interpretations. "For indigenous peoples, what needs to be presented is a picture of a decolonized future."[9] To decolonize our own perspectives and values— to "look forward"—it is necessary to first understand how imperialism and colonialism have impacted us in the past and present. It is not that the focus should only be on colonization, but that colonization must be present and critiqued. Although some Indigenous leaders may fear that this hindsight will be interpreted as a form of victimization, we must look at the past in order to move forward. History indeed bears this out: colonizers invaded our lands and stole and exploited resources while committing genocide of Indigenous peoples. What is at stake for those who have colonized and benefited from colonization is the ability to ignore the colonial past and negate the Indigenous past. What is at stake for Indigenous people is our future—not simply survival in the present.

Making Indigenous history "present" is an important mission for Indigenous peoples and scholars. Wilma Mankiller, former principal chief of the Cherokee Nation, in a recent speech at the Tulsa Press Club spoke about "misunderstandings about tribes [as] a problem."[10] Speaking about the need to change the perceptions many Americans hold about American Indians, she remarked that this would have a more positive impact on tribal and non-Indian relationships and policies. With one million visitors in its first five months, the NMAI could have a dramatic impact on public policy. Because of her position, Mankiller's statement is more readily reported and publicized, yet many Indigenous scholars, community members, activists, and others have called for the reclaiming and rewriting of Indigenous history, a history that not only reclaims but critiques imperialism and colonialism and its impacts on Indigenous worldviews, cultures, and existences.[11]

The dehumanizing processes of colonization continue to have far-reaching impacts on Indigenous life and America society. Many of the social problems attributed to reservation life or Indigenous existence result from the legacy of conquest and colonization. Indigenous scholar Lisa Poupart notes, "Virtually nonexistent in traditional tribal communities prior to European invasion, contemporary American Indian communities struggle with devastating social ills including alcoholism, family violence, incest, sexual assault, fetal-alcohol syndrome, homicide, and suicide at startling rates similar to and sometimes exceeding those of white society."[12] In addition to poverty, depression, diabetes, cancers, and myriad other ills, many of our people have internalized oppression, withdrawing from, resisting, and condemning traditional forms of knowledge to adapt their views to colonizing ideologies.

One particular exhibit demonstrates that the NMAI has the ability to educate Indigenous audiences, as well as the general public, on decolonization. The Tohono O'odham display, Desert Walk for Health, 2000, is an interactive, multimedia presentation that illustrates the importance of traditional desert foods, not only for the health of the Tohono O'odham people, but for other uses. The exhibit's video explains the walk:

> In March 2000, the Tohono O'odham Indians walked 240 miles to the Sonoran desert to Mexico from Tucson. The purpose, to raise awareness about diabe-

tes which afflicts many of our people. We also wanted to promote the use of traditional desert foods and medicinal plants. We were once a healthy people that ran, walked, and worked in the fields. We didn't have TV. We didn't sit a lot. Now we have to do drastic things like walk 240 miles in the desert to make our people realize that many of our illnesses come from not eating healthy. Our people have to get back to eating foods from the desert.

Walking 240 miles raised awareness among the Tohono O'odham community about the impacts of colonization and created a renewed impetus for traditional elder knowledge and traditional relationships with the desert environment.

Even here, though, the historical context that would provide a better understanding of why the Tohono O'odham diet and lifestyles so drastically changed is lacking. For example, the exhibit does not describe (at length) the forced confinement that makes it difficult to continue traditional running. Even more important, it does not address the theft of water that restricted traditional farming. Losing the river impacted agriculture, health, and culture, not to mention the dramatic shift of the biodiversity with loss of the river. While the critique is limited, its strength is in encouraging Indigenous peoples to search for solutions within our traditional, cultural contexts.

Elders have been saying for a long time that diabetes is a symptom of losing touch with the O'odham (humdag). These foods will allow us to return to a state of wellness. In speaking to schoolchildren over the years, I have found that many of them at first thought that eating the traditional foods, the desert foods, was taking a step backward, and I've reminded them, "Actually no, we are taking a step forward back to where we should be. We took a step backwards when we [were] eating the Western diet foods."[13]

Significantly, this statement rejects the linear narrative of progress that the museum's director has imposed on the NMAI. The assumed progress of European foods is rejected, recognizing that our traditional foods have important nutritional and cultural value. Additionally, without victimization, the Tohono O'odham are clear about the impact Spanish colonialism and Catholicism had on them as a people. Rather than taking a step backward, returning to Indigenous technologies and knowledge about foods and medicines allows the Tohono O'odham to do more than simply survive. Moving beyond the concept of simply surviving within colonization pushes us toward empowerment through decolonization.

Thus, much more than policy relationships are at stake by transforming "American" misconceptions of Indigenous peoples. Retelling and reclaiming our Indigenous histories and images can transform Indigenous lives, self-esteem, health, and empowerment. Waziyatawin Angela Wilson has called for "reclaiming our humanity . . . to restore health and prosperity to our people by returning to traditions and ways of life that have been systematically oppressed."[14] Importantly, our histories illustrate that Indigenous peoples have legitimate claims and rights to lands, culture, and religious freedoms. How does one teach a public whose knowledge of Indigenous peoples derives mostly from racist, dehumanizing images, movies, Academy Awards performances, mascots, and museums portraying over five hundred years of colonization? Individuals who understand the tenuous history of Indigenous peoples and museums, or who have gone to museums and recognized dehumanizing exhibits, comprehend that building a museum with a different perspective—one that differs from traditionally Eurocentric perspectives—is a realistic and necessary goal. It is vital that Indigenous communities freely discuss (and even debate) the history and impacts of colonization to begin healing and move toward the decolonization of Indigenous peoples. Taken in a different direction, the NMAI can be a space to bring Indigenous peoples together to reflect on our history, transform our communities, heal and thrive.

Notes

1. Caroline Chung Simpson, *An Absent Presence: Japanese Americans in Postwar American culture, 1945–1960* (Durham NC: Duke University Press, 2001), 4.
2. *We Are the Evidence*, video, NMAI.
3. Our Universes, NMAI; italics added.
4. *National Museum of the American Indian*, pamphlet distributed at the NMAI.

5. *We Are the Evidence.*

6. Juan Williams, correspondent, "American Indian Museum Prepares for Opening," *Morning Edition*, NPR, March 26, 2004.

7. Philip Burnham, "A Place of Reconciliation: Talking with W. Richard West," *Indian Country Today*, July 14, 2004.

8. Williams, "American Indian Museum Prepares for Opening."

9. Waziyatawin Angela Wilson and Michael Yellow Bird, eds., *For Indigenous Eyes Only: A Decolonization Workbook* (Santa Fe NM: School of American Research, 2005), 3.

10. S. E. Ruckman, "Perception Key for Indians," *Tulsa World*, March 15, 2005.

11. See Taiaiake Alfred, *Peace, Power, Righteousness: An Indigenous Manifesto* (New York: Oxford University Press, 1999); Taiaiake Alfred, *Wasáse Indigenous Pathways of Action and Freedom* (Peterborough, Ontario: Broadview Press, 2005); Vine Deloria Jr., The World We Used to Live In: Remembering the Powers of the Medicine Men (Golden CO: Fulcrum Publishers, 2006); Lisa Poupart, "Familiar Face of Genocide: Internalized Oppression among American Indians," *Hypatia* 18, no. 2 (2003); Linda Tuhiwai Smith, *Decolonizing Mythologies: Research and Indigenous Peoples* (New York: St. Martin's Press, 1999); Waziyatawin Angela Wilson and Michael Yellow Bird, eds., *For Indigenous Eyes Only: A Decolonization Handbook* (Santa Fe NM: School of American Research, 2005); Waziyatawin Angela Wilson, *Remember This! Dakota Decolonization and the Eli Taylor Narratives* (Lincoln: University of Nebraska Press, 2005).

12. Lisa Poupart, "A Familiar Face of Genocide: Internalized Oppression among American Indians," *Hypatia* 18, no. 2 (2003): 88.

13. Tohono O'odham, "Desert Walk for Health, 2000," NMAI.

14. Angela Cavender Wilson, "Reclaiming Our Humanity," in *Indigenizing the Academy: Transforming Scholarship and Empowering Communities*, ed. Devon Abbott Mihesuah and Angela Cavender Wilson (Lincoln: University of Nebraska Press, 2004), 71.

12. "Acknowledging the Truth of History"

Missed Opportunities at the National Museum of the American Indian

Amy Lonetree

The Columbian Legacy, now 510 years and counting, is by many accounts genocidal. The atrocities committed by Columbus, those under his command, and those who followed him are legion. In the name of God or science, in the pursuit of gold or glory, and in the services of imperialism or manifest destiny, the bodies and beliefs of the Indian peoples of the Western Hemisphere, along with their possessions and their lands, were plundered and debased. And a substantial portion of the American Indian collections hoarded in museums is made up of that tainted bounty.

—Craig Howe[1]

Museums are indeed very painful sites for Native peoples, as they are intimately tied to the colonization process. The study of the relationship between Indigenous peoples and museums—both the tragic stories of the past as well as examples of successful Native activism and leadership within the museum profession that are happening today—have preoccupied my professional life both inside and outside the academy. The museum world has changed significantly from the days when museums were considered "ivory towers of exclusivity"[2] to today, when Indigenous people are actively involved in making museums more open and community-relevant sites.

We can certainly see this new development reflected in exhibitions, the "most prominent and public of all museum offerings."[3] Native Americans have witnessed a shift from curator-controlled presentations of the

American Indian past to a more inclusive or collaborative process, with Native people actively involved in determining exhibition content. As the art historian David Penney writes, "Today, when museums consider organizing an exhibition with an American Indian topic, there are nearly always three major agents at work: the institution of the museum and the representatives of living American Indian communities . . . both of whom address the third agent, the 'object' of the exhibition."[4] This new relationship of "shared authority" between Native people and museum curators has changed the way Indigenous history and culture are represented and defines our relationship with museums.

During the course of my research I have found that one of the primary objectives of those working with museums is to have the exhibition not only serve as an important site of "knowledge making and remembering"[5] for their own communities, but also to challenge the commonly held stereotypes about American Indian history and culture that are predominant in our society. These stereotypes were often reinforced by museum displays of the past that tended to obscure the great historical, cultural, and linguistic diversity of tribal nations by dividing Native people into cultural groups—giving a sense that all tribes are the same or at least the same within one particular region. Exhibitions tended to reinforce the view of static, unchanging culture. Certainly the diorama, a popular display technique used in natural history museums, tended to do this by keeping Indians frozen in a particular time period and by displaying them near the dinosaurs and other extinct animals.[6] Exhibitions also defined Indian societies by their functional technology (we are only what we made) and displayed sacred and sensitive objects and information. Most tragically, even our ancestors' remains often served to emphasize the notion of Indians as a vanishing race, an idea prevalent at the time when the collecting of Native American material culture began. The movement by tribal communities to be involved in the development of exhibitions today is recognition that controlling the representation of their cultures is linked to the larger self-determination movement and cultural survival.

While collaborative efforts on the surface appear to be a positive direction—and there are certainly success stories to note—these successes are uneven at best.[7] The story is not that simple, as the historical legacy of the relationship between American Indians and museums is difficult to overcome. We suffered great injustices in the colonization process and in the name of Western science, both of which are intimately linked with the museum world. The Smithsonian's National Museum of the American Indian (NMAI), the self-proclaimed "Museum Different," reflects this still complicated and evolving relationship.

Museum Collaborations: The NMAI in Context

One of the most important works to emerge in recent years on the processes of collaboration is Ruth Phillip's essay "Collaboration in Exhibitions: Toward a Dialogic Paradigm." In the essay, she asserts that there is "a spectrum of models . . . bracketed by two distinct types."[8] She is careful, however, to acknowledge that there is no prototypical model or single collaborative process. Each project is firmly rooted in the institutional history of the particular museum and also dependent on relationships between individuals in the museums and on the community advisory boards. Even though each project is unique, Phillips notes two models that most collaborative projects fall into: the multivocal model and the community-based model. Throughout the NMAI's history the museum has followed both or a combination of these models for its exhibitions.

According to Phillips, the multivocal exhibit model allows for multiple perspectives in the exhibitions. The voices of curators, scholars, and Indigenous people are all present in the interpretative space, offering their own interpretation on the significance of the pieces and themes presented. The NMAI's George Gustav Heye Center in New York employed this approach in its display Creations Journey: Masterworks of Native American Identity and Belief that opened in 1994. The gallery focused on the museum's masterworks (determined by Western standards of aesthetic quality) and showcased the perspectives of anthropologists and art historians who offered their view of the objects from their own disciplinary lens. At the same time, Native labels offered the tribal perspective on the relevance of these pieces. This very ambitious enterprise by the NMAI was critiqued by many as failing to address the needs of the audience, and visitors were often confused over the display techniques. As one of the staff members told me when we discussed the NMAI's evolving museology, "There were just too many voices talking at once in that exhibition."[9] A reviewer with the *New York Times* recognized the beauty of the five hundred objects on display but felt they were "sabotaged by an over produced installation."[10] Margaret Dubin, in her review of the Heye Center exhibits, included commentary from visitors expressing confusion over the display techniques, which compelled one visitor to write, "Organization seems confused, the presentation was horrendous—very cramped, chaotic media blitz, no sense of scale, not enough space and information incomplete."[11] The criticisms of this exhibition strategy may have been one factor that led the NMAI to choose a different method for its exhibitions on the National Mall in Washington DC, one that falls into what Phillips calls the community-based model.[12]

In the community-based approach "the role of the professional museum curator or staff member is defined as that of a facilitator who puts his or her disciplinary and museological expertise at the service of community members so that their messages can be disseminated as clearly and as effectively as possible."[13] The community is given final authority in all decisions related to the exhibition, from the themes and objects that will be featured to the design of the actual exhibition. The tribal perspective has primacy in interpretation in this model, and exhibition text is typically in the first person. This strategy is reflected in each of the three community-curated sections of the permanent galleries at the DC site that opened in September 2004. The effectiveness of this strategy is discussed in the following section.

One further point needs to be made in regard to museum collaborations. The NMAI has become the most visible model for community collaborative exhibitions with Indigenous groups. But what I want to emphasize here is that the NMAI is only part of an evolving new relationship between Native Americans and museums, one in which tribal nations collaborate in the development of exhibitions on their history and culture. Other museums pursued this approach prior to the creation of the NMAI, and the institution is not unique in this regard.[14] The NMAI's founding director, W. Richard West, has noted this, saying, "Most smaller museums who work with first nations or native communities or tribes invoke the native voice in interpretation and representation." But West has also noted that what makes the NMAI unique is that it "is the first institution of this size to take this approach on this scale."[15]

My own experience and the research of others have demonstrated that collaboration in museum exhibitions is becoming more the norm than the exception and that the NMAI's claim to uniqueness does indeed rest in the scale in which it employed this approach. The NMAI represents the most ambitious of these collaborative projects to date. For the exhibitions on the National Mall that opened on September 21, 2004, the museum "co-curated" with twenty-four tribal nations from across the Western hemisphere for its three permanent galleries: Our Universes (focusing on Native American philosophies), Our Peoples (examining tribal history), and Our Lives (addressing contemporary identity). Each of these three galleries contains sections in which the tribal communities were asked to present their respective community's story and a "thematic spine" in which NMAI curators provide an overarching framework.[16] The collaborative process of developing these exhibitions has been applauded by many (myself included) and represents the NMAI's desire to chart a new course in our relationship to museums by sharing curatorial authority. The process of community collaboration is important and is not in dispute, but the question remains, How effective are the inaugural exhibitions at the NMAI in advancing the public's knowledge concerning Native American history, identity, and philosophies?

Reflections on the Gallery Space: Missed Opportunities

The NMAI's community-based approach for the DC site is the topic of much discussion and has been both widely praised and critiqued. The museum's ambitious "new Indian museology"[17] has been praised by several scholars and journalists for offering a complicated, nuanced, and ultimately effective presentation of Indigenous philosophy, history, and identity as told from the perspective of Indigenous communities. But for many, something is missing. Voices of individuals from all cultural and professional backgrounds express dissatisfaction at what they view as ineffective and vastly disappointing exhibitions that are confusing, unengaging, and lacking in historical context.[18]

As many scholars have argued, the NMAI emerged out of a growing movement within museums that include more thematic rather than object-based exhibitions, more storytelling and first-person voice, collaborative methods that bring "source communities'" perspectives to the forefront, and a de-centering of the authority that museum curators have held. As I walked through the NMAI, I did see these most important new directions in the museum world on display in the state-of-the-art film presentations, first-person text panels, large images of Native people everywhere, emphasis on twentieth-century survival, more thematic and storytelling than object-based exhibitions—all of the markers of a museum that has embraced the new exhibition practices of the past several decades. But what I had hoped for were more moments of wonder and places that touched my heart and more of an emphasis on truth telling—a site where the difficult stories could finally be told to a nation with a willed ignorance of the past five hundred years of ongoing colonization.

Several contributors to this volume have given considerable attention to the silences around the subject of genocide and the hard truths of colonization and its lasting impact in Indigenous communities. This is also a noticeable absence for me, and as a result I am profoundly disappointed about this missed opportunity to truly challenge the American Master Narrative—a narrative that has silenced and even erased the memory of the genocidal policies of America's past and present. That the National Museum of the American Indian allows for silences around these issues, articulates an abstract historical message that is confused and confusing, and does not hold accountable those who walk through this museum for the colonization of Native Americans speaks to a historical amnesia that is tragic for a national museum of such prominence and one that has such potential as a site where new understandings of American history could have taken place.

It is important to keep in mind that several scholars argue that the museum does indeed include these stories.[19] According to them, the stories are told implicitly, which they suggest reflects an Indigenous way of knowing and teaching. The stories are there, they assure us, the museum just presents them in a manner that makes the visitor work for it. But is this really an effective way to present Native American history and culture to a nation and a world with a willed ignorance of this history? Or to a society that carries with them so many stereotypes about who we are as Indigenous people and to a nation that has defined itself by "playing Indian"? From the glass cases in Our Peoples filled with stone figures, gold, swords, treaties, Bibles, and guns to a bizarre storm display that, as Myla Vicenti Carpio argues, problematically uses a metaphor that is caused by *nature* to equate what happened to Indigenous people at the hands of the U.S. government and its citizens,[20] this museum fails to tell the painful stories and serves to obscure an important message to visitors that should have been presented powerfully and prominently.

In comparison, the specifics of the difficult and painful history of the Jewish Holocaust are not sacrificed at the United States Holocaust Memorial Museum; that museum did not obscure the specifics of the Jewish people's painful past, the violence they suffered at the hands of the Nazis, to make a larger theoretical argument about how history is constructed. The curators present the specifics in a moving narrative that does not surrender coherency to make some sort of relativistic argument in the service of postmodernism.[21]

The stories that are most prevalent at the NMAI are those emphasizing Native survival, or "survivance," which serve to tackle head-on the "vanishing race" stereotype that predominated in earlier museum representations. But the museum fails to provide the fundamental context for survival. To understand survival and Indigenous agency (another popular theme in the museum) in the wake of government policies designed to destroy us, one must have a clear understanding of what we were up against. The more painful stories of the past five hundred years of colonization are excluded, or if they are there they are not prominently displayed. I agree with the American Indian movement activists who criticized the museum for not telling the story of the American Indian Holocaust along with our stories of survival. As they stated, "The museum falls short in that it does not characterize or does not display the sordid and tragic history of America's holocaust against the Native Nations and peoples of the Americas."[22]

The museum allows for silences around the tragedies of what took place, and founding director West argues that this was the intention because this period of tragedy is only a small portion of our time in the Americas: "Here's what I want everyone to understand. As much, and as important as that period of history is—the centuries of war, disease and exile—it is at best only about 5 percent of the period we have been in this hemisphere. We do not want to make the National Museum of the American Indian into an Indian Holocaust Museum."[23]

If "the centuries of war, disease, and exile" is "only about 5 percent" of the broad sweep of our history, as West claims, where is our earlier history? There is no extensive treatment in this museum of our pre-Columbian past in any of the galleries. So although West seems to be implying that the thousands of years before contact are critical and that the museum will give equal emphasis to the entire span of our history (not just the past five hundred years), those earlier periods are not reflected on the exhibition floor. The time depth argument is important and could serve as the principal illuminator of our deep history in these lands, but treatment of our ancestral past is not presented prominently at the NMAI in any of the three inaugural exhibitions.

Furthermore, while it is accurate to say that the past five hundred years of "war, disease, and exile" are not the entire span of Indigenous history, it is critical to acknowledge that it has had a disproportionate impact on our communities and cultures. And the impact this period had on our communities continues: colonization is not over, nor has the holocaust in the Americas ever been recognized. The continuing legacies of those policies in Indian Country are very much a part of our contemporary experience. This may be only a short period of time, but it has had the greatest impact.

Abstraction, Postmodernism, and Audience Confusion

One of the most interesting arguments made by several scholars is that the museum is advancing an Indigenous way of knowing in the exhibitions, "an indigenous museology," that non-Natives and even some Native people are not working hard enough to understand.[24] They argue that the exhibitions are designed to be challenging, reflecting engagements with both postmodernist and postcolonial critiques, as well as decolonizing strategies. I agree that many of the very thoughtful displays at the institution are indeed there to challenge us, to provide us with new insights through the presentation of Indigenous knowledge from the Indigenous perspective. But why is this new knowledge system at work in the institution not clearly conveyed? Given that the public carries with them so many stereotypes about who we are as Native people, isn't it critical that the museum staff engage those issues right away? Reviews of the exhibitions have indicated that visitors are often left feeling overwhelmed, confused, and frustrated by the display techniques. If the museum is to truly challenge stereotypes that have long dominated in the representation of our histories and cultures, then content, design, text, and images must be clear, consistent, and coherent.

The museum's failure to tell the more painful stories of colonization, as well as the curators' inability to convey their ideas clearly to the public, is prevalent throughout the Our Peoples gallery, which focuses on tribal history. There are eight "community-curated" sections in Our Peoples, as well as sections curated by NMAI staff.

The importance of the NMAI-curated site titled Evidence cannot be emphasized enough. Curator Paul Chaat Smith has stated that the content to be covered in this exhibit "is the *raison d'etre* for the existence of the museum itself" and comprises roughly half of the gallery space in Our Peoples. This gallery is meant to tell the "biggest untold story of all": that contact between vastly different worlds changed everything.[25] The exhibition deals with the aftermath of "contact"; disease, warfare, dispossession of lands and resources, and the role Christianity played in the process. Evidence is a very object-based exhibition, but without any labels associated with individual objects.

At the entrance to the gallery the word "Evidence" is emblazoned on a large frosted-glass wall with objects buried underneath, designed to suggest that the exhibit itself is an "excavation site . . . where history is buried, lost and found."[26] From there you find a case with large black letters stating "1491" filled with figurines that are there to supposedly represent the diversity of tribal nations before contact. Next are cases filled with gold and other riches of the Americas, symbolizing the great wealth in abundance throughout the hemisphere. From there you see weapons such as swords and guns, which one could assume were used to plunder these resources. Behind the gun display is a case filled with Bibles, and around the corner is a case filled with treaties. The guns, Bibles, and treaties form the Storm installation that represents the forces—weapons, foreign governments, and Christianity—that all tribal nations in the Western hemisphere faced after invasion.

Some have argued that all of these "symbols of power" are just meant to overwhelm visitors; hence the reason for the lack of labels with identifying information including tribal affiliations, provenance, and dates.[27] In her review essay Gwyn Isaac argues that this gallery reflects an engagement "with the postmodern discourse on the history of colonialism—a discourse which stems from the academic critique of how history is created, constructed and controlled." She further states, "In Our Peoples [curator] Paul Chaat Smith does not want us to learn the details of Native American history, he wants us to question our ethnocentric ideas about history itself."[28] This certainly reflects the words of Smith's co-curator, Jolene Rickard: "There are other places where you can learn the exact dates of the Trail of Tears. It's less important to me that someone leave this museum knowing all about Wounded Knee than that they leave knowing what it takes to survive that kind of tragedy."[29]

This may be a valid role for a museum. But it is important to keep in mind that it took Isaac, a highly trained academic, two different encounters with this institution to come to these conclusions about the intended meaning of this exhibition. Should an exhibition require a person be well schooled in postmodernist theory to engage effectively with the displays? It is one thing for a curator or academic to understand this theory-laden argument; it is another thing entirely to be able to convey that message to the general public in an engaging, moving, and compelling manner. A majority of the estimated four million people a year coming to this museum will have only one opportunity to engage with the exhibition—only one— and do not bring with them an extensive background on postmodern theory or museum training. One has to wonder if this is the most effective manner in which to frame the eight community-curated history presentations in the remaining part of the Our Peoples gallery that Evidence was designed to accomplish.

The decision to pursue an abstract storyline in connection with a postmodernist critique was a poor choice for the museum. Abstraction is not an effective method of presentation for a museum hoping to educate a nation with a willed ignorance of its treatment of Indigenous peoples and the policies and practices that led to genocide in the Americas. Our survival, as many people have argued, is one of the greatest untold stories, and the specifics of this difficult and shameful history need to be told.

To illustrate my point on the dangers of representing history in the abstract manner that the NMAI did in the Evidence gallery, I would like to offer my recollection of an encounter that took place in front of the gun display in the gallery in 2005. My impression of that case remains the same as on the first night that I walked through this exhibit in September 2004. As a Native woman, historian, and museum professional I found this case to be very problematic, and I was seriously worried whether the intended message of the display would reach the audience or would be "read" by the audience as another example of Indigenous people as war-like savages engaged in a futile battle to evade encroachment on their lands. Or, just as problematically, whether it would be read as a glorification of weaponry that fails to illuminate these weapons' broader meaning and devastating impact on Indigenous people.

Every time I return to this gallery and stand in front of the gun case I notice who is standing with me. On these occasions, numbering more than twenty, I am almost always standing with men. Time and time again they stare in awe and intense concentration on the case densely packed with guns. From my vantage point it looks as though they are focusing on the objects themselves instead of reading the text panels. Those panels might have given visitors the context that other scholars claim is there: that these guns were used against Native people as one of the three forces they faced after invasion, while at the same time Native people "transformed the tools of colonialism into the instruments of integration, empowerment, and even liberation."[30]

On this particular October afternoon, one year after the museum's official opening, I stood in front of the case with several middle-aged men and two young schoolboys around ten years of age. The boys were excitedly chatting to each other and pointing to various guns in the case. Their animated conversation was interrupted abruptly by a middle-aged woman who told them loudly that they were not to be there. At this point, I decided to go over and introduce myself to the woman, explaining that I am a historian conducting research on the museum, and I couldn't help but overhear their conversation. I mentioned that I heard her say that they shouldn't be here and I was wondering why. She proceeded to tell me that she was their teacher and the school has a policy that forbids the children from entering this gallery to view the gun case, but somehow they still manage to hear about it anyway and many are determined to find it. It was at this moment that one of the boys asked her, "If you could have any one of these guns, which one would you choose?" She quickly responded, "None," and told them that they must return to the group. That the children were banned from viewing the case while on a school field trip because of the violence these guns embody speaks volumes about the problems of "implicitly" attempting to make a point to the audience.

I think this observation is very revealing. It is a manifestation of the problems inherent in using an abstract, object-based exhibition with very little contextual information to convey a complex history. The text that is included does not connect this abundance of information to a larger narrative of systematic violence against Indigenous people. I worried on several occasions that the larger argument that the curators were trying to make here would be lost to the visitor. Given the many misconceptions that the general public has regarding Native people, there is great risk in these messages being "hijacked" and read "on the basis of . . . misinformation and stereotypes."[31]

The intended arguments that I assume the curators attempted to convey appeared lost on those I spoke with that day, and I remain greatly concerned that the intended messages will be "hijacked" and read within ethnocentric narratives. The absence of labels in this installation is strategic, according to Claire Smith, as this reflects an Indigenous way of imparting knowledge, in which knowledge has to be earned. As she argues, "People have to work at understanding the exhibits and perhaps this is the point. They have been given the power to determine what is important for themselves, and this will vary according to each individual. . . . . This is an Indigenous, not a Western, route to knowledge."[32] Not only is this a problematic and essentialist argument, but it also presumes far too much about the knowledge base of visitors. What happens when the visitors who are supposed to come to their own conclusions bring with them deeply embedded myths and stereotypes of Indigenous communities? What happens when the audience is completely unaware that another knowledge system exists or is at work in the museum? Audience evaluations will help demonstrate what visitors are taking away and if they do indeed understand the knowledge system at work in the museum.

I would like to bring in an example from a study by Oxford University anthropologist Laura Peers, who has recently completed an impressive ten-year ethnographic study on living history sites in the Great Lakes region. Her book *Playing Ourselves: Interpreting Native Histories at Historic Reconstructions* critically examines the complex process of representing Native American and First Nations' history at reconstructed historic sites. This is the first major study focusing exclusively on the role of Indigenous interpreters working to incorporate Native themes into the programming at these sites. Peers's study captures the complexities of how these histories are negotiated and produced and provides insights on their impact at shaping the public's understanding of Native American history.

One of the most important conclusions that Peers draws from this study is the problem inherent in not providing enough context for visitors to work with when they encounter what for many is actually new information on the Indigenous past and present at these sites. Peers discusses how, even with the best of intentions, the revisionist messages that are presented at these sites can be hijacked. A case in point is a new interpretative strategy developed at Colonial Michilimackinac in Michigan, a reconstructed eighteenth-century fur trading post. The manager at this site wanted to include a war post as part of the interpretation, with the intended message conveying a more nuanced argument on "the participation of the upper Great Lakes Indians in the American Revolution. . . . [and] to explain how Michilimackinac functioned as a recruitment and staging center for Indian warriors in the 1770s."[33] Even though the intended message is historically accurate and appropriate for this site, Peers found that interpreters she interviewed claimed that "most visitors did not have this knowledge . . . and often made comments indicating that they associated [the war post] with stereotypes about savages, scalping, and the warpath, as well as with the much-emphasized 1763 Ojibwa attack on the fort." A well-intentioned idea designed to combat stereotypes and challenge visitors to new understandings became recast in the stereotypical narratives that visitors bring with them to these sites. As Peers argues, "While the stories suggested by artifacts are crucial, it is dangerous to let them remain implicit, for—as with the war post—they can be 'read' by visitors as easily within misinformed narratives as they can within intended ones."[34]

Peers's study acknowledges the embeddedness of the many myths and stereotypes concerning the Indigenous past and present that visitors bring with them; she emphasizes throughout her study that these stereotypes and cultural baggage must be challenged explicitly. There is danger in letting messages in exhibitions remain implicit, especially given how misunderstood and misrepresented Indigenous communities and our history have been. Interestingly, the video in the NMAI's Evidence section acknowledges this very point. In *Making History*, narrator Floyd Favel Starr movingly tells visitors that Native people have long had our histories framed, and powerful representations formed, by forces not of our own making. As he states, "The subjects here, us, have been portrayed from the outside. Our stories told by others to explain or justify their own agendas. Or we've been considered people without a history. The truth is we care passionately and have fought at great cost to reclaim knowledge of the past. We are left then with this paradox: for all our visibility, we have been rendered invisible and silent. A history-loving people stripped of their own history."[35]

Disappointingly, though, the history that is conveyed in the rest of the Evidence section does not fulfill the promise of the video and fails to provide a hard-hitting analysis of the forces associated with the colonization process that have sought to silence our versions of the past. The death caused by guns and swords, the forced conversions and abuse at the hands of Christian churches, the devastation that resulted from European diseases (some deliberately spread), the colonial policies and practices of foreign governments that attempted to destroy our worlds—these stories are not explicitly told. Instead, we get cases of guns and swords, Bibles, and treaties in an abstract object-driven display that fails to connect these objects of power to the forces of power that devastated our worlds. The museum missed an important opportunity to make explicit the manifestation of colonization throughout the hemisphere.[36]

Decolonizing History: Truth Telling in a National Space

What is at stake in not speaking the hard truths? The NMAI has long stood by its story that the emphasis on contemporary survival in the exhibitions is what Native people asked for and that the museum honored this request. The message that "we are still here" is an important one to convey. But by failing to tell the hard truths of colonialism this message loses its most important context and the primary reason why the message of survival is so amazing and worthy of celebration. We did survive a holocaust in North America—even though this nation refuses to take responsibility for this act— and we as Indigenous people must name this history for what it was: genocide. Apache scholar Nancy Mithlo bravely calls into question why we fail to face this history and the dangers of continually emphasizing our survival without sufficiently explaining what we were surviving: "Couldn't the concept of the holocaust museum be just as appropriate for recognizing the genocide of American Indians? Why are we always celebrating the survival of Native American culture, instead of truly understanding just how much we have lost and how we have lost it? It is this type of representation I am interested in and as far as I know, no museums are talking about my people truthfully in this manner."[37]

This call for truth telling in the context of museums is important; speaking the truth of what has happened is part of a growing call for decolonization in Native communities. Indigenous scholars Waziyatawin Angela Wilson and Michael Yellowbird recently assembled a collection of essays focusing on decolonizing Native communities. In the volume *For Indigenous Eyes Only: A Decolonization Handbook* nine intellectuals from a range of tribal and disciplinary backgrounds provide insights into the work that needs to take place in Indian Country to bring about decolonization and healing for our communities. The purpose of the volume is to encourage critical thinking skills so as to "mobilize a massive decolonization movement in North America."[38]

In a compelling final essay, Wilson calls for a truth commission in the United States, similar to truth commissions that took place in South Africa and other parts of the world, to address the ongoing and systematic attacks on Indigenous bodies, land, sovereignty, and lifeways that have occurred throughout the Western hemisphere. She states that truth-telling is necessary to bring about the healing of our communities and to empower future generations of Indigenous people. The only way for Native people to heal from the historical trauma that we have experienced—genocidal warfare, land theft, ethnic cleansing, disease, the attempted destruction of our religious and ceremonial life at the hands of the government and Christian churches—is for us to speak the truth about what has happened, document the suffering and name perpetrators of the violence in our history. As she argues, "Since the truth about injustices perpetrated against Indigenous peoples has been largely denied in the United States, truth telling becomes an important strategy for decolonization."[39] By naming and speaking these truths, we are moving out of victimry and seeking justice for the past and the present.

Furthermore, in speaking the truth about the violence in our history we are also ensuring that future generations can never claim ignorance of this history. As Archbishop Tutu states regarding the South African Truth Commission, "No one in South Africa could ever begin to say, 'I didn't know,' and hoped to be believed."[40] I am afraid that the narratives told at the NMAI serve only to reinforce this sense of not knowing that pervades our society. And it is this missed opportunity to speak the hard truths that makes the NMAI so incomplete.

As the NMAI charts its course for the future, it is imperative that the institution take seriously the calls for historical narratives that serve to challenge deeply embedded stereotypes—not just the ones of Native disappearance in the wake of westward expansion in the nineteenth century, but the willed ignorance of this nation to face its colonialist past and present. The truths need to be told specifically instead of the passive-voice presentation of the colonizing forces in our history that predominate at the NMAI. W. Richard West has stated that this museum "make[s] possible the true cultural reconciliation that until now has eluded American history."[41] But how can this "cultural reconciliation," or any form of reconciliation for that matter, be achieved without an acknowledgment of what actually took place? Reconciliation cannot be set in motion, as scholar Rebecca Tsosie has argued, "without an acknowledgement of responsibility for the historical wrongs and their continuing effect."[42] The message coming from the NMAI is that the historical trauma that we have suffered as Indigenous people is a closed chapter, yet there has been no formal acknowledgment of or apology for the harms suffered by Indigenous people by the U.S. government and its citizens. Nor have we as Native communities had a forum in which to tell these painful stories.

Claire Smith has erroneously referred to the National Museum of the American Indian as a "decolonizing museum."[43] But how can it be a decolonizing museum without a discussion of colonization? This is critical, for as Wilson and Yellowbird argue, "The first step toward decolonization is to question the legitimacy of colonization."[44] Until this institution and its exhibitions describe the genocidal acts committed against Indigenous peoples, until we name the specifics of a shameful history that every American should be held accountable for, until we tell the truth to a nation and a world that has willfully ignored this history or tried to silence our versions of the past, this museum on the National

Mall in Washington DC will remain a museum that serves the interests of the nation-state. If we assess this museum in relation to the growing movement for decolonization, for which telling the truth of our past and present is critical, this museum fails in its mission to move us forward in our efforts for decolonization and reparative justice. As this institution charts its course for the future it is imperative that it serve as a place for education, commemoration, and truth telling in a national space.

Notes

This is an expanded version of my essay "Missed Opportunities: Reflections on the NMAI *" that appeared in* American Indian Quarterly *30, no. 4 (2006). Additionally, two paragraphs are from a shorter review of the* NMAI *titled "Continuing Dialogues: Evolving Views of the National Museum of the American Indian,"* Public Historian *28, no. 2 (Spring 2006): 57–61.*

1. Craig Howe, "The Morality of Exhibiting Indians," in *Embedding Ethics: Shifting the Boundaries of the Anthropological Profession*, ed. Lynn Meskell and Peter Pels (Oxford: Berg, 2005), 220.
2. Gail Anderson, "Introduction: Reinventing the Museum," in *Reinventing the Museum: Historical and Contemporary Perspectives on the Paradigm Shift*, ed. Gail Anderson (Walnut Creek CA: AltaMira Press, 2004), 1.
3. Kathleen McLean, "Museum Exhibitions and the Dynamics of Dialogue," in Anderson, *Reinventing the Museum*, 193.
4. David W. Penney, "The Poetics of Museum Representations: Tropes of Recent American Indian Art Exhibitions," in *The Changing Presentation of the American Indian: Museums and Native Cultures*, ed. National Museum of the American Indian Smithsonian Institution (Washington DC: Smithsonian Institution and University of Washington Press, 2000), 47.
5. This quote is taken from one of the most important studies of a Native American tribal museum, Patricia Pierce Erikson with Helma Ward and Kirk Wachendorf, *Voices of a Thousand People* (Lincoln: University of Nebraska Press, 2002), 30. Also see Patricia Pierce Erikson, "A-Whaling We Will Go: Encounters of Knowledge and Memory at the Makah Culture and Research Center," *Cultural Anthropology* 14, no. 4 (1999): 556–83.
6. Richard Hill, "The Museum Indian: Still Frozen in Time and Mind," *Museum News*, May/June 2000, 40–44, 58–63, 66–67, 74.
7. For a recent examination of the involvement of Native people in the museum world, see Nancy Marie Mithlo, "Red Man's Burden: The Politics of

Inclusion in Museum Settings," *American Indian Quarterly* 28, nos. 3–4 (Summer–Fall 2004): 743–63.

8. Ruth B. Phillips, "Collaboration in Exhibitions: Toward a Dialogic Paradigm," introduction in *Museums and Source Communities: A Routledge Reader*, ed. Laura Peers and Alison K. Brown (London: Routledge, 2003) 158.

9. NMAI staff person, personal communication, August 2000.

10. Holland Cotter, "New Museum Celebrating American Indian Voices," *New York Times*, October 28, 1994.

11. Margaret Dubin, *Native America Collected: The Culture of an Art World* (Albuquerque: University of New Mexico Press, 2001), 94.

12. For other scholarly reviews of the NMAI's George Gustav Heye Center, see Allison Arieff, "A Different Sort of (P)Reservations: Some Thoughts on the National Museum of the American Indian," *Museum Anthropology* 19, no. 2 (Fall 1995): 78–90; Richard White, "Representing Indians: Art, History, and the New Museums," *New Republic*, April 21, 1997, 28–34; Patricia Penn Hilden and Shari M. Huhndorf, "Performing 'Indian' in the National Museum of the American Indian," *Social Identities* 5, no. 2 (1999): 161–83; and Shari M. Huhndorf, *Going Native: Indians in the American Cultural Imagination* (Ithaca NY: Cornell University Press, 2001), 199–202.

13. Phillips, "Collaboration in Exhibitions," 163.

14. For discussion of other collaborative projects, see Jocelyn Wedll, "Learn about Our Past to Understand Our Future: The Story of the Mille Lacs Band of Ojibwe," in *The Changing Presentation of the American Indian: Museums and Native Cultures*, ed. National Museum of the American Indian (Washington DC: Smithsonian Institution Press, 2000), 89–98; Amy Lonetree, "American Indian Self-Determination and the Emergence of Tribal Museums: The Development of the Mille Lacs Indian Museum," unpublished manuscript; Gerald T. Conaty, "Glenbow's Blackfoot Gallery: Working toward Co-existence," in Peers and Brown, *Museums and Source Communities*, 227–41; Michael Ames, "How to Decorate a House: The Renegotiation of Cultural Representations at the University of British Columbia Museum of Anthropology," in Peers and Brown, *Museums and Source Communities*, 171–80.

15. Judy Stoffman, "Natives Tell Their Own Story at Smithsonian: Controversy in Calgary Led to Collaboration; Native Groups Consulted on Every Aspect of Museum," *Vancouver Sun*, August 21, 2004.

16. Douglas Evelyn, "The Smithsonian's National Museum of the American Indian: An International Institution of Living Cultures," *Public Historian* 28, no. 2 (Spring 2006): 53.

17. Gerald McMaster used this term when describing the NMAI's evolving exhibition strategy. Gerald McMaster, deputy assistant director for cultural resources, tape-recorded interview with the author, December 11, 2001.

18. For scholars' critiques, see Robin Delugan, Myla Vicenti Carpio, and Sonya Atalay in this volume. For reviews by journalists and cultural critics, see Marc Fisher, "Indian Museum's Appeal, Sadly, Only Skin Deep," *Washington Post*, September 21, 2004; Paul Richard, "Shards of Many Untold Stories: In Place of Unity, a Melange of Unconnected Objects," *Washington Post*, September 21, 2004; Edward Rothstein, "Who Should Tell History: The Tribes or the Museums?" *New York Times*, December 21, 2004; Tiffany Jenkins, "The Museum of Political Correctness," *Independent Review*, January 25, 2005; Joel Achenback, "Within These Walls, Science Yields to Stories," *Washington Post*, September 19, 2004; Timothy Noah, "The National Museum of Ben Nighthorse Campbell: The Smithsonian's New Travesty," *Slate*, September 29, 2004, http://slate.msn.com/id/2107140/ (accessed October 13, 2004).

19. Claire Smith, "Decolonising the Museum: The National Museum of the American Indian in Washington, DC," *Antiquity* 79, no. 304 (2005): 424–39; Debra Ann Doyle, "National Museum of the American Indian Opens in Washington, DC," *Perspectives* November 2004, online, accessed May 2005; Amanda J. Cobb, "The National Museum of the American Indian as Cultural Sovereignty," *American Quarterly* 57, no. 2 (June 2005): 485–506; Amanda J. Cobb, "The National Museum of the American Indian: Sharing the Gift," *American Indian Quarterly* 29, nos. 3–4 (Summer–Fall 2005): 361–83; Elizabeth Archuleta, "Gym Shoes, Maps, and Passports, Oh My! Creating Community or Creating Chaos at the NMAI?," *American Indian Quarterly* 29, nos. 3–4, (Summer–Fall 2005): 426–49.

20. Myla Vicenti Carpio, "(Un)disturbing Exhibitions: Indigenous Historical Memory at the NMAI," *American Indian Quarterly* 30, nos. 3–4 (2006): 625.

21. For an excellent study of the United States Holocaust Memorial Museum, see Edward T. Linenthal, *Preserving Memory: The Struggle to Create America's Holocaust Museum* (1995; New York: Columbia University Press, 2001).

22. Signed statement by American Indian movement leaders Floyd Red Crow Westerman, Dennis Banks, Clyde Bellecourt, and Vernon Bellecourt, quoted in Jodi Rave, "Indian Museum Looks at Life, Death, " *Bismarck Tribune*, September 26, 2004.

23. Quoted in Achenback, "Within These Walls."

24. Smith, "Decolonising the Museum"; Doyle, "National Museum of the American Indian."

25. "Curator's Talk: Paul Chaat Smith," *Smithsonian TV*, Smithsonian's National Museum of the American Indian, http://smithsonian.tv/videos/nmai/Curator_Talks/2005-03-04_ChaatSmith.htm (accessed May 14, 2005).

26. Ibid.

27. Gwyneira Isaac, "What Are Our Expectations Telling Us? Encounters with the National Museum of the American Indian," *American Indian Quarterly* 30, nos. 3–4 (Summer–Fall 2006): 585.

28. Isaac, "What Are Our Expectations Telling Us?," 586.

29. Quoted in Richard Lacayo, "A Place to Bring the Tribe," *Time*, September 20, 2004, 70.

30. Joanne Barker and Clayton Dumont, "Contested Conversations: Presentations, Expectations, and Responsibility at the National Museum of the American Indian," *American Indian Culture and Research Journal* 30, no. 2 (2006): 124.

31. Laura Peers raises these important concerns in her review, "Native Americans in Museums: A Review of the Chase Manhattan Gallery of North America," *Anthropology Today* 16, no. 6 (2000): 11.

32. Smith, "Decolonising the Museum," 433.

33. Philip Porter, "Interpreters' Manual: Indian Encampment, Colonial Michilimackinac," internal document for site use, 1992, quoted in Laura Peers, *Playing Ourselves: Interpreting Native Histories at Historic Reconstructions* (Lanham MD: AltaMira Press, 2007), 100.

34. Peers, *Playing Ourselves*, 100, 104.

35. *Making History*, video, script written by Paul Chaat Smith, NMAI.

36. Amy Lonetree, "Continuing Dialogues: Evolving Views of the National Museum of the American Indian," *Public Historian* 28, no. 2 (Spring 2006): 60.

37. Nancy Mithlo, "History Is Dangerous," *Museum Anthropology* 19, no. 2 (1995): 57.

38. Waziyatawin Angela Wilson and Michael Yellowbird, "Beginning Decolonization," in *For Indigenous Eyes Only: A Decolonization Handbook*, ed. Waziyatawin Angela Wilson and Michael Yellowbird (Santa Fe NM: School of American Research Press, 2005), 3.

39. Wilson and Yellowbird, "Beginning Decolonization," 7.

40. Desmond Tutu, quoted in Waziyatawin Angela Wilson, "Relieving Our Suffering: Indigenous Decolonization and a United States Truth Commission," in Wilson and Yellowbird, *For Indigenous Eyes Only*, 204.

41. W. Richard West, "Remarks on the Occasion of the Grand Opening Ceremony," National Museum of the American Indian, Washington, DC, Sep-

tember 21, 2005, available at http://newsdesk.si.edu/kits/nmai (accessed August 23, 2006).

42. Rebecca Tsosie, "The BIA's Apology to Native Americans," in *Taking Wrongs Seriously: Apologies and Reconciliation*, ed. Elazar Barkan and Alexander Karn (Stanford: Stanford University Press, 2006), 201.

43. Smith, "Decolonising the Museum."

44. Wilson and Yellowbird, "Beginning Decolonization," 2.

Conversation 4
Questions of Nation and Identity

13. The National Museum of the American Indian as Cultural Sovereignty

Amanda J. Cobb

Beginnings

On September 21, 2004, more than twenty-five thousand Native Americans gathered together on the Washington Mall to celebrate the opening of the National Museum of the American Indian (NMAI). As a citizen of the Chickasaw Nation of Oklahoma, I too participated in that moment, which was beautiful for so many reasons: because of the physical beauty of the NMAI building and grounds, because of the cultural significance and even sacred connotation of so many objects in the museum, because of the more than sixty-five thousand non–Native Americans who joined the celebrations, and because the sun came out that morning after a solid week of rain. The thousands of people present that day seemed to understand that the National Museum of the American Indian is more than just a museum. As NMAI Director W. Richard West (Southern Cheyenne) reflected, "There was just this kind of power in the air for Native people. But somehow it was almost the same for non-Indians who were there. They sensed, lots of them, the sixty-five thousand who watched the procession, that there was something very fundamental going on that day."[1]

Even in 1989, when Congress passed Public Law 105-189 establishing a National Museum of the American Indian as part of the Smithsonian, those involved knew something fundamental was occurring. Introduced by Senator Daniel Inouye of Hawai'i and Representative Ben Nighthorse

Campbell (Northern Cheyenne) of Colorado, the bill significantly embodied the cultural resurgence that had been growing in Indian Country for a number of years, a resurgence that took a more clearly limned shape and form and a stronger, more insistent voice in the public arena.[2] This consciousness recognized and acknowledged, in the words of poet Simon Ortiz (Acoma), that "this America has been a burden of steel and mad death" but also saw, in the "flowers and new grass and . . . spring wind rising," a different future for Native peoples.[3] This outpouring from Native Americans manifested itself in everything from the Red Power movement to the growth of American Indian studies in academe, the renaissance of contemporary Native American art, literature, and film, the emergence of tribal museums and cultural centers, the upsurge in economic development, and the increased exercise of tribal sovereignty in legal and political arenas. The congressional bill, which appropriated funds for three museum facilities—the Gustav Heye Center in New York City, the Cultural Resources Center in Suitland, Maryland, and the National Museum of the American Indian in Washington DC—was one of the many institutional changes wrought by Native cultural resurgence and revitalization and one of the most significant because it involved *museums*, which have served as powerful colonizing forces throughout Native America.

The NMAI as an Exercise of Native Cultural Sovereignty

As I walked through the NMAI, I was particularly struck by a display in Our Peoples: Giving Voice to Our Histories, one of the three permanent exhibitions. The installation consisted of long, curvilinear glass cases, one of which was filled to overflowing with guns, one with Bibles, and one with government treaties. The accompanying wall text argues that the three major forces of colonization were warfare, churches, and government, and through the display of literally hundreds of guns, Bibles, and treaties, the exhibit demonstrates how all three served as instruments of dispossession. But the exhibit goes on to say that these same objects—in the hands of Native Americans—served also as instruments of resistance, resilience, and survival. Armies may have used guns and warfare to seize land and conquer tribes, but Native peoples used guns to protect their communities and fight back. Missionaries and school-teachers may have used churches and Bibles to "civilize" Native individuals in their attempt to destroy elements of Native cultures, but Native Americans, in an exercise of profound cultural agency, either rejected the imposed religion or adapted elements of it into existing religious and spiritual traditions, using religion as a common thread to bind the community together. Government officials may have used treaties to forge alliances and force the cession of land, but Native nations learned to use these documents to fight for continued federal recognition of their sovereign status.

An ironic and unspoken aspect of the display was striking—that is, that this argument was being made in a museum, an institutional tool of culture that quite possibly could serve as the fourth major force of colonization after guns, God, and government. I was therefore struck by the fact that in creating the NMAI, Native Americans have *again* turned an instrument of colonization and dispossession into something else—in this case, into an instrument of self-definition and cultural continuance.

Native Americans have a tortured relationship with museums. Museums offer significant bodies of scholarship and knowledge that cannot be discounted; nevertheless, museological practices are underpinned by Western epistemologies, systems of classification, and ideological assumptions that, when applied to Native Americans, have functioned in exploitive, objectifying, and demeaning ways. By using a historically unquestioned authority to take Native objects and remains and to define who and what Native Americans are, museums have, in many ways, trapped Native Americans behind their glassed-in cases, rendering vital, contemporary Native voices silent, dynamic Native cultures invisible, and abstract concepts of legal and cultural sovereignty difficult to exercise in meaningful ways. At the same time, however, many Native Americans care very deeply about museums because they hold Native remains, sacred objects, and objects of cultural heritage and patrimony. Native peoples care very deeply about the continued existence and appropriate care of these objects in spite of the often tragic ways in which they were acquired.

Since the repatriation movement of the 1980s and 1990s, however, museums have begun to acknowledge their power as institutional colonizers; as a result, museum theory and practice have made significant strides in revising the relationship between museums and Native Americans, particularly as Native individuals have entered the arena as curators. Significantly, the years since the passage of the Native American Graves Protection and Repatriation Act (NAGPRA) have seen the emergence of the "new museology" as well as the development of a number of tribal museums and cultural centers. Based on actually incorporating criticism of museums into exhibitions, the new museology throws the authority of museums into question, thus subtracting some, but by no means all, of their power.[4] The simultaneous emergence of a number of tribal museums and cultural centers both contributed to and borrowed from the new museology and provided a place to test new museological methods. However, "indigenizing" the National Museum of the American Indian was a complicated project on a much grander scale—a project through which the NMAI carries forward the new museological paradigm in dramatic ways. After all, museums have served as one of the most compelling definers of Native Americans; the creation of the NMAI represented a major chance for Native peoples to redefine museums while defining themselves on an international stage.

Richard West, who was appointed NMAI director in 1990 and who worked in collaboration and consultation with NMAI staff and Native communities across the Americas, had a very clear sense of how to turn an instrument of dispossession into one of self-definition, thus truly making the national museum of American Indians. Those involved in developing the museum's guiding principles knew that the museum should celebrate, protect, and support the living Native cultures of the Americas, not study, classify, or objectify them. They also knew that the museum should include Native peoples of North and South America, recognizing that the boundaries of contemporary nation-states in no way reflect tribal cultural boundaries. Furthermore, they knew that a museum of Americans developed by American Indians would never take 1492 as its historical beginning point; American Indian history since European contact is only a small part of a much deeper history. In addition, they knew that their "views, voices, and eyes" should be woven into every facet of the museum, from the ground up. Finally, they knew that a museum of and for American Indians should bring exhibitions to Indian Country, thus establishing what is referred to as the "fourth museum." Each element of the museum, from the landscape to the building design to the exhibits, stems from these principles, all of which are based on Indigenous peoples' knowledge, core values, and definitions of themselves.[5]

In other words, every aspect of the museum, including its very purpose and function, had to be filtered through Native core cultural values and adapted accordingly. Consequently, the "something very fundamental" described by West was the recognition of the significance of the National Museum of the American Indian as an exercise of what filmmaker and scholar Beverly Singer (Santa Clara) calls "cultural sovereignty."[6] Such exercise requires the use of traditions as a map for the future by making the "old ways" part of contemporary life. In the case of the NMAI, that means integrating the old ways and core cultural values and traditions into the very concept of what a museum is and can be—changing what has historically been a cabinet of curiosities into a community-centered gathering place for the celebration of living cultures.

It is true that the museum as a specific concept is foreign to Native peoples; however, caring for and cherishing cultural patrimony is not, regardless of commonly held scholarly views on that matter. Sadly, as Christina Kreps has noted, the assertion that "non-western people are not concerned with the collection, care, and preservation of their cultural property . . . has frequently been used to justify the collection (or some would say plunder) and retention of non-western people's cultur-

335

al property in museums."[7] Caring for cultural property is hardly a new idea for Native people, and indeed, may exist at the center of many cultures. Consequently, adapting the old ways to museums is not the same as adapting the old ways to a new or foreign idea. Instead, it is about adapting new and foreign methods of collection, care, and preservation to a very old idea. After all, as Robert Warrior (Osage) has written, "To understand what the 'real meaning' of traditional revitalization is . . . American Indians must realize that the power of those traditions is not in their formal superiority but in their adaptability to new challenges."[8] Making a large-scale, national museum such as the NMAI into a "Native place" presented such a challenge.

Creating the NMAI

To create a museum truly based on these guiding principles, the NMAI developed an elaborate process of community collaboration and consultation, a process that marked each phase of development and decision making, from the design of the space to the content and style of the exhibitions and the choice of food in the cafeteria. Initially, rather than invite individual representatives of Native communities to travel to New York City or Washington DC, the NMAI staff chose to travel to Native communities. During the early 1990s, the staff held dozens of community consultations at different sites in Indian Country. At each consultation, participants voiced their ideas for the building, landscape, and overall tone of the museum, going far beyond what was originally asked of them. The comments generated during those sessions were recorded and compiled into a landmark planning document titled "The Way of the People," which continues to guide the NMAI in its plans for the future.[9]

An excellent example of applying the old ways to a contemporary challenge was the way the NMAI reconceptualized the idea of a museum as a space. Because the NMAI occupies the last available space on the National Mall, it ironically occupies the first space directly across from the Capitol. Consequently, the NMAI both symbolically and physically reclaims Washington DC, as Indian Country. The reclamation is made ever more apparent by the distinctive elements of the landscape surrounding the building and the building itself, both of which effectively demonstrate the conceptual link between the natural and built environments that is so central to most Native worldviews.

To remind all visitors to the Capitol that America—all of the Americas—was once and still is Indian Country, the designers took great pains to re-create the local natural environment as it was before European contact. As a result, the museum grounds consist of four indigenous habitats, which are a home for more than thirty-three thousand plants of 150 different species. The specific habitats are (1) a forest environment that includes such species as red maple, sumac, and white oak; (2) a wetlands environment, featuring wild rice and morel mushrooms; (3) a meadow environment in which sunflowers and panic grass can be found; and, perhaps most significant, (4) a traditional croplands area in which the "three sisters"—beans, squash, and corn—are raised using Native agricultural methods.[10]

Other notable features of the landscape are the cardinal direction markers and the grandfather rocks. The cardinal direction markers, four large stones placed on the grounds along the north-south and east-west axes of the site, signify the Native peoples of the Americas and were brought from corresponding communities. For example, the northern stone is from the Northwest Territories, Canada; the southern from Punto Arenas, Chile; the eastern from Great Falls, Maryland; and the western from Hawai'i. Furthermore, the axes on which the stones are placed intersect with markers inside the building at the center of the Potomac room, the huge circular space on the ground floor that represents the museum's heart. The grandfather rocks, large boulders that traveled from Alma, Canada, symbolize the "elders of the landscape." These more than forty uncarved rocks evoke the long relationship of Native peoples to place.[11]

In many ways, the museum building itself functions as part of the landscape. Stressing a relationship between natural and built environments, the curvilinear building—built of sand-colored limestone and occupying 250,000 square feet—stands in stark contrast to the white marble, straight lines, and sharp edges of the other monuments on the Washington Mall. The carved tiers of the five-story building resemble a jagged rock, smoothed and shaped over time by wind and water, a resemblance further enhanced by a waterfall featured in the northwest corner. At the same time, however, the structure's curved lines, tiers, and dome call to mind the very best of contemporary architecture, thus underscoring that Native cultures are both ancient and thoroughly present in the here and now.[12]

The craftsmanship and artistry that mark the museum's exterior pervade the interior, making the entire space function as a sort of exhibition in and of itself. For example, while visitors can find exquisite examples of contemporary Native art in Native Modernism, a retrospective of the work of George Morrison (Chippewa) and Allan Houser (Chiricahua), they can also find superb examples in the basketry-inspired wall of woven copper that encircles the Potomac room, or in the adzed wood of the museum stores. The natural color palette and textures throughout the museum were taken from plants and animals of special significance to Native peoples, for example, corn, beans, squash, and salmon. Abstractions from astronomy and specific celestial references are themes found time and again throughout the museum, including the floor of the Potomac, the oculus in the Potomac dome, and the eight glass prisms on the south wall designed to let light enter on certain days, at certain times, and in certain seasons. Such particularized design elements were considered in every detail of the museum, from the curved lines (supposedly, there is only one right angle in the entire structure) to the elevator doors, which feature bird motifs and cardinal direction markers.[13]

The attention to design and detail, both inside and on the grounds, is one way the NMAI reconceptualizes space in its reconceptualization of the entire museum project, making this museum more of a living gathering place than a repository for cultural property. Organizing the content of the museum further challenged the NMAI to engage more fully and broadly in the exercise of cultural sovereignty. To turn the museum from an instrument of dispossession into an instrument of self-definition, the NMAI aggressively carried forward propositions first tested in smaller tribal museums and cultural centers as well as in the Heye Center of New York, which opened in 1994.

First, the NMAI is based on the proposition that a museum-as-gathering-place or a museum-as-cultural-center must consist of more than exhibitions. In other words, a place that celebrates and contributes to the continuance of living cultures must make space for living cultures. To that end, the NMAI provides a welcome wall that includes greetings in hundreds of Native languages, a special place in the Potomac for dancing, performing, and demonstrations, as well as designated spaces for conferences and special programming. For example, the NMAI houses a Main Theater for musicians, theater companies, film festivals, and storytellers, as well as the Lelawi Preparatory Theater and a Resource Center, which is open seven days a week and offers a library, an interactive learning center with eighteen public access computers, and a technologically equipped classroom. Virtual and traveling exhibitions, which make up the "fourth museum," emphasize that the NMAI is a space that living Native cultures can access whether or not they are able to travel to Washington.

Furthermore, the Mitsitam Native Foods Café (Piscataway for "Let's eat"), which takes up a substantial portion of the first floor, offers Native foods, prepared using traditional techniques, from five geographic regions. Visitors might sample tamales from South America, buffalo burgers from the Great Plains, enchiladas from Mesoamerica, salmon from the Northwest Coast, and succotash from the Northern Woodlands. All of these features—in particular the welcome wall, fourth museum, and restaurant—emphasize community and hospitality, which are important Indigenous values across the Americas, and contribute to the NMAI's mission as a place of contemporary cultural continuance.[14]

Second, the NMAI is based on the proposition that while museums have objects and exhibitions, those objects and exhibitions must be curated collaboratively with the Native peoples they seek to represent. As a result of such collaborative curation, the museum employs "nontraditional" (by museological standards) methods of care and preservation, display, and classification and privileges Native conceptualizations of history and truth. This framework was established early on in the consultation process and carried throughout the NMAI's development.

Consequently, the Cultural Resource Center in Suitland, Maryland, one of the primary storage facilities for the massive collection, became the center of NMAI's object care and preservation efforts. Those efforts relied on "traditional care" techniques, which were developed by the NMAI and other tribal museums since NAGPRA. These techniques are based on the belief that many cultural objects are alive rather than inanimate and often require curators to allow them to "breathe" rather than suffocate in sealed plastic containers, to move or store objects so that they are facing a particular direction, and to provide tribal citizens with the ability to visit their objects and to "feed" them, often with pollen, or perform ceremonies with them. Many museums, tribal and nontribal, have integrated these techniques into the curation of their collections in recent years, though certainly not on such a grand scale as the NMAI has done.[15]

Traditional care highlights the fact that Native peoples care deeply about their cultural property, just as Eurocentric museums do, but not always for the same reasons. Whereas Western museology is concerned with an object's "physical integrity and attributes as evidence of cultural, historical, or scientific phenomena," Native traditional care is concerned with an object's spiritual integrity and meaning and function within its community.[16] The integration of these methods in non-Native museums indicates the extent to which museology is willing to change its relationship with Native peoples and the ways in which the NMAI has served and continues to serve as a role model for other institutions.

To carry forward the second proposition of community collaboration in exhibition development, the NMAI developed an elaborate protocol of community curation. During the consultation process, Native community members stressed that no one discipline—for example, history, anthropology, or art—provided the necessary knowledge base required for self-definition. Instead, these individuals suggested that elements of those disciplines be incorporated into Native ways of knowing based on Native resources, including oral traditions, elders, and spiritual leaders.[17] The core thematic content of the three permanent exhibitions, Our Universes: Traditional Knowledge Shapes Our World, Our Peoples: Giving Voice to Our Histories, and Our Lives: Contemporary Lives and Identities, is based on this principle.

Each of the three permanent exhibitions is characterized by Native points of view and takes as its focus a specific theme developed through the early consultation process. Each exhibition is displayed on a curvilinear model, consistent with the building's overall design. Each consists of a "spine," or center installation, developed by NMAI curators, that offers an explanation and analysis of that exhibition's theme. The function of the spine is to share an experience or worldview common to the Indigenous peoples of the Americas. Eight circular, community-curated installations surround each spine. In these installations, a specific Native nation narrates the ways its community has experienced or understands a given theme. Thus, the combination of the spine and community-curated installations demonstrates that the Native peoples of the Americas share some common values, worldviews, and experiences but remain culturally distinct and diverse.

To create the community-curated installations, the NMAI first invited twenty-four Native communities, representative of geographic regions, to participate. After the communities accepted the invitation, NMAI curatorial staff traveled to each to discuss the project and process. Then each tribal community delegated members to serve as community curators who traveled to the NMAI to view all of the museum's holdings of that community's objects and to work with NMAI curators to decide how to use those objects within a given exhibition's theme. As a result, each community-curated installation makes use of interdisciplinary and inventive methods of exhibition and organizational structures.[18]

Few visitors will be very familiar with the interdisciplinary nature of the exhibitions. Historically, Native American exhibits have been firmly curated within the disciplinary boundaries of particular types of institutions, for example, art museums, anthropological museums, or history museums, the last being the most pervasive and accessible, as they flourish in large cities and small towns throughout the country. According to James Nason, the most common exhibition styles with regard to Native Americans are (a) the geographical exhibit, in which objects are grouped by region or specific cultural affiliation, giving visitors the chance to "tour" the exhibit as they would on vacation in another country; (b) the history period display, which categorizes objects chronologically, thereby showing the "development" or "evolution" of Native peoples as they "progress" toward a Western perception of civilization; (c) the habitat exhibit, which frequently consists of dioramas designed to allow visitors a glimpse into a way of life in a particular moment; and (d) the open-storage display, in which visitors are shown as many objects as possible regardless of the object's region, age, or other disciplinary criterion. Overwhelmingly, these exhibition styles emphasize Native Americans as peoples of a distant past; this is particularly true of dioramas, which "freeze" Native people in a particular moment in time. Furthermore, all four of the styles tend to establish Native American peoples as "other" and frequently, whether intentionally or not, as exotic and inferior.[19]

The NMAI's professional curators, who have likely all had some sort of specific disciplinary training, have stressed that strict disciplinary approaches have brought important knowledge to bear, but that no single discipline has offered the multiple perspectives required to fully share Native worldviews and bodies of knowledge. Such worldviews and knowledge bases tend to emphasize connection, not disjuncture, among knowledges. Because NMAI and community curators wanted to emphasize the distinctiveness of individual Native cultures as well as cultural dynamism, they worked in tandem to create exhibitions that demonstrated community specificity and community vitality.

The twenty-four community-curated installations make use of historical objects, contemporary art and cultural production, wall text, video and/or audio features, photographs, and interactive features, as well as materials, fabrics, textures, colors, and built mock-ups or structures (but not dioramas) meant to describe a way of life or evoke a particular response. The community-curated installations do not offer the revisionist, "this is the story you were told; this is our version of the story" lessons many visitors might expect. As a matter of fact, the installations do not offer narratives with clear beginnings, middles, and ends at all. Instead, the selected objects, text, photographs, and so on work together to form an image or collage that, ultimately, becomes an elaborate self-portrait.

Our Universes: Traditional Knowledge Shapes Our World concentrates on Native cosmology and the relationship Native peoples have with the natural world, thus spotlighting Native philosophical worldviews and the time depth of Native cultures. The installations in Our Universes follow the path of one solar year and demonstrate how ceremonies and seasonal celebrations were developed and are shaped by the movements of the sun, moon, and stars. Moving through a solar year, each of the eight community-curated installations demonstrates how that principle is manifested in a particular tribal experience in a particular season and offers that community's symbols and interpretation of the order of the world. The eight communities are the Pueblo of Santa Clara (New Mexico), the Anishinaabe (Canada), the Lakota (South Dakota), the Quechua (Peru), the Hupa (California), the Q'eq'chi' Maya (Guatemala), the Mapuche (Chile), and the Yup'ik (Alaska). The spine of the exhibit encapsulates the communities' emphasis on the ancient bodies of knowledge and wisdom, maintained in oral traditions that continue to inform Native cultures today, and the balanced relationship of humans and the natural world.

Special features include abstractions of celestial references on the ceiling and walls, as well as examples of ancestral Native teachings, including an extended video of a Tlingit story, "How Raven Steals the Sun," which is accompanied by an exquisite blown and sand-carved glass piece by Preston Singletary (Tlingit), symbolizing the raven. The installations include descriptions and photographs of seasonal celebrations, such as the Day of the Dead, to illustrate the ways in which ancient knowledge continues to inform contemporary daily life.

Our Peoples: Giving Voice to Our Histories centers on Native peoples' experiences resulting from European contact, highlighting survivance strategies in the face of colonizing forces. The eight communities—the Seminole (Florida), Kiowa (Oklahoma), Tohono O'odham (Arizona), Eastern Band of Cherokee (North Carolina), Nahua (Mexico), Ka'apor (Brazil), and Wixarika, or Huichol (Mexico)—describe the five hundred years since European contact from each community's own point of view. This particularly moving exhibition examines how European contact changed the world. The spine of the exhibit describes the effects of European contact on Native peoples using the metaphor of a hurricane and focuses not solely on the devastation wrought by the hurricane, but the methods Native peoples used for cultural survivance. The exhibition explicitly asks visitors to consider history—what it is, who writes it, and how the writing of it affects our lives.

This exhibition has several particularly notable features in addition to the guns, churches, and government installation described earlier. For example, one large wall, inscribed with the name of every known Native nation in the Americas, simply, yet eloquently, bears witness to Native survivance. Another highlight is the Storm installation, which consists of curvilinear walls arranged in a circle. Each wall is made up entirely of blue video screens, some of which depict a hurricane impacting a coastline. Visitors hear the hurricane in the background, and every few minutes, a voice-over describes European contact, using the storm as a metaphor. This installation is made especially effective by the fact that visitors are forced to stand in the center of the storm, with no place to sit, which evokes feelings of helplessness and inevitability, making the emphasis on survivance strategies all the more powerful.

Our Lives: Contemporary Life and Identities focuses on present-day individual and communal identity issues, examining both imposed and self-determined identities by emphasizing language, place, and legal policies. In this installation the eight communities—the Campo Band of Kumeyaay Indians (California), the urban Indian community of Chicago (Illinois), the Yakama Nation (Washington State), the Igloolik (Canada), the Kahnawake (Canada), the Saint-Laurent Métis (Canada), the Kalinago (Carib Territory, Dominica), and the Pamunkey Tribe (Virginia)—accentuate the hard but deliberate choices they have made when challenged by very often harsh realities marked by poverty and social dysfunction that affect their identities, as individuals and communities. The spine of the exhibition directly asks visitors, Who is Indian? and What does it mean to be Indian? by explicitly calling into question preconceived notions of authenticity and racial purity as well as popular and abidingly destructive stereotypes.

Our Lives, as the exhibition with the most overtly contemporary focus, plays with exhibition style somewhat more than the other permanent exhibitions. Highlights include a wall of dozens and dozens of individual photographs of the faces of Native Americans, of every imaginable age and phenotype; a glassed-in case displaying objects that symbolize the Red Power movement, such as an original copy of Vine Deloria's *Custer Died for Your Sins*; many pieces of contemporary Native art; and even a mock-up of the urban Indian center in Chicago.

In addition to the three main exhibitions, the NMAI's current installations include *Who We Are*, a multimedia, preparatory film experience showing inside the circular Lelawi Theater; The Jewelry of Ben Nighthorse, on display in a gallery that will later be used as a gathering or conference space for Native Americans on business in Washington; a major retrospective, Native Modernism: The Art of George Morrison and Allan Houser, on display until the fall of 2005 in the changing exhibitions gallery; and Window on Collections, glass-fronted cases featuring more than three thousand items from the NMAI collection arranged by the following thematic groups: arrowheads, dolls, beads, peace medals, objects featuring animals, and containers.

The celebratory attitude of the twenty-five thousand Native Americans who traveled from as far north as Alaska and as far south as Chile to attend the opening ceremony and First Americans Festival underscores that no one understands the significance of the NMAI as a monument to and symbol of the survivance of Native peoples better than Native peoples themselves. For the National Museum of the American Indian to be *of* American Indians and *for* American Indians, the NMAI had to fundamentally alter what museums have always meant to Native people in every way, and in this, the NMAI succeeded.

The display of guns, Bibles, and treaties in the Our Peoples exhibition powerfully demonstrates that objects are imbued with their meaning by the community and context in which they are used. The traditional care techniques employed by NMAI curators make the same point: it is not the object itself, but the community's use of an object that lends it its significance. To turn guns, Bibles, treaties, and museums from instruments of dispossession into instruments of resistance, resilience, survival, and self-definition, Native peoples did not inherently change the object; instead, they changed its use, which made all the difference. By focusing on use or process over object or product in its own form and function, the NMAI highlights the vitality and dynamism of Native peoples —agents engaged in acts of self-definition and cultural sovereignty, living cultures modeling the survivance strategies that have enabled their cultural continuance. For Native Americans, the National Museum of the American Indian not only announces "We are still here," but it also demonstrates the process that made this fact possible.

By Native criteria, the NMAI is by and large successful. Much of the early criticism of the content of the museum from specific Native communities centered not on the design of the grounds or building or on the community-curated installations, but on the extent to which that community was able to find its own representation and cultural objects. That individual community representation was the chief criticism, given the tremendous number of Native communities in North and South America, suggests that, for Native audiences, the NMAI probably succeeded in many other ways, including its overall mission to serve as a forum for living cultures. Early non-Native responses, on the other hand, were not as generous.

The NMAI and Non-Native Responses

Museum critics, like the four million visitors the NMAI is expecting each year, who may not understand or appreciate the museum's significance as a practice of cultural sovereignty, judge it by very different standards. The criteria by which critics judge the museum were made explicit in the early reviews published in the *New York Times* and the *Washington Post*. Those reviews were predominantly characterized by confusion, disappointment, and a sense of failed expectations. Edward Rothstein of the *Times* and Paul Richard and Marc Fisher of the *Post*, in particular, found much to criticize; they specifically alleged a lack of "scholarship," or "crisp lessons" in the exhibits. According to Rothstein, "The notion that tribal voices should 'be heard' becomes a problem when the selected voices have so little to say." He continues by noting that the museum "seems satisfied with serving a sociological function. . . . Understanding . . . is not a matter of whose voice is heard. . . . It is a matter of scholarship."[20] Fisher, in a similar vein, declares, "The Smithsonian accepted the trendy faux-selflessness of today's historians and *let* the Indians present themselves as they wish to be seen" (emphasis added).[21] Richard continues this line of criticism, stating that "the museum doesn't nourish thought," that "the exhibitions are a blur" and "the labeling is awful," and that because the museum is neither "an art museum" nor "a history museum," it is "ahistorical."[22]

Clearly all three of these critics begin their critiques from the assumptions that museums consist of exhibitions and that exhibitions must meet the standards of discrete disciplines and must teach crisp, cleanly labeled lessons—assumptions that are based on years of experience with Western museums and academic disciplines. Rothstein indicates that the narratives told in tribal voices get in the way of scholarship or meaning, demonstrating that he does not consider Native bodies of knowledge valid or equal to Western bodies of knowledge. Furthermore, his assertion that it does not matter "whose voice is heard" suggests that, for him, identity does not equal knowledge. Identity may not equal knowledge, but Rothstein's knowledge of museums certainly does not equal insight into the processes at work in the National Museum of the American Indian. Perhaps most patronizing, Fisher's comment that historians "let" the Indians tell their own stories signals that there are no Native American historians and that the privileging of tribal voices is an example of irresponsible scholarship. Finally, Richard's claim that the NMAI is "ahistorical" invalidates the Native versions of history and truth the Our Peoples exhibit asks visitors to consider and question.

For critics like Rothstein, Richard, and Fisher, the NMAI fails because it does not adhere to long-standing Western museological standards. It does not seem to matter to these critics that those museological standards have exploited and objectified Native Americans in very specific ways. Nor does it seem to matter to these critics that the NMAI telegraphed its intentions to be a "museum different" for years prior to its opening. The critics judged the NMAI based on the purpose they wanted it to serve rather than the purpose it serves. The perceived "avoidance of scholarship" noted by Rothstein is particularly interesting because the NMAI may well be among the most heavily and self-consciously theorized museums in existence. However, the theorizing, which is based on a combination of Native worldviews and postmodernity, led away from the more standard and much more familiar forms of display and organization and toward a dialogic system that demands the critical engagement and interpretation of its visitors. Rothstein seemingly failed to recognize the new system and the theoretical foundations on which it is based. He argues that museums should offer lessons for visitors to learn. His resistance to, or lack of recognition of, the NMAI's mission, theory, and organizational system indicates that he may not be as interested in learning something new as he is in validating his own knowledge.

That these critics do not recognize the theory and scholarship at work in the NMAI, much less the symbolic importance of the entire project, is maddeningly disappointing and in many ways outright infuriating. Nonetheless, all three make an important point: many visitors will find the new museological paradigm at work in the exhibitions unfamiliar and confusing. The unfamiliarity of the narrative structure and classification system in combination with stereotypical (and sadly racist) imaginings about Native Americans will inevitably lead to a certain amount of disappointment on the part of some visitors.

Although the interdisciplinary organizational structure may be difficult for some visitors, it is not beyond comprehension. West, for example, suggests that visitors approach a given exhibition as they would an impressionist painting, not searching for the meaning in each object or swirl of paint but stepping back and seeing how the objects function together to complete the picture.[23]

The literary scholar Elizabeth Archuleta (Yaqui) uses a quote from writer Leslie Marmon Silko (Laguna) to explain the epistemology that underpins the NMAI exhibitions: "For those of you accustomed to a structure that moves from point A to point B to point C, this presentation may be somewhat difficult to follow because the structure of Pueblo expression resembles something like a spider's web—with many little threads radiating from a center, criss-crossing each other. As with the web, the structure will emerge as it is made and you must simply listen and trust, as the Pueblo people do, that meaning will be made."[24]

Archuleta uses this quote to describe her own interpretation of the exhibits: "Rather than structure the exhibits in a way that guides visitors and 'teaches' them about Indians, leading them from point A to point B to point C, museum curators structured them like the 'many little threads' of a spider web with each strand adding to the larger picture." She goes on to say that this organizational strategy requires visitors to "set aside notions they previously held about museums and Indians, 'listen' to the stories being told in the exhibits, and trust that meaning will be made if they become involved in the storytelling process."[25]

Unfortunately for the NMAI, few visitors are likely to understand the level of dialogic interaction that is expected of them, and those who do may be resistant to "trusting" that meaning will be made. Furthermore, visitors steeped in Hollywood stereotypes may not realize that they have something new to learn. In fact, as I walked through the NMAI, I asked the guest consultants working the floor what question visitors asked them the most. The answer: "Where are the teepees?"

The NMAI should not attempt to offset visitor frustration by reverting to the more familiar exhibition styles; to do so would be tantamount to calling the entire project—a project so significant to cultural sovereignty and continuance—a failure. Instead, I recommend that the NMAI find ways (perhaps through audio or video) to prepare visitors for what they will experience, letting them know that they will be asked to "read" differently and asking them to rise to the occasion. Making such a strategy available is crucial, not only because 99 percent of the four million expected visitors a year will be non-Native and it would be good for business, but also because the entire NMAI project provides an important opportunity for Native and non-Native Americans. American museums, especially the Smithsonian museums, aggressively promote an American national identity. For Native Americans, the NMAI—a Smithsonian institution—promotes *Native American national identities*. For non–Native Americans, the NMAI provides a real chance to consider what those national identities mean in the context of American identity. As Richard West so movingly stated in his remarks at the opening ceremony, Native Americans "remain a part of the cultural future of the Americas, just as we were a part of its past and fought so hard to be a part of its present." Because of that, the NMAI opens up the possibility for "the true cultural reconciliation that until now has eluded American history."[26]

Notes

Several paragraphs of this review appeared in the American Indian Quarterly by permission of the University of Nebraska Press. © 2005 by the University of Nebraska Press.

1. W. Richard West, interview by author, January 14, 2005.
2. *National Museum of the American Indian: Map and Guide* (Washington DC: Scala and Smithsonian, 2004), 16–17.
3. Simon Ortiz, untitled poem, in *From Sand Creek* (Tucson: University of Arizona Press, 1981), n.p.
4. Margaret Dubin, *Native America Collected: The Culture of an Art World* (Albuquerque: University of New Mexico Press, 2001), 83–99.
5. West interview.
6. Beverly Singer, *Wiping the War Paint Off the Lens: Native American Film and Video* (Minneapolis: University of Minnesota Press, 2001), 2.
7. Christina Kreps, *Liberating Culture: Cross-Cultural Perspectives on Museums, Curation, and Heritage Preservation* (New York: Routledge, 2003), 46.
8. Robert Warrior, *Tribal Secrets: Recovering American Indian Intellectual Traditions* (Minneapolis: University of Minnesota Press, 1995), 93–94.
9. George Horse Capture, "The Way of the People," in *Spirit of a Native Place: Building the National Museum of the American Indian*, ed. Duane Blue Spruce (Washington DC: National Geographic and Smithsonian, 2004), 31–45.
10. *National Museum of the American Indian: Map and Guide*, 22–23.
11. *National Museum of the American Indian: Map and Guide*, 23.
12. *National Museum of the American Indian: Map and Guide*, 24–26.
13. *National Museum of the American Indian: Map and Guide*, 29.
14. *National Museum of the American Indian: Map and Guide*, 39.
15. Kreps, *Liberating Culture*, 91–93.
16. Kreps, *Liberating Culture*, 93.
17. Horse Capture, "The Way of the People," 46.
18. West interview.
19. James Nason, "'Our Indians': The Unidimensional Indian in the Disem-

bodied Local Past," in *The Changing Presentation of the American Indian*, ed. W. Richard West (Washington DC: Smithsonian Institution, 2000), 34–39.

20. Edward Rothstein, "Museum Review: Museum with an American Indian Voice," *New York Times*, September 21, 2004, E1.

21. Marc Fisher, "Indian Museum's Appeal, Sadly, Only Skin-Deep," *Washington Post* online, http://www.washingtonpost.com/wp-dyn/articles/A3681 –2004Sep20.html (accessed March 1, 2005).

22. Paul Richard, "Shards of Many Untold Stories: In Place of Unity, a Mélange of Unconnected Objects," *Washington Post* online, http://washingtonpost.com/ wp-dyn/articles/A36886–2004Sep20.html (accessed March 1, 2005).

23. West interview.

24. Leslie Marmon Silko, quoted in Elizabeth Archuleta, "Gym Shoes, Maps, and Passports, Oh My! Creating Community or Creating Chaos at NMAI?," *American Indian Quarterly* 29, nos. 3–4, (Summer–Fall 2005): 426.

25. Archuleta, "Gym Shoes," 429–30.

26. W. Richard West, "Remarks on the Occasion of the Grand Opening Ceremony," National Museum of the American Indian, Washington DC, September 21, 2005, available at http://newsdesk.si.edu/kits/nmai/ (accessed March 1, 2005).

14. Performing Reconciliation at the National Museum of the American Indian

Postcolonial Rapprochement and the Politics of Historical Closure

Pauline Wakeham

In his meditation *On Cosmopolitanism and Forgiveness*, Jacques Derrida argues that "scenes of . . . confession, forgiveness, or apology . . . have multiplied on the geopolitical [stage] . . . in an accelerated fashion in the past few years." While Derrida focuses on performances of apology taking place in "the theatrical space[s]" of war crimes tribunals and truth and reconciliation proceedings,[1] I would like to suggest another space of performance that warrants critical consideration: the public forum of museums dedicated to the Indigenous peoples of ostensibly postcolonial nation-states. A particularly complex example is the Smithsonian's eighteenth museum, an institution intended to represent Indigenous peoples across the entire Western hemisphere and yet collapsed within the appropriative rubric of the National Museum of the American Indian (NMAI).[2] Built on the stage of the Washington Mall, the NMAI, according to Director Rick West, constitutes a "profound" symbol of "cultural reconciliation" by representing Native peoples via a museological monument occupying the last available site on the "Nation's front lawn."[3] On September 21, 2004, the NMAI was inaugurated with pageantry and performance in the form of a week-long First Americans Festival featuring Indigenous dancers, singers, storytellers, and artisans. The celebrations began with a Native Nations Procession—what the NMAI web site described as "a highly symbolic walk of indigenous cultural expression" involving twenty-five thousand participants from five hundred Native groups who collectively traversed the distance from the Smithsonian Castle to the U.S. Capitol.[4] Declaring it "the largest gathering of Native peoples in modern history," Smithsonian and NMAI officials framed the procession as a demonstration of rapprochement between First Peoples and the state.[5] In the process, the "official" discourse contouring the grand opening seems to have bypassed any performance of apology for colonial injustices and moved straight to a joyous, depoliticized celebration of reconciliation.

While the proliferating "scenes of confession . . . and apology" of which Derrida writes are not without their own substantial problems, I am concerned about the ways that such moments of a state's explicit grappling with its past and ongoing colonialist policies may be evaded by celebratory performances that stage ostensibly postcolonial reconciliation as a fait accompli.[6] In so doing, such triumphant pageants impose a kind of historical closure on colonial violence, thereby attempting to silence recognition— and calls for redress—of the continued power asymmetries and systemic racism that affect Indigenous peoples and their struggles for social justice today. In recent years, museums have increasingly become imbricated in such processes, serving as important sites for the staging of postcolonial rapprochement. This observation is not intended to dismiss the significant (but also complex) changes that have occurred in the relations between museums and Indigenous peoples in the United States over the past few decades, including the flourishing of tribal museums and cultural centers, the critical application of postcolonial theory to museology and anthropology, and the ratification of federal repatriation legislation (the Native American Graves Protection and Repatriation Act) in 1990.[7] Such transformations, rehearsed here in abbreviated form, have become well-worn terrain for most museum scholars and curators. What is less frequently analyzed, however, is how these changes have at times been collectively assembled in a narrative of scholarly and institutional progress that extends its teleology into descriptions of the current era as one in which the promise of institutional and representational change has been largely fulfilled, thereby achieving a kind of museological reconciliation between dominant cultural institutions and Indigenous peoples. Such a hasty celebration of these changes as a watershed period of transformation may enable scholars, curators, and the general public to feel overly confident in the benefits of an imagined postcolonial critical hindsight. What is at risk here is a failure to vigilantly consider how the gestures of incorporating postcolonial theory and collaborative approaches into exhibition design and museum policy might engender new representational problems while also dissimulating ongoing power asymmetries that continue to structure dominant museological institutions.

A second and related problem with such narratives of progress concerns the way they may be utilized to effect a conflation of museological reconciliation with broader forms of political reconciliation between the nation-state and Indigenous peoples. Museums are inherently politicized spaces that have the potential to reinforce or resist the *grand récits* of Western imperial history and associated ideological assumptions about "otherness." That said, transformations in museum policy and practice are only one aspect of broader cultural, socioeconomic, and political changes crucial to reckoning with colonial violence in North America and working toward a future of social justice. As a result, the celebratory discourse of museological reconciliation lends itself to complicity with and co-optation by the state for the purposes of staging postcolonial rapprochement via the cultural milieu of museums while circumventing further restitution in the form of land claims, rights to natural resources, and compensation for the state's destruction of the environment on reservation territory, to cite only a few examples.

The grand opening of the National Museum of the American Indian in September 2004 brought these dynamics to life in powerful ways, dramatizing the scene of supposedly postcolonial rapprochement against "the dramatic backdrop of the U.S. Capitol building on the National Mall."[8] While the concepts of museological and political reconciliation could be analyzed in relation to many aspects of the NMAI, including the museum's managerial and institutional structure, its repatriation policies, and its purportedly collaborative approach to installation design, each of these topics warrants critical attention far beyond the scope of one essay. I want to focus instead on the inaugural celebrations of the museum and what I have been explicitly casting as the *performance* of reconciliation that took place on the National Mall precisely because the grand opening—rather than constituting an exception to the NMAI's everyday modus operandi—throws into relief the museum's complex and widespread mobilization of performative strategies as museological heuristics throughout the building. Described by Rick West as an "institution of living cultures," the NMAI attempts to foreground its "liveness" by dedicating much of its space to performance, from the heart of the building, referred to as the Potomac, where artisans, dancers, and singers frequently share their arts with the public, to the Rasmuson Theater, used for films, dramatic groups, and musicians, and the Lelawi Theater on the fourth floor that features an introductory film and orientation to the museum.[9] I seek to read between and across performative tactics mobilized both inside the museum and on the Mall during the grand opening, thereby interrogating the multiple ways the NMAI stages performances of reconciliation. I consider how such performances may (at times unwittingly) serve to reinforce the colonial status quo, and I also endeavor to demonstrate how alternative performative tactics might be mobilized to engender new possibilities for anticolonialist and antiracist resistance.

The Lives and Afterlives of Performance

As a way of proceeding, I want to outline a few crucial thoughts prompted by autobiographical caveats. In researching and writing this essay, I have been conscious of my position as a Euro-Canadian academic who is approaching the NMAI with a mixture of cautious hope and critical scrutiny regarding the institution's ability to combat stereotypes of Native peoples and to play a role in grappling with colonial oppression. In particular, I am painfully aware that my critique of the NMAI grand opening problematizes an event that many Indigenous participants—as I've seen on video footage and read on web sites and listservs and in academic articles—did find to be meaningful and empowering.[10] The convergence of so many diverse Indigenous people on the National Mall and the opportunities this event afforded for the building of solidarity and the exchange of ideas among Native people are indeed significant. My critique of the dominant discourses framing the grand opening, however, does not stand in necessary contradiction to this fact, nor does it intend to foreclose the ways Native people may have exercised agency within the constraints of the festivities. Rather, I hope that my attempts to destabilize the hegemonic narrative framing Indigenous participation in the grand opening might work to create spaces for alternative perspectives about the NMAI—articulated from multiple locations— to emerge.

A second crucial caveat concerns my absence at the First Americans Festival. I did not attend due to the financial and time constraints imposed on a doctoral student sequestered up in northwestern Canada with a defense deadline looming. Consequently, my encounters with the Native Nations Procession are primarily with its compromised afterlife, its uncanny mediation through a dominant archive of mainstream media coverage, raw footage filmed by NMAI-contracted videographers, and the commercial product of that footage now repackaged as *Welcome Home*, a DVD sold at NMAI gift shops. As previously mentioned, I have also attempted to locate sources currently excluded from the dominant archive, such as personal photographs and listserv commentary. For Peggy Phelan, who argues that "the ontology of performance" hinges on the liveness of the event that escapes the economy of reproduction, it is perhaps a grave contradiction for me to examine the NMAI's grand opening with such an emphasis on its compromised afterlives, corrupt copies of the vanished performative event that such copies labor, in futility, to capture.[11] And yet it is precisely on the edge of this precarious contradiction that I want to hover. For performance, particularly in the current era of proliferating technologies of dissemination, does have diverse forms of afterlife that powerfully reframe the ostensibly lost event in and for the social imaginary. Such afterlives, I argue, have important political implications for understanding the imbrication of performance within historical processes—something crucial to the project of reckoning with colonial genocide and the reinscription of colonial power in narratives of postcolonial reconciliation.

Rethinking performance's ontological condition in relation to its afterlives of technological dissemination and re-presentation enriches consideration of performance's imbrication not only in historical processes but also in material, or social, political, and economic networks. While I agree with Phelan that a live performance and its archival copy are not the same thing—that something is altered in the attempt to transfer the live event to a celluloid, digital, or textual document—I am cautious of the way her emphasis on performative liveness risks fetishizing an idealized notion of the "pure" event that somehow transcends material constraints and compromises.[12] For example, Phelan argues that performance's defining quality is its "independence from mass reproduction, technologically, economically, and linguistically." In other words, "performance resists the balanced circulations of finance. It saves nothing; it only spends."[13] Lapsing into a discussion of capital in largely metaphorical terms—as a figure of thought used to denote abstracted concepts of "saving" and "spending," "reproduction" and "loss"—Phelan distances performance from the material systems that necessarily shape it. In the process, her theory risks juxtaposing the purportedly pure event of live performance against the archival documentation or mass mediation of that event in terms of an oppositional anticapitalist versus complicitous capitalist binary. Such a dichotomy is far too simplistic for understanding the complex ways that both the lives and afterlives of performance are crucially shaped by material constraints and, in turn, how both might be appropriated for politically conservative, status quo projects as well as for the purposes of counterhegemonic resistance.

José Muñoz further complicates the privileging of the supposedly "distinctive oppositional edge" of live performance in his discussion of how "subaltern subjects negotiate" what he refers to as the "burden of liveness"—"a particular hegemonic mandate that calls the minoritarian subject to 'be live' for the purpose of entertaining elites."[14] Rather than signaling the attainment of social recognition, minoritarian performance, according to Muñoz, is often encouraged *"especially* when human and civil rights disintegrate" and subaltern subjects are denied access to other forms of social representation. Moreover, "the 'burden of liveness' affords the minoritarian subject an extremely circumscribed temporality. To be only in 'the live' means that one is denied history and futurity."[15] Muñoz's theory incisively points to the ways that a privileging of performative liveness may be linked to a fetishization of racialized, exoticized bodies presented "in the flesh" and presented within a contained moment of time: the always vanishing present tense. Although I find Muñoz's argument persuasive, I want to complicate his critique of performance's temporal containment within the tense of liveness by suggesting that while this is certainly one way in which racist ideology attempts to frame minoritarian performance, I believe that Indigenous bodies and Indigenous performance may also be spectacularized as performances of pending death and extinction.

That said, Muñoz's overarching postulation about the fetishization of performative liveness and the particular constraints it places on minoritarian subjects and their temporal range—their recourse to histories and futures—is extremely apt. Broaching these concerns from a related but somewhat different vantage point, I want to consider both performative liveness and its afterlife mediations in relation to historical processes and the reframing of performative events over time. In this context, it is important to underscore that performance's lives and afterlives are not always strictly distinguished from one another; the borders between these categories are blurred due to the fact that "live performance now often incorporates mediatization such that the live event itself is a product of reproductive technologies."[16] Such was the case at the grand opening of the NMAI, as JumboTrons were positioned at key sites around the Mall, displaying scenes from the Native Nations Procession and the First Americans Festival and close-ups of Smithsonian, NMAI, and political officials presenting speeches at the opening ceremonies. As a result, this interimbrication of mediatization and live performance demonstrates that neither performance's lives nor afterlives may lay claim to always already being defined by a certain "purity," a particular ontological constitution defined by an ability to transcend material constraints.

En route to applying these theoretical propositions to the grand opening of the NMAI, I want to first take a strategic detour and consider a complex scene of performance's afterlives staged inside the museum that provokes thought about the political implications of performative liveness and reproduction. On the third floor of the NMAI, a permanent installation titled Our Lives grapples with crucial issues affecting Indigenous peoples in the contemporary era, from approximately 1960 to the present. Approaching questions such as the relation between cultural tradition and hybridity, the complexities of identity construction, and the meaning of survivance for Native peoples, Our Lives demonstrates a savvy incorporation of postcolonial and poststructural theory into exhibition design. Such theoretical reflexivity poses a challenge for intellectual critique, as the installation's conscious differences from conventional anthropological and natural history museum models are so refreshingly apparent that it is easy to follow the exhibition's own logic without rigorously considering the implications of such new museological approaches. Rather than passively approving of such representational changes, it is important to think critically about how the incorporation of postcolonial and poststructural theory into museum space might engender new representational conundrums. In so doing, I aim to take up the invitation offered by actor Floyd Favel Starr in a movie screened in the Our Peoples installation. Here Starr, ostensibly speaking on behalf of the museum, states, "View what's offered with respect, but also skepticism. Explore this gallery, encounter it, reflect on it, argue with it."[17]

One of the conventional museological strategies that Our Lives attempts to challenge is the reliance on artifactual displays: exhibits that use as their focal points Indigenous material culture objectified in the form of "artifacts." Attempting to create alternative modes of display, Our Lives frequently takes recourse to re-presenting past events of Native performance via the use of photographs and text panels that interpret the images' meaning and significance. In so doing, the exhibit seeks to re-present these events as heuristic anecdotes that help to illustrate the installation's discussion of identity, stereotypes, and survivance. In contrast to the more literalized forms of performance involving live singers, dancers, and artisans enacted throughout the NMAI, Our Lives reproduces performance via the afterlife medium of the museum display. It is precisely this difference that makes Our Lives such an important site for considering the complex and ideologically loaded ways that performances are mediated, reproduced, and reframed.

In a section entitled On Display that seeks to grapple with the colonial history of rendering Native peoples objects of spectacle, an exhibit attempts to re-present Luiseño artist James Luna's 1987 performance, The Artifact Piece. Describing Luna's work, a text panel comments:

> The artist . . . lay motionless in a 19th-century museum display case. Labels commented on the scars on his body. Nearby cases contained Luna's family photographs, Luiseño medicine objects, and other personal items, laid out like early anthropological displays of arrowheads, pottery shards, and tools.
>
> This work of performance art . . . was first shown in 1987 at the Museum of Man in San Diego. In it, Luna subverts the practice of regarding Native Americans as objects or artefacts. By placing his living body on display, he criticizes museums that display Native cultures as dead or solely part of the past.

Beside the explanatory text, an oversized photograph of Luna lying in the display case is back-lit with an eerie orange-sepia glow, depicting the body as a ghost of the always already ghostly dead "Indian" qua anthropo-

logical specimen. Here, the question of performative liveness and reproduction takes on particular importance due to the fact that Luna's original *Artifact Piece* hinged on a strategic play between the categories of
"life" and "death"—a tactic based on assuming the guise of death while
simultaneously emitting subtle vital signs that disturb the museological representation of the dead "Indian." The afterlife re-creation of *The
Artifact Piece* in the Our Lives installation, however, flattens out this play
between life and death with an imposing photograph of Luna's body
that appears very much dead. While the explanatory text panel informs
the viewer that Luna was alive in this ghostly pose, the overwhelming
focal point of the display is the image of what appears to be a racialized
corpse. As a result, the re-presentation of *The Artifact Piece* unintentionally risks reinscribing the iconology of the dead Indian in its very attempt
to challenge such stereotypes.

In a related vein, On Display creates a *mise-en-abyme* effect (a scene
within a scene within a scene) through which a series of temporal refrac-
tions reshape the political and ideological implications of the exhibit.
Through layers of re-presentation, Luna's performative reconstruction of
nineteenth-century museological depictions of indigeneity inside a 1980s
museum is reframed yet again as an object of display within the NMAI
(and, admittedly, reframed once more in this essay). Across these strata of historical refraction, the performative and pedagogical effects of
The Artifact Piece are altered. While Luna initially intended his art to effect
a shock of recognition that would underscore the persistence of nineteenth-century modes of anthropological display and their concomitant
ideological assumptions in the 1980s, the NMAI's museumification of
this performative event produces a historical distance between the cultural climate of the 1980s and that of 2004. Such distance diffuses the
powerful defamiliarizing effect that Luna's performance was intended
to provoke, enabling the new visitor of the NMAI to imagine himself or
herself as self-reflexively meditating on racist dynamics that have supposedly now been reckoned with. In the process, the NMAI exhibit risks

suggesting that the radical performative tactics employed in The Artifact
Piece are themselves "artifacts" of a time prior to the present tense of so-
called reconciliation.

Moving further back in time, another display in Our Lives titled Breaking
Out re-presents a distinctly periodized era of Native cultural resurgence
and political activism. An introductory text panel sets the scene: "In
the turbulent 1960s and 1970s, survivance went public. After nearly 500
years of occupation and subjugation, Indians broke out culturally, spiritually, and politically. It was a time of Red Power, the American Indian
Movement, Akwesasne Notes, and a world of possibilities. . . . Native intellectuals told our history while poets and artists imagined our future."

This text is superimposed on an oversized photo-collage of black- and-
white images of Indigenous protest, including posters for the Native
Caravan of 1974 and pictures of American Indian movement members
in Washington DC during the Longest Walk in 1978, with an image of
the Capitol prominently in view. The entire mural is washed in large
streaks of acid green, hot pink, and purple, recalling the psychedel-
ic colors of the era. Here, the performance of "survivance [gone] public" is identified as taking the shape of protests and rallies, sit-ins and
occupations. In a small text panel titled "Thinking Indian," such protests are described in the following terms: "In the 1970s, Native activists . . . took part in landmark actions—the occupation of Alcatraz and
Wounded Knee, the Bureau of Indian Affairs takeover, and the Longest
Walk—that changed the politics and culture of the United States." The
explanatory narrative for this exhibit therefore repeatedly discusses Native
activism in the past tense while also instating an air of finality to the
way these events "changed" American politics. My point is not to detract
from the work and achievements of Indigenous protesters in this era but
to question the periodization— and potential historical containment
of—activism and change within the decades of the 1960s and 1970s.
The exhibit text is visually reinforced by a display of objects mounted on
a black backdrop and protected behind glass, including items such as

Vine Deloria Jr.'s *God Is Red* and *Custer Died for Your Sins*, along with photographs and pamphlets. The display of protest memorabilia behind the iconic museological glass panel inscribes the semiotics of artifactualization, further reinforcing the sense of pastness attributed to Native activism. In perhaps an even more direct way than the re-presentation of Luna's *Artifact Piece*, the Breaking Out exhibit risks "museumizing" protest as a potentially obsolete Indigenous activity from a prior era—a time long before the current climate of reconciliation ostensibly symbolized by the NMAI itself.

In critiquing the representational and ideological effects of the exhibit's pedagogical strategy of re-creating past performances via the medium of the museum display, I do not want to imply, as Phelan's analysis sometimes suggests, that performance's afterlives—mediations of once-live events—are always already politically regressive. Although the exhibit's attempt to rethink the museological dependence on artifacts is laudable, the act of substituting narratives of Indigenous performance for spectacularized Indigenous material objects cannot alone transform museum politics if the overarching (and overdetermined) historical frame of the museum exhibit itself—the language of pastness and periodization, the semiotics of the glass display case, and the iconology of "dead" Native bodies—are not more aggressively combated. Although I appreciate much of what Our Lives attempts to do in broaching complex questions of identity and survivance through introducing visitors to performance art informed by postmodern and postcolonial thinking, the installation sets up an ironic temporal reversal in which the showcasing of that which is relatively "new" or "contemporary" in Indigenous cultures (that is, the work of Belmore, Luna, and others) becomes historically contained within a past prior to the NMAI's present tense. As I argue in the next section, the temporal reversal effected in Our Lives unintentionally sets the stage for the NMAI to define a new kind of Indigenous performance proper to the epoch of supposedly postcolonial reconciliation as a recuperation of "tradition."

Reconciliation and the Return to Performative Purity?

If the Our Lives installation implicitly periodizes the eras of Native activism (Breaking Out's 1960s and 1970s) and politicized, postmodern Indigenous performance art (The Artifact Piece's 1980s), the opening celebrations of the museum in September 2004 became a significant event in the formation of the NMAI's vision for Indigenous performance of the new millennium. As Smithsonian Secretary Lawrence Small described it in his opening ceremonies speech, the Native Nations Procession was a "joyful" celebration that put "Native cultures . . . vibrantly on display."[18] The aspect of putting "native cultures on display" most frequently highlighted in NMAI press releases and the mainstream media was the fact that many procession participants wore "full tribal regalia"—the key sartorial semiotics of supposedly authentic "Indianness."[19] More crassly summed up by Hank Stuever in a Washington Post article, the opening festivities fulfilled their implied promise: "Everyone came to see Indians, and everyone got to see some."[20] It is this "traditional" regalia-clad image of Indianness that the NMAI's commercial film Welcome Home showcases during its brief thirteen-minute feature presentation and its DVD extras consisting largely of performances from the First Americans Festival. While the raw video coverage of the grand opening filmed by NMAI-contracted videographers spends a great deal of time surveying tourists and onlookers (the majority of whom are white) eagerly documenting the events via their own cameras and camcorders, the edited presentation in Welcome Home focuses its gaze primarily on the most colorful and costumed Indigenous participants. The dominant representations surrounding the NMAI's opening festivities consequently risk reinforcing what Muñoz has diagnosed as a "cultural imperative within the majoritarian public sphere that denies subalterns access to larger channels of representation, while calling the minoritarian subject to the stage, performing her or his alterity as a consumable . . . spectacle."[21]

In contrast to the politicized Indigenous performances of protest and confrontational art that are temporally contained within the Our Lives installation, the grand opening was framed by the mainstream press as being without controversy. As Stuever elaborated, "Rare is the large-scale event on the Mall that isn't trying to noisily prevent something (a war, gun-related violence, the reversal of *Roe v. Wade*). And so the opening festival for the National Museum of the American Indian had to it a meandering, pleasing friendliness."²² If Stuever was "pleased" by the procession's "meandering friendliness," so too, NMAI officials suggested, were its Indigenous participants. Rick West retrospectively interpreted Indigenous responses to the festival in the following terms: "My sense of it, anecdotally admittedly—we did not run a formal survey saying how did you like the procession—is that Native people just felt so good."²³ In citing West's comment, my point is not to suggest that Native people should not have "felt so good" during the First Americans Festival. Rather, my concern centers on how state apparatuses and their agents stage the drama of reconciliation in ways that may enforce a powerful imperative for Native peoples to perform "good feeling" on behalf of the American nation, thereby silencing differences of opinion and voices of dissent. According to Elizabeth Povinelli, such a performance of "good feeling" is inextricably bound up with the performance of "a domesticated non-conflictual 'traditional' form of sociality and (inter)subjectivity"—a protest-free demonstration of imagined Indigenous authenticity.²⁴ The NMAI web site intensified these dynamics by assuming the authority to interpret the emotive inspirations and interior desires of Indigenous participants in the following terms: "Native Americans from North, Central, and South America realize[d] a long-awaited dream to share and honor their vibrant cultures with visitors from throughout the world."²⁵ Here, dreams for self-determination and for reparations for the colonial expropriation of land and natural resources are eclipsed by the NMAI's construction of a politically neutralized collective longing to share in the multicultural romance of free cultural expression ostensibly unhindered by the problems of stereotyping and spectacle. According to this logic, the new era of Indigenous performance that the NMAI inaugurates is actually a return to a phantasmatically imagined realm of unguarded and pure cultural expression, a return to "traditional" regalia and "traditional" dances performed without the political confrontation at stake in public protest and in performance art such as Luna's *Artifact Piece*.

Further interpreting the significance of the First Americans Festival for the public, Rick West took the podium during the opening ceremonies and asserted in the first-person plural, "We have lived in these lands and sacred places for thousands of years. We thus are the original part of the cultural heritage of every person hearing these words today, whether you are Native or non-Native."[26] While West's first sentence offers an important affirmation of Indigenous peoples' long-standing inhabitation of the continent, the second statement strikes me as a troubling non sequitur. It is true that Indigenous peoples' histories and cultures should be acknowledged and respected, but it does not follow that such histories and cultures belong to all groups that currently occupy the Western hemisphere. West's statement consequently lapses into an invitation to appropriate Indigenous cultures and to claim them as "the original part of the cultural heritage of every person." What is at stake here is a multicultural fantasy in which, to borrow Povinelli's words, the concept of indigeneity is used to provide "the nation [with] an experience of [a time] 'before nationalism'"—an experience that, rather than constituting a "counternational form," is appropriated by the state to "purify" and "redeem" "the ideal image of the nation."[27] In this way, the U.S. nation-state is able to appropriate what West describes as the rich "time depth" or cultural heritage of Indigenous peoples of the Western hemisphere developed over a span of roughly "twenty thousand years" and claim it in the service of the American imperialist mythology of rightful belonging in the so-called New World.[28]

A closer examination of the NMAI's grand opening demonstrates that the multicultural fantasy of pure, unhindered Indigenous expression actually dissimulates ongoing colonial power asymmetries that structure this Smithsonian museum as well as federal policies vis-à-vis Native peoples.

While the name Native Nations Procession suggests that this walk symbolically affirms the sovereignty of indigenous groups, Welcome Home's film coverage, as well as the hours of raw video footage housed at the Cultural Resources Center in Suitland, Maryland, demonstrate the procession's hierarchical structure affirming the hegemony of white America. The procession was led by Smithsonian Secretary Small, a Euro-American anthropologist dressed in a suit, flanked on either side by NMAI Director West and Republican Senator Ben Nighthorse Campbell (R-Colorado), both dressed in the tribal regalia of their Cheyenne nation. As the three men walked ahead of the masses, Campbell prominently carried the American flag, symbolizing which nation remained hegemonic, subsuming the subsequent Indigenous nations within its imperialist grasp.

The dominance of the United States as a governing authority was also reinforced in prior scenes of border crossing in which Indigenous people from foreign countries had to participate in order to congregate on the Washington Mall. The Native Nations Procession Participant Guide, published by the NMAI, encourages Indigenous people to wear their "traditional regalia," but "international visitors" are warned:

> There are a variety of sea mammals, bird feathers, shells, coral, plant matter such as cocoa leaves, and other animal/wildlife products that may not be legally brought into the U.S. Such articles could be seized by the U.S. authorities upon entry to the United States and subject the individual bringing them to fines and/or other penalties. For these reasons, Procession participants should consider not bringing any ceremonial objects, regalia, or other traditional clothing containing such material. . . . The NMAI is not responsible for actions that may be taken against Procession participants or their possessions by governmental authorities at the border.[29]

Thus, while the Native Nations Procession was framed by a white fantasy of a return to pure, unguarded cultural expression, the regulations outlined in the Participant Guide demonstrate the continued ways that the United States circumscribes and monitors Indigenous cultural practices. Moreover, the scene of border crossing underscores the fact that the Indigenous peoples of the Western hemisphere whom the NMAI claims to unite continue to be separated in substantial ways by geopolitical boundaries created as part of the colonial enterprise.

The NMAI's fantasy of hemispheric unity celebrated via a supposedly emancipated return to pure Indigenous performance is further troubled in the following example. Another display in the NMAI's Our Lives installation depicts the afterlife of Ojibwe artist Rebecca Belmore's 1991 *Speaking to their Mothers (Ayum-ee-aawach-Oomama-mown)* performance piece. After weaving a giant megaphone, Belmore "set it up at political pressure points across . . . Canada and invited Native people to . . . speak to their mother, the earth." The exhibit juxtaposes a photograph of Belmore's megaphone with a display of shells behind glass. As a text panel explains, "These ancient shells remind us that conch trumpets were used across the Americas to summon people and spirits." The exhibit's juxtaposition of "ancient" and "postmodern" "artifacts" of the conch-blowing ceremony help to illuminate the kinds of performance foregrounded in dominant archival representations of the Native Nations Procession. The procession officially began with a return to what the DVD liner notes to *Welcome Home* term the "traditional ritual of the Conch Shell Ceremony," as performed by Native Hawaiians Calvin and Kawai Hoe.[30] *Welcome Home* presents this event as its own way of commencing its coverage of the ceremonies. The camera zooms in on the Hoe brothers standing on a second-floor balcony of the Smithsonian Castle and blowing their shells, and then pans down to the approving faces of Rick West and other Smithsonian and NMAI officials presiding over the procession.[31] Reading this scene in conjunction with the Our Lives installation, what becomes clear is that the type of conch-blowing performance enacted for the NMAI's grand opening is quite different from Belmore's ironic and politicized megaphone performance: it appears to be much more like a return to "ancient tradition."

At the same time that *Welcome Home* refers to the conch-blowing ceremony as a "traditional ritual," the staging of this scene from the balcony of the neogothic Smithsonian Castle seems to appropriate the Hoe brothers' performance not as a "call to the people"—a call for solidarity among Indigenous groups—but as a troubadour-like salute to the authority of the Smithsonian Institution and its kingdom of the National Mall. Moreover, while NMAI and Smithsonian officials attempt to depict the First Americans Festival as a celebration of the harmonious uniting of colorful Indigenous diversity from across the hemisphere, the presence of Native Hawaiians at this festival was contoured by far more complex political circumstances. In her incisive essay "Contradictions and Celebrations: A Hawaiian Reflection on the Opening of the NMAI," J. Kēhaulani Kauanui argues that Native Hawaiian participation in the opening ceremonies was freighted with debates about the proposed Native Hawaiian Reorganization Act, a piece of legislation that seeks to include Hawaiians in federal Native American policy. According to Kauanui, this Act "undercuts . . . [Hawaiian] sovereignty rights under international law, especially since there has not been any manner of formally extinguishing the rights of Hawai'i as an independent nation-state," thereby opening the door for the extinguishment of Hawaiians' title to their national territory. "Because the federal Office of Hawaiian Affairs [a state apparatus in support of the Reorganization Act] took charge of organizing the Hawaiian contingent for the Native Nations Procession," Kauanui further contends, Hawaiian participation in the grand opening consequently "signalled a particular political stance—one assumed to be in line with U.S. federal policy's application to the situation of Hawaiians."[32] Thus, far from constituting a politically neutral version of Indigenous cultural expression, the conch shell blowing performance as well as the performances of Hawaiian singers, dancers, and participants in the Native Nations Procession was shaped by profound questions of continued American imperial aggression.

A closer investigation of the dominant discourses framing the grand opening of the NMAI as well as the material conditions affecting Indigenous participation in these events demonstrates that both the lives and the afterlives of performance are shaped profoundly by political and material constraints. Moreover, the fantasy of transcending such constraints or being somehow able to operate outside the conditions of capitalism and colonialism may actually play right into the hands of dominant institutions and governing bodies. The First Americans Festival is a striking case in point, as it is precisely the illusion of politically neutralized and unguarded Indigenous celebration that the NMAI and the Smithsonian—and, by extension, the U.S. nation-state—mobilizes to dissimulate ongoing colonial violence. Rather than suggesting that the colonial status quo is unchallengeable, my analysis up to this point has been focused on charting the terrain of constraints that contour the current political field as a way of preparing the groundwork for thinking about anticolonial resistance. It is to matters of counterhegemonic possibilities and struggles for social justice that I now turn.

Rethinking Visibility Politics/Re-visioning the Political Field

The power asymmetries contouring Native participation in the opening celebrations raise important questions about the possibilities and limits of visibility politics—or the political potential of increased visibility in the public sphere—for Indigenous peoples today. Describing the logic underpinning visibility politics, Peggy Phelan comments:

> Arguing that communities of the hitherto under-represented will be made stronger if representational economies reflect and see them, progressive cultural activists have staked a huge amount on increasing and expanding the visibility of racial, ethnic, and sexual "others." It is assumed that disenfranchised communities who see their members within the representational field will feel greater pride in being part of such a community and those who are not in such a community will increase their understanding of the diversity and strength of such communities.[33]

The potential problem with such a logic, as Phelan sees it, is that "while there is a deeply ethical appeal in the desire for a more inclusive representational landscape and certainly under-represented communities can be empowered by an enhanced visibility, the terms of this visibility often enervate the putative power of these identities." Phelan's comments are apt for identifying the problems at stake in the Native Nations Procession: namely, the fact that the terms of visibility offered for Indigenous participants by Smithsonian and NMAI officials co-opted Native performance for dominant agendas. That said, I remain cautious of the alternative to increased visibility that Phelan theorizes. In her attempt to revalue the negative, she proposes that "there is real power in remaining unmarked" or rendering oneself "invisible" to the public sphere. Admittedly, Phelan is quite careful to emphasize that her argument does not seek to theorize a passive form of invisibility but, rather, "an *active* vanishing, a deliberate and conscious refusal to take the payoff of visibility."[34] Despite her insistence on the active and agential quality of such a disappearing act, this strategy raises particularly complex questions when considered in relation to the history of colonial invasion on this continent—an invasion that first rendered Indigenous peoples invisible under the gaze of terra nullius and then sought to naturalize genocide via recourse to the volatile trope of the "vanishing Indian." Such deeply sedimented historical layers of forced Native disappearance, as well as the continued discursive purchase of tropes of Aboriginal vanishing, leave me skeptical of the possibility of new forms of Indigenous invisibility that are not overdetermined by colonialist techniques of eclipsing Native presence.

If recourse to increased visibility in the public sphere leaves Indigenous cultural expression open to co-optation by the state, and, on the other hand, "active vanishing" does not adequately consider the history of forced Native disappearance and its ramifications today, what possibilities remain in the struggle for meaningful political recognition of and social justice for Indigenous peoples? In proposing an alternative, I am cognizant of my status as a Euro-Canadian academic seeking to engage with the dilemma of visibility politics for Indigenous peoples without wanting to prescribe a course of action for such individuals and groups. As a result, the alternative I am formulating is a critical practice that could be mobilized for anticolonialist intellectual work by cultural critics across many locations and subject positions—spaces from which

I can intervene. I want to underscore, however, that this strategy also holds possibilities for performative praxis, and I invite people to appropriate it for those purposes.

If the "unmarked" is defined by what it is not, it is crucial to return critical pressure to the dominant term rather than to overestimate its coherence or stability. In this vein, I want to formulate a critical practice that seizes hold of the concept of the "marked" and intervenes in the dominant field of vision by deliberately re-marking it with a proliferation of alternative scenes: resistant performances that have been eclipsed from view due to their potential to disrupt the hegemonic social imaginary. In the case of the Native Nations Procession, this strategy could rupture the dominant staging of unfettered reconciliation by reactivating disturbing scenes from the history and present tense of U.S. imperialism and articulating them to the field of vision. In contrast to the Our Lives installation that mediates performance's afterlives through a museumizing temporal logic that emphasizes pastness and inscribes historical containment, I propose a critical strategy that seeks to reanimate performance's afterlives as disruptive traces that actively haunt the hegemonic staging of so-called postcolonial progress. Rather than attempting to evacuate Indigenous presence from the dominant field of vision (as Phelan might suggest), I want to obscure the hegemonic scene of reconciliation by rendering it shot through with alternative traces of colonial violence and Native resistance—disruptive "markings" that bombard and saturate the representational field with haunting reminders of historical and ongoing state-sanctioned racism against Indigenous peoples.

This strategy is inspired in part by Diana Taylor's notion of "hauntology," which she formulates in response to Phelan's "ontology of performance." In this context, Taylor argues:

> My view of performance rests on the notion of ghosting, that visualization that continues to act politically even as it exceeds the live. Like Phelan's definition, it hinges on the relationship between visibility and invisibility, or appearance and disappearance, but comes at it from a different angle. For

> Phelan, the defining feature of performance—that which separates it from
> all other phenomena—is that it is live and disappears without a trace. The
> way I see it, performance makes visible (for an instant, live, now) that which
> is always already there: the ghosts, the tropes, the scenarios that structure
> our individual and collective life.

For Taylor, therefore, "ghosting" is a way of understanding and making visible performance's imbrication in historical processes. Rather than constituting a phenomenon that can never occur again, performance brings to visibility, intensifies, and refocuses attention on the political and social dynamics—the "scenarios," or "meaning-making paradigms" for embodied social encounters[35]—that "structure" and haunt "our individual and collective life."

Appropriating Taylor's concept of performative hauntology for the critical strategy of re-marking the dominant field of vision, I want to invoke the scenario of the organized Indigenous walk, a particular historical paradigm of social encounter that has yet been malleable in its reiterations, in order to complicate the scene of the Native Nations Procession. By recalling to visibility this scenario, I seek to challenge dominant framings of the NMAI procession as historically unprecedented, as unlike anything else. Such master discourses seek to inscribe a kind of historical exceptionality to the NMAI-orchestrated gathering on the Mall in a way that frames September 21, 2004, as the inauguration of a new era of reconciliation while simultaneously occluding from view the history of colonial violence that the idea of postcolonial rapprochement should necessarily recognize. Re-marking the dominant vision of the Native Nations Procession with the scenario of the organized Indigenous walk ruptures the hegemonic narrative of one-of-a-kind-ness and overlaps the scene of the NMAI festivities with the specter of forced migration under colonial oppression. Here, the amnesia of the seemingly joyous, politically neutralized walk of the NMAI's 2004 procession is ruptured by the historical traces of U.S. policies of Indian removal, the 1838 Cherokee Trail of Tears, the Navajo Long Walk of the 1860s, the multiple relocations of the

Delaware and Lenape, as well as the Anishinabe, to name only a few of many such traumatic journeys. Invoking the scenario of the organized Indigenous walk is not about staging victimry; rather, it is a remembrance of survivance and resistance. This scenario also calls to mind the specter of Native American activism and protest, most notably, the Trail of Broken Treaties in 1972 and the Longest Walk in 1978, both of which converged on the National Mall and reoccupied the space of the capital in radical ways, such as the conversion of the Bureau of Indian Affairs into the Native American Embassy.[36] By layering these other scenes from the history of organized Indigenous walking over the Native Nations Procession and reactivating their traces in the present, I seek to defamiliarize the politically neutralized scene of September 2004 and ask how the staging of reconciliation might jeopardize the vital project of remembering and continuing to recognize colonial violence as well as envisioning the future of social justice.

In fleshing out the concept of strategically re-marking the visual field, I want to call attention to a brief scene from *Welcome Home* that reveals how this tactic might be put into performative praxis. Billy Frank, a member of the Nisqually Nation and chairman of the Northwest Indian Fisheries Commission, reflects on the significance of the grand opening of the NMAI. While Frank articulates his support for the work of Senator Daniel K. Inouye (D-Hawai'i) and Director Rick West in developing the museum, he also proceeds to re-vision the scene taking place on the Mall and to reactivate the haunting traces of colonial violence that elsewhere seem to be eclipsed by the festivities. In this context, Frank comments, "Now this is just a great, great day for all of us to have a museum put right here on the Mall in our country. I see all of our 63 million Indian people that was killed. They're here, they're sitting on these buildings and they're with us today."

In the raw footage filmed by NMAI-contracted videographers, the camera focuses intently on Frank as he slowly and emotively speaks these words and gestures to the buildings and sites around him, as if to point to the ancestors he is naming. In the commercial product of *Welcome Home*, however, strategic editing alters Frank's commentary in striking ways. At the very moment that Frank reimagines the scene of the National Mall with the presence of Native Americans killed by colonial forces, *Welcome Home* attempts to minimize the impact of his powerful words and bodily gestures by cutting away from his image and letting only his voice persist in a mixed soundtrack alongside the noises of people walking and talking. In turn, the image track overwrites Frank's face with a scene of U.S. hegemony—the Smithsonian secretary leading the procession with an American flag carried nearby—such that Frank's gesture of pointing to the absences he seeks to make present is occluded from view. Rather than allowing *Welcome Home* to eclipse the power of Frank's commentary, I want to mark and deliberate on this moment of resistance and revision, to seize hold of Frank's image of the dead returned, precisely as it flashes up at this moment of danger (as Walter Benjamin would say).[37] Such may be the beginnings of a performative hauntology that recalls the scene of colonial genocide without reinscribing victimry and, instead, actively enables the invisible to re-mark and to reoccupy the space of the National Mall.

Afterlives of the Future

One year after the First Americans Festival took place on the National Mall, I visited the NMAI on the occasion of its first anniversary. Delivering a speech from the museum's stage-like atrium known as the Potomac, Rick West recalled the scene of the opening ceremonies as a historic event. A birthday cake was cut and shared with visitors. The crowd joined hands with West and other NMAI staff and danced around the Potomac. *Welcome Home* was screened for the first time for a public audience in the Rasmuson Theater and released for sale in the Roanoke Gift Shop.

Across the street, on a traffic triangle carved out by the intersection of Maryland Avenue, Independence Avenue, and Third Street, a different kind of performance was occurring. A small group sponsored by the Gwich'in

Nation was staging a "drumming, singing, dancing vigil . . . in honor of the calving and nursery ground of the Arctic National Wildlife Refuge" and in protest against a congressional budget resolution that paved the way for future legislation to sanction oil drilling in the region.[38] With often fewer than ten members present on the traffic island, the activists drummed and sang day after day from August 13 to the end of September. On the one-year anniversary of the NMAI, crowds flocked to the museum, and as they exited the building, some turned to notice the activists, though only a small percentage of the NMAI's visitors crossed Maryland Avenue to learn more about the Wildlife Refuge. Visitors appeared more interested in viewing the performances of Indigenous dancers and artisans inside the museum than supporting the environmental concerns of Native activists. The positioning of the Gwich'in Nation members directly across from the NMAI and yet separated by Maryland Avenue seemed to mark a distancing and marginalization of this group from the hub of activity located at the museum. Explaining the activists' location, Evon Peter, a member of the Gwich'in Nation from Arctic Village, Alaska, and chairman of the Native movement, commented to me that the group was stationed on the traffic island because Smithsonian and NMAI policy prohibited protesting on Smithsonian property.[39] Peter's comments throw into striking relief the ongoing implications of the historical containment of protest within the NMAI's Our Lives installation and the exclusion of politicized activism elsewhere throughout the museum. If the NMAI is, as it claims to be, an "institution of living cultures" (to recall Rick West's words) that creates a space for those dynamic cultures to be shared, why is Indigenous activism not considered just as valid a form of Native cultural expression as the dancing and singing the museum showcases? If the NMAI has a "special responsibility to contribute to the continuance of Native communities,"[40] why does the museum fail to support protest against state policies that could jeopardize Native lifeways?

If my narrative reframing of the Gwich'in Nation's "drumming, singing, [and] dancing vigil" of September 2005 in honor of the Arctic

National Wildlife Refuge constitutes a textual mediation, an academic afterlife, of this performative event, then the act of linking it to the NMAI's grand opening in 2004 will prompt it to return from the future to haunt the scene of reconciliation staged by NMAI and Smithsonian officials on that day. For the strategy of performative hauntology I have been developing in this essay should not be limited to one forward-driven temporal direction circumscribed by Western notions of chronology and linearity. Retrospectively linking the scene of Gwich'in activism to the First Americans Festival serves to rupture the hegemonic fantasy of postcolonial reconciliation fulfilled—of joyous, politically neutralized Indigenous dancing and singing performed on behalf of the good feeling of the U.S. nation-state. At the same time, the Gwich'in campaign for the Arctic Refuge might point a way forward to a future of social change. In subsequent e-mail correspondence, Evon Peter noted that although the Smithsonian and NMAI institutional policies prohibited protest on museum grounds, certain Indigenous staff members and volunteers working inside the NMAI used their location to lend a hand by crossing the street to offer water and support and by distributing pamphlets in the third-floor media center. The Gwich'in activists' persistence in the face of institutional constraints and their use of the NMAI as a space for developing informal networks with other Indigenous supporters is beginning to prompt larger gains, such as the NMAI New York's recent agreement to screen the film *Homeland: Four Portraits of Native Action*, which portrays Gwich'in efforts to protect the Refuge.

As much as the Gwich'in campaign offers an inspiring example of the political potential of Indigenous action, it should also serve as a powerful challenge to the NMAI to rethink its policies and programs and to consider more carefully whose political interests they serve. Rather than celebrating forms of political and social reconciliation that have not yet arrived, the task for museums that purport to represent Indigenous peoples is to interrogate their own celebratory narratives of progress, to resist imposing forms of historical closure on the era of colonialism, and to underscore the radical incompleteness of the project of colonial reckoning.

Notes

Many thanks are owed to Michael Pahn, media archivist at the NMAI's Cultural Resources Center, for facilitating my research with the video footage of the grand opening. Thank you also to Edward Hanecak for checking the citations in this essay.

1. Jacques Derrida, *On Cosmopolitanism and Forgiveness*, trans. Mark Dooley and Michael Hughes (New York: Routledge, 2001), 28, 29.
2. Amanda Cobb reads the significance of the museum's name differently. She argues that because "the museum is international in scope" it "enhances the meaning of the name of the institution, allowing for us to interpret the 'National Museum of the American Indian' as a museum of the many Native nations of the Americas, recognizing cultural relationships rather than political separations and underscoring sovereignty and nationhood." Amanda Cobb, "The National Museum of the American Indian: Sharing the Gift," *American Indian Quarterly* 29 (Summer–Fall 2005): 366. While I find Cobb's interpretation to be interesting and hopeful, I fear that this alternative reading may perhaps too optimistically overlook the power asymmetries contouring the museum, as well as the fact that the term "national museum" on the Washington Mall is powerfully inscribed as meaning the American nation's museum (the National Museum of Natural History, the National Museum of American History, the National Air and Space Museum, etc.). In addition, the NMAI is frequently referred to as the Smithsonian's National Museum of the American Indian, which clearly locates the institution as belonging to the white philanthropic and state powers that continue to control political and cultural agendas in the United States.
3. W. Richard West, *Opening Ceremony Program*, pamphlet, National Museum of the American Indian and Smithsonian Institution, Washington DC, 2004; W. Richard West, *An Evening to Celebrate*, pamphlet, National Museum of the American Indian and Smithsonian Institution, Washington DC, 2004.
4. National Museum of the American Indian, http://www.nmai.si.edu (accessed July 20, 2004).
5. Amy Drapeau, "Facts and Figures from the Grand Opening of the Smithsonian's National Museum of the American Indian," *NMAI Grand Opening Press Kit*, National Museum of the American Indian, http://www.nmai .si.edu/press/releases/10-29-04_Facts_and_figures_opening.pdf.

6. I am aware of the debates surrounding the invocation of the category of "the postcolonial" in relation to the political situation of Native Americans whose territory is located within the geopolitical borders of the United States. In reciting various arguments about the rubric of "the postcolonial," Arnold Krupat (speaking of literary classifications in particular) comments, "Contemporary Native American literatures cannot quite be classed among the postcolonial literatures of the world for the simple reason that there is not yet a 'post-' to the colonial status of Native Americans. Call it domestic imperialism or internal colonialism; in either case, a considerable number of Native people exist in conditions of politically sustained subalternity." Arnold Krupat, "Postcolonialism, Ideology, and Native American Literature," in *Postcolonial Theory and the United States: Race, Ethnicity, and Literature*, ed. Amritjit Singh and Peter Schmidt (Jackson: University Press of Mississippi, 2000), 73. Understood in these terms, the application of the category "postcolonial" to the American political context risks denying the fact that Native Americans still live under colonial governance. Although this is one possible interpretation of the category of "the postcolonial," many scholars have argued that the status and meanings of the "post" are still very much under debate and that the term does not seek to overwrite the many ways colonial and neocolonial power asymmetries persist in the present tense. By invoking the category of "the postcolonial" in relation to my discussion of discourses of reconciliation, I do not intend to suggest that the current political situation of Native Americans is satisfactory or that colonial oppression has ceased to exist in the United States. Rather, I invoke the term "postcolonial" in this essay precisely to signal the ways hegemonic discourses of reconciliation falsely imply that the era of colonial violence is now over and that certain ideals of justice and equity are being fulfilled in contemporary American society.

7. Here I am briefly reciting examples only from the United States. Similar transformations have occurred in other countries, such as Australia, New Zealand, and Canada, to name a few. For further discussion of changes in Canadian museum policies and practices, please refer to Ruth B. Phillips and Mark Salber Phillips, "Contesting Time, Place, and Nation in the First People's Hall of the Canadian Museum of Civilization," in *Race and Empire in Public Space*, ed. Lisa Mayer Knauer and Daniel Walkowitz (Durham NC: Duke University Press, forthcoming), and Moira McLoughlin, *Museums and the Representation of Native Canadians: Negotiating the Borders of Culture* (New York: Garland, 1999).

8. National Museum of the American Indian, http://www.nmai.si.edu.9. W. Richard West Jr., "A New Idea of Ourselves: The Changing Presentation of the American Indian," in *The Changing Presentation of the American Indian: Museums and Native Cultures*, ed. Ann Kawasaki (Seattle: National Museum of the American Indian, Smithsonian Institution, in association with University of Washington Press, 2000), 8. Amanda Cobb further describes the museum's foregrounding of performance in the following terms: "conceiving of the NMAI as a forum or gathering place for living cultures dedicated to continuance allowed for the development of programs such as live demonstrations, performances, readings, lectures, and film screenings." Cobb, "Sharing the Gift," 366–67.

10. The video footage I consulted constituted many hours of raw footage of the NMAI grand opening filmed by NMAI-contracted videographers, held in the NMAI Cultural Resources Center in Suitland, Maryland. In January 2005, I also sent an open query soliciting reflections on the grand opening to the H-NET H-AMINDIAN listserv accessible to scholars and Native peoples.

11. Peggy Phelan, *Unmarked: The Politics of Performance* (London: Routledge, 1993), 146.

12. In a similar vein, Philip Auslander argues, "Much as I admire Phelan's commitment to a rigorous conception of an ontology of liveness, I doubt very strongly that any cultural discourse can actually stand outside the ideologies of capital and reproduction or should be expected to do so." Philip Auslander, "Liveness: Performance and the anxiety of simulation," in *Performance and Cultural Politics*, ed. Elin Diamond (London: Routledge, 1996), 197.

13. Phelan, *Unmarked*, 149, 148.

14. Phelan, *Unmarked*, 148; José Muñoz, *Disidentifications: Queers of Color and the Performance of Politics* (Minneapolis: University of Minnesota Press, 1999), 182.

15. Muñoz, *Disidentifications*, 187, 189.

16. Auslander, "Liveness," 197.

17. Floyd Favel Starr, quoted in Cobb, "Sharing the Gift," 379.

18. Lawrence M. Small, "National Museum of the American Indian Opening Ceremony Remarks," in NMAI *Grand Opening Press Kit*, National Museum of the American Indian, http://www.nmai.si.edu/press/releases/09-22-04 _Small_remarks.pdf.

19. Paul Schwartzman, "Native Americans March to Museum of Their Lives," *Washington Post*, September 22, 2004, A1. Similarly, the NMAI Web site sug-

gests that "thousands of indigenous peoples from North, Central, and South America, many in their traditional clothing, will walk in unison to the stage of the Grand Opening ceremony." National Museum of the American Indian, http://www.nmai.si.edu. An NMAI press release also reported that "many participants wore traditional regalia." Drapeau, "Facts and Figures." Raju Chebium and Faith Bremner referred to the Native Nations Procession as a "colorful spectacle." "Day of Celebration Ushers in Museum," USA Today, September 22, 2004, A16. The Knight Ridder report described "thousands of Indigenous peoples gathered in traditional dress." "American Indian Museum a Smithsonian 'Monument'," Edmonton Journal, September 22, 2004, sec. A.

20. Hank Stuever, "A Family Reunion: Opening Day on the Mall Brings Tradition into the Light of Today," Washington Post, September 21, 2004, C1.

21. Muñoz, Disidentifications, 182. Indeed, the spectacle staged by the NMAI during the First Americans Festival did spark significant economic consumption, as the "museum set a Smithsonian record with more than $1 million in sales at the two museum stores." Drapeau, "Facts and Figures."

22. Stuever, "A Family Reunion," C1.

23. Rick West, quoted in Amanda Cobb, "Interview with W. Richard West, Director, National Museum of the American Indian," American Indian Quarterly 29 (Summer–Fall 2005): 532.

24. Elizabeth A. Povinelli, The Cunning of Recognition: Indigenous Alterities and the Making of Australian Multiculturalism (Durham NC: Duke University Press, 2002), 6. Povinelli's argument is developed in specific reference to what she analyzes as "liberal forms of multicultural . . . domination" in contemporary Australian society (6). Her work develops a nuanced theoretical understanding of how "liberal discourses and identifications are elaborated in colonial . . . worlds" and is salient for thinking about the context of the contemporary United States as well (6).

25. National Museum of the American Indian, http://www.nmai.si.edu.

26. W. Richard West Jr., "Remarks on the Occasion of the Grand Opening Ceremony, National Museum of the American Indian," in NMAI Grand Opening Press Kit, National Museum of the American Indian, http://www.nmai .si.edu/press/releases/09-22-04_WRW_Remarks.pdf.

27. Povinelli, The Cunning of Recognition, 26.

28. Rick West, quoted in Cobb, "Interview," 518, 521.

29. Native Nations Procession Participant Guide (Washington DC: Smithsonian Institution and the National Museum of the American Indian, 2004), 25.

30. Welcome Home, DVD, National Museum of the American Indian, Smithsonian Institution, Washington DC, 2005.

31. Although the footage of the conch-blowing ceremony shown in *Welcome Home* does not feature a clear shot of Smithsonian Secretary Lawrence Small, raw video footage of the event confirms that Small was standing near West, also acting as one of the key officials.

32. J. Kéhaulani Kauanui, "Contradictions and Celebrations: A Hawaiian Reflection on the Opening of the NMAI," *American Indian Quarterly* 29 (Summer–Fall 2005): 501, 496–97.

33. Phelan, *Unmarked*, 7.

34. Ibid, 7, 6, 19.

35. Diana Taylor, *The Archive and the Repertoire: Performing Cultural Memory in the Americas* (Durham NC: Duke University Press, 2003), 143, 28.

36. For a more detailed discussion of Native activism and protest during the 1960s and 1970s, please refer to Paul Chaat Smith and Robert Allen Warrior, *Like a Hurricane: The Indian Movement from Alcatraz to Wounded Knee* (New York: New Press, 1996).

37. In "Theses on the Philosophy of History," Benjamin formulates his method of historical materialism: "To articulate the past historically does not mean to recognize it 'the way it really was' (Ranke). It means to seize hold of a memory as it flashes up at a moment of danger" —a moment that risks being lost to historical amnesia due to the forces of dominant historiography that would make events conform to the chronological master narrative of Western progress. Walter Benjamin, "Theses on the Philosophy of History," in *Illuminations: Essays and Reflections*, ed. Hannah Arendt, trans. Harry Zohn (New York: Schocken Books, 1968), 255.

38. Gwich'in Steering Committee, "DC Action Flyer," Drum, Sing, Dance, Protect, http://www.drumforthearcticrefuge.info/dcannouncement.html.

39. I emailed Leslie Wheelock, special assistant to the Executive Office of the NMAI, to verify the accuracy of Peter's statement. Wheelock provided the following response on February 8, 2006:

> I have checked with the Smithsonian's Director of the Office of Protection Services. He explained that the Smithsonian does not allow demonstrations on our property. If anyone shows up with signs our security officers do not let them in the buildings and will move them off of Smithsonian property. If they are in a building and pull out signs our security officers ask them to put the signs away or they could be subject to arrest.
>
> As a Smithsonian museum, the NMAI follows these practices.

40. Cobb, "Sharing the Gift," 366.

15. "South of the Border" at the National Museum of the American Indian

Robin Maria DeLugan

The National Museum of the American Indian (NMAI) stands in nearly unobstructed proximity to the U.S. Capitol, arguably the grandest symbol of U.S. political power. The fluid, organic, warm-toned architecture of the museum contrasts sharply with the staid monumentality and winter-white hue of the Capitol. As the latest addition to the Smithsonian's cluster of national museums,[1] the NMAI is an institution of the U.S. federal government. Symbolizing the often uneasy, if not contentious, relationship between North American Indians and the United States, the intent of the NMAI is to honor Native peoples.[2] However, for some the NMAI stands on the National Mall as a reminder of Native endurance from invasion, imperialism, and modern nation building; for others it signifies the destruction of Native sovereignty and the co-optation of Native cultures in a gesture of nation-state largesse.

First-time visitors to the NMAI may be unaware of the museum's hemispheric scope. By creating a museum for Native peoples from the Arctic north to the tip of South America, the NMAI extends our conventional notion of "American Indian," a term historically associated with tribes and nations within the United States. At the NMAI, "American Indian" signifies all Native peoples throughout the Americas. This essay specifically examines how the NMAI engages Native peoples from Latin America. I argue that more than showcasing the diversity of Native cultures, the museum is an important platform for reporting Indian and nation-state tensions and other struggles and victories. By situating the realities of Native peoples from "south of the border" in local, transnational, and global matrices, the NMAI highlights factors and conditions that unite Native North, Central, and South America.[3] Because a broad lens on the conditions that affect Native communities invites a critique of U.S. geopolitical engagements with Latin America, the limits of the NMAI as a federal institution to wholly represent Native realities are tested.

Indians, Museums, and the Nation-State

[Museums are] powerful and subtle authors and authorities whose cultural accounts are not easily dislodged. . . . [They are institutions that] inevitably bear the imprint of social relations beyond their walls and beyond the present.[4]

The NMAI attempts to transform a long history of museum practices wherein non-Native experts determined representations of Native peoples with a tendency to privilege non-Native interests or priorities.[5] Since the late 1980s the ongoing self-reflective critical turn in the museum profession and the protest of Native peoples to have their own voices heard have led to an examination of past, present, and future representational practices. Issues of voice and authority are debated by museum professionals and policy makers who endeavor to correct the imbalances that influenced the knowledge that museums produced about Native peoples.[6] In certain regions, Native people are increasingly taking roles in public museums. Meanwhile tribal museums have emerged as important vehicles for Native self-representation. The tribal museum strengthens Indian communities while allowing Native people to determine what they want the world to know about their particular group, tribe, or nation. When Natives author what museums communicate about Native peoples, the exhibition is enriched from the insider's perspective and sensibility about Native cultures and communities.

However, a national museum (such as the NMAI) is not a tribal museum. By definition a national museum exists to serve the nation-state and to advance nation-state interests, and the national museum functions as a powerful tool for promoting official ideas about national history, culture, and society. Regardless of whether or not a national museum makes reference to the region's Indigenous population, the museum as an extension of modern nation building and nation-state authority will always congeal ambiguous or tension-laden historical and contemporary relations between Native people and the nation-state. The official narratives that national museums promote are palimpsests of Native invasion, colonization, oppression, and exclusion.

National museums stand foremost as a symbol of the nation-state. Both through architectural splendor and exhibition content, national museums reveal the nation-state's spheres of power and influence. National museums exist to communicate official meanings and, as Benedict Anderson asserts, to consolidate the relationship between national territory, state, and the population associated with a given national territory.[7] The consolidation is often accomplished by promoting ideas about a shared national culture, history, and identity. As a technology of modern nation building, it is clear that national museums have rarely functioned on behalf of Native communities. This is particularly true of how national museums function throughout Latin America.

In the mosaic of territories and populations that constitute Latin America, the relationships between states, national societies, and Native populations vary tremendously. The history of Latin American nations is distinct from the history of the United States. In general, Latin American nations did not establish treaties in recognition of First Nations people or Native tribes. In some Latin American countries, national societies were based on complex ideas of *mestizaje*, the racial and cultural blending of Indian and Spanish. For example, in Mexico, the national ideology of *lo Mexicano* (the Mexican) is to celebrate the blending of the Indian and the Spanish and the forging of a "cosmic" national race.[8] Other countries, such as Costa Rica and Argentina, moved into nationhood with extremely small Native populations. Still other countries, such as Bolivia, Ecuador, and Guatemala, continue as territories with a majority Native population even though Native peoples in these countries rarely hold the reins of political or economic authority. It is important to comment that just because certain countries forged national societies and cultures from a historical melding of Indian with Afro, Iberian, or other European populations, this did not equate to a positive accent placed on contemporary Indian culture and identity. Throughout Latin America, Native populations live in conditions of great impoverishment and marginalization.

The highly charged relationship between Native populations and the nation-state in Latin America is often reflected in exhibits at national museums. While early nation building in Latin America extended largely from struggles for independence between the generations of Spaniards born in the Americas (criollos) and the Spanish Crown, a common ideological strategy for the early nation builders was to promote ancient Native American culture not only as a symbol of the unique nation but as justification for the independent nation to exist. However, at the same time that ancient Native culture was exalted, contemporary Native Americans were consistently denied meaningful participation in emerging national societies. Instead, the material and symbolic system of domination ushered in by invasion and colonization, codified through the idea of race and producing the new social category and identity of "the Indian," was perpetuated by and even fundamental to earlier projects to constitute new nation-states and national identities.[9] The ability of Native communities in Latin America to stay intact during epochs of nation building was assailed by national policies and ideas about the "modern" nation that attempted to eliminate Native rights and Native difference while co-opting ancient Native culture as symbolic of a unique and original deep history useful for representing national identity.

Exhibitions in national museums in Latin America today often repeat this same representational strategy that communicates an ambiguous relationship of Indigenous peoples to the nation-state. In national museums, Native Americans often symbolize the deepest history of the nation. Yet while exhibitions locate American Indians in primordial space and time, the inclusion or representation of a contemporary American Indian population is much less guaranteed. This is because ideologies of nation building and modernity in Latin America are tied to the promotion of a dominant, homogeneous non-Native national culture and society. Contemporary Indians disrupt these goals. In El Salvador, Central America, where I conduct research that follows the rebuilding of a polarized and war- torn society, new post–civil war national museums still situate Indians in a certain past, refusing to acknowledge their place in contemporary national life.[10] Museum exhibitions that keep Indians in a past time or that make Indians gradually disappear from view often closely match the national government's refusal to officially recognize the nation's Indigenous population. At the Museo Nacional de Antropologia in Mexico City, for example, the impressive display of the grandeur of Ancient Civilizations appears much more a symbol of domination and appropriation when considering the historic and ongoing problematic relations between Mexico's Indigenous peoples and the nation-state.[11] This is added to the fact that the Mexican state forges national identity by promoting an ideology of mestizaje—a blending of Indian and Spanish bodies and cultures intended to transform each into something distinct and new.[12] Let me reiterate: because national museums are by definition in the service of the nation-state, they rarely function for the benefit of Native Americans.

What makes the NMAI a unique national museum is that by including Native participation from throughout the Americas, the museum creates a platform otherwise unavailable to Native peoples within their respective nation-state contexts. Some view the NMAI as a positive advance in American Indian and U.S. government relations, especially through its effort to include Native peoples, to respect Native cultures, and, to a certain degree, to recognize historical rights and wrongs. The NMAI may be compared with admirable efforts at other national museums, such as the

Grand Hall of the Canadian Museum of Civilization, which has outstanding exhibitions that honor Native peoples. But other national museums do not match the NMAI's commitment to solely present Native cultures and to have their exhibits based primarily on Native authorship and collaboration. As a federal institution the NMAI directly embodies the histories of American Indians and their relationship with the U.S. government, and the potential of improved American Indian and nation-state relations communicated by the very existence of the NMAI bears most directly on Native communities within the United States. It is a potential for improved relations that is still not afforded to most Native peoples in Latin America. This reality makes the NMAI extremely valuable, for it provides Native peoples south of the border a forum for self-representation of issues of interest and concern otherwise unavailable to them.

The history of strained relations between nation-states, national museums, and American Indians makes the NMAI and its hemispheric mission important. In this national museum, American Indians will express in their own voices the histories that are to be told. They will introduce their communities as they see fit. They will raise issues of concern, and this will mean speaking out against past and present policies that threaten Native communities. Still, as a national museum the subtext of the NMAI will always and unavoidably be Indian and nation-state relations. In what follows I explore this subtext by focusing on the NMAI as a proxy space where Native peoples from south of the border can articulate local issues, including Indian and nation-state relations. I examine how the exhibitions at the NMAI refer to ways that Native peoples throughout the Americas interact with nation-states and with each other to ultimately transform our understanding of who is an American Indian. Finally, I suggest that the conditions that impact Native communities in Latin America must be understood at the nation-state level but also in terms of regional and global dynamics. In this expanded context, the role of U.S. power and imperialism comes into focus. This necessarily complicates an understanding of the NMAI as a forum for expressing south of the border Native realities. I explore the limits that seem to be set for the NMAI, a federal institution of the U.S. government, to wholly serve the interests of Native peoples of Latin America.

The NMAI: Serving Communities South of the Border

Within the three main exhibition halls—Our Universes, Our People, and Our Lives—there are smaller rooms that focus in detail on specific communities. In these community exhibitions, the NMAI staff collaborated with community curators who authored displays of their respective community. Our Universes, Our Peoples, and Our Lives accommodate only a very small number of community exhibitions. The close-up view of particular communities that the community exhibitions provide is extremely valuable; however, overall the design logic severely limits the NMAI's ability to represent the many hundreds of Native communities throughout the hemisphere. What minute handful of communities will be selected for representation, and why? The NMAI staff hopes to eventually rotate community exhibitions into and out of the three main halls so that new communities will be able to participate. However, because of the great public demand to visit the original exhibitions, coupled with the financial demands of producing new community exhibits, it may be five or more years before the current community installations in the three main exhibition halls are changed.[13] In terms of the representation of Native peoples from Latin America, only nine groups have community exhibits. These exhibits are briefly described in the following paragraphs.

In Our Universes community curators from a Mapuche community from Temuco, Chile, a Quechua community from Cuzco, Peru, and a Q'eq'chi Maya community from Cobán, Guatemala, have separate walled-in spaces within which displays inform the museum visitor how the cosmos orients the daily life of the communities. Each space emanates unique spoken language, music, and song. For every community exhibit there is a distinctive cosmogram, a graphic illustration of colors, symbols, and elements drawn to represent the community's understanding of their place on earth and in the universe. Here one is struck by the commonalities of Native cosmology that link Native communities throughout the hemisphere. Characteristic is the linking of cardinal directions to specific colors and specific qualities and forces, all woven into a unity to express concepts of spiritual and social being and belonging.

In Our Peoples community curators from two small Amazonian tribes, the Tapirapé and Ka'apor, tell of centuries of struggle to reclaim territory. There is a presentation of the recent victories and regaining of homeland. While every Native struggle and victory is important, the curatorial decision to include both of these very small, somewhat neighboring tribes instead of inviting a different community from a distinct Latin American context seems like a lost opportunity. Based on my conversations with NMAI staff, the reason for having two small Amazonian tribes may have been an artifact of an earlier, abandoned exhibition concept rather than a deliberate, though misguided, selection aiming for regional representation.

Also to be found in Our Peoples is an exhibit by Wixarika (Huichol) community curators of Mexico that presents the complex ways that power and authority infuse the community's telling of who they are. Intertwined in Wixarika narratives of community identity are mestizos (people of mixed Indian and Spanish ancestry) and santos (religious icons of the Catholic Church). Both, we are told, demonstrate the heavy imprint of invasion and colonization on Wixarika culture and identity. Wixarika curators remind us that the struggles of power and authority revealed through a careful examination of community narratives do not mean that struggles emanate solely from the past. Today's struggles are also presented. The exhibition communicates how the arrival of mestizo settlers and policies of the Mexican government are reducing the Wixarika's land base. Here is an example of the NMAI as a forum for Native protest against nation-state polices that endanger the well-being of their communities.

The final Latin America–based community exhibit in Our Peoples is from a Nahua community from Guerrero, Mexico. Community curators tell the history of ancient Nahua migrations through North and Central America. The primordial narratives of origin and relocation illustrate geographic links and suggest deep cultural ties between American Indians from within the United States and Mexico today. Although the reasons for ancient migrations are not explained, the exhibition also tells of the reverse migration that is occurring today. The community curators name the economic and demographic pressures that are forcing the migrations northward into the United States as the Nahua seek sheer survival. Beyond historical and contemporary nation-state tensions, it is increasingly understood that a negative effect of the North American Free Trade Agreement (NAFTA), a policy that emanates from the U.S. government, has been to usher into Mexico corporate-sponsored agricultural products and activities (including genetically modified crops) that threaten the survival of small farmers (Native and non-Native) and traditional agricultural practices. However, the Nahua community exhibition refrains from naming NAFTA as a source of community woes. Does this illustrate the limit of the NMAI—a U.S. federal institution— to wholly serve Native communities south of the border?

The exhibition hall Our Lives emphasizes a multitude of contemporary Native issues. A total of eight groups from throughout the hemisphere were invited to create community exhibits within Our Lives. Of this tiny number only two have ties to Latin America. The Kumeyaay Nation represented by the Campo band tells the museum visitor how California statehood in 1848 split Kumeyaay families between the United States and Mexico and how strict immigration laws today continue to impact the Kumeyaay Nation. We can imagine how post–9/11 security fears and the increasing militarization of the U.S.-Mexican border newly impact the divided Kumeyaay Nation. There is no specific reference to how heightened U.S. security in a post–9/11 era entrenches the separation of Kumeyaay kin.

The second Native community with ties to Latin America appearing in Our Lives is the Kalinago (Carib) from the Caribbean Island of Dominica.

The theme of the community exhibition is loss and survival. Ravaged from early contact with Europeans, Kalinago Indians and African slaves melded bloodlines and cultural practices. The Kalinago know their forefathers are from South America, and they look to Native peoples on the continent for instruction and inspiration as they strengthen their Native identity. In 2002 the Kalinago hosted the Reunion of the Condor and Eagle Indigenous Action Summit, where Native leaders from all over the Americas gathered. With the condor symbolizing the Native people of the Southern hemisphere and the Eagle the Native people from the North, the Kalinago summit expresses the solidarities that are increasingly being forged between Native peoples of the Americas.

Apart from the distinct community exhibits described here, the NMAI depicts issues of concern to Native peoples from Latin America in ways that connect communities south of the border with Native peoples throughout the hemisphere, if not around the globe. In addition to the community exhibitions, the main exhibition halls emphasize overarching topics such as European invasion, Christianity, and the impact of capitalism to reference historical experiences and conflicts shared by many Native peoples throughout the hemisphere. The hall Our Lives touches on migration, the forging of international law on behalf of Native peoples, and international solidarities, all of which highlight south of the border realities as well as the increasing links between North, Central, and South American Indians.

Before examining a variety of these representations in detail, it is necessary to remark that the information I cull from the NMAI about south of the border communities and hemispheric ties may not be obvious or easily accessible to the casual museum visitor. I visited the NMAI deliberately seeking this material, and my analysis required cobbling together random texts and inconspicuous references. In much the same way that the museum is limited in its ability to introduce the numerous diverse communities of the Americas, the experiences and conditions that influence Native peoples in contemporary societies is also myriad and therefore difficult for one museum to capture. The NMAI does provide a unique forum for articulating the realities and concerns of Latin America's Indigenous populations and hemispheric ties; however, the forum does have limitations. Nonetheless, in the next section I continue my review of the NMAI to explore both its promise and limits to serve Native communities from Latin America.

Wars, Genocide, and Displacement

For centuries and all across the continent, Native peoples have been displaced by social and political pressures wrought by newcomers who treated the Americas as virgin terrain without regard for the lives and worlds of Indigenous peoples. As mentioned earlier, the Kumeyaay Nation teaches us how the construction of a border between Mexico and the United States divided Kumeyaay territory and Kumeyaay families. The violence to Native peoples that accompanied the arrival of new nation-states is not merely a matter of new geographical borders but the creation of social, cultural, and economic conditions that continue to pose threats to the well-being of Native communities. It is no secret that even in nation-states where Native peoples constitute the majority population, national policies have historically denied and continue today to deny Native interests.[14]

Native peoples from Latin America have struggled for centuries. More recently, the 1970s and 1980s were an especially devastating period as many regions of Latin America were ravaged by repression and armed conflict. In Guatemala, where Maya Indians constitute the majority population, a civil war erupted and the state retaliated against Indian communities. Acts of genocide took more than two hundred thousand lives and destroyed more than eight hundred villages. The civil war displaced hundreds of thousands of Indigenous people, who became refugees and who moved from their villages to remote areas or into cities as they sought safety or a livelihood.[15] At the NMAI, commemorating this devastating history is a painting by artist Diego Isais Hernandez Mendez (Tz'utuhil Maya) titled *Dolor y Llanto por Difuntos* (translated as "Sorrow and Tears for the Deceased"). The painting depicts the horror of violence and expresses the grief of a community. Not provided in this commemoration is information about how the U.S. government backed Guatemala's repressive military government for decades. Mentioned, however, is the displacement and migration caused by the region's devastating civil wars. In Guatemala many Maya refugees sought a safe haven from social, political, and economic violence by coming to the United States. Today Guatemala Mayans are a growing Indigenous population in the United States.[16]

The civil wars in Guatemala, Nicaragua, and El Salvador have ended, but economic instability in Latin America now forces many Indians to leave their communities in order to survive. Today poverty and hunger are the greatest generators of migration in Latin America. In an attempt to illustrate how Native people are disproportionately impacted by conditions of poverty, a small, somewhat inconspicuous wall panel in Our Lives displays the poverty rates in select countries of the Americas. In the display each country has two statistics; the first is the general poverty rate, and the second is the poverty rate for Indians—a number that in each case is markedly higher.[17] Here the disparity between powerful and less powerful nations in the hemisphere is matched by the disparity of poverty between national averages and the conditions suffered by Native peoples. Not mentioned in the panel is how, throughout much of Latin America, poverty has been compounded by national economic policies that respond to pressure by the United States and other international political and financial bodies to adopt neoliberal economic models and reforms. Among the results of neoliberalism are the privatization to corporate interests of formerly state-administered services such as water and power and the undermining of the strength of local agricultural economies. All contribute to an increase in Indian poverty. The NMAI does not name the contemporary geopolitical and economic factors, including the authority of the U.S. government, that contribute to the increased poverty and displacement of Native communities.

The need for work and food has motivated massive migration from rural villages into the cities, as well as movement across national borders as Indians migrate by the thousands to "El Norte."[18] If we read carefully among the patchwork of multiple text panels, large and small, of Our Lives, we learn that Latin American Indians collectively form the third largest Indigenous group in the United States today. The migration of Native people from Latin America to the United States is bringing Indigenous people from North, Central, and South America geographically, if not socially, closer together. While transnational ties to the homeland may enable Indians to maintain their connection to their communities back home, there is no guarantee that this connection will last.[19] There is a photograph of Quechua and Aymara miners in Bolivia who reaffirm their identity through the Diablo dance. Next to the photograph Carlos Sanchez (Aymara), who lives in New York, speaks about the dance and about migration: "Indigenous families that leave their homeland often find that traditions are hard to preserve for the next generation." Migrations and the displacements of Native peoples do not have to result in loss of cultural traditions or Native community. One example of the survival of cultural traditions is presented in the outer hall of Our Universes, where a video displays Day of the Dead ceremonies in Santa Maria Huatulco, Mexico, and Los Angeles, California. The video demonstrates how an important cultural event that is celebrated in Latin America is also having an increasing presence in the United States. Here we might compare Latin American migrations with the many forced relocations of American Indians by the U.S. government, not only in terms of cultural and community disruption, but also in terms of the resiliency of Native people who forge inclusive communities that unite American Indians from many nations in new spaces, be they urban, international, or transnational.[20]

Native Autonomy and International Solidarities

The NMAI offers a place for reporting on various struggles of Native peoples south of the border. For some communities, such as the Ka'apor and

Tapirapé, the struggle to reclaim territory resulted in victory. From other Native communities with control over their territory we learn about ongoing efforts to assert autonomy. Our Lives includes the briefest report on the Kuna, who, between 2001 and 2003, worked with the nongovernmental organization Native Lands to create their own map of their land: the Comarca Kuna Yala. Throughout the globe, Native mapping is reemerging as a practice of autonomy and sovereignty. It is an important tool of decolonization that privileges the fundamental contribution of Indigenous knowledge production as inscribed upon the representation of Native land. Whether through projects of decolonization, self-determination, or participation in a plurinational society, the political landscape for Indigenous people in Latin America is dynamic. Increasingly Native peoples are pressuring nation-states for rights, equal protection, and policies that respect Native interests. In countries such as Ecuador, Bolivia, Mexico, Guatemala, and Colombia, Indigenous movements demand constitutional reforms to recognize the multiethnic and plurinational composition of their countries. Indigenous movements challenge national ideologies long based on assimilation and the formation of homogeneous societies. In the process they are redefining ideas about citizenship and society.[21]

When nation-states in Latin America continue to refuse Native autonomy or to provide meaningful representation and participation within national societies, international efforts are increasingly applying pressure to national governments to recognize and safeguard the interests of Indigenous people. In the process, international entities such as the United Nations assist in the building of new alliances among the world's Native peoples. Entities such as the International Working Group for Indigenous Affairs exist to engage in global struggles for Native survival, well-being, and self-determination.[22] The NMAI acknowledges the growing international solidarity of Indigenous people through the display of a handful of photographs from the first (2002) and second (2004) sessions of the U.N. Permanent Forum on Indigenous Peoples. Accompanying these photographs are the words of Rigoberta Menchu Tum (Q'eq'chi' Maya) as she accepted the Nobel Peace Prize in 1992: "Let there be freedom for the Indians, wherever they may be because while they are alive, a glow of hope will be alive as well as a true concept of life."

This reference to Menchu Tum's words links the struggles of American Indians from North, Central, and South America to the struggles of Indigenous peoples worldwide.

A New Tomorrow

The historical conditions of repression and marginalization that characterize Indian and nation-state relations throughout Latin America are being challenged today as never before. In *La Emergencia Indígena en Latin America* (2000), anthropologist José Bengoa recounts how Indians are gaining increasing visibility and authority.[23] What he describes as "emergence" is partially explained as the inability of ideological projects and recent revolutionary struggles to subsume Indians under broad categories: *campesino*, peasant, communist, and so on.

In 1994 the Maya uprising in Chiapas, Mexico, brought the Zapatista movement international attention and solidarity. The rebellion coincided with the implementation of NAFTA, a Washington DC–based policy that has wreaked havoc on the well-being of Indigenous communities and others in Mexico by introducing cheap imports of corn and other agricultural products from the United States, impairing Indigenous participation in the agricultural economy. As a revolutionary Indigenous movement, the Zapatista National Liberation Army fights against social inequality and in favor of self-determination. By highlighting the suffering of Indigenous peoples, the Zapatistas propose a different model of sociality and justice to promote a worldview that will better humanity as a whole. Negotiations with the Mexican government have yet to result in acceptable policy changes. However, the Zapatistas continue to influence the national imaginary. In 2005–6, they mounted an alternative to the formal national presidential elections campaign. Through

La Otra Campaña ("The Other Campaign"), the Zapatistas reached out to the citizens of Mexico. Listening to the concerns of others in support of Indians and other subalterns, the Zapatistas promote a unique vision for a better tomorrow, a vision that is putatively grounded in Indigenous philosophy and cosmology.

In 2006, Evo Morales was elected president of Bolivia. As he is Aymara, Indigenous language and ceremony were incorporated into the inauguration, raising the promise that an Indian president will approach leadership of the nation-state in a distinct manner. With Morales as president, the people of Bolivia have a historic opportunity to address the needs and interests of Bolivia's majority Indigenous population. In neighboring Ecuador Indians are increasingly active in efforts to reshape the political and economic conditions of the nation-state. Through the Confederation of Indigenous Nationalities of Ecuador Ecuador's Indians organize in protest of neoliberal economic agendas that threaten to privatize natural resources. Shutting down Ecuador's "business as usual," Indigenous activism is largely responsible for ousting three presidents since 1997.

As suggested, through protest, activism, and political participation Indigenous people of Latin America are demanding a better tomorrow. The alternative visions they promote are often in direct challenge to the hegemonic policies of the United States. Whether it is resistance to Washington-based free trade agreements, U.S.-supported neoliberal policies that aim for privatization of natural resources, or U.S. military presence cloaked in antidrug or antiterrorism campaigns, the glaring clash between the priorities and interests of Indigenous people south of the border and that of the U.S. government is increasingly evident. The current exhibitions at the NMAI give little hint of the revolutionary activities that are transforming Indian and nation-state relations in Latin America. Nor do the exhibitions highlight the opposition mounted by Indigenous people against U.S. government policies or the economic interests of U.S.-based transnational corporations.

Conclusion

As a national museum, the NMAI endeavors to distinguish itself from a much longer history of national museum practices that foremost served nation-state interests instead of the interests of Native peoples. The very existence of the NMAI is entangled with the complex and often tension-laden relationships between American Indians and the United States. However, as a museum with a hemispheric mission, the NMAI offers a unique platform for Native peoples throughout the Americas to report on their particular nation-state entanglements. In this essay, I examined how the NMAI serves Native peoples south of the border, arguing that the NMAI offers an important forum not locally available for reporting on struggles, issues, and realities of importance to their communities.

The NMAI is unable to adequately represent the great diversity of Native communities of the Americas. However, a handful of communities are introduced in greater detail through collaboration with community curators who invite the museum visitor to learn more about their community's history, cultural identity, and specific issues of concern. Other representational practices at the NMAI emphasize historical forces and experiences of invasion and colonization shared by Native communities throughout the hemisphere. Placing contemporary Native communities in local, national, and even global matrices, the NMAI tells how state violence, displacements, and migrations impact many Latin American Indigenous communities. The museum provides a glimpse into the process by which new Indian communities are forged across nation-state boundaries, including through strengthening transnational ties. Further, the museum nods to the new international solidarities that are being formed in the struggle for Indigenous autonomy, sovereignty, and increased participation in national society. Depicting the shared historical and contemporary (often heart-wrenching) conditions that Native peoples in the Americas experience, the NMAI draws Native peoples throughout the hemisphere closer together.

As illustrated, a very attentive visit to the NMAI not only reveals a glimpse into the diversity of communities south of the border, but also provides important information on the dynamic relationship of Indians to Latin American nation-states. However, our current global model, defined by a patchwork of nation-states, is but the latest extension of earlier colonial practices and capitalist encroachment upon Native worlds. "Democratic" and even "postcolonial" national societies that have emerged have done so largely at the expense of Native communities. In today's global model, the U.S. government acts as an imperial power, and as such it plays a crucial role in the maintenance and perpetuation of a range of political and economic policies that negatively affect Native peoples throughout the hemisphere.

To acknowledge the conditions that impact American Indians south of the border will require examination of the role of U.S. policies and practices. The degree to which the NMAI will be willing or able to take on this important examination remains to be seen and may point to the limits of a federal institution in Washington to wholly serve the interests of American Indians.

Notes

This is an expanded version of an essay of the same title that appeared in Amer-ican Indian Quarterly 30, no. 4 (2006).

1. The NMAI joins the following Smithsonian museums: National Museum of Natural History, National Museum of American History, National Air and Space Museum, National Museum of African Art, National Gallery of Art, Freer Gallery of Art and Arthur M. Sackler Gallery, and Hirshhorn Museum and Sculpture Gallery,

2. Ben Nighthorse Campbell, "A Long Time Coming," *Smithsonian*, September 2004, 59–62.

3. Gabrielle Tayac reminds us that geographic borders are artificially constructed, arbitrary, and contingent. However, they are no less powerful in shaping ideas about "us" and "them." Gabrielle Tayac, "We Rise, We Fall, We Rise," *Smithsonian*, September 2004, 63–64.

4. Sharon Macdonald and Gordon Fyfe, eds., *Theorizing Museums* (Cambridge MA: Blackwell, 1994), 4.

5. For examples of the transformation of museum representational practices, see National Museum of the American Indian, *The Changing Presentation of the American Indian: Museums and Native Culture* (Washington DC: Smithsonian Institution Press, 2000).

6. James Clifford and George E. Marcus, eds., *Writing Culture: The Poetics and Politics of Ethnography* (Berkeley; University of California Press, 1986); Ivan Karp and Steven Lavine, eds., *Exhibiting Cultures: The Poetics and Politics of Museum Display* (Washington DC: Smithsonian Institution, 1990).

7. Benedict Anderson, *Imagined Communities: Reflections on the Origins and Rise of Nationalism* (1983; London: Verso, 1991).

8. Manuel Gamio, *Forjando Patria (pro nacionalismo)* (1916; Mexico City: Editorial Porrua, 1960).

9. Anibal Quijano argues that not only did the construction of the category of race that legitimated exploitation of Indians and others have roots in European contact with the Americas, but that it was fundamental to the European-centered world capitalist project. In the historical process, normative meanings and practices around Eurocentric and hegemonic notions of race, gender, sex, class, and religion have perpetuated social inequality throughout the Americas and elsewhere. Anibal Quijano, "Coloniality of Power: Eurocentrism and Latin America," *Nepantla: Views from the South* 1, no. 3 (2000): 533–80.

10. Robin Maria DeLugan, "Re-Imagining the Ties That Bind: State Practices of Nation-building in Post–Civil War El Salvador (1992–2000)," Ph.D. diss., University of California, Berkeley, 2004. See also Henrietta Riegel, "Into the Heart of Irony: Ethnographic Exhibitions and the Politics of Difference," in *Theorizing Museums*, ed. Sharon Macdonald and Gordon Fyfe (Cambridge MA: Blackwell, 1986).

11. Nelson Graburn. "Art and Pluralism in the Americas," in *Anuario Indigenista: Problemas Etnicos de la Sociedad Contemporanea* 30 (Mexico City: Instituto Indigenista Interamericano, 1970), 191–204.

12. Ana María Alonso, "Conforming Disconformity: 'Mestizaje,' Hybridity and the Aesthetics of Mexican Nationalism," *Cultural Anthropology* 19, no. 4 (2004): 459–90.

13. NMAI staff, personal communication, 2004.

14. Carol A. Smith, *Guatemalan Indians and the State, 1540–1988* (Austin: University of Texas Press, 1990); Mark Thurner, *From Two Republics to One Divided: Contradictions of Postcolonial Nationmaking in Andean Peru* (Durham NC: Duke University Press, 1997); Florencia Mallon, *Peasant and Nation: The Making of Post-Colonial Mexico and Peru* (Berkeley: University of California Press, 1995).

15. Beatriz Manz, *Paradise in Ashes: A Guatemalan Journey of Courage, Terror and Hope* (Berkeley: University of California Press, 2004).

16. Xóchitl Castañeda, Beatriz Manz, and Alison Davenport, "Mexicaniza-tion: A Survival Strategy for Guatemalan Mayans in the San Francisco Bay Area," *Migraciones Internacionales* 1, no. 3 (2002): 103–23; Alan Burns, *Maya in Exile: Guatemalans in Florida* (Philadelphia: Temple University Press, 1993); Jacqueline Maria Hagan, *Deciding to Be Legal: A Maya Community in Houston* (Philadelphia: Temple University Press, 1994); Norita Vlach, *The Quetzal in Flight: Guatemalan Refugee Families in the United States* (Westport CT: Praeger, 1992).

17. Examples of the difference in national and Native poverty rates displayed on the exhibition panel include Bolivia, where the general poverty rate is 48.1 percent and the poverty rate for Indians is 64.3 percent (1994 figures); Mexico, where the general poverty rate in 2003 was 17.9 percent and for Indians 80.5 percent; and the United States, where the general poverty rate was 12.1 percent but for Indians was 24.5 percent (averaged between 1999 and 2001).

18. Jonathan Fox and Gaspar Rivera Salgado, eds., *Indigenous Mexican Migrants in the United States* (San Diego: Center for Comparative Immigration Studies, University of California, San Diego, 2004); Beatriz Manz, Xóchitl Castañe-da, Allison Davenport, Ingrid Perry-Houts, and Cecile Mazzacurati, *Gua-temalan Immigration to the San Francisco Bay Area*, Working Paper 6, no. 1, (Berkeley: Center for Latino Policy Research, Regents of the University of California, 2000).

19. The 1993 video *Transnational Fiesta: 1992*, produced by Paul Gelles and Wil-ton Martinez, captures the dynamic of transnational cultural ties by accom-panying Peruvian Andean immigrants living in Washington DC on their visit back to Peru to sponsor and participate in an important traditional village celebration. David Brooks and Jonathan Fox, *Cross-Border Dialogues: U.S.-Mexico Social Movement Networking* (San Diego: Center for U.S. Mexi-can Studies, University of California, San Diego, 2002). Research in this volume highlights broad structural conditions that influence migration and other hemispheric interactions. Selections also attend to the partic-ular experience of the Indigenous migrant from Latin America as well as organizing and alliances of human rights and other mobilizations around issues of concern to Indigenous communities.

20. My ongoing collaboration with Indigenous community leaders from North, Central, and South America working together in the San Francisco Bay Area of California to forge a multinational, multicultural Indian alliance attests to the creation of new Indigenous communities in the United States.

21. Deborah J. Yashar, *Contesting Citizenship in Latin America: The Rise of Indigenous Movements and the Postliberal Challenge* (Cambridge, England: Cambridge University Press, 2005).

22. Suhas Chakma and Marianne Jenson, eds., *Racism against Indigenous Peoples*, IWGIA Document No. 105 (Copenhagen: International Work Group for Indigenous Affairs and Asian Indigenous and Tribal Peoples Network, 2001).

23. José Bengoa, *La Emergencia Indígena en América Latina* (Mexico City: Fondo de Cultura Economica).

16. Inside Out and Outside In

Re-presenting Native North America at the Canadian Museum of Civilization and the National Museum of the American Indian

Ruth B. Phillips

For Native North Americans, the new millennium began with a big museological bang when the national museums of the United States and Canada opened new and radically revised exhibitions on the Indigenous peoples of the Americas. The First Peoples Hall of the Canadian Museum of Civilization (CMC), which opened in February 2003, occupies almost 35,000 square feet in Canada's national museum of history and anthropology in Gatineau, Quebec. The Smithsonian Institution's National Museum of the American Indian (NMAI), which opened in September 2004, is an even larger project, occupying a new four-story building on the Mall in Washington DC. From the outside, the buildings that house the new installations are close cousins. Both were designed in the signature style of Douglas Cardinal, a Canadian architect of Blackfoot and Métis ancestry. Cardinal's organic forms reflect his deep conviction of the integral bonds linking humans to the natural world and the topographies of land.[1] Both on the banks of the Ottawa River and on the Mall in Washington, the undulating strata of Cardinal's buildings and the warmth of their gold-hued stone stand out against the rectilinearity and gray historicism of nearby government buildings.

On the inside, however, the new exhibitions display as many differences as similarities. On the one hand, there are a number of striking convergences in the themes and display approaches adopted for the two exhibitions. These similarities, I will argue, testify to the epochal changes in the power relations between Indigenous peoples and settler institutions that took place inside and outside both museums during the last two decades of the twentieth century. These changes participate in a global movement toward a postcolonial museology powered by the anticolonial activism of Indigenous peoples in informal alliance with academic poststructuralist critics of museum representation.[2] The contrasts between the new exhibitions, on the other hand, point to historically contingent differences in the relationships between Indigenous peoples and the institutions and governments of Canada and the United States. These result from more local and idiosyncratic processes of decolonization that have been shaped by distinctive national and institutional histories. To explore both the global and the local resonances of the new exhibitions, I ask two kinds of questions. The first has to do with power: What are the structural problems inherent in mounting revisionist exhibitions within national museums, and to what degree can Indigenous peoples who have been marginalized within modern nation-states use national museums as effective sites for political contestation? The second, related question has to do with poetics: In what ways do contestatory politics intervene in the modernist display paradigms of art and artifact that, as we will see, are held to have been compromised by their historical deployment in colonial museology? I will not, of course, be able to explore either of these questions exhaustively in this essay. Rather, by looking briefly at the historical contexts of both exhibitions and by comparing their thematic structures and several specific installations, I hope to provide a fruitful analytical framework for thinking about Native North American museum representation, not only in Washington and Ottawa, but also in Europe.

Contexts: Institutional, Personal, Political

Museum exhibitions begin with abstract conceptual plans, but they are realized by individuals who must negotiate particular institutional histories, who bring to the table their prior experiences of exhibition development, and who are ultimately answerable to external sponsors and government agencies. It is therefore useful to position the First Peoples Hall and the NMAI's Mall museum's long-term displays in relation to the modernist twentieth-century exhibitions that preceded them, to several critical events that had formative impacts on key individuals who worked on the new exhibitions, and to the late twentieth-century identity politics that shaped the expectations of external sponsors.

Although the permanent installations replaced by the new exhibitions differed in numerous details, both were informed by the assumptions about universal progress and cultural evolution that were fundamental to twentieth-century modernist museum anthropology. The Museum of the American Indian and the National Museum of Canada installations were organized according to a standardized system of culture areas that was closely associated with environmental determinism, and they employed a taxonomic approach to artifacts derived from natural history classification that objectified and dehumanized Aboriginal people and their cultures. Their exhibits located Native North Americans in an idealized and fictive past prior to contact with the West and, whether overtly or implicitly, conveyed the message that Aboriginal people had lost their authenticity and that their traditions were incompatible with modernity and were fated to disappear.[3] The crowded cases of the Museum of the American Indian seemed to epitomize the greed of Western collectors, their fetishization of rare and old objects, and—through their public displays of human remains and sacred objects—their disrespect for Indigenous beliefs and sensitivities.

The almost exclusive reliance of these typical twentieth-century installations on displays of historical material objects has been analyzed by Tony Bennett in his searching discussion of the connections that link evolutionist museum narratives, colonialism, and "new liberal" political agendas of Victorian Britain and its colonies:

The museum's task was, so to speak, to batten down a new order of things by reassembling the objects comprising the artefactual domain (bones, fossils, minerals, tools, pottery, etc.) in gradual and continuous lines of evolutionary development. This comprised the central exhibition rhetoric through which the "evolutionary showmen" sought to display the orders of nature and culture, and the relations between them, in ways that would regulate progress by providing a template for its smooth and uninterrupted advance.[4]

Although Bennett's focus in this passage is on museums at the turn of the twentieth century, the reliance on objects and texts that he describes and the "orders of nature and culture" they charted remained largely undisturbed for most of the twentieth century. When opportunities arose in the United States and Canada to build new national museums, however, the link between material culture display and oppressive colonial discourses of race, history, and time, long naturalized by modernist museum displays, would become a key site for reformist attacks.

The active development of both the CMC's and the NMAI's exhibits began during the period of heightened Native North American cultural activism of the late 1980s and early 1990s. In both countries, change in museum representation had been identified by Aboriginal leaders as a visible and immediately obtainable goal useful to broader, long-term political agendas. In Canada, an Aboriginal boycott and national controversy over The Spirit Sings: Artistic Traditions of Canada's First Peoples, a high-profile "super show" of Native art and culture organized for the 1988 Calgary Winter Olympics, provided the catalyst for the creation of a national Task Force on Museums and First Peoples. The central recommendation of its report, issued in 1992, was that partnerships between museums and First Nations be established to guide all future projects related to Aboriginal peoples, including exhibitions, research, and the care of collections.[5] During the same period, Indigenous activism in the United States resulted in the creation of a legal instrument for repatriation rather than a more general policy, when the Native American Graves Protection and Repatriation Act (NAGPRA) was passed by the U.S. Congress in 1990. Despite these different points of departure, during the past fifteen years museums in both countries have moved in similar directions; in U.S. museums, collaboration with Native American communities or curators is increasingly normative, while in Canada repatriation has proceeded both under the guidelines included in the Task Force report and as part of the treaty and land claims negotiations that were renewed in the early 1990s.[6]

A third important event that lies in the background of the new exhibitions was the 1992 Columbus quincentenary, which provided occasions for Native American contestations of settler historical narratives. In retrospect, several specific projects can be seen as opening salvos in the reformist campaigns that resulted in the First Peoples Hall and the NMAI's exhibits. These include Indigena: Contemporary Aboriginal Perspectives, co-curated for the CMC by Gerald McMaster (Plains Cree) and Lee-Ann Martin (Mohawk);[7] The Submuloc Show/Columbus Wohs, organized by Atlatl-National Native Arts Network; and the National Gallery of Canada's Land/Spirit/Power: First Nations at the National Gallery, codeveloped by a team of Aboriginal and non-Aboriginal curators. Together, the artworks, installations, and texts stimulated by the Columbus quincentenary constituted a powerful corpus of revisionist historical work which, in Canada, was situated inside the space of two national museums.[8]

The 1992 exhibitions were important formative experiences for several Aboriginal artists and curators who would go on to play key roles in conceptualizing the new CMC and NMAI exhibitions. McMaster, for example, served as the initial cochair of the First Peoples Hall and then as special assistant to the director for Mall exhibitions at the NMAI; Tuscarora artist, curator, and academic Jolene Rickard, who contributed artwork to the 1992 exhibitions, would co-curate two of the NMAI's three permanent exhibitions, Our Lives and Our Peoples. The experience gained in 1992 helped to shape a sense of common cause among Indigenous cultural producers as well as an understanding of how contemporary art and installation could be used as effective rhetorical strategies for political contestation and historical revisionism.

New Museums and New Opportunities

The occasion for a comprehensive rethinking of the CMC's installations arose in the early 1980s, when the government of Prime Minister Pierre Trudeau allocated long-awaited funds to create new buildings for the National Museum of Man and the National Gallery of Canada on the Quebec and Ontario sides of the Ottawa River, adjacent to Parliament Hill. The initial program of permanent exhibitions developed for the new national museum, renamed the Canadian Museum of Civilization,[9] was informed by the vision of its director, Dr. George MacDonald, a specialist in Northwest Coast archaeology, and was influenced by his passionate admiration for Northwest Coast arts and cultures and by the populist communication theory of his early mentor, Marshall McLuhan. The two major exhibitions that were installed for the museum's official opening in 1988 were, accordingly, a Grand Hall devoted to Northwest Coast arts and cultures and a Canada Hall devoted to settler history that was modeled on the streetscape environments of the Milwaukee Public Museum, the Royal British Columbia Museum, and Epcot Center at Disney World.

The elongated oval of the Grand Hall is the museum's most prestigious space, and its windowed outer wall provides spectacular views of Parliament Hill. Along the opposite wall and facing out over the expanse of a polished stone floor designed to suggest the surface of water MacDonald installed the museum's outstanding collection of totem poles and a line of Northwest Coast house fronts. These were commissioned from contemporary Native artists in the traditional styles of six different coastal peoples. The historicism and the fictive unity of these houses seems at first to evoke the frozen time of the "ethnographic present" that has been deconstructed by Johannes Fabian and others. Yet, arguably, in the Grand Hall, this impression of timelessness converges with an important goal of the First Nations artists and experts who collaborated in its creation and who have insisted that museums represent their cultures as both traditional and living. It could be argued that important aspects of the Grand Hall were accomplished through partnership models avant la lettre.

Early in the CMC's planning process, a huge space behind the Grand Hall was allocated for a First Peoples Hall that would present exhibits on Indigenous peoples outside the Northwest Coast. Initially this was envisioned as a set of standard culture-area displays using dioramas and scientific and ethnographic information focused primarily on historical lifestyles and traditional subsistence patterns. During the 1980s, the museum's non-Native ethnology and archaeology curators completed detailed plans for the exhibits, but implementation was put on hold so that the museum could devote its resources to getting the Grand Hall and the Canada Hall ready for the 1989 opening. By the time the museum returned to the First Peoples Hall project in the early 1990s, the boycott of The Spirit Sings and the Task Force report had radically altered the familiar modernist terrain of Canadian museum anthropology. Three of the CMC's curators were members of the Task Force and had helped to develop the new model of partnership between Aboriginal communities and museums. The CMC board endorsed the Task Force report just as the museum was resuming work on the First Peoples Hall, and, in accordance with its recommendations, the museum appointed an Aboriginal advisory committee to work with the team of museum curators in the development of the new hall. Although the CMC had worked closely with many Aboriginal consultants on early exhibits, this structure marks a defining break with the traditional academic and disciplinary structures of curatorial authority because it fundamentally altered the power relations embedded in earlier consultative processes.[10]

The power structure put into place for the development of the NMAI Mall museum involved an even more radical shift in power relations than occurred at the CMC. When the U.S. Congress agreed to transfer the collections amassed by George Heye to a new National Museum of the American Indian created within the Smithsonian Institution, it entrusted the project to a Native American–dominated directorate and board who put in place a curatorial process that reversed the power relationships characteristic of modernist museum anthropology. In contrast to the past, when the Native "informants" consulted by professional ethnologists in the course of fieldwork or exhibition development had no authority over the end product, the NMAI set up a series of "vetting sessions" during which Native and non-Native experts were invited to Washington to critique the story lines being developed by the museum's Aboriginal-led curatorial team.[11] Whereas the CMC's First Peoples Hall took shape as the result of a process of negotiation and compromise, at the NMAI ultimate decision-making power was unambiguously in the hands of senior Native American staff. As we will see, these different curatorial structures and power relations have resulted in different narratives and modes of display.

Power structures operate not only intra-but also interinstitutionally, especially in national museums. In setting up the NMAI, Congress had followed the precedent set earlier by the Smithsonian's National Museum of African Art and the United States Holocaust Memorial Museum, both of which accommodate the representational needs of ethnic minorities through separate institutions operating under the Smithsonian umbrella. As would be the case with the NMAI, the National Museum of African Art came into being when Congress accessioned the collection of a private museum with chronic funding problems and empowered a new, African American–led institution to display as works of art objects very similar to those already being displayed as ethnographic artifacts by the anthropology division of the Smithsonian's National Museum of Natural History.[12] The National Holocaust Memorial Museum has a historical and commemorative mandate rather than an ethnographic focus and is governed by members of the Jewish community it represents. The system of special interest museums is accompanied by its own politics. The Canadian model of collaboration requires negotiation, whether among staff belonging to different professional and ethnic communities working within a single institution or between the institution and outside cultural communities. The separate museums dedicated to particular cultural interests that have been developing within the Smithsonian museums must also negotiate the space between the more homogeneous subject positions of their staff members and the majoritarian views and ideologies promoted by the governing institution. Arguably, the difference between the museum structures developed in Canada and the United States in response to late twentieth-century identity politics results from Canada's much smaller population and resources. It is also possible, however, that the Canadian model of internal negotiation reflects its different political history and a national culture of negotiation that has developed in response to unresolved issues of federal-provincial, French-English, and Aboriginal-Canadian power and sovereignty. Timothy Luke has addressed questions of power in the museum in his book, *Museum Politics: Power Plays at the Exhibition*. He underscores the importance of looking at both the macro and the micro level of exhibitionary events—at both the larger issues of power they engage and the individual choices and decisions through which their intents are realized. Successful exhibitions, he argues,

> are always already shows of force that articulate new plays of political power in their presentations of "culture," "history," "nature," or "technology" for the museum. Which images and objects are mobilized, how they are displayed, where they are situated, and why they are chosen all constitute powerful rhetorical strategies for governmentalizing maneuvers, especially at those sites, like the Smithsonian Institution or the American Museum of Natural History, where the authoritative pretense is maintained that these sites are where "the nation tells its story."[13]

Revisionist exhibitions can backfire, as Luke demonstrates in his analyses of two widely publicized controversies that developed at the Smithsonian around the National Museum of American Art's 1991 The West as America and the National Air and Space Museum's 1995 planned *Enola Gay* exhibit. Both provoked conservative reactions inside and outside Congress, revealing the limits of institutional tolerance for historical revisionism in the 1990s just as the planning process for the NMAI was beginning.

National museums, funded by national governments and directed by their appointees, have no choice but to navigate official ideologies and politics. The framing strategies of the Smithsonian's minority-interest museums can be detected in specific elements of their installations. One of the first installations visitors encounter at the Holocaust Museum, for example, is a display of the flags of U.S. battalions that liberated concentration camps, an exhibitionary gesture that links the European story told inside the building to American history. Native American histories are, of course, indigenous to the United States by definition, but it is nevertheless important to establish forms of alliance with dominant political forces to counterbalance the revisionist thrusts of their Indigenous historical narratives—as seen in the prominence of U.S. Senator Ben Nighthorse Campbell (a Native American and a Republican) at the museum's opening ceremonies and in its opening exhibitions.

The First Peoples Hall was begun in the midst of what political scientist Alan Cairns has referred to as a "revolution" in Aboriginal peoples' relationship with Canada. This revolution has been advanced through a series of contestations, political negotiations, and legal decisions, including the federal government's withdrawal of its 1969 White Paper on Indian policy, which, as Cairns argues, finally ended the century-old official policy of directed assimilation.[14] Among the landmark settlements and negotiated agreements that followed are the 1982 enshrinement of Aboriginal sovereignty in the Canadian Constitution; the reestablishment in the early 1990s of a federal-provincial treaty process for the negotiation of land claims after a hiatus of nearly a century; the institutionalization of new forms of territorial sovereignty and self-government with the Nisga'a agreement of 1997 and the establishment of the eastern Arctic territory of Nunavut in 1999; and the federal government's formal "statement of regret" and compensation agreement in 1998 and 2007 for the damage wrought by the residential school system. The past few decades have also witnessed violent confrontations between Natives and non-Natives, most notably at Oka, Quebec, in 1990, when a group of Mohawk and their supporters opposed plans to build a golf course on a traditional burial ground, and at Burnt Church, New Brunswick, in 1999 and 2000, when Mi'kmaq exercised treaty rights to fish commercially as well as for their own use, as upheld by a recent Supreme Court of Canada decision. Direct references to many of these events are found inside the exhibition.

The legal and political issues facing Native Americans during this period have been somewhat different. On the one hand, title to major tracts of unceded Indian land in the United States had been settled with California tribes after World War II and in Alaska in the 1970s. Arguably, however, endemic problems of racism, poverty, and stereotyping faced by Aboriginal people have had a relatively low profile in the United States, where Native American issues must compete for attention with those of numerically larger African American and Hispanic American minorities. During the last decades of the twentieth century two federal initiatives intended to clarify issues of Indian identity under the law have instead exacerbated existing ambiguities and injustices, according to many Native Americans. The federal recognition process established by the Bureau of Indian Affairs in 1978 to enable unrecognized tribes to claim legal status as Indians has proved controversial and is widely regarded as overly stringent in its requirements and political in its implementation.[15] The Indian Arts and Crafts Act of 1990, which was intended to prevent appropriation and false advertising by authorizing only enrolled members of recognized tribes to exhibit or sell work as made by Native Americans, is also regarded as having made matters worse.[16] Thus, while land claims dominate the agenda of Aboriginal people in Canada, issues of identity come to the fore among Indigenous people in the United States.

The First Peoples Hall at the
Canadian Museum of Civilization

It is not surprising to find that the issue of land claims confronts the visitor at the entrance to the First Peoples Hall. Visitors come first to a billboard-size panel bearing words of welcome. In conformity with a protocol that has become widely established in Canadian museums during the past decade, this welcome is issued not by the museum or its sponsor, the government of Canada, but by the Kitigan Zibi Circle of Elders, the representatives of the First Nation recognized as the traditional owners of the land on which the museum sits. It is inscribed over a mural-size picture that seamlessly combines an early nineteenth-century watercolor with a contemporary photograph of the same site. Through the use of digital wizardry, the image proposes an impossible fiction that collapses time and allows two bodies to occupy the same space. In the lower half of the panel, a group of Aboriginal people dressed in the clothing of the early nineteenth century stands on the bank of a river looking across at the opposite shore. We, the museum visitors, stand behind these Aboriginal figures in the space of the gallery, and, as our eyes follow the direction of their gazes, we become aware of two things in quick succession. First, these nineteenth-century Algonquians are standing on the site of the museum, where we are standing now; second, the upper half of the image is filled with something that they could not have seen, the neogothic buildings of the Canadian Parliament. These buildings, constructed between 1860 and 1922, symbolize the historical process by which Aboriginal peoples' sovereignty was supplanted and their lands appropriated. We realize that these Aboriginal figures stand before us not only in pictorial space, but also temporally, and their priorness begins to open the questions of other claims to priority— to land, power, and voice—that will be affirmed in the exhibits of the First Peoples Hall.

The advisory committee established four themes for the introductory zone of the Hall: (1) we are diverse, (2) we are still here, (3) we contribute, and (4) we have an ancient relationship with the land. The themes are articulated through a series of individual text panels and visual materials that focus on the achievements of prominent contemporary Aboriginal people. Repeatedly, the headers tie the themes to the issue of land:

> We celebrate our long history in this land. | We celebrate our work, our creativity, our creations. | We celebrate our differences, our similarities, and

our survival as Aboriginal people. | We have not forgotten the land. . . . |
We have an Ancient Bond with the Land. | Our bond with the land is forged
in knowledge. | Our bond with the land is forged in centuries of hard work.
| Our bond with the land is forged in the prayers, offerings, and dances that
hold our connections with other living beings of the earth. | We speak of our
bond with the land in the things we make, in the memories of our Elders and
in the voices of our own experience.

This is the only section of the exhibition that foregrounds the beautifully crafted and artistically elaborated objects that are today featured
not only by anthropology museums, but also by art galleries. However,
instead of the hushed quietude typical of the rhetoric of the "art" installation and that is intended to foster an appreciation of aesthetic singu-
larity, or the typological groupings that promote the kind of analytical
clarity characteristic of the earlier exhibits described by Bennett, the First
Peoples Hall presents us with a party—cheerful, noisy, and crowded.
The theme of diversity is illustrated by a jumble of objects from different
times and places that jostle each other in chaotic but purposeful confusion, creating an impression of color, variation, and vitality but denying
the possibility of focusing on the objects individually. Across the way, a
thematically structured installation spells out the advisory committee's
key messages through a sequence of text panels and through visual materials that focus on the achievements of contemporary individuals.

In the next section of the exhibition, Ways of Knowing, these affirmations and assertions are addressed in more depth and through a strategy
of calculated juxtaposition with the findings of Western ethnology and
archaeology. The message of this section is the equivalent authority of
traditional Indigenous knowledge—particularly as articulated through
oral traditions and stories— to Western scientific knowledge. This is conveyed by inverting the usual proportion of space devoted to traditional
Indigenous knowledge and Western anthropological and archaeological
knowledge. The hall's main archaeological installation is surrounded by
an array of Indigenous storytelling forms: Norval Morrisseau's painted
account of Ojibwa cosmology, *A Separate Reality;* Shelley Niro's sculpture

417

of the Iroquois creation story, *Sky Woman*; a storytelling booth; and a large theater in which CMC curator and Mi'kmaq elder Stephen Augustine narrates parts of the Gloosecap trickster-hero cycle.

The archaeological exhibit is also theatrical. Through glass floor panels we see and walk over the re-created artifactual deposits museum archaeologists have found at Bluefish Caves in the Yukon Territory, a twenty-five-thousand-year-old site containing the oldest deposits of human-made tools in Canada. Adjacent text panels describe the excavations and research, as well as the scientific arguments for climate changes thought to have controlled the movements of people into North America across the Bering Straits from Asia. In Ways of Knowing, then, the visitor is presented with two different kinds of stories that account for the human habitation of North America, but no attempt is made to resolve their discrepancies. Rather, they are presented side by side as coexistent, alternative, and competing forms of explanation. Two bodies occupying the same space.

When we enter the third section of the First Peoples Hall, An Ancient Bond with the Land, we could be forgiven for thinking that the initial 1980s plan for the First Peoples Hall had survived after all. As the introductory panel informs us, its six large semicircular bays "explore the role of whaling, fishing, communal hunting, farming and trading in supporting Aboriginal societies across the northern half of North America." Structured according to classical anthropological frameworks, it purports to explain the traditional lifestyles of regional Aboriginal groups in terms of the interdependence of ecology, Indigenous subsistence systems, technologies, and material culture. Large scrims evoking the natural environment form the backdrops for tableaux of precontact tools, hunting and fishing equipment, and dwellings. On closer inspection, however, we find numerous interventions and negotiations of these standard ethnographic tropes. In the People of the Longhouse bay, for example, the focus is on the role of women in Iroquois society, a revisionist stress that intervenes in the dominant patriarchal discourse of colonial anthropology. But the juxtapositions are often uneasy. A text discussing "changing human-plant relationships" and the importation of corn from Mexico seven thousand years ago is followed by others identifying the earth as Turtle Island and discussing "Clans and Clan Mothers" and "Women's Influence on the Men's World."

Adjacent to each bay, furthermore, is a small booth containing a video, texts, and artifacts that address contemporary issues. The booth adjacent to People of the Longhouse focuses on the 1990 Oka crisis and shows modern-day clan mothers assuming traditional leadership roles. Its artifact label reads, "Razor wire/1990/Used at Kahnawake (near Montreal) by the Canadian Armed Forces during the Oka Crisis/steel/Loan from the Kanien'kehaka Onkwawenna Raotitiohkwa" —a standard "tombstone" label that verges on postcolonial mimicry in its deadpan reference to the violent history associated with the object. Similarly, the booth adjacent to the People of the Maritimes bay focuses on the confrontations between Native and non-Native fishermen at Burnt Church that followed the Supreme Court's Donald Marshall decision.

This video so well illustrates the complex negotiations of tradition and innovation, history and politics, and memory and modernity that characterize the First Peoples Hall that it is worth looking at in detail. As the video opens, the voice of a young man begins to tell a story from the Gloosecap cycle about the lobster and the eel. The voice of an elder takes it up, explaining how the two sea creatures at first tried to inhabit the same river but found in the end that each had to find its own seasonal habitation in order to coexist in harmony. While we listen we watch children in a modern-day Mi'kmaq school making enormous full-body masks with which they will enact the story for an annual festival. We then hear about the Donald Marshall case and watch familiar though still shocking newsreel footage of the tense confrontations and boat rammings that occurred during the summer of 2000 when angry non-Native fishermen found they had to compete with Native fishermen on new terms for dwindling Atlantic fish stocks. The narrator concludes, "Today the

Mi'kmaq are still waging political battles. Today the lobster and the eel continue to avoid each other, returning to the river at different times of the year." The solution that is being offered here to the two-body problem is spatial separation and parallelism that is, as Cairns notes, the favored option of many contemporary Aboriginal political leaders.

The final section of the hall is devoted to The Arrival of Strangers and the enormous changes that have been enforced on Aboriginal people in the course of five centuries of contact with settler society. In installation terms, the displays in this section adopt conventional didactic forms: text panels and a rich array of artifacts, images, and documents shown behind glass and on the walls, organized along a linear path and clearly structured according to thematic topics. Yet these themes reflect, summarize, and reduce to digestible proportions a generation of revisionist historical and ethnographic research, not only about the Fur Trade, the Explorers, and the Retention of Traditional Beliefs, but also about Conversion, Residential Schools, High-Steel Workers, Canneries, Gambling, the adoption of Western farming, Legislation, Rodeos, and Veterans. Although created by ten different curators, Native and non-Native, the installation speaks to the visitor in the singular, anonymous voice of the modernist museum.

The First Peoples Hall closes with a display on Aboriginal humor, complete with stand-up comedians and a montage of cartoons, and a wall of contemporary paintings and sculptures presented as an important site of Indigenous resistance and discourse. The words of Aboriginal elder statesman George Erasmus are mounted at the exit of the Hall: "The history of our people needs to be told. We need to present accurately what happened in the past, so that we can deal with it in the future. I don't like what has happened over the last 500 years. We can't do much about that. But what are we going to do about the next 500 years? What are we going to do about the next ten years?" His eloquent, authoritative words issue a challenge to use the experience of the visit to the First Peoples Hall to carry forward the process of change that has linked the hall's varied and heterogeneous installations both as counterpoint and as thematic.

The NMAI's Exhibits

The NMAI's long-term exhibits are divided into three large thematic areas. Our Universes focuses on Indigenous cosmologies and belief systems, Our Lives explores issues of lifestyle and identity, and Our Peoples addresses the heavy legacy of history since European contact. In each of the three sections there is a central core of installations created by named NMAI curators that explicate the general theme. A series of smaller exhibits, which will rotate over time, open off this core. Each is created by a group of nonprofessional curators from a different Aboriginal community. In the opening round of exhibits the communities represented ranged from Chile to the Canadian Arctic. As at the CMC, one of the main messages of the exhibits, taken as a whole, is diversity. Not only recognized tribes are included, but also the unrecognized Pamunkey of Virginia, a Métis or half-breed community from Manitoba, and an ethnically diverse urban Indian community in Chicago. Also as in the First Peoples Hall, the theme of contemporaneity is everywhere. Despite the unparalleled richness of the NMAI's collections, the large majority of objects that serve as adjuncts to the busy, didactic photo murals and text panels that feature the faces and voices of contemporary community members are from the second half of the twentieth century—a period that had been excluded from most previous exhibitions by the modernist paradigm of authenticity.

These two emphases can be illustrated by looking more closely at the exhibit curated by a team from the Mohawk community of Kahnawake as part of the Our Lives section. It is particularly useful to the comparative thrust of this essay because one of the team members, Kanatakta, also served as a member of the advisory committee for the First Peoples Hall and contributed to the People of the Longhouse exhibit discussed earlier. The differences and similarities between these two modules are illuminating of larger patterns that emerge from a contrast of the two exhibits. Invited to contribute to the Our Lives section, the Kahnawake curatorial group chose to highlight their history as iron workers, and large steel girders provide the visual focus of their exhibit. Kahnawake men have worked on skyscrapers in major cities in the United States and Canada—they helped both to put up and take down the World Trade Center, for example—and this focus allows them to emphasize their integration into modernity. A counterbalancing stress is also placed on the role of Mohawk women in protecting traditional ways of life and in starting the Kahnawake survival school for their children. One text reads:

> Women and men in one community have always had different but complementary roles. In the early years, men ventured away from the village to hunt and trade. Women stayed in the village as heads of households, raising children, and managing community affairs.
>
> These roles are still carried out in Kahnawake, but we're going through a period of change where women's and men's roles are becoming more intertwined. While men still work outside Kahnawake—mainly as ironworkers—a greater number are staying in the community and have become more involved in child rearing and community decisions. Women remain active in community and home affairs, though full time jobs have changed their responsibilities, too.

At CMC, similar points about women's roles were made in the highly politicized context of a display about Oka, but the major emphasis was on premodern Hodenosaunee lifestyles and women's former roles in traditional agriculture. Strikingly, the objects on display in the Kahnawake module at NMAI do not present any of the museum's rich collections of historical beadwork, cradleboards, or other objects. Rather, what we see are the artifacts of contemporary industrial and urban life. Plans on file in the CMC archives show that, except for the Contemporary Issues Booth display on the Oka crisis, the People of the Longhouse exhibit is very similar to the installation designed by the museum's non-Native ethnologists and archaeologists in the 1980s, before the collaborative process was introduced. The contrast between NMAI, where the community curators had a free hand, and the CMC, where they had to negotiate the museum's modernist museum anthropology traditions, illustrates the different end products produced by the multivocal and community-curated models of collaboration.[17]

The central thematic area of Our Lives elucidates the problematics of identity and contemporaneity. As you enter the space you walk through a corridor onto whose walls are projected images of contemporary Native people walking past you on city streets. "Anywhere in the Americas, you could be walking with a twenty-first century Native American," you read. The long, curving "Faces wall" in the center of the space was designed by curator Jolene Rickard, who is both an academic and a noted contemporary photographic and installation artist. The elements of her installation underscore the opening message: you cannot tell a Native American by his or her physiognomy; contemporary Native American identities are complex, but authentic. The face in one image is adorned with traditional face painting that divides it into four quadrants. Another face is broken up by digital video into a mosaic of separate squares. When these fragments resolve into the unified image of a single woman, she smiles.

The use of techniques from contemporary art and installation is even more in evidence in the large, introductory thematic exhibits created one floor above, for the Our Peoples section. It is here that history is confronted. No attempt at a linear chronology is made, nor, more surprisingly, does the exhibit provide a narrative of the precontact civilizations of the Americas. Rather, the aims of the installations are to deconstruct the histories that visitors already "know" and to provide a site for commemoration and mourning. It is in Our Peoples that the model of the Holocaust Museum is most fully felt. On the frosted glass wall through which the visitor enters the word "EVIDENCE" is etched in large letters rendered in a classic typeface. A series of installations are mounted in long curving walls of glass cases that spiral off to the right. The first is filled with ceramic figurines from archaeological sites throughout the Americas. None is individually identified within the cases, for their primary purpose is not to invite aesthetic contemplation or to convey specific historical facts, but rather to evoke in a more general way the populous, pre-epidemic vitality of the Americas. "They aren't 'Indians,'" the text panel tells us. "They have never heard of 'America.' The figures standing before you knew this world. Many spent centuries underground until farmers, tomb raiders, road builders, and archaeologists brought them to light. Like their human descendants they are survivors of a buried past." Similar arrays fill the next cases: objects made of gold, guns, Bibles, and treaties and other legal documents—all artifactual "evidence" that comes from the interspaces of colonial contact, not from hermetically sealed-off "native cultures." The power of these installations derives from the additive strategy of the curators, from the cumulative weight of the objects, and they recall the haunting displays of the shoes and hair of Holocaust victims that visitors pass as they enter the exhibits at the Holocaust Museum.

Facing these installations another historical legacy is exposed, that of the romanticization of the American Indian through stereotypes embedded in art, film, and museum displays. The focus here is a re-creation of George Catlin's mid-nineteenth-century Indian Gallery. Video screens the same size as the framed portraits are interspersed. On them the stereotypical images of Indians flicker as we hear commentary spoken by Plains Cree playwright Floyd Favel Starr. "This gallery is about history and the past—two different things. What they all have in common—They were not created by Native Americans." In classic trickster fashion an adjacent text panel issues a warning: "We are left then with this paradox. For all our visibility we have been rendered invisible. And silent. A history-loving people, stripped of their own history. This Gallery is making history. And like all other makers of history it has a point of view, an agenda. What is found here is our way of looking at the Native American experience. So view what is offered with respect, but also with skepticism." The installation thus reproduces the vertically stacked hang of Catlin's original exhibition only to intervene in and disrupt its historical integrity. In so doing, it ventures even more aggressively into the revisionist terrain of The West as America. Yet, in marked contrast to the controversy that greeted that exhibition in 1991, the NMAI's critique of a well-loved and iconic corpus of nineteenth-century American art went relatively unremarked—a barometer, I would argue, of a sea change that occurred during the intervening years. At the beginning of the twenty-first century there appears to be a wider acceptance of postcolonial perspectives and of the role played by the Smithsonian's special interest museums as sites where alternative viewpoints can be presented.

Conclusions

The aspects of the NMAI's exhibitions that have met with criticism are its refusal of the standard modernist rhetorical strategies of art and artifact display. The reviewers from major newspapers who attended the NMAI opening fully expected to see more of the museum's famous collections used as anchors for its narratives about history, art, and culture. As Paul Richard wrote in the *Washington Post*, "The museum owns 800,000 Indian objects. Where are they? Mostly absent. Mostly absent, too, is the brain food one expects from good museums. . . . The eye should have been offered a feast of many courses," he lamented. "Instead it's served a stew."[18] Edward Rothstein of the *New York Times* agreed. Citing one of the community-curated exhibits, he complained, "One does not learn what daily life is like or even what the tribe's religious ceremonies consist of. . . . The notion that tribal voices should 'be heard' becomes a problem when the selected voices have so little to say."[19]

The lacks these reviewers felt are the result of deliberate choices made by the NMAI staff. While non-Native art and anthropology curators have wrangled over the relative merits of the art and artifact paradigms, many Native North Americans have found both approaches fetishizing and appropriative because they involve radical decontextualizations and disruptions of holistic Aboriginal expressive cultures. In the numerous talks NMAI director Richard West Jr. gave about his museum project during its development, he insisted that its exhibits "would not be object-driven."[20] Similarly, one of the principles adopted by the CMC's Aboriginal Advisory Committee states, "In developing the exhibits, we are working with ideas. While we recognize and treasure the skill, knowledge and aesthetic quality represented in the objects in the collections, in exhibits the role of objects will be to illustrate ideas. The shape of the collection will not determine or limit the character of exhibits."[21] As we saw, in the sections of the First Peoples Hall most closely overseen by the advisory committee cultural artifacts are grouped in ways that disrupt both standard anthropological taxonomies and modes of aesthetic appreciation. And, as at the NMAI, contemporary objects are much more prominent than in the installations that preceded it. In his assessment of the Mall museum, museum historian Stephen Conn argues that the NMAI has lost an opportunity by failing to exploit the natural relationship between object display and the fundamental rhetorical strategy available to museums:

> Objects are simply not at the center of what visitors experience. That's too bad, and not only because the Heye Collection is such an extraordinary resource. Museums have always tried to tell stories with objects. We might and should argue over which stories get told and how, but the notion that original objects can convey an immediacy and a "realness" to a narrative is at the very heart of what a museum is. Nowhere at NMAI are we asked to pause to consider an object, to study it, to admire it, ask questions of it. Apparently the curators at the NMAI have little faith in the power of objects to convey meaning.[22]

As Bennett's historical study also demonstrates, the evolutionary installations that so demeaned and dehumanized Indigenous peoples were highly constructed, produced by attaching certain texts and meanings to items of material culture that were, in and of themselves, innocent. From this perspective, both "art" and "artifact" paradigms can be understood as technologies that can be used to convey many different kinds of messages. By the late twentieth century, however, they had become guilty by association with colonial ideologies of nation, race, citizenship, and property, promoted to serve the needs of Western nation-states.

But the different histories of Aboriginal people in Canada and the United States have also led to contrasting emphases in the new exhibitions, which used the potential of the museum to serve as a "site of struggle" to advance more local agendas. In Canada, the large and unresolved issue of land claims provides the central thematic spine of the First Peoples Hall. I would argue that at the NMAI the relative lack of attention given to Native American issues in comparison with those of larger visible minorities and lack of official acknowledgment of the past oppression have resulted in a relatively greater stress on problems of identity and stereotyping, on the one hand, and on the creation of a site for public commemoration, on the other. The historic shift in power that has allowed these new representations to take the material form of exhibitions is the hard-won achievement of activist movements of resistance. Positioned close to the symbolic centers of governmental power—the NMAI next to the Capitol and the CMC across from the Parliament buildings—the new exhibitions are landmarks in the ongoing Native North American struggle against the legacy of five centuries of death, loss, and compromised identity. They will only gain in rhetorical power in the future if they deploy the Aboriginal heritage of historical materials—objects, texts, and traditional Indigenous knowledge—more fully in the service of Native North American goals.

Notes

This essay incorporates and expands on two shorter discussions, "Disrupting Past Paradigms: The National Museum of the American Indian and the First Peoples Hall at the Canadian Museum of Civilization," in Review Roundtable: The National Museum of the American Indian, Public Historian 28, no. 2 (2006): 75–80; and "Double Take: Contesting Time, Place, and Nation in the First Peoples Hall of the Canadian Museum of Civilization," coauthored with Mark Salber Phillips, in American Anthropologist 107, no. 4 (December 2005): 694–704. A version of this essay was delivered as a lecture at the University of Illinois at Urbana-Champagne, October 2005.

1. On Cardinal's architecture, see Trevor Boddy, The Architecture of Douglas Cardinal (Edmonton, Canada: NeWest Press, 1989).
2. See, for example, Ivan Karp and Steven D. Lavine, eds., Exhibiting Cultures: The Poetics and Politics of Museum Display (Washington DC: Smithsonian, 1991), and Ivan Karp, Christine Mullen Kreamer, and Steven D. Lavine, eds., Museums and Communities (Washington DC: Smithsonian, 1992), which fea-

tures Cardinal's CMC building on its cover. See also Donald Preziosi and Claire Farrago, eds., *Grasping the World: The Idea of the Museum* (Aldershot, England: Ashgate Press, 2004).

3. Johannes Fabian has termed this the "ethnographic present." *Time and the Other: How Anthropology Makes Its Object* (New York: Columbia University Press, 1983). For an example of cultural evolutionist narrative in the Iroquois displays of the Museum of the American Indian during the 1980s, see Ruth B. Phillips, *Trading Identities: The Souvenir in Native North American Art from the Northeast, 1700–1900* (Seattle: University of Washington Press, 1998).

4. Tony Bennett, *Pasts beyond Memory: Evolution, Museums, Colonialism* (New York: Routledge, 2004), 165.

5. The Task Force was funded by the Canadian federal government through the Ministry of Communications and was sponsored by the Canadian Museums Association and the Assembly of First Nations, which formally adopted its report on behalf of their members. On the controversy raised by The Spirit Sings, see Julia Harrison, "Completing a Circle: 'The Spirit Sings'," in *Anthropology, Public Policy and Native Peoples in Canada*, ed. Noel Dyck and James B. Waldram (Montreal: McGill-Queen's University Press, 1993). The task force report, *Turning the Page: Forging New Partnerships between Museums and First Peoples. A Report Jointly Sponsored by the Assembly of First Nations and the Canadian Museums Association, Ottawa*, is available from the Canadian Museums Association in Ottawa. On the task force, see Trudy Nicks, "Partnerships in Developing Cultural Resources: Lessons from the Task Force on Museums and First Peoples," *Culture* 12, no. 1 (1992): 87–94. For a comparison of initial impacts of NAGPRA and the task force report, see Michael M. Ames, "Are Changing Representations of First Peoples in Canadian Museums and Galleries Challenging the Curatorial Prerogative?," in National Museum of the American Indian, *The Changing Presentation of the American Indian: Museums and Native Cultures* (Seattle: University of Washington Press, 2000), 73–88.

6. Aboriginal bands that never concluded treaties for the alienation of their land can negotiate for the return of cultural property held by federal and provincial institutions as part of the larger land claims process.

7. Gerald McMaster and Lee-Ann Martin, eds., *Indigena: Contemporary Native Perspectives* (Vancouver: Douglas and McIntyre, 1992).

8. The catalogue for *Land/Spirit/Power: First Nations at the National Gallery* was edited by the curators, Diana Nemiroff, Robert Houle, and Charlotte Townsend-Gault (Ottawa: National Gallery of Canada, 1992).

9. The Human History Division of the National Museum of Canada was split off from the natural history divisions and renamed the National Museum of Man in 1968. Its name was changed again, in 1986, to the Canadian Museum of Civilization.

10. On the differences in power relations, see Michael M. Ames, "How to Decorate a House: The Renegotiation of Cultural Representations at the University of British Columbia Museum of Anthropology," *Museum Anthropology* 22, no. 3 (1999): 41–51.

11. The author participated in several of these vetting sessions. See also Judith Ostrowitz, "Concourse and Periphery: Planning the National Museum of the American Indian," *Museum Anthropology* 25, no. 2 (2002): 21–37.

12. The National Museum of African Art employs an art paradigm, in contrast to the artifact paradigm used at the National Museum of Natural History's (NMNH) African exhibits prior to the mid–1990s. Similarly, when the NMAI was created the NMNH North American exhibits resembled those at the old Museum of the American Indian in New York and at the National Museum of Man in Ottawa. Plans to redo the North American exhibits at the NMNH were, however, in progress at the time of the founding of the NMAI. They had to be canceled because of a lack of funding, and after the old exhibits were taken down the NMAI became the only Smithsonian museum to exhibit comprehensive long-term displays of Native North American materials. The older African exhibits were reconceptualized using a collaborative curatorial model and replaced with the African Voices exhibit in 1999. See Mary Jo Arnoldi, Christine Mullen Kreamer, and Michael Atwood Mason, "Reflections on 'African Voices' at the Smithsonian's National Museum of Natural History," *African Arts* 34, no. 2 (2001): 16–35, 94; and Ruth B. Phillips, "Where Is 'Africa'?: Re-Viewing Art and Artifact in the Age of Globalization," *American Anthropologist* 104, no. 3 (2002):11–19.

13. Timothy Luke, *Museum Politics: Power Plays at the Exhibition* (Minneapolis: University of Minnesota Press, 2002), 226–27.

14. Alan C. Cairns, *Citizen Plus: Aboriginal Peoples and the Canadian State* (Vancouver: University of British Columbia Press, 2000), 51–53; Sally Weaver, *Making Canadian Indian Policy: The Hidden Agenda, 1968–1970* (Toronto: University of Toronto Press, 1980).

15. This process is administered by the Branch of Acknowledgment and Research in the Department of Interior and the Bureau of Indian Affairs. It requires applicants or communities to prove continuous identification as American Indians from historical times, evidence of a governing system, politi-

cal influence, and a list of tribal members whose status has never been formally terminated and who are not members of any other tribe. See http://www.nativehawaiians.com/uspolicy.html.

16. For a summary of the Indian Arts and Crafts Act, see http://www.doi.gov/iacb/act.html.

17. I have proposed this model in "Community Collaboration in Exhibitions: Toward a Dialogic Paradigm. Introduction," in *Museums and Source Communities*, ed. Laura Peers and Alison K. Brown (London: Routledge, 2003).

18. Paul Richard, "Shards of Many Untold Stories," *Washington Post*, September 21, 2004, C1–C2.

19. Edward Rothstein, "A Museum That Speaks with an American Indian Voice," *New York Times*, September 21, 2004, B5.

20. For example, Richard West Jr., "Native Women and Art: Survival and Sovereignty," a talk presented at the Stanford University symposium organized by Aldona Jonaitis, May 9, 2000.

21. CMC Aboriginal Advisory Committee, "CMC Principles for Development of the First Peoples Hall (Created 1998, edited 2002)", copy provided the author by Dr. Andrea Laforet.

22. Stephen Conn, "Heritage vs. History at the National Museum of the American Indian," *The Public Historian* 18, no. 2 (2006): 71.

17. The National Museum of the American Indian and the Siting of Identity

Mario A. Caro

The nationalist function of museums has been the topic of much scholarly attention.[1] In the United States, the collection of museums in Washington DC, serves as a prime example of how these institutions prompt visitors to identify along national affiliations. As we enter the museum, we are asked to identify as either a foreign visitor, an outsider learning about the host nation, or a domestic patron, an insider whose sense of belonging is reinforced by these institutions.[2] Once inside, we may find that the museum's architecture and exhibitions tell a story that attempts to cohere into a narrative of the nation.

These engagements, however, are not always so simple. The nationalist binary of "us" and "them" is not always so straightforward and may include visitors whose national identity is multiple or in transition: immigrants whose national identification is in the process of shifting from an old to a new homeland; expatriates who continue to have a historical connection to the old country; and those with multiple citizenship and, therefore, multiple allegiances. The case of Native American visitors is also one that often produces a complicated response to the question of national identity. A Native individual may negotiate between a national identification based on tribal or cultural affiliation, which itself may be multiple, and an identification aligned with U.S. nationalism.

While these complicated and, at times, fluid processes of national identity may be at play during a visit to a national museum, what I would like to explore in this essay is how a notion of belonging to a place, especially our connection to a particular place that provides for us a sense of "homeland," contributes to our understanding of ourselves as national subjects. Specifically, I would like to explore how the trip to a national museum is a journey that emphasizes a visitor's national identity by pointing to the connection between two sites: the site of "home" and that of the museum. The route taken traces a trajectory that delineates the space conceived as "here" from that found "there," a function similar to the nationalist distinction made between "us" and "them." I begin by discussing the ideological implications of the museum as an institution whose history is imbricated with the history of colonialism. I then discuss how the location of the National Museum of the American Indian (NMAI), its specific relationship to its site, can be discussed in light of recent scholarship on site-specific works of art and their possibilities for producing communal identities. This is a discussion that I then apply to Gerald McMaster's conceptualization of "Reservation X" as a site that complicates a stable sense of place. This analysis leads me to consider the differences between the ways the location of tribal museums, perceived as having an immediate, and often contiguous, relationship to their communities, differs from the location of the NMAI. I end by considering how an installation by Jolene Rickard, found at the threshold of the Our Lives gallery within the NMAI, can lead us to reflect further on some of the complex dynamics between place and the affirmation of identity.

Always Already Nationalist

The ideological implications of the representation of Native cultures within museums have been the focus of recent scholarship, much of it critically analyzing the display practices that take place within these museums.[3] Many historical accounts of the museum trace a development from its origins as exclusive, private rooms used to exhibit personal collections full of wondrous curiosities—often gathered from colonial enterprises carried out around the world—to the more recent establishment of public museums that display materials that reify a nation's patrimony. The contemporary emphasis on the nationalist implications of the museum is particularly important when considering the ideological implications of the colonial legacy marked by the practice of collecting Native cultural products.[4] It is especially relevant to an analysis of the NMAI, an institution that in itself forms a national collection of Native nations. A focus of this recent scholarship has often been on the practices of curating, on the meaning produced by establishing relationships among objects, and also the interplay between them and the spaces they occupy within the museum. One should keep in mind, however, that the museum itself is an object on display and that the building's placement, its geographic location, is a major factor in establishing a viewer's engagement with the institution's nationalist narrative.[5]

Lost Origins

The presentation of any museum is, of course, a major consideration for its architects, who consider not only the building's aesthetic profile but also how it fits its surroundings. In terms of the NMAI, the architects chose a strategy that highly contrasts the aesthetic profile of the building with the many neoclassical structures nearby, including the iconic Capitol, which is situated directly across from the museum. The curvilinear design of the NMAI and its rough limestone façade, originally conceived by the prominent Native architect Douglas Cardinal, refer to a southwestern landscape, which adds to this sense of disjuncture. These contrasts, however, are highly productive; they help to connote dislocation and relocation, key concepts in considering the histories of Native nations. They also disrupt the associations that neoclassical architecture makes to ancient Greece as an origin for Western cultural heritage. Instead, the NMAI's architecture indexes a different place and time as its source, one set in a landscape distinctively recognizable as located in North America. The lack of fit between the site referenced by the architecture of the NMAI and that referenced by the surrounding buildings works to emphasize the visitor's engagement with the building, an engagement that indexes points of origin. However, it is an indexical tug of war that posits origins elsewhere. Lost is the visual index that locates this place as the traditional home of the original inhabitants of the area, the Piscataway and Delaware nations. The NMAI, as well as the rest of the structures located on the Mall, are therefore out of place, marked not as autochthonous sites but as unanchored destinations. This is a place produced for perpetual tourism, a process of consumption that depends on a visitor's sense of the uncanny, the unsettling feeling of being out of place, away from home—the Unheimlich.

You Are Here

The tourist's journey, however, depends on relating an unfamiliar destination with a sense of home. It often involves an ongoing process of orientation. When a map shows your location with a note that reads "You are here," you construct a path to your destination mindful that you may have to return to that same spot to make your way home. "You are here" marks a spot that, like Ariadne's thread, leads you safely out of the labyrinth. This process of stringing your way to and from your destination is one that helps to place you in context. This was made evident during the opening ceremonies on September 21, 2004, when thousands of people from many parts of the globe came together to celebrate the opening of the NMAI.

In many ways, the people participating in the opening ceremonies represented a condensed version of the variety of audiences that will eventually come to visit the museum. The diversity of the museum's visitors was most apparent during the part of the opening ceremonies billed as the Native Nations Procession.[6] Representatives from Native nations all over the world had been invited to take part in the procession. It was an opportunity for Native people to come together and celebrate their commonalities while also appreciating their differences. The result was a grand procession of more than twenty-five thousand participants, most of them wearing traditional regalia, marching through the Mall toward the museum. The regalia, flags, and banners were visual signs used to denote the variety of Native identities on display. This sight, however, was not intended for an audience of tourists expecting to see "real Indians" on display. Instead, this was a demonstration that worked to visually affirm Native sovereignty and identity.[7] This affirmation occurred among the marchers as well as between them and the spectators. Whether Native or non-Native, the emphasis on the visuality of identity demanded a response, requiring the viewer to geographically map the visual signs being presented.

What I would like to emphasize is how the process of location required of the visitor to the NMAI depends on a starting point: on the visitor's relation to a notion of "home." The visitor's connection to a place of origin leads us to consider the significance of the placement of the NMAI, the meaning produced by its citing in the mall—its site-specificity. It is essential to consider the site-specificity of museums in general in order to complicate the workings of the narratives produced inside. It is also productive to think about the site-specificity of museums in taking into account their relationship to the communities they address and those they represent.

Essential Sites

A recent study that is helpful in thinking about the idea of site-specificity as it relates to the formation of communal identity is a book by Miwon Kwon titled *One Place after Another: Site-Specific Art and Locational Identity*. In it, Kwon theorizes the "spatio-political problematic [of the] nexus between the subject/object and location."[8] One of the issues she examines is the relationship of public art to community. Although Kwon is mainly addressing site-specificity to discuss works of art that are produced for and gain meaning from a particular location, her discussion can be useful for my discussion of the meaning produced by the siting of the NMAI. Because she considers issues that pertain to art produced

435

in urban settings—which often involve negotiations between the artist, the community, and art institutions—her discussion is relevant to my analysis of the negotiations between viewer, museum, and communities. The most applicable of her insights for my project is her discussion of the location and production of community, of community as site.

One of Kwon's caveats is against the possibility that the production of public art that purports to engage a particular community's concerns will reify, and therefore commodify, that community. Her deconstruction of the concept of community critiques what she characterizes as the essentialist production of space, a space occupied by "authentic" communities. As she states:

> It seems historically inevitable that we will leave behind the nostalgic notion of a site and identity as essentially bound to the physical actualities of a place. Such a notion, if not ideologically suspect, is at least out of sync with the prevalent description of contemporary life as a network of unanchored flows. Even an advanced theoretical position . . . predicated on the belief that a particular site/place, with its identity-giving or identifying properties, exists always and already prior to whatever new cultural forms might be introduced to it or emerge from it [seems dated].[9]

Kwon's analysis, based on the "prevalent description of contemporary life as a network of unanchored flows," leads her to the conclusion that "reckoning with the impossibility of community . . . may be the only way to imagine past the burden of affirmational siting of community to its critical unsiting."[10] In other words, the fragmentary nature of identity cannot sustain a unitary notion of community, and, subsequently, its siting.

The irony of Kwon's project— to think "beyond and through the impossibility of community"[11]—is that, at least in terms of Native identity, "the notion of site and identity as essentially bound to the physical actualities of a place" is precisely the belief often advocated by those looking to maintain homelands or, alternatively, regain territories taken away by force.[12]

Siting Reservation x

It is the survival of such place-bound identities that Gerald McMaster addressed when he curated Reservation x: The Power of Place in Aboriginal Contemporary Art in 1998. For this exhibition, he chose the Native reservation as the operative site of engagement. The exhibition featured the work of eight Native artists (Mary Longman, Nora Naranjo-Morse, Marianne Nicolson, Shelley Niro, Jolene Rickard, Mateo Romero, and C. Maxx Stevens) who McMaster believed exemplified efforts by Native artists "to merge the legacy of individualism with the dynamic and affirming bond of community. They no longer see the appeal of being marginalized iconoclasts but prefer to become active participants, where community and individual growth are not incompatible but complementary goals."[13]

McMaster was fully aware of the contradictions present in actual reservations, which denote "a negotiated space set aside for Indian people by oppressive colonial governments to isolate them, to extricate them from their cultural habits, and to save them from the vices of the outside world." He presented the dual nature of the reservation as "both sanctuary and prison," as a place that "will always be both a symbolic and real home for most Indian people."[14] The reservation is the site, real or imagined, to which many Native communities have an essential relationship. This is true even of those Native communities that have been so severely displaced that they lack access to their homeland.[15] Even then, the locus of the reservation functions dialectically as formative of Native identity. To designate the place of this ambivalent site, McMaster uses the term "Reservation x."[16] As he elaborates: "The urban and rural now make up two discursive spaces or communities that form the new reservation narrative."[17] This is a narrative that, unlike the urban-centered analysis proposed by Kwon, acknowledges the complicated relationships of various sites to the formation and affirmation of identity.

Authentic Places/Essential Identities

The discursive production of Reservation x outlined by McMaster's project is further affirmed by the claims of authenticity that are often made for such spaces by Native communities themselves. It is at this point that a project such as Kwon's, which is explicitly informed by postmodernist discourses, reveals the incommensurabilities between Western aesthetics and those theories centered on Indigenous notions of identity. The former espouses an anti-essentialism that is wary of the "cultural valorization of places as the locus of authentic experience and coherent sense of historical and personal identity," and endorses, instead, a fluid notion of identity that is constituted at the nexus of site and performance, while the latter may appeal to a sense of identity dependent on the stability of history and place.[18] It is important to realize, however, that Indigenous claims to authentic sites and essential identities are not necessarily strategic; they are often fundamental to Native epistemologies.[19]

Whereas notions of authenticity and essentialism become limiting burdens for artists attempting to avoid ghettoization in today's global art market, many Indigenous artists eschew this Western problematic. The art critic Ian McLean has noted how these different approaches function in the presentation of Aboriginal art in Australia: "The burden of authenticity felt so heavily by postcolonial artists . . . is, for Indigenous artists, a liberation and essential component of their identity. The old desert painters wear this authenticity lightly because it is so much a part of them. Far from being a burden hoisted on them by Eurocentric intellectuals wanting to legitimise their own modernity, it is and always has been the secret of the success of Indigenous art."[20]

McLean makes a crucial distinction between the Indigenous artists, whom he describes as belonging to a traditional culture, and the position occupied by the postcolonial artists, whom he identifies as those who "work across a range of styles and ideas in a deliberate hybrid fashion that is global and temporal in outlook." Postcolonial art, according to McLean, "is a syncretic modernism that, in the spirit of modernism, is grounded in the temporality and spatiality of modernity," which he contrasts to art emerging from traditional cultures and characterized by "the specificity of place and locality."[21] This is a provocative distinction, particularly since it does not account for the location of artists, such as the participants in Reservation x, who strongly identify with a specific place and yet participate in the production of what McLean considers postcolonial art.[22]

McLean's discussion of the essentialism involved in claiming authenticity explicitly points to a paradigmatic chasm between certain Indigenous perspectives based on essentialist notions of identity and those espousing a (post)modern perspective that depends on anti-essentialism. As my discussion of Reservation x illustrates, this distinction (essentialist/traditional versus anti-essentialist/postcolonial) becomes complicated when discussing the use of postmodern aesthetics to express traditional beliefs. As Linda Tuhiwai Smith, a Maori cultural studies scholar, explains, Indigenous notions of essentialism are complex:

> The essence of a person is also discussed in relation to indigenous concepts of spirituality. In these views, the essence of a person has a genealogy which can be traced back to an earth parent, usually glossed as an Earth Mother. A human person does not stand alone, but shares with other animate, and in the Western sense, "inanimate" beings, a relationship based on a shared "essence" of life. The significance of place, of land, of landscape, of other things in the universe, in defining the very essence of a people, makes for a very different rendering of the term essentialism as used by indigenous peoples.[23]

For Smith, a Native perspective often includes the notion that one's land is a site of authenticity that engenders essential identities; it represents the place essential to identity.

Been There/Being There: Visiting Tribal Museums

The propriety of place, the relationship of Native bodies to sites that ground identity, can be explored by examining the experience of the non-Native visiting a tribal museum.[24] The sites of these museums, often located on reservations, help to produce narratives that are greatly influenced by the visitor's approach and departure from the building, which often involves negotiating a Native space, a space often clearly designated as sovereign. This relationship to place, to the setting that provides a prologue for the museum's narration, is crucial for noting the differences in the ways museums function on the reservation versus off the reservation. This is especially true for the non-Native visitor whose performance of the tribal museum can be a somewhat uncanny experience, the infelicitous experience of not belonging to a place, of being a foreigner.

In his analysis of the museum as site, James Clifford describes the museum as a "contact zone," a term he borrows from Mary Louise Pratt, who defines it as "the space of colonial encounters, the space in which peoples geographically and historically separated come into contact with each other and establish ongoing relations, usually involving conditions of coercion, radical inequality, and intractable conflict."[25] In "Museums as Contact Zones," Clifford's focus is on the relationships produced within the space of the Western museum, and particularly the exchanges between Native communities and Western museums whose holdings include their cultural property. He is careful to acknowledge the power inequalities that constitute these relationships. These are not places for benign cultural encounters. Instead, these are sites that collect "particular histories of dominance, hierarchy, resistance, and mobilization." To address these inequalities, he advocates the enacting of the Western museum as a site for negotiation where the "contact work" of "active collaboration and a sharing of authority" can occur.[26]

In an earlier essay, titled "Four Northwest Coast Museums," Clifford compared the display strategies of two Western museums, the University of British Columbia Museum of Anthropology and the Royal British Columbia Museum, with those of two smaller tribal museums, the U'mista Cultural Centre and the Kwagiulth Museum and Cultural Centre.[27] Although all four museums feature materials belonging to various Northwest Coast communities, the two tribal museums have an unusual history. They were formed in the late 1970s as part of an agreement to repatriate items confiscated during a potlatch ceremony held in 1921, a ceremony that by that time had been outlawed.[28] These Native museums are also different in terms of their relationship to the cultures they represent. Clifford notes the significant difference it makes to belong to the immediate community represented by the tribal museums, the difference it makes to how the museum's narrative is performed. As he states, "Objects here are family and community memorabilia. To an outsider, at least, a great part of their evocative power—beyond their formal, aesthetic values—is the simple here. . . . In a local museum, 'here' matters."[29]

Clifford's experience can be useful not only in thinking about an outsider's engagement with a tribal museum, a site where "here" matters, but also as a contrast to a museum such as the NMAI, where "here" also matters. Although there is no doubt that in many respects the NMAI functions much like a Western museum, particularly in terms of its site, there are many other aspects of it, such as the careful landscaping that references cosmologically significant directions, that invoke "home" to many Native visitors. As I suggested earlier, it is precisely this dislocation from home that makes visitors aware of their relationship to the processes of identification.

If we return to McMaster's formulation of Reservation x as a discursively produced site—one that functions as both sanctuary and prison, can be real or imagined, and accommodates urban and rural Native populations—what can we say about its relationship to the NMAI? Is it possible to conceive of the museum as located on such a site? How would non-Native visitors respond to such a siting? The answers to these questions will become apparent only as visitors themselves help to determine the use value of the institution. The museum will, of course, also play a major role in how it invokes, rather than just represents, Native notions of home and identity.

At the Threshold of Identity

There is one particular element of the NMAI's interior design that stands out as a work that enacts the process of identification that I have been describing. As one reaches the third level of the museum, there is an entrance to the left that leads into the Our Lives gallery, which is meant to "illustrate how Native Americans, despite many challenges, continue to exist as distinct communities."[30] Although the various displays inside are powerful illustrations of the complexities of negotiating contemporary Native identity, it is the entranceway to the gallery that first involves the visitor in actually experiencing these complicated processes of identification.

The work is designed by Jolene Rickard (Tuscarora), an artist, curator, and scholar whose work is well known for addressing the intricate relationships between visual representation and Native identity. In this installation, Rickard emphasizes the performative aspect of Native identity, particularly the ways identity is produced through the process of recognition. The work consists of two large screens, approximately twelve feet long and eight feet high, on either side of the entrance onto which are projected life-size images of people who seem to walk alongside visitors as they enter and exit the gallery. The people depicted are diverse; they include individuals representing a spectrum of ages, skin tones, and sizes. There are images of women, children, and men dressed in suits, uniforms, sports clothes, traditional regalia, and more. In short, they represent a wide demographic of Native peoples. The work is subtle in the way it addresses the visitor. These images do not confront the viewer but appear, almost imperceptibly, beside the visitor. It is only after entering the passageway that one becomes aware of the projected images, and then only when one takes a sideward glance. It is a brief encounter, a momentary vision of a fellow traveler, but one that demands a quick and unconscious process of recognition.

It may be helpful to compare the performance of identification that Rickard's work demands and that enacted during the Native Nations Procession. One could have read the dynamics of identity played out during the procession as having to do with a simple notion of identity. A superficial glance at the activities could have perceived the participants eager to photograph themselves and others wearing traditional regalia as enacting a simple notion of identification, one in which identity is simply worn and easily framed within the camera's viewfinder. Participants in the event, however, were aware of the complicated nature of the processes of identification. Sorting through the many visual markers may have been a daunting task, particularly for those intending to identify who was and was not Native. However, the strong distinction between those wearing cultural markers of identity and the rest only frustrated any easy act of recognition.

The distinction I am trying to emphasize is between a fixed notion of identity and one that is aware of identification as a dynamic process. The theorist Diana Fuss has discussed the process of identification as "set[ting] into motion the complicated dynamic of recognition and misrecognition that brings a sense of identity into being." Although this process may imply a "narrowing in" on identity, she emphasizes the uncertainty of the process, which "immediately calls that identity into question."[31] It is the uncertainty of identification that is enforced by passing through Rickard's threshold. The fluid nature of recognition is emphasized by the aesthetic strategies employed; the artist has produced an effect by which the images momentarily come into focus and then slowly blur away. There is an emphasis on the spatiotemporal dimensions of motion, on those aspects of the brief encounter that literally blur the "here and now" with the "there and then." The sign accompanying this threshold reads, "Anywhere in the Americas, you could be walking with a 21st-century Native American." This "anywhere" could be everywhere; it all depends where, and how, you find yourself.

At Home and Away

The instability of the process of recognition that this work emphasizes can be seen as contrasting sharply with the essentialist notions of home discussed earlier. However, it is precisely this difference that works to reinforce a sense of identity that is place-bound. The fluidity and instabil-

443

ity of identification performed at the site of the NMAI can, in turn, work to affirm a Native identity based on a fixed notion of home.

While visitors' responses to the NMAI may range from feelings of alienation and indifference to pride, it is the journey that has led them there that will inform their attachment to the museum and its contents. It is likely that a visit to the NMAI will challenge those whose ideas of Native identity depend on the recognition of stable markers of identity. It is also possible that for these visitors the cultural objects found within will only help to reify their ideas of indigeneity. Others, however, may consider the museum as yet another passage leading them back home.

Notes

I want to thank Tina Kuckkahn for her helpful insights and suggestions on an earlier draft of this essay.

1. For a selection of essays on the nationalist role of the museum, see David Boswell and Jessica Evans, eds., *Representing the Nation: A Reader, Histories, Heritage and Museums* (New York: Routledge, 1999). Also see Carol Duncan, *Civilizing Rituals: Inside Public Art Museums* (London: Routledge, 1995). For an earlier analysis of the use of Native American material as part of the nation's patrimony, see Curtis M. Hinsley Jr., *The Smithsonian and the American Indian: Making Moral Anthropology in Victorian America* (Washington DC: Smithsonian Institution Press, 1981).

2. One way to think about the ways institutions contribute to the production of identity is to consider the Marxist notion of interpellation, an ideological call to an individual, a summons to occupy a subject position prescribed by a state institution. Louis Althusser, *Lenin and Philosophy, and Other Essays* (London: New Left Books, 1971), 174.

3. Much has been published on museums, particularly during the past decade. A selection of works relevant to the display of Native cultures includes Tim Barringer and Tom Flynn, eds., *Colonialism and the Object: Empire, Material Culture and the Museum* (New York: Routledge, 1998); Eilean Hooper-Greenhill, *Museums and the Interpretation of Visual Culture* (New York: Routledge, 2000); Christina F. Kreps, *Liberating Culture: Cross-Cultural Perspectives on Museums, Curation and Heritage Preservation* (New York: Routledge, 2003); W. Richard West, ed., *The Changing Presentation of the American Indian: Museums and Native Cultures* (Seattle: University of Washington Press and National Muse-

um of the American Indian, 2000); Lynda Jessup and Shannon Bagg, eds., *On Aboriginal Representation in the Gallery* (Hull: Canadian Museum of Civilization, 2002); Miriam Clavir, *Preserving What Is Valued: Museums, Conservation, and First Nations* (Vancouver: University of British Columbia, 2002); Laura Peers and Alison K. Brown, eds., *Museums and Source Communities: A Routledge Reader* (New York: Routledge, 2003).

4. On the development of major Native collections, a process that has often involved the aid of academic disciplines such as anthropology, archaeology, and art history, see Douglas Cole, *Captured Heritage: The Scramble for Northwest Coast Artifacts* (Seattle: University of Washington Press, 1985). A more recent critical assessment is found in Margaret Dubin, *Native America Collected: The Culture of an Art World* (Albuquerque: University of New Mexico Press, 2001).

5. For a discussion of the historical relationship between art and architecture, see Douglas Crimp, "The Postmodern Museum," in *On the Museum's Ruins* (Cambridge MA: MIT Press, 1993), 282–325.

6. For the museum's coverage of the opening ceremonies, see its official publication *National Museum of the American Indian* (Winter 2004). Also see *Native Peoples* 17, no. 6 (September/October 2004).

7. This was most obvious when noticing how important it became for participants to photograph themselves taking part in the event. For a lively account from a photographer's perspective, see Dugan and Liz Aguilar, "The Opening of the National Museum of the American Indian," *News from Native California* 18, no. 2 (Winter 2004–5): 4–12.

8. Miwon Kwon, *One Place after Another: Site-Specific Art and Locational Identity* (Cambridge MA: MIT Press, 2002), 2, 8.

9. Kwon, *One Place*, 164.

10. Kwon, *One Place*, 155.

11. Kwon, *One Place*, 154.

12. Kwon is basing her ideas of community on an approach outlined by Jean-Luc Nancy, which posits that "only a community that questions its own legitimacy is legitimate" (155). See Jean-Luc Nancy, *The Inoperative Community* (Minneapolis: University of Minnesota Press, 1991). The efficacy of this skeptical approach to communal identity is questionable from a Native perspective, especially when considering the oppressive conditions faced by Indigenous peoples in the Americas.

13. Gerald McMaster, "Living on Reservation X," in *Reservation X*, ed. Gerald McMaster (Seattle: University of Washington Press and Canadian Museum of Civilization, 1998), 23.

14. McMaster, "Living on Reservation X," 19, 22, 19.

15. For an overview of the history of Native dislocation and the status of Native land claims see Ward Churchill, "The Earth Is Our Mother: Struggles for American Indian Land and Liberation in the Contemporary United States," in *The State of Native America: Genocide, Colonization and Resistance*, ed. M. Annette Jaimes (Boston: South End Press, 1992). For a discussion of the establishment of community-based museums in the United States by immigrant communities, see Moira G. Simpson, "Remembering Homeland," in *Making Representations: Museums in the Post-Colonial Era* (London: Routledge, 1996).

16. McMaster borrowed this name from Shelley Niro, who uses it as the setting for her film *Honey Moccasins* (1998).

17. McMaster, "Living on Reservation X," 21.

18. Kwon, *One Place*, 52.

19. On the Western production of the concepts of authenticity and primitivism, see Shelly Errington, *The Death of Authentic Primitive Art and Other Tales of Progress* (Berkeley: University of California Press, 1998). For an analysis of authenticity and contemporary Aboriginal art, see Marcia Langton, "Dreaming Art," in *Complex Entanglements: Art, Globalisation and Cultural Difference*, ed. Nikos Papastergiadis (Sydney, Australia: Rivers Oram Press, 2003.) Langton argues that the representation of landscapes in various Native art practices, including those by traditional Aboriginal desert painters, forms a genre that requires a different scope of reception, one mindful of an Indigenous perspective. For an analysis of the ideological implication of this genre in Australia, see Geoff Levitus, ed., *Lying about the Landscape* (Sydney, Australia: Craftsman House, 1997). I am grateful to Ian McLean for bringing Langton's article to my attention.

20. Ian McLean, "Postcolonial Traffic: William Kentridge and Aboriginal Desert Painters," *Third Text* 17, no. 3 (September 2003): 239–40.

21 McLean, "Postcolonial Traffic," 228.

22. McLean goes on to complicate this distinction by concluding, "We need to be wary of a postcolonial primitivism inherited from modernist times that precludes the Indigenous from the postcolonial" ("Postcolonial Traffic," 240).

23. Linda Tuhiwai Smith, *Decolonizing Methodologies: Research and Indigenous Peoples* (London: Zed Books, 1999), 74. See Peter Nabokov, ed., *Sacred Land Reader* (La Honda CA: Sacred Land Film Project, 2002), for an overview of issues dealing with Native religions in relation to sites considered sacred.

24. For an overview of the complicated development of Native representa-

tion in museums, see Janet C. Berlo and Ruth B. Phillips, "'Our (Museum) World Turned Upside Down': Re-presenting Native American Arts," *Art Bulletin* 77, no. 1 (1995): 6–10.

25. Mary Louise Pratt, cited in James Clifford, "Museums as Contact Zones," in *Routes: Travel and Translation in the Late Twentieth Century* (Cambridge MA: Harvard University Press, 1997), 192.

26. Clifford, "Museums as Contact Zones," 213, 210.

27. James Clifford, "Four Northwest Coast Museums," in *Routes*, 107–45.

28. Repatriation, which can be described as the re-siting of cultural objects to their proper place, has been a long struggle for many Native communities who have lost their cultural treasures through unethical collecting. On repatriation, see Devon A. Mihesuah, *Repatriation Reader: Who Owns American Indian Remains?* (Lincoln: University of Nebraska Press, 2000); Ann M. Tweedie, *Drawing Back Culture: The Makah Struggle for Repatriation* (Seattle: University of Washington Press, 2002); Elazar Barkan and Ronald Bush, eds., *Claiming the Stones/Naming the Bones: Cultural Property and the Negotiation of National and Ethnic Identity* (Los Angeles: Getty Publications, 2002).

29. Clifford, "Four Northwest Coast Museums," 126.

30. National Museum of the American Indian, press release, September 3, 2004.

31. Diana Fuss, *Identification Papers* (New York: Routledge, 1995), 2.

The Contributors

Elizabeth Archuleta (Yaqui/Chicana) is an assistant professor in women and gender studies at Arizona State University. She is a member of the Advisory Board for the American Native Press Archives/Sequoyah Research Center and the author of several journal articles and forthcoming chapters in edited collections.

Sonya Atalay (Ojibwe) is an assistant professor of anthropology at Indiana University. She is the chair of the Society for American Archaeology's Committee on Native American Relations, and in this capacity is active in bringing Native American voices and perspectives to the archaeological community. Her work relates to Indigenous archaeology, particularly community-based participatory research (CBPR), decolonization, NAGPRA and "culturally unidentifiable" ancestral remains, intellectual property, and archaeological ethics. Dr. Atalay maintains active archaeological fieldwork in the Great Lakes region of North America, working on collaborative projects with Anishinaabek communities. She is currently preparing a book on applications of participatory research methods within archaeology.

Janet Catherine Berlo is a professor of art history and visual and cultural studies at the University of Rochester. She holds a PhD in history of art from Yale University. Her many books include *Spirit Beings and Sun Dancers: Black Hawk's Vision of a Lakota World* (2000), *Native North American Art* (1997, with Ruth Phillips), and the exhibition catalogue *Plains Indian*

Drawings 1865–1935: Pages from a Visual History (1996). Her most recent book is *American Encounters: Art, History and Cultural Identity* (2008, with A. Miller, B. Wolf, and J. Roberts). Janet Berlo has taught Native American art history as a visiting professor at Harvard, Yale, and UCLA and has received grants for her scholarly work from the Guggenheim Foundation, the Getty Foundation, and the National Endowment for the Humanities.

Mario A. Caro is a historian and critic of contemporary Indigenous art. His recent work has analyzed the intersections of aesthetics and nationalism within the workings of globalization. He is currently completing a manuscript dealing with these issues titled *Decolonizing Aesthetics: Art, History, Nationalism and the Native as Image.*

Cynthia Chavez Lamar (San Felipe Pueblo/Hopi/Tewa/Navajo) is currently the director of the Indian Arts Research Center (IARC) at The School for Advanced Research on the Human Experience in Santa Fe, New Mexico. She served as an associate curator at the Smithsonian's National Museum of the American Indian from 2000 to 2005, where she led the development of the inaugural exhibition, Our Lives: Contemporary Life and Identities, which currently remains on exhibit at the NMAI on the National Mall in Washington DC. She was then recruited to become the museum director at the Indian Pueblo Cultural Center in Albuquerque, New Mexico, where she revitalized the educational programming and exhibits.

Chavez Lamar has an MA in American Indian Studies from the University of California, Los Angeles, and a PhD in American Studies from the University of New Mexico. Much of her personal and professional experience has focused on fostering collaborative projects between Native peoples, organizations, and institutions.

Amanda J. Cobb (Chickasaw) is an associate professor of English at Oklahoma State University. She serves as the editor of *American Indian Quarterly*. She has recently returned to Oklahoma to serve the Chickasaw Nation as the administrator of the Division of History, and Culture. In this role she oversees the Chickasaw Cultural Center and the Chickasaw Press, the first tribal press of its kind. Cobb's book, *Listening to Our Grandmothers' Stories: The Bloomfield Academy for Chickasaw Females, 1852–1949* (2000), received the North American Indian Prose Award as well as the American Book Award.

Robin Maria DeLugan (Cherokee, Lenape) is an assistant professor at the University of California, Merced. She has teaching and research interests that cross the borders of anthropology, Latin American studies, Native American studies, and comparative ethnic studies. Her research in El Salvador examines how reflections on post–civil war national history, culture, and identity intersect with Native efforts for official recognition. In northern California she is working with Indigenous immigrants from Latin America as they join and build Native communities in a new homeland.

Patricia Pierce Erikson is a cultural anthropologist and Native American studies scholar whose career has crossed back and forth between museums and universities. In collaboration with the Makah community of Neah Bay, Washington, she wrote *Voices of a Thousand People: The Makah Cultural and Research Center* (2002), a book that documents the importance of their tribal museum to the tribe's self-determination efforts. While working as Curator and Head of Education for the Washington State History Museum, she collaborated with the Nisqually Tribe in creating online lesson plans that serve the K–12 public school system statewide. Dr. Erikson teaches in the University of Southern Maine–Portland's American and New England Studies Department. When she is not consulting with museums, she is writing her next book, set in Greenland.

Gwyneira Isaac received her DPhil at Oxford University in 2002 and is assistant professor and director of the Museum of Anthropology at the School of Human Evolution and Social Change, Arizona State University. Her research is focused on the relationships people develop with their past through material culture, leading her to explore the history of anthropology, photography, and the development of tribal museums in the Southwest. Her publications include *Mediating Knowledges: Origins of a Zuni Tribal Museum* (2007).

Ira Jacknis is a research anthropologist at the Phoebe A. Hearst Museum of Anthropology, University of California, Berkeley. He has a doctorate in anthropology from the University of Chicago (1989). Before coming to the Hearst Museum in 1991, he worked for the Brooklyn Museum, the Smithsonian, the Field Museum, and the Newberry Library. His research specialties include museums and the arts and cultures of the Native peoples of western North America.

Art historian **Aldona Jonaitis** received her PhD in art history from Columbia University in 1976. An expert in Northwest Coast Native art, she has published several books, including *Art of the Northern Tlingit* (1986), *From the Land of the Totem Poles: Northwest Coast Art at the American Museum of Natural History* (1988), *Chiefly Feasts: The Enduring Kwakiutl Potlatch* (1991), *The Yuquot Whalers' Shrine* (1999), and *Art of the Northwest Coast* (2006). Currently in press is *The Northwest Coast Totem Pole: History and Myth*, coauthored with Aaron Glass. She was on the faculty and served as an administrator at the State University at Stony Brook from 1975 to 1989, then became Vice President for Public Programs at the American Museum of Natural History, where she stayed for four years. Currently she serves as Director of the University of Alaska Museum of the North in Fairbanks and is a Professor of Anthropology at the University of Alaska, Fairbanks.

Amy Lonetree is an enrolled citizen of the Ho-Chunk Nation of Wisconsin. She earned a PhD in ethnic studies from the University of California, Berkeley, where she specialized in Native American history and museum studies.

Her scholarly work focuses on the representation of Indigenous people in both national and tribal museums, and she has conducted research on this topic at the Smithsonian's National Museum of the American Indian, the Minnesota Historical Society, the Mille Lacs Indian Museum, the Ziibiwing Center of Anishinabe Culture and Lifeways, and the British Museum. She has published articles based on this research in the *American Indian Quarterly* and the *Public Historian*. She is currently an Assistant Professor of American Studies at the University of California, Santa Cruz.

Judith Ostrowitz is the author of *Interventions: Native American Art for Far-Flung Territories* (2008) and *Privileging the Past: Reconstructing History in Northwest Coast Art* (1999), as well as numerous articles about Native American art. She is an adjunct associate professor who has taught at Columbia University, Yale, New York University, and the City College of New York. She is a contractual lecturer for the Metropolitan Museum of Art and is a former assistant curator at the Brooklyn Museum of Art. She was the recipient of a J. Paul Getty Postdoctoral Fellowship in the History of Art and Humanities, 1997–98.

Ruth B. Phillips is Canada Research Chair and a professor of art history at Carleton University, Ottawa. Her publications include *Trading Identities: The Souvenir in Native North American Art from the Northeast* (1998); *Native North American Art* (with Janet Catherine Berlo, 1998); *Unpacking Culture: Art and Commodity in Colonial and Postcolonial Worlds*, coedited with Christopher B. Steiner (1999); and *Sensible Objects: Colonialism, Museums, and Material Culture*, coedited with Elizabeth Edwards and Chris Gosden (2006). She has also curated a number of exhibitions and served as director of the University of British Columbia Museum of Anthropology. Currently she directs the Great Lakes Alliance for the Study of Aboriginal Arts and Cultures (GRASAC), a major international collaboration of researchers in Indigenous communities, museums, and universities.

Beverly R. Singer (Tewa/Diné) is an associate professor of Anthropology and Native American Studies at the University of New Mexico, Albuquerque. She resides at Santa Clara Pueblo. She is the author of *Wiping the Warpaint Off the Lens* (2001). Her work as a filmmaker has received wide acclaim.

Paul Chaat Smith (Comanche) is associate curator at the Smithsonian's National Museum of the American Indian. His projects have included the museum's permanent history exhibit in Washington and the 2005 international symposium "Vision, Space, Desire: Global Perspectives and Cultural Hybridity." His exhibitions and essays have explored the work of Richard Ray Whitman, Baco Ohama, James Luna, Faye Heavy Shield, Shelley Niro, Erica Lord, and Kent Monkman. Smith is coauthor of *Like a Hurricane: The Indian Movement from Alcatraz to Wounded Knee* (1996). His second book, a collection of essays, will be published by the University of Minnesota Press in 2009.

Myla Vicenti Carpio (Jicarilla Apache, Laguna, Isleta) is an assistant professor in American Indian studies at Arizona State University.

Pauline Wakeham is an assistant professor in the Department of English at the University of Western Ontario. Her book *Taxidermic Signs: Reconstructing Aboriginality* (2008) decodes the practice of taxidermy as it was performed in North America from the late nineteenth century to the present, revealing its connection to a matrix of colonial, ecological, and racial discourses that conflate the signs of "animality" and "aboriginality" in the service of anthropocentric hierarchies of white supremacy. Her current research engages in a comparative analysis of the institutional mediation of discourses of reconciliation between First Peoples and the nation-state at the Canadian Museum of Civilization and the National Museum of the American Indian.

Index

National Museum (*cont.*)

vault of, 106–7, 111, P4; as exhibit in itself, 338; façade of, 110; as gathering place, 338–39, 381n8; gift shops of, 75, 214–15, 216, 250, 382n21; holistic vs. object-oriented focus of, 113–14, 310, 425–26; independence of, 23, 63; Indians as minority in, 141–42; and individuality of tribes, 107–8, 113, 114–15; mission statement of, 122n11, 271; as monument, 89; name of, xxvi–xxvii, 379n2; narrative of, 73–75, 77–78, 322; as national tribal museum, 29–32, 41n77, 42n83; Native access to design of, 116–17; Native material culture and, 69–71; nature referenced in, 111, 337–38; non-Native architecture of, 112, 118; opening of, 3, 183–84, 208, 241–42, 253–54, 346; overview of interior, 249–50, 338–39; performance as focus of, 356, 381n8; Potomac space of, 107–8, 111, 112, 213–14, 216, 337, 338, 339, 356, P4; repatriation of objects by, 30; Resource Center of, 339; review process of design, 124n17, 125–26n46; rooftop habitats of, 105; sacred objects in, 30, 103, 333–34, 335–36, 340, 346; site design of, 104–5, 107, 111–12, 212–13, 337–38, 433–34, 441; as site of national conversation, 132, 142; size of collection of, 26–27; as transnational site, xxvi, xxviii–xxix; trustees of, 23, 63, 99, 122n11; unstructured starting point in, 249, 250–51. *See also* authority of Native Americans; collaboration; exhibits; Cultural Resources Center (CRC); Fourth Museum; Heye Center for the American Indian; National Museum of the American Indian (NMAI)

national museums: ambiguity of term, 24–25; homogeneity and noncontroversiality in, 185, 413; of Latin America, 386–88; location of, 24; media expectations for, 184; minority free-standing institutions within, 24, 412–13, 414, 425; nationalist interests and, xxvi–xxvii, xxviii, 385–88, 389–90, 400–401, 412–14, 431–33; as owned by nation-state, 24–25; scope of collection and, 25; size of collection and, 24

National Park Service, 172, 175
national security, 274–75, 392
national symbolic, 203
national unity, 86

nations, indigenous: name wall of, 344; numbers of, 293; as preferred term, 295
nation-states, national museums of, xxvi–xxvii, xxviii, 385–88, 389–90, 400–401, 412–14, 431–33
Native American architecture: basketry, 97; booklet guiding, 94; circular forms, 97; consultation process as prerequisite for, 92–93, 94; convergent values in, 95; directional symbolism in, 97; as genre, 93; inception of, 94; intertribal borrowings and, 98, 99; nature, 95, 97; as principle-based, 98; qualities common to, 93–98; traditions of architecture and, 93, 94–96, 97
Native American Design Collaborative (NADC), 98, 102
Native American Graves Protection and Repatriation Act (NAGPR), xviii, 30, 62, 63, 277–78, 334
Native American museum movement: definition of, 47; effectiveness of, 77–78; and knowledge making, 47–49; NMAI as tribal museum of, 30–32; overview of, xviii–xix; and proposed renovation, 54–55; repatriation and, xviii–xix, 66–67, 334; stereotypes and, 46–47, 54; as trend, 47. *See also* representation
Native criticism of NMAI: collection and display issues, 278; on community representation, 347; general, 76; on intellectual and cultural property rights, 278; potential for co-optation and silencing, 76–77; repatriation issues, 277–78; on stereotypes, 282, 285, 306, 311, 312, 313, 317–19, 322–23. *See also* academic critical discourse; media coverage
Native Hawaiian Reorganization Act, 370
Native Modernism (exhibit), 227–29, 251–53, 338, 346, P19, P20
Native Nations Procession. *See* First Americans Festival
Native Nations Procession Participant Guide (for NMAI), 368
"Native Peoples of North America: Cultures in a Changing World," 54
Native space, 196–97
Native voice: archaeology controversies and, 281; and collaboration process, 154–55, 163n21; commonalities in, 210–11; definition of, 154; new museology and, 210;